Mastering ASP.Net From Beginner To Web Developer

Anshuman Mishra

Published by Anshuman Mishra, 2025.

HOW TO STUDY THIS BOOK AND BENEFIT FROM IT

WHO THIS BOOK IS FOR:

THIS BOOK IS CRAFTED TO SERVE A WIDE SPECTRUM OF LEARNERS, FROM ABSOLUTE BEGINNERS TO INTERMEDIATE USERS WHO ASPIRE TO BECOME PROFICIENT ASP.NET DEVELOPERS. HERE'S A BREAKDOWN OF WHO WILL BENEFIT THE MOST:

1. BEGINNERS WHO WANT TO BUILD DYNAMIC WEBSITES USING ASP.NET

IF YOU HAVE LITTLE OR NO BACKGROUND IN PROGRAMMING OR WEB DEVELOPMENT, THIS BOOK IS STRUCTURED TO GUIDE YOU FROM THE VERY BASICS. YOU'LL BE INTRODUCED TO FUNDAMENTAL CONCEPTS SUCH AS HTML, CSS, AND JAVASCRIPT BEFORE DIVING INTO ASP.NET. WITH CLEAR INSTRUCTIONS, SIMPLIFIED EXPLANATIONS, AND HANDS-ON EXAMPLES, YOU'LL FIND YOURSELF GAINING CONFIDENCE IN WRITING YOUR FIRST ASP.NET APPLICATIONS BY THE END OF UNIT I.

2. STUDENTS AND LEARNERS OF BCA, BSC-IT, MCA, AND ENGINEERING COURSES

THIS BOOK IS IDEAL FOR ACADEMIC PURPOSES. IT COMPLEMENTS THE CURRICULUM OF MOST UNDERGRADUATE AND POSTGRADUATE COMPUTER SCIENCE AND IT PROGRAMS. EACH CHAPTER NOT ONLY ALIGNS WITH CORE SYLLABI BUT ALSO INCLUDES PRACTICAL ELEMENTS OFTEN REQUIRED IN LAB EXAMINATIONS AND PROJECT WORK. STUDENTS CAN USE THE EXERCISES AND MINI-PROJECTS FOR SEMESTER PROJECTS, ASSIGNMENTS, OR VIVA PREPARATION.

3. WORKING PROFESSIONALS SEEKING TO TRANSITION INTO ASP.NET DEVELOPMENT

PROFESSIONALS FROM OTHER DOMAINS WHO WANT TO SWITCH TO ASP.NET-BASED DEVELOPMENT WILL FIND THIS BOOK ESPECIALLY HELPFUL. THE CONTENT IS STRUCTURED TO MINIMIZE LEARNING GAPS. CONCEPTS ARE EXPLAINED THROUGH REAL-WORLD ANALOGIES, AND HANDS-ON EXAMPLES ARE INCLUDED TO HELP YOU UNDERSTAND THE USE OF ASP.NET IN ENTERPRISE-LEVEL PROJECTS.

4. HOBBYISTS AND FREELANCERS AIMING TO GAIN REAL-WORLD ASP.NET WEB DEVELOPMENT SKILLS

FOR THOSE WHO ENJOY PROGRAMMING AS A HOBBY OR WISH TO OFFER WEB DEVELOPMENT SERVICES AS FREELANCERS, THIS BOOK PROVIDES A STRONG FOUNDATION. WITH EXAMPLES FOCUSED ON SMALL-SCALE APPLICATIONS, YOU CAN QUICKLY CREATE PORTFOLIO PROJECTS OR OFFER ASP.NET DEVELOPMENT SERVICES CONFIDENTLY.

STUDY APPROACH

LEARNING A TECHNOLOGY LIKE ASP.NET IS MOST EFFECTIVE WHEN APPROACHED WITH A STRATEGY. THIS BOOK FOLLOWS A CAREFULLY DESIGNED PROGRESSION OF CONCEPTS THAT MIRROR HOW APPLICATIONS ARE BUILT IN THE REAL WORLD. HERE'S HOW YOU CAN MAKE THE MOST OF THIS BOOK:

1. READ UNIT BY UNIT (PROGRESSIVE LEARNING)

EACH UNIT IN THIS BOOK IS LAID OUT IN A PROGRESSIVE STRUCTURE, MOVING FROM SIMPLER TO MORE COMPLEX TOPICS. START WITH UNIT I, EVEN IF YOU HAVE PRIOR PROGRAMMING EXPERIENCE. THIS ENSURES YOU BUILD ON A SOLID FOUNDATION. EACH CHAPTER BUILDS UPON THE LAST:

- UNIT I INTRODUCES YOU TO WEB TECHNOLOGIES, VISUAL STUDIO, AND THE BASIC STRUCTURE OF AN ASP.NET APPLICATION.
- UNIT II MOVES INTO WEB FORMS, CONTROLS, VALIDATION, AND DESIGN ELEMENTS.
- UNIT III COVERS DATA ACCESS, A CRUCIAL PART OF WEB APPLICATION DEVELOPMENT.
- UNIT IV TRANSITIONS YOU INTO ASP.NET MVC, WHICH IS HIGHLY SOUGHT-AFTER IN THE PROFESSIONAL WORLD.

TAKE YOUR TIME WITH EACH UNIT. DO NOT SKIP CHAPTERS, ESPECIALLY IF YOU'RE NEW TO THE TECHNOLOGY.

2. PRACTICE CODE SNIPPETS ACTIVELY

EVERY CHAPTER INCLUDES HANDS-ON CODE SNIPPETS AND PROJECTS. YOU'RE ENCOURAGED TO REPLICATE EACH ONE MANUALLY RATHER THAN COPYING AND PASTING. TYPING CODE REINFORCES UNDERSTANDING AND MUSCLE MEMORY.

STEPS TO FOLLOW:

- SET UP VISUAL STUDIO AND CONFIGURE YOUR ENVIRONMENT AS DESCRIBED.
- MANUALLY TYPE OUT CODE EXAMPLES.
- TRY MODIFYING VALUES AND OBSERVING THE OUTPUT.
- DEBUG ERRORS THAT OCCUR AND TRY TO UNDERSTAND WHAT WENT WRONG.

DOING THIS WILL HELP YOU:

- IMPROVE DEBUGGING SKILLS.
- GAIN A DEEPER UNDERSTANDING OF HOW ASP.NET WORKS UNDER THE HOOD.
- INCREASE CONFIDENCE IN WRITING ORIGINAL CODE.

3. WORK ON MINI PROJECTS

AFTER COMPLETING EACH UNIT, TRY TO BUILD A SMALL-SCALE APPLICATION BASED ON WHAT YOU'VE LEARNED. HERE ARE A FEW IDEAS:

- AFTER UNIT I: CREATE A SIMPLE PERSONAL PORTFOLIO WEBPAGE.
- AFTER UNIT II: DEVELOP A CONTACT FORM WITH VALIDATIONS.
- AFTER UNIT III: BUILD A CRUD (CREATE, READ, UPDATE, DELETE) APPLICATION USING SQL SERVER.
- AFTER UNIT IV: CREATE A BASIC E-COMMERCE CART USING MVC.

THESE MINI-PROJECTS:

- CONSOLIDATE YOUR KNOWLEDGE.
- PROVIDE CONCRETE OUTCOMES THAT CAN BE INCLUDED IN YOUR PORTFOLIO.
- HELP YOU UNDERSTAND HOW MULTIPLE CONCEPTS INTEGRATE IN REAL-WORLD PROJECTS.

4. REVISE KEY CONCEPTS

EACH CHAPTER CONCLUDES WITH:

- A SUMMARY
- KEY POINTS
- CHECKLISTS
- QUICK REVISION QUESTIONS

USE THESE TOOLS ACTIVELY. REWRITING SUMMARIES IN YOUR OWN WORDS, CREATING FLASHCARDS, OR TEACHING A FRIEND THE CONCEPT ARE EXCELLENT WAYS TO REINFORCE YOUR LEARNING.

YOU CAN ALSO KEEP A SEPARATE REVISION NOTEBOOK OR DIGITAL DOCUMENT WHERE YOU JOT DOWN:

- FREQUENTLY USED SYNTAX.
- DEFINITIONS AND DIFFERENCES (E.G., VIEWSTATE VS SESSION).
- CODE PATTERNS AND TEMPLATES (E.G., HOW TO CONNECT TO SQL SERVER).

5. EXPERIMENT AND EXPLORE BEYOND THE BOOK

DON'T LIMIT YOURSELF TO WHAT'S WRITTEN. EXPLORE THE WORLD BEYOND EACH CHAPTER:

- TRY DIFFERENT PROPERTIES OF THE CONTROLS.
- USE EXTERNAL LIBRARIES OR NUGET PACKAGES.

- CUSTOMIZE THE UI USING BOOTSTRAP OR MATERIAL DESIGN.
- INTEGRATE THIRD-PARTY APIS OR PAYMENT GATEWAYS.

THIS KIND OF EXPLORATION HELPS YOU:

- STAND OUT IN INTERVIEWS AND ON THE JOB.
- BUILD APPLICATIONS WITH RICHER FEATURES.
- UNDERSTAND THE ECOSYSTEM OF ASP.NET AND FULL-STACK DEVELOPMENT.

BENEFITS OF STUDYING THIS BOOK

STUDYING THIS BOOK OFFERS A WIDE ARRAY OF ADVANTAGES THAT EXTEND BEYOND JUST ACQUIRING TECHNICAL SKILLS:

1. BUILD STRONG FOUNDATIONAL AND ADVANCED SKILLS IN ASP.NET

FROM SETTING UP YOUR ENVIRONMENT TO CREATING MVC-BASED WEB APPLICATIONS, THIS BOOK ENSURES THAT YOU DEVELOP SKILLS AT EVERY LAYER OF ASP.NET DEVELOPMENT. IT EMPHASIZES BOTH THEORY AND PRACTICE, ENSURING YOU'RE NOT JUST READING ABOUT CODE—YOU'RE WRITING IT.

YOU'LL LEARN TO:

- CREATE WEB FORMS.
- USE VALIDATION CONTROLS.
- WORK WITH STATE MANAGEMENT.
- INTERACT WITH SQL DATABASES USING ADO.NET.
- BUILD MVC APPLICATIONS.

2. GAIN PRACTICAL EXPOSURE TO REAL-WORLD ASP.NET APPLICATIONS

EACH CONCEPT IS PRESENTED ALONGSIDE A REAL-WORLD ANALOGY OR A BUSINESS SCENARIO. YOU'LL LEARN TO:

- CREATE LOGIN PAGES.
- VALIDATE FORMS FOR SECURE USER INPUTS.
- MANAGE SESSIONS IN A MULTI-USER ENVIRONMENT.
- BUILD DASHBOARDS AND ADMIN PANELS.

ALL THESE EXAMPLES HELP YOU RELATE WHAT YOU'RE LEARNING WITH WHAT'S USED IN PROFESSIONAL ENVIRONMENTS.

3. UNDERSTAND FULL-STACK WEB DEVELOPMENT USING MICROSOFT TECHNOLOGIES

THOUGH THIS BOOK IS ASP.NET-CENTRIC, IT LAYS THE GROUNDWORK FOR BECOMING A FULL-STACK DEVELOPER IN THE MICROSOFT ECOSYSTEM. HERE'S HOW:

- FRONTEND: HTML, CSS, JAVASCRIPT, RAZOR VIEWS
- BACKEND: ASP.NET WEB FORMS AND MVC
- DATABASE: ADO.NET AND SQL SERVER

IN LATER STAGES, YOU CAN EXTEND YOUR SKILLS INTO:

- BLAZOR FOR SPA DEVELOPMENT
- AZURE FOR CLOUD DEPLOYMENT
- ENTITY FRAMEWORK FOR ORM
- WEB APIS FOR RESTFUL SERVICES

4. BE PREPARED FOR INTERNSHIPS, JOB INTERVIEWS, AND PROFESSIONAL WEB DEVELOPMENT

YOU'LL BUILD PROJECTS, UNDERSTAND REAL-WORLD APPLICATIONS, AND GET FAMILIAR WITH PROFESSIONAL TOOLS LIKE VISUAL STUDIO. THIS POSITIONS YOU WELL FOR:

- TECHNICAL INTERVIEWS
- CODING CHALLENGES
- INTERNSHIP AND JOB OPPORTUNITIES

THIS BOOK PREPARES YOU TO ANSWER QUESTIONS LIKE:

- EXPLAIN VIEWSTATE VS SESSION STATE.
- HOW DOES MVC ROUTING WORK?
- WHAT IS THE DIFFERENCE BETWEEN WEB FORMS AND MVC?
- HOW TO BIND DATA USING ADO.NET?

MASTERING ASP.NET: FROM BEGINNER TO WEB DEVELOPER

TABLE OF CONTENTS

UNIT IV: ASP.NET MVC FRAMEWORK

ABOUT THE AUTHOR:

ANSHUMAN KUMAR MISHRA IS A SEASONED EDUCATOR AND PROLIFIC AUTHOR WITH OVER 20 YEARS OF EXPERIENCE IN THE TEACHING FIELD. HE HAS A DEEP PASSION FOR TECHNOLOGY AND A STRONG COMMITMENT TO MAKING COMPLEX CONCEPTS ACCESSIBLE TO STUDENTS AT ALL LEVELS. WITH AN M.TECH IN COMPUTER SCIENCE FROM BIT MESRA, HE BRINGS BOTH ACADEMIC EXPERTISE AND PRACTICAL EXPERIENCE TO HIS WORK.

CURRENTLY SERVING AS AN ASSISTANT PROFESSOR AT DORANDA COLLEGE, ANSHUMAN HAS BEEN A GUIDING FORCE FOR MANY ASPIRING COMPUTER SCIENTISTS AND ENGINEERS, NURTURING THEIR SKILLS IN VARIOUS PROGRAMMING LANGUAGES AND TECHNOLOGIES. HIS TEACHING STYLE IS FOCUSED ON CLARITY, HANDS-ON LEARNING, AND MAKING STUDENTS COMFORTABLE WITH BOTH THEORETICAL AND PRACTICAL ASPECTS OF COMPUTER SCIENCE.

THROUGHOUT HIS CAREER, ANSHUMAN KUMAR MISHRA HAS AUTHORED OVER 25 BOOKS ON A WIDE RANGE OF TOPICS INCLUDING PYTHON, JAVA, C, C++, DATA SCIENCE, ARTIFICIAL INTELLIGENCE, SQL, .NET, WEB PROGRAMMING, DATA STRUCTURES, AND MORE. HIS BOOKS HAVE BEEN WELL-RECEIVED BY STUDENTS, PROFESSIONALS, AND INSTITUTIONS ALIKE FOR THEIR STRAIGHTFORWARD EXPLANATIONS, PRACTICAL EXERCISES, AND DEEP INSIGHTS INTO THE SUBJECTS.

ANSHUMAN'S APPROACH TO TEACHING AND WRITING IS ROOTED IN HIS BELIEF THAT LEARNING SHOULD BE ENGAGING, INTUITIVE, AND HIGHLY APPLICABLE TO REAL-WORLD SCENARIOS. HIS EXPERIENCE IN BOTH ACADEMIA AND INDUSTRY HAS GIVEN HIM A UNIQUE PERSPECTIVE ON HOW TO BEST PREPARE STUDENTS FOR THE EVOLVING WORLD OF TECHNOLOGY.

IN HIS BOOKS, ANSHUMAN AIMS NOT ONLY TO IMPART KNOWLEDGE BUT ALSO TO INSPIRE A LIFELONG LOVE FOR LEARNING AND EXPLORATION IN THE WORLD OF COMPUTER SCIENCE AND PROGRAMMING.

Copyright Page

Title **MASTERING ASP.NET: FROM BEGINNER TO WEB DEVELOPER**

Author: Anshuman Kumar Mishra

CHAPTER 1: INTRODUCTION TO WEB TECHNOLOGIES

Web technologies form the foundation of all modern web applications. Whether you're building a blog, an e-commerce platform, or a large enterprise application, understanding how web technologies work is crucial. This chapter lays the groundwork by explaining basic concepts, tools, and the evolution of web development technologies.

📌 1. Basics of Web Development

Web Development is the multifaceted process of creating and maintaining websites and web applications that are accessible and functional through web browsers. It encompasses a wide range of activities, from designing the user interface to managing the server-side infrastructure. For a comprehensive understanding, web development is broadly categorized into three main areas: Frontend Development, Backend Development, and Full Stack Development.

1. Frontend Development: The User's Experience (UI/UX)

- **What it is:** Frontend development, also known as client-side development, focuses on everything the user directly sees and interacts with on a website or web application. This includes the visual design, layout, interactive elements, and overall user experience (UX) and user interface (UI). The goal of a frontend developer is to create a seamless, intuitive, and visually appealing experience for the end-user.
- **Analogy:** Think of a physical store. The frontend is like the storefront, the displays, the layout of the aisles, the cash register, and how you, as a customer, navigate and interact with everything.
- **Key Responsibilities:**
  - **Implementing the design:** Translating visual designs (often created by UI/UX designers) into functional web pages.
  - **Creating interactive elements:** Developing buttons, forms, animations, and other interactive components that respond to user actions.
  - **Ensuring responsiveness:** Making sure the website or application looks and functions correctly on various devices and screen sizes (desktops, tablets, smartphones).
  - **Optimizing for performance:** Ensuring the website loads quickly and runs smoothly in the browser.
  - **Accessibility:** Making the website usable by people with disabilities.
- **Core Technologies:**
  - **HTML (HyperText Markup Language):** The structural foundation of every web page. It defines the meaning and structure of the content (e.g., headings, paragraphs, images, links). Think of it as the skeleton of the website.
    - **Example:** Using `<p>` tags to define a paragraph of text, `<h1>` to define a main heading, `<img>` to embed an image, and `<a>` to create a hyperlink.

- **CSS (Cascading Style Sheets):** Used to control the visual presentation of the HTML content. This includes colors, fonts, layout, spacing, animations, and responsiveness. Think of it as the clothing and aesthetics of the website.
    - **Example:** Setting the background color of a button to blue, changing the font size of a heading, or defining how elements should be arranged on different screen sizes using media queries.
  - **JavaScript (JS):** A powerful scripting language that adds interactivity and dynamic behavior to websites. It allows for manipulating the HTML and CSS in response to user actions, making asynchronous requests to the backend, and much more. Think of it as the behavior and intelligence of the website.
    - **Example:** Making a dropdown menu appear when a button is clicked, validating user input in a form before submission, or updating the content of a page without requiring a full reload.
- **Frameworks and Libraries:** Frontend developers often utilize frameworks and libraries built on top of these core technologies to streamline development and build complex user interfaces more efficiently. Examples include React, Angular, Vue.js, and jQuery.

2. Backend Development: The Application's Engine (Server-Side Logic)

- **What it is:** Backend development, also known as server-side development, focuses on the behind-the-scenes functionality that powers the website or web application. This involves managing the server, database, and application logic. It's responsible for processing user requests, handling data, ensuring security, and making sure the frontend has the information it needs to display.
- **Analogy:** Continuing the store analogy, the backend is like the stockroom, the accounting department, the security system, and the staff that manages inventory and processes transactions. Customers don't directly see it, but it's essential for the store to function.
- **Key Responsibilities:**
  - **Building and maintaining the server-side infrastructure:** Setting up and managing servers that host the application.
  - **Developing the application logic:** Writing code that handles user requests, processes data, and implements the core functionality of the application.
  - **Managing databases:** Storing, retrieving, and manipulating data using database systems.
  - **Ensuring security:** Protecting the application and its data from unauthorized access and cyber threats.
  - **Developing APIs (Application Programming Interfaces):** Creating interfaces that allow the frontend to communicate with the backend.
- **Core Technologies (Examples):** Backend developers have a wide range of programming languages and frameworks to choose from, depending on the project requirements and their preferences.
  - **ASP.NET (C#):** A powerful framework developed by Microsoft for building web applications.
  - **PHP:** A widely used scripting language particularly suited for web development.
  - **Python:** A versatile language with popular frameworks like Django and Flask for backend development.

    - **Node.js (JavaScript):** Allows developers to use JavaScript on the server-side, creating a consistent language across the frontend and backend.
    - **Ruby on Rails (Ruby):** A developer-friendly framework known for its convention-over-configuration approach.
    - **Java (Spring):** A robust and scalable language with the Spring framework for enterprise-level applications.
- **Databases (Examples):** Backend development heavily relies on databases to store and manage application data.
    - **SQL Server:** A relational database management system developed by Microsoft.
    - **MySQL:** A popular open-source relational database management system.
    - **PostgreSQL:** Another powerful open-source relational database management system.
    - **MongoDB:** A NoSQL database that stores data in flexible, document-like structures.
    - **Firebase (Firestore):** A NoSQL cloud database offered by Google.

3. Full Stack Development: The Hybrid Approach

- **What it is:** A full stack developer possesses skills in both frontend and backend development. They are capable of working on all layers of the application, from the user interface down to the database and server logic.
- **Analogy:** In the store analogy, a full stack developer is like a versatile employee who can handle tasks on the sales floor (frontend) as well as manage inventory in the back (backend).
- **Advantages:**
    - **Increased efficiency:** One person can handle various aspects of the project.
    - **Better understanding of the whole system:** Facilitates better communication and collaboration within a team.
    - **Faster development cycles for smaller projects.**
- **Challenges:**
    - **Requires a broad skillset:** Staying proficient in both frontend and backend technologies can be demanding.
    - **May not have deep expertise in every area:** Specialists in frontend or backend might have more in-depth knowledge in their respective domains.

Example Breakdown (BBC News):

- **Frontend (What you see and interact with):**
    - The overall **layout** of the website, including the header, navigation menus, sidebars, and footer.
    - The **text** content of the news articles, headlines, and captions.
    - **Buttons** for navigation, sharing articles, and interacting with comments.
    - **Images** and videos embedded within the articles.
    - The **styling** (colors, fonts, spacing) that makes the website visually appealing and consistent with the BBC brand.

    - The **interactive elements** like dropdown menus, search bars, and potentially live updates.
    - How the website **adapts** to different screen sizes (desktop, mobile).
- **Backend (What powers the application behind the scenes):**
    - **Fetching news from a database:** When you click on a news category, the backend logic queries a database to retrieve the latest articles related to that topic.
    - **Handling logins:** When you create an account and log in, the backend verifies your credentials against a database of user information.
    - **Managing user comments:** When you submit a comment on an article, the backend receives, stores, and displays it.
    - **Serving the website content:** The backend processes requests from your browser and sends the necessary HTML, CSS, JavaScript, and images to be displayed.
    - **Handling search queries:** When you use the search bar, the backend processes your query and searches its database for relevant articles.
    - **Managing the content management system (CMS):** The backend provides tools for BBC journalists and editors to create, edit, and publish news articles.

📌 2. Client-side vs Server-side Programming

The distinction between client-side and server-side programming is a core concept in web development. It defines where the code is executed and what responsibilities each side handles in the process of delivering a functional web experience to the user. Think of it as a conversation between your web browser (the client) and a distant computer (the server).

Here's a detailed breakdown of the differences, as summarized in your table, along with illustrative examples:

Aspect: Executed on

- **Client-side:** Code executed directly on the **user's web browser**. This means the processing happens on the device (computer, phone, tablet) that the user is using to view the website.
    - **Analogy:** Imagine ordering food at a restaurant. The client-side is like you, the customer, looking at the menu, filling out an order slip, and interacting with the waiter at your table. The actions you take and the immediate feedback you receive (like seeing the menu) happen "on your side."
- **Server-side:** Code executed on a **web server**, which is a remote computer that hosts the website and its associated applications. The processing happens on this powerful machine, and the results are then sent back to the user's browser.
    - **Analogy:** In the restaurant scenario, the server-side is like the kitchen, the chefs, the inventory management system, and the payment processing system. You don't directly see these processes, but they are crucial for your order to be prepared, your payment to be processed, and the overall restaurant operation.

Aspect: Languages

- **Client-side:** Primarily uses **HTML (HyperText Markup Language)** for structuring content, **CSS (Cascading Style Sheets)** for styling and presentation, and **JavaScript**[1] **(JS)** for adding interactivity and dynamic behavior.
  - **HTML:** Defines the structure and meaning of the content (e.g., headings, paragraphs, images, links).
    - **Example:** `<button onclick="changeText()">Click Me</button>` defines a button.
  - **CSS:** Controls how the HTML elements are displayed (e.g., colors, fonts, layout).
    - **Example:** `button { background-color: blue; color: white; }` styles the button.
  - **JavaScript:** Adds dynamic functionality and handles user interactions directly in the browser.
    - **Example:** The `changeText()` function in JavaScript could modify the text content of an element on the page when the button is clicked, without needing to communicate with the server.

Server-side: Employs a variety of programming languages such as **ASP.NET (often with C# or VB.NET), PHP, Node.js (JavaScript on the server), Python (with frameworks like Django or Flask), Ruby (with Ruby on Rails), Java (with Spring), and many others.** The choice of language depends on factors like project requirements, developer expertise, and performance considerations.

  - **ASP.NET (C#):** Used for building robust and scalable web applications, often integrated with Microsoft technologies.
    - **Example:** Code that handles user authentication, interacts with a SQL Server database, and generates dynamic HTML.
  - **PHP:** A popular language for web development, often used for content management systems like WordPress.
    - **Example:** Code that processes form submissions, queries a MySQL database, and generates dynamic web pages.
  - **Node.js (JavaScript):** Allows using JavaScript for both frontend and backend development, enabling code sharing and a more unified development experience.
    - **Example:** Code that handles real-time communication using WebSockets or builds RESTful APIs.
  - **Python (Django/Flask):** Known for its readability and extensive libraries, often used for complex web applications and APIs.
    - **Example:** Code that defines data models, handles URL routing, and interacts with a PostgreSQL database.

Aspect: Used for

- **Client-side:** Primarily responsible for **user interface (UI) interactions**, making the website dynamic and responsive to user actions without constant server requests. It's also used for **client-side validation**, checking user input in forms before submitting it to the server, improving user experience and reducing server load.

  - **Example (UI Interaction):** Animating a button when a user hovers their mouse over it, displaying a dropdown menu when a user clicks, or creating interactive maps.
  - **Example (Validation):** Using JavaScript to check if a user has entered a valid email format in a registration form *before* sending it to the server for processing. If the format is incorrect, an error message is displayed immediately in the browser.

- **Server-side:** Handles **database access**, allowing the application to store, retrieve, and manipulate data persistently. It also implements the core **business logic** of the application, which includes the rules and processes that govern how the application functions (e.g., processing orders, managing user accounts, calculating prices).
  - **Example (Database Access):** Retrieving a user's profile information from a database to display on their account page, or storing a new blog post submitted through a form.
  - **Example (Business Logic):** Implementing the logic for calculating the total price of items in a shopping cart, applying discounts, or verifying user credentials during login.

Example Workflow:

This example clearly illustrates the interplay between client-side and server-side programming:

1. **A user fills out a form on a website (client-side).**
   - The user interacts with HTML form elements (text fields, dropdowns, checkboxes) rendered in their browser. This is purely a client-side operation.
2. **JavaScript checks if all fields are filled (client-side validation).**
   - Before the form data is sent to the server, JavaScript code running in the user's browser can quickly verify if required fields have been filled and if the data format is correct (e.g., a valid email address). This provides immediate feedback to the user without needing to contact the server.
3. **The form is submitted to the server (server-side request).**
   - Once the client-side validation (if any) is successful, the browser sends the form data as an HTTP request to the web server.
4. **ASP.NET stores the data into SQL Server (server-side processing).**
   - The web server, running ASP.NET code in this example, receives the form data. The ASP.NET application then processes this data, likely performing tasks like:
     - Sanitizing the input to prevent security vulnerabilities.
     - Validating the data again on the server-side (as client-side validation can be bypassed).
     - Connecting to the SQL Server database.
     - Executing SQL commands to insert the submitted data into the appropriate tables.
5. **A confirmation message is sent back to the browser (client-side response).**

- After successfully processing the form data and storing it in the database, the ASP.NET application on the server generates a response (often in the form of an HTML page or a JSON/XML data structure). This response is sent back to the user's browser.
- The browser then renders this response, which could be a simple confirmation message ("Your data has been submitted successfully") or a redirect to another page. JavaScript on the client-side might also be used to dynamically update the current page with the confirmation message without a full page reload.

In essence:

- The **client-side** focuses on the user's direct experience, making the website interactive and visually engaging within the confines of the user's browser.
- The **server-side** handles the heavy lifting behind the scenes, managing data, implementing business logic, and ensuring the application functions correctly and securely.

Both client-side and server-side programming are crucial for creating modern web applications. They work in tandem to deliver a rich and functional user experience. Understanding their individual roles and how they interact is a fundamental step in becoming a proficient web developer.

📌 3. Overview of HTML, CSS, JavaScript: The Client-Side Triad

HTML, CSS, and JavaScript are the fundamental building blocks of the World Wide Web, forming what is often referred to as the "client-side triad." They work together in the user's web browser to create the structure, style, and interactivity of virtually every webpage you encounter. Let's break down each technology in detail with examples.

1. HTML (HyperText Markup Language): The Structure of Web Pages

- **What it is:** HTML is the standard markup language for creating web pages. It provides the semantic structure and meaning to the content displayed in a web browser. It's not a programming language in the traditional sense; rather, it uses a system of tags to describe and organize the different parts of a webpage.
- **Purpose:** To define the content and structure of a webpage. This includes identifying headings, paragraphs, lists, images, links, forms, and other elements. It tells the browser what the content *is*, not how it should *look*.
- **Key Concepts:**
  - **Elements:** The fundamental building blocks of HTML. They are defined by tags. Most elements have a start tag and an end tag, with content in between (e.g.,

<p>This is a paragraph.</p>). Some elements are self-closing (e.g., <br /> for a line break).
    - **Tags:** Keywords enclosed in angle brackets (< and >). Start tags indicate the beginning of an element, and end tags (with a forward slash) indicate the end.
    - **Attributes:** Provide additional information about HTML elements. They are specified in the start tag and consist of a name and a value (e.g., <img src="image.jpg" alt="My Image">).
    - **Document Structure:** Every HTML document follows a basic structure:
        - <!DOCTYPE html>: Declares the document type as HTML5.
        - <html>: The root element[1] of the HTML page.
        - <head>: Contains meta-information about the HTML document, such as the page title, character set, links to CSS files, and scripts. This information is usually not displayed directly on the page.
        - <body>: Contains the visible page content.
- **Example Breakdown:**

HTML

```
<!DOCTYPE html>
<html>
<head>
  <title>My First Web Page</title>
</head>
<body>
  <h1>Welcome to Web Development</h1>
  <p>This is an example of HTML structure.</p>
  <a href="https://www.example.com">Visit Example Website</a>
  <div>
    <img src="my_image.png" alt="A descriptive image">
    <ul>
      <li>Item 1</li>
      <li>Item 2</li>
    </ul>
  </div>
</body>
</html>
```

```
* `<!DOCTYPE html>`: Tells the browser that this is an HTML5 document.
* `<html>`: The root element, encompassing all other HTML content.
* `<head>`:
    * `<title>My First Web Page</title>`: Sets the title that appears in the browser tab or window title bar.
* `<body>`: Contains the visible content of the webpage:
    * `<h1>Welcome to Web Development</h1>`: Defines a main heading (level 1).
    * `<p>This is an example of HTML structure.</p>`: Defines a paragraph of text.
    * `<a href="https://www.example.com">Visit Example Website</a>`: Creates a hyperlink (anchor tag) that, when clicked, will navigate the user to the specified URL. The `href` attribute specifies the link destination.
    * `<div>`: Defines a generic container element that can be used to group other HTML elements for styling or scripting purposes.
    * `<img src="my_image.png" alt="A descriptive image">`: Embeds an image. The `src` attribute specifies the path to the image file, and the `alt` attribute provides alternative text if the image cannot be displayed.
```

```
    * `<ul>`: Defines an unordered list (bulleted list).
    * `<li>Item 1</li>` and `<li>Item 2</li>`: Define list items within the
unordered list.
```

2. CSS (Cascading Style Sheets): The Styling of Web Pages

- **What it is:** CSS is a stylesheet language used to describe the presentation of an HTML (or XML, including in XML dialects like SVG, MathML) document. It controls how the elements defined in HTML are displayed in the browser.
- **Purpose:** To separate the content (HTML) from the presentation (styling). This makes web development more organized, maintainable, and allows for consistent styling across multiple pages.
- **Key Concepts:**
    - **Selectors:** Target specific HTML elements that you want to style (e.g., `body`, `h1`, `p`, `.my-class`, `#my-id`).
    - **Properties:** The aspects of an element you want to style (e.g., `background-color`, `font-family`, `color`, `width`, `margin`).
    - **Values:** The settings you apply to the properties (e.g., `lightblue`, `Arial, sans-serif`, `navy`, `100px`, `10px`).
    - **Ruleset (or Style Rule):** A combination of a selector and one or more declarations (property-value pairs) enclosed in curly braces `{}`.
    - **Cascading:** The "cascading" aspect refers to how styles from different sources (browser defaults, external stylesheets, internal styles, inline styles) are applied to elements. Stylesheets are applied in a specific order, and more specific styles can override less specific ones.
- **Example Breakdown:**

CSS
```css
body {
  background-color: lightblue;
  font-family: Arial, sans-serif;
}

h1 {
  color: navy;
}

p {
  font-size: 16px;
  line-height: 1.5;
}

.important-text {
  font-weight: bold;
  color: red;
}

#main-heading {
  text-align: center;
}
```

```
* `body { ... }`: Styles the `<body>` element (the entire visible page
content). It sets the background color to light blue and the default font to
Arial or a generic sans-serif font if Arial is not available.
* `h1 { ... }`: Styles all `<h1>` (main heading) elements, setting their text
color to navy.
* `p { ... }`: Styles all `<p>` (paragraph) elements, setting the font size
to 16 pixels and the line height to 1.5 for better readability.
* `.important-text { ... }`: Styles any HTML element that has the class
attribute set to "important-text" (e.g., `<p class="important-text">This is
important.</p>`). It makes the text bold and red.
* `#main-heading { ... }`: Styles the HTML element that has the ID attribute
set to "main-heading" (e.g., `<h1 id="main-heading">This is a centered
heading</h1>`). It centers the text within the element.
```

3. JavaScript (JS): Making Pages Interactive

- **What it is:** JavaScript is a dynamic, high-level, often just-in-time compiled, and multi-paradigm scripting language that is essential for web development. It allows you to add interactivity, dynamic behavior, and complex functionality to websites.
- **Purpose:** To make web pages respond to user actions, manipulate the HTML structure (DOM - Document Object Model) and CSS styles dynamically, handle asynchronous requests to the server (AJAX), and build complex single-page applications (SPAs).
- **Key Concepts:**
  - **Variables:** Used to store data.
  - **Data Types:** Different kinds of data that can be stored (e.g., numbers, strings, booleans).
  - **Operators:** Symbols used to perform operations on data (e.g., +, -, *, /, ==, ===).
  - **Control Flow Statements:** Structures that control the order in which code is executed (e.g., `if...else`, `for`, `while`).
  - **Functions:** Reusable blocks of code that perform specific tasks.
  - **Objects:** Collections of key-value pairs, representing entities and their properties.
  - **Events:** Actions that occur in the browser (e.g., clicking a button, hovering over an element, submitting a form). JavaScript can "listen" for these events and execute code in response.
  - **DOM (Document Object Model):** A programming interface for HTML and XML documents. It represents the page structure as a tree of objects, allowing JavaScript to access and manipulate the content, structure, and styles of the webpage.
- **Example Breakdown:**

JavaScript

```
function greet() {
  alert("Welcome to ASP.NET Web Development!");
}

let button = document.querySelector('button'); // Selects the first button
element
if (button) {
  button.addEventListener('click', greet); // Attaches the greet function to
the button's click event
}
```

```
function changeBackgroundColor() {
  document.body.style.backgroundColor = 'yellow'; // Changes the background
color of the body
}

let anotherButton = document.getElementById('changeBgButton'); // Selects an
element by its ID
if (anotherButton) {
  anotherButton.addEventListener('click', changeBackgroundColor);
}
```

* `function greet() { ... }`: Defines a function named `greet`. When called, it will display an alert box with the message "Welcome to ASP.NET Web Development!".
* `let button = document.querySelector('button');`: Uses the `querySelector` method to select the first `<button>` element in the HTML document and stores it in the `button` variable.
* `if (button) { button.addEventListener('click', greet); }`: Checks if a button element was found. If so, it attaches an event listener to the button. This means that when the button is clicked (`'click'` event), the `greet` function will be executed.
* `function changeBackgroundColor() { ... }`: Defines a function that changes the `backgroundColor` style of the `document.body` (the `<body>` element) to 'yellow'.
* `let anotherButton = document.getElementById('changeBgButton');`: Uses the `getElementById` method to select the HTML element with the ID attribute set to "changeBgButton" and stores it in the `anotherButton` variable.
* `if (anotherButton) { anotherButton.addEventListener('click', changeBackgroundColor); }`: Attaches the `changeBackgroundColor` function to the click event of the element with the ID "changeBgButton".

The Client-Side Triad in Action:

These three technologies work together seamlessly in the browser:

1. **HTML provides the structure and content of the webpage.**
2. **CSS styles that content, making it visually appealing and organized.**
3. **JavaScript adds interactivity and dynamic behavior, making the page respond to user actions and update without requiring constant reloads.**

For example, imagine a simple form:

- **HTML** would define the input fields (text boxes, buttons).
- **CSS** would style the form (layout, colors, fonts).
- **JavaScript** could be used to:
    - Validate the user's input as they type.
    - Submit the form data to the server when the submit button is clicked.
    - Display a dynamic "thank you" message after submission without reloading the entire page.

Understanding HTML, CSS, and JavaScript is the crucial first step for anyone embarking on a journey into web development. They form the foundation upon which more advanced frontend frameworks and libraries are built.

📌 4. Evolution from Classic ASP to ASP.NET

The journey of web development within the Microsoft ecosystem saw a significant leap forward with the introduction of ASP.NET, succeeding its predecessor, Classic ASP. While Classic ASP served as a foundational technology in the late 1990s, the rise of the .NET framework brought about ASP.NET, addressing many of the limitations of its earlier counterpart and offering substantial improvements in performance, security, and developer productivity.

Here's a detailed comparison of Classic ASP and ASP.NET based on the features outlined in your table:

Feature: Language

- **Classic ASP:** Primarily used **VBScript (Visual Basic Script)** as its scripting language. VBScript was an interpreted language, meaning the code was executed line by line at runtime.
    - **Characteristics:** Relatively easy to learn, especially for those familiar with Visual Basic. However, its interpreted nature contributed to slower performance compared to compiled languages. It lacked strong object-oriented programming (OOP) features.
    - **Example:** As shown in your example, embedding VBScript directly within HTML was common.
- **ASP.NET:** Primarily utilizes **C# (C Sharp)** and **VB.NET (Visual Basic .NET)** as its main programming languages. These are powerful, compiled languages that are part of the .NET framework.
    - **Characteristics:** Offers significantly better performance due to compilation. Provides robust support for object-oriented programming (OOP), allowing for better code organization, reusability, and maintainability. The .NET framework also offers a vast library of pre-built classes and functionalities.
    - **Example:** The ASP.NET example uses C# syntax within an ASP.NET Web Forms control.

Feature: Compilation

- **Classic ASP:** Code was **interpreted** by the web server each time a page was requested. This meant that the server had to read, parse, and execute the VBScript code on every hit, leading to overhead and slower execution times, especially for complex applications.
    - **Analogy:** Imagine a chef having to read a recipe line by line and figure out each step every time they need to cook a dish.

- **ASP.NET:** Code is **compiled to IL (Intermediate Language)** the first time a page is accessed or when the application is built. This IL is then further compiled to native machine code by the Common Language Runtime (CLR) for execution. This pre-compilation significantly improves performance as the server doesn't have to interpret the code on every request.
    - **Analogy:** Imagine the chef having a pre-written set of instructions (the compiled IL) that they can quickly follow each time they need to prepare the dish.

Feature: Code Separation

- **Classic ASP:** Often involved **mixing HTML markup directly with scripting code (VBScript)** within the same `.asp` file. This could lead to messy and hard-to-maintain code, making it difficult to separate the presentation logic (HTML) from the application logic (VBScript).
    - **Analogy:** Imagine the restaurant menu having the cooking instructions embedded directly within the description of each dish. This would make the menu very long and confusing.
- **ASP.NET:** Introduced the **code-behind model**, which separates the user interface (HTML in `.aspx` files for Web Forms, or Razor syntax in `.cshtml` or `.vbhtml` files for MVC/Razor Pages) from the application logic (C# or VB.NET code in separate `.aspx.cs` or `.aspx.vb` files for Web Forms, or controller/page model files for MVC/Razor Pages). This separation of concerns improves code organization, readability, and allows developers and designers to work on different parts of the application independently.
    - **Analogy:** The restaurant has a separate menu (HTML/Razor) for customers and detailed recipes (code-behind) for the chefs in the kitchen.

Feature: Error Handling

- **Classic ASP:** Provided **limited** built-in mechanisms for error handling. Developers often had to rely on basic error trapping and logging, which could be cumbersome and less robust. Unhandled errors could lead to cryptic messages or application crashes.
    - **Analogy:** If something goes wrong in the kitchen, the customer might just get a burnt dish without knowing what happened or if the issue was resolved.
- **ASP.NET:** Offers a comprehensive **try-catch exception handling** mechanism. This allows developers to gracefully handle errors that occur during runtime, log them, display user-friendly error messages, and prevent application crashes. The .NET framework provides a structured way to manage and respond to exceptions.
    - **Analogy:** If something goes wrong in the kitchen, the staff can identify the problem, try to fix it, and perhaps offer the customer an apology or an alternative.

Feature: OOP Support

- **Classic ASP:** Had **minimal** support for object-oriented programming (OOP). While it was possible to simulate some OOP concepts, it lacked the robust features and structure provided by true OOP languages.

    - **Analogy:** The restaurant might have some basic organizational structures, but it's not built around well-defined roles and responsibilities.
- **ASP.NET:** Is built upon the **.NET framework**, which provides full support for object-oriented programming (OOP) principles like encapsulation, inheritance, and polymorphism. OOP allows developers to create more modular, reusable, and maintainable code, leading to more scalable and complex applications.
    - **Analogy:** The restaurant is organized with clear roles for chefs, waiters, managers, and a well-defined hierarchy, making operations more efficient and scalable.

Classic ASP Example Breakdown:

VBScript
```
<%
  Response.Write("Hello from Classic ASP")
%>
```

- `<%` and `%>`: These delimiters enclose the VBScript code that needs to be executed on the server.
- `Response.Write("Hello from Classic ASP")`: This VBScript statement sends the text "Hello from Classic ASP" back to the client's browser as part of the HTML response.

ASP.NET Example (C# Web Forms) Breakdown:

HTML
```
<asp:Label ID="lblMessage" runat="server" Text="Hello from
ASP.NET"></asp:Label>
```

- `<asp:Label>`: This is an ASP.NET Web Forms server control. Server controls are special elements that are processed on the server and render HTML output to the browser.
- `ID="lblMessage"`: This assigns a unique identifier to the Label control, allowing it to be referenced in the code-behind file (e.g., in C#).
- `runat="server"`: This crucial attribute indicates that this control should be processed on the web server.
- `Text="Hello from ASP.NET"`: This sets the initial text content of the Label control. This value can also be dynamically changed in the code-behind file.

Why ASP.NET? (As highlighted in your text):

- **Better performance through compiled code:** As discussed, compilation leads to significantly faster execution compared to interpreted code.
- **Code-behind architecture:** The separation of presentation and logic improves code organization and maintainability.
- **Support for modern frameworks (MVC, Web API):** ASP.NET evolved beyond Web Forms to include powerful architectural patterns like Model-View-Controller (MVC) and Web API for building modern web applications and services.

- **Built-in security and state management:** ASP.NET offers features like form validation controls, membership and role management, and various state management options to simplify development and enhance security.
- **Visual Studio integration:** ASP.NET is tightly integrated with Visual Studio, a powerful Integrated Development Environment (IDE) that provides excellent tooling for coding, debugging, and deployment.

Real-World Use Cases:

- **Classic ASP:** Due to its age and limitations, Classic ASP is primarily found in **legacy applications** that were built in the late 1990s and early 2000s and may still be running for various reasons (e.g., cost of migration, specific functionality). However, it is generally not used for new development.
- **ASP.NET:** Powers a vast range of **modern portals** and enterprise-level applications, including:
    - **Banking systems:** Secure online banking platforms.
    - **Enterprise dashboards:** Internal tools for data visualization and business intelligence.
    - **Intranets:** Internal communication and collaboration platforms for organizations.
    - E-commerce websites, content management systems, and many other types of web applications.

□ Summary

- Web development involves building both client-facing and server-side applications.
- HTML, CSS, and JavaScript are essential for frontend development.
- ASP.NET is a robust framework for backend development using Microsoft technologies.
- Understanding the evolution from Classic ASP to ASP.NET helps appreciate its powerful features.

WRITE 10 PRACTICAL EXAMPLES WITH SOLUTION

1. Simple Portfolio Website (HTML & CSS - Client-Side Focus)

- **Problem:** Create a basic online portfolio showcasing personal information, skills, and projects.
- **Solution:**
    - **HTML:** Structure the content with sections for "About Me," "Skills," and "Projects" using appropriate tags (`<header>`, `<nav>`, `<section>`, `<h1>`, `<p>`, `<ul>`, `<li>`, `<img>`, `<a>`).
    - **CSS:** Style the layout, typography, colors, and responsiveness of the portfolio to create a visually appealing and user-friendly design using selectors, properties, and values.
    - **Code Snippet (Illustrative HTML):**

HTML

```
<!DOCTYPE html>
<html>
<head>
    <title>My Portfolio</title>
    <link rel="stylesheet" href="style.css">
</head>
<body>
    <header>
        <h1>John Doe</h1>
        <nav>
            <ul>
                <li><a href="#about">About</a></li>
                <li><a href="#skills">Skills</a></li>
                <li><a href="#projects">Projects</a></li>
            </ul>
        </nav>
    </header>
    <section id="about">
        <h2>About Me</h2>
        <p>A passionate web developer with a focus on...</p>
    </section>
    </body>
</html>
```

- **Learning Outcome:** Understanding HTML structure and CSS styling for basic website layout and presentation.

2. Interactive To-Do List (HTML, CSS, JavaScript - Client-Side Interactivity)

- **Problem:** Build a simple to-do list where users can add, remove, and mark tasks as complete without page reloads.
- **Solution:**
    - **HTML:** Create input fields for adding tasks, a button to add, and an unordered list to display tasks.
    - **CSS:** Style the to-do list for better visual organization.
    - **JavaScript:**
        - Listen for the "click" event on the add button.
        - Dynamically create new list items (`<li>`) with the entered task text.
        - Add functionality to mark tasks as complete (e.g., by toggling a CSS class).
        - Implement a "remove" button for each task to delete it from the list.
    - **Learning Outcome:** Applying JavaScript to manipulate the DOM (Document Object Model) and handle user interactions for dynamic client-side behavior.

3. Basic Form Validation (HTML & JavaScript - Client-Side Validation)

- **Problem:** Implement client-side validation for a simple registration form (e.g., checking for empty fields, valid email format).

- **Solution:**
  - **HTML:** Create input fields for username, email, password, etc., and a submit button.
  - **JavaScript:**
    - Listen for the "submit" event on the form.
    - Prevent the default form submission behavior.
    - Write functions to check if each required field is filled.
    - Implement a regular expression to validate the email format.
    - Display error messages next to the invalid fields.
    - Only allow form submission if all validations pass.
  - **Learning Outcome:** Understanding the importance and implementation of client-side validation using JavaScript to improve user experience and reduce server load.

4. Displaying Dynamic Content (HTML, CSS, JavaScript - Client-Side Data Manipulation)

- **Problem:** Fetch an array of product names (simulated in JavaScript) and display them as a styled list on the webpage.
- **Solution:**
  - **HTML:** Create an empty unordered list (`<ul>`) with a specific ID.
  - **CSS:** Style the list and list items.
  - **JavaScript:**
    - Create an array of product names.
    - Get a reference to the empty `<ul>` element using its ID.
    - Loop through the product array.
    - For each product, create a new `<li>` element, set its text content to the product name, and append it to the `<ul>` element.
  - **Learning Outcome:** Using JavaScript to dynamically generate and manipulate HTML content based on data.

5. Simple Login System (Client-Side Form, Server-Side Authentication - Client-Server Interaction)

- **Problem:** Create a basic login form on the client-side that sends credentials to a server for authentication and receives a response.
- **Solution:**
  - **HTML:** Create input fields for username and password, and a submit button.
  - **CSS:** Style the login form.
  - **JavaScript (Client-Side):**
    - Listen for the "submit" event on the form.
    - Prevent default submission.
    - Collect username and password values.
    - Use `fetch` or `XMLHttpRequest` to send a POST request to a server-side endpoint (e.g., `/login`) with the credentials in the request body (likely in JSON format).

        - Handle the server's response (success or error) and display appropriate messages to the user.
    - **Backend (Conceptual - Server-Side):**
        - Create a server-side endpoint (`/login`) using a language like Python (Flask), Node.js (Express), or ASP.NET.
        - Receive the username and password from the client request.
        - Query a database to check if the username exists and if the provided password matches the stored hash.
        - Send a JSON response back to the client indicating success or failure.
    - **Learning Outcome:** Understanding the fundamental client-server interaction for form submission and authentication.

6. Displaying Data from a Server (Client-Side Request, Server-Side Response - Client-Server Data Fetching)

- **Problem:** Fetch a list of users from a server-side API and display their names on the webpage.
- **Solution:**
    - **HTML:** Create an empty unordered list (`<ul>`) to display the user names.
    - **CSS:** Style the list.
    - **JavaScript (Client-Side):**
        - Use `fetch` or `XMLHttpRequest` to make a GET request to a server-side API endpoint (e.g., `/api/users`).
        - Handle the promise returned by `fetch` to get the response.
        - Parse the response data (likely in JSON format).
        - Loop through the array of user objects in the response.
        - For each user, create a new `<li>` element with the user's name and append it to the `<ul>`.
    - **Backend (Conceptual - Server-Side):**
        - Create a server-side API endpoint (`/api/users`) using a backend framework.
        - Retrieve user data from a database.
        - Send the user data back to the client in JSON format.
    - **Learning Outcome:** Understanding how the client-side can asynchronously fetch data from a server and dynamically update the webpage.

7. Simple Counter Application (HTML, JavaScript - Client-Side State Management)

- **Problem:** Create a webpage with a button and a display that increments a counter each time the button is clicked.
- **Solution:**
    - **HTML:** Create a button and a `<span>` or `<p>` element to display the counter value.
    - **CSS:** Style the button and display.
    - **JavaScript:**
        - Declare a variable to store the counter value (initialized to 0).

        - Get references to the button and the display element.
        - Add an event listener to the button's "click" event.
        - Inside the event listener function:
            - Increment the counter variable.
            - Update the text content of the display element with the new counter value.
    - **Learning Outcome:** Understanding basic client-side state management using JavaScript variables and event handling.

8. Classic ASP "Hello World" vs. ASP.NET "Hello World" (Evolution Illustration)

- **Problem:** Demonstrate the basic syntax difference between Classic ASP and ASP.NET for a simple output.
- **Solution:**
    - **Classic ASP (`.asp` file):**

      VBScript

      ```
      <%
          Response.Write("Hello from Classic ASP!")
      %>
      ```

    - **ASP.NET (C# Web Forms - `.aspx` file with code-behind `.aspx.cs`):**
        - **`.aspx`:**

          HTML

          ```
          <%@ Page Language="C#" AutoEventWireup="true"
          CodeBehind="HelloWorld.aspx.cs"
          Inherits="WebApp.HelloWorld" %>

          <!DOCTYPE html>
          <html>
          <head>
              <title>ASP.NET Hello</title>
          </head>
          <body>
              <form id="form1" runat="server">
                  <div>
                      <asp:Label ID="lblMessage"
          runat="server"></asp:Label>
                  </div>
              </form>
          </body>
          </html>
          ```

        - **`.aspx.cs` (Code-Behind):**

          C#

```
using System;
using System.Web.UI;
using System.Web.UI.WebControls;

namespace WebApp
{
    public partial class HelloWorld : Page
    {
        protected void Page_Load(object sender, EventArgs
e)
        {
            lblMessage.Text = "Hello from ASP.NET!";
        }
    }
}
```

- **Learning Outcome:** Understanding the fundamental syntax and structural differences, particularly the code-behind model in ASP.NET compared to the embedded scripting in Classic ASP.

9. Basic Website Layout using HTML and CSS (Frontend Structure and Styling)

- **Problem:** Create a webpage with a header, navigation, main content area, sidebar, and footer using semantic HTML and CSS for layout.
- **Solution:**
  - **HTML:** Use semantic tags like `<header>`, `<nav>`, `<main>`, `<aside>`, and `<footer>` to structure the different sections of the page. Use `<div>` elements for further organization if needed.
  - **CSS:** Use CSS layout techniques like Flexbox or Grid to arrange the different sections into a responsive and visually appealing layout. Style the colors, fonts, and spacing.
  - **Learning Outcome:** Applying HTML for semantic structure and CSS for advanced layout management.

10. Simple Image Gallery (HTML, CSS, JavaScript - Client-Side Image Display)

- **Problem:** Create a webpage that displays a gallery of images, allowing users to click on thumbnails to view a larger version.
- **Solution:**
  - **HTML:** Create a container for thumbnails (using `<img>` tags within `<a>` tags) and a separate area to display the larger image (initially empty or with a placeholder).
  - **CSS:** Style the thumbnails and the large image area.
  - **JavaScript:**
    - Add event listeners to each thumbnail.
    - When a thumbnail is clicked:
      - Prevent the default link behavior.
      - Get the `src` attribute of the clicked thumbnail.
      - Set the `src` attribute of the large image display area to the thumbnail's `src`.

    - Optionally add animations or modal-like behavior for the larger image.
- **Learning Outcome:** Combining HTML for structure, CSS for styling, and JavaScript for handling user interactions and dynamically updating image sources.

30 multiple-choice questions with answers covering the topics of Basics of Web Development, Client-side vs. Server-side Programming, Overview of HTML, CSS, and JavaScript, and the Evolution from Classic ASP to ASP.NET.

1. Which of the following is NOT a core technology of frontend development? a) HTML b) CSS c) JavaScript d) PHP * Answer: d) PHP

2. Which language is primarily used for structuring the content of a web page? a) CSS b) JavaScript c) HTML d) XML * Answer: c) HTML

3. Which language is used for styling the presentation of a web page? a) HTML b) JavaScript c) CSS d) XML * Answer: c) CSS

4. Which language is used to add interactivity to a web page? a) HTML b) CSS c) JavaScript d) XML * Answer: c) JavaScript

5. Which of the following is executed on the user's browser? a) Server-side code b) Client-side code c) Database queries d) Server configurations * Answer: b) Client-side code

6. Which of the following is executed on a web server? a) HTML b) CSS c) JavaScript d) PHP * Answer: d) PHP

7. Which of the following is NOT a server-side language? a) Python b) Node.js c) C# d) JavaScript * Answer: d) JavaScript

8. Which of the following is NOT a client-side language? a) HTML b) CSS c) JavaScript d) SQL * Answer: d) SQL

9. What is the primary purpose of HTML? a) To define the styling of a web page b) To define the structure of a web page c) To add interactivity to a web page d) To manage server-side logic * Answer: b) To define the structure of a web page

10. What does CSS stand for? a) Common Style Sheet b) Cascading Style Sheet c) Computer Style Sheet d) Creative Style Sheet * Answer: b) Cascading Style Sheet

11. What is the purpose of JavaScript? a) To structure web pages b) To style web pages c) To make web pages interactive d) To manage databases * Answer: c) To make web pages interactive

12. Which HTML tag is used to define a heading? a) <p> b) <div> c) <h1> d) <span> * Answer: c) <h1>

13. Which HTML tag is used to define a paragraph? a) <h1> b) <div> c) <span> d) <p> * Answer: d) <p>

14. Which CSS property is used to change the text color of an element? a) font-size b) background-color c) color d) text-align * Answer: c) color

15. Which CSS property is used to change the background color of an element? a) font-size b) background-color c) color d) text-align * Answer: b) background-color

16. Which of the following is NOT a valid CSS selector? a) .my-class b) #my-id c) my-tag d) @my-rule * Answer: d) @my-rule

17. In JavaScript, which method is used to display a message in an alert box? a) console.log() b) document.write() c) alert() d) print() * Answer: c) alert()

18. What does DOM stand for? a) Document Object Model b) Data Object Model c) Digital Output Management d) Dynamic Object Management * Answer: a) Document Object Model

19. Which of the following is an example of a client-side scripting language? a) PHP b) ASP.NET c) JavaScript d) SQL Server * Answer: c) JavaScript

20. Which of the following is an example of a server-side scripting language? a) JavaScript b) HTML c) CSS d) PHP * Answer: d) PHP

21. Which of the following is a server-side technology developed by Microsoft? a) JavaScript b) PHP c) ASP.NET d) Node.js * Answer: c) ASP.NET

22. Which language was primarily used in Classic ASP? a) C# b) VB.NET c) VBScript d) JavaScript * Answer: c) VBScript

23. How is code executed in Classic ASP? a) Compiled b) Interpreted c) Transpiled d) Optimized * Answer: b) Interpreted

24. How is code executed in ASP.NET? a) Interpreted b) Compiled c) Transpiled d) Optimized * Answer: b) Compiled

25. Which feature was introduced in ASP.NET to separate presentation from logic? a) Inline scripting b) Code-behind c) Server-side includes d) Client-side scripting * Answer: b) Code-behind

26. Which of the following is a benefit of ASP.NET over Classic ASP? a) Simpler syntax b) Better performance c) Interpreted code d) Limited error handling * Answer: b) Better performance

27. Which of the following is a common use case for ASP.NET? a) Static websites b) Simple HTML pages c) Modern web portals d) Client-side animations * Answer: c) Modern web portals

28. Which of the following is NOT a characteristic of Classic ASP? a) Interpreted language b) VBScript c) Strong OOP support d) Mixed HTML and script * Answer: c) Strong OOP support

29. Which of the following is a key advantage of compiled code (like in ASP.NET) over interpreted code (like in Classic ASP)? a) Easier debugging b) Faster execution c) More flexible syntax d) Smaller file size * Answer: b) Faster execution

30. What is the primary advantage of the "code-behind" model in ASP.NET? a) Improved client-side performance b) Better code organization and maintainability c) Simpler syntax for scripting d) Direct database access from HTML * Answer: b) Better code organization and maintainability

10 medium-sized questions with answers, covering the topics you requested:

1. Explain the roles of HTML, CSS, and JavaScript in web development, and provide a simple example of how they work together.

- **Answer:**
  - **HTML (HyperText Markup Language):** Provides the structure and content of a web page. It uses tags to define elements like headings, paragraphs, images, and links.
  - **CSS (Cascading Style Sheets):** Controls the visual presentation of the HTML content. It defines styles like colors, fonts, layout, and spacing.
  - **JavaScript:** Adds interactivity and dynamic behavior to web pages. It can manipulate HTML and CSS, respond to user events, and [1] communicate with servers.

  - **Example:**

    HTML

```
<!DOCTYPE html>
<html>
<head>
    <title>My Webpage</title>
    <style>
        h1 { color: blue; }
    </style>
</head>
<body>
    <h1>Welcome</h1>
    <p>This is a paragraph.</p>
    <button onclick="myFunction()">Click Me</button>
    <script>
```

```
            function myFunction() {
                alert("Hello!");
            }
        </script>
    </body>
    </html>
```

        ▪ HTML structures the page.
        ▪ CSS styles the heading.
        ▪ JavaScript displays an alert when the button is clicked.

2. Describe the key differences between client-side and server-side programming, and provide examples of languages used in each.

- **Answer:**
    - **Client-side:** Code executes in the user's browser. It's responsible for UI interactions, validation, and enhancing user experience.
        - Languages: HTML, CSS, JavaScript.
    - **Server-side:** Code executes on the web server. It handles database access, business logic, security, and processing requests.
        - Languages: PHP, Python, Java, ASP.NET (C#), Node.js.
    - **Example:** A user fills out a form (client-side - HTML, JavaScript validation). The data is sent to the server (request). The server (server-side - PHP, ASP.NET) processes the data, stores it in a database, and sends a confirmation back.

3. Explain the concept of the Document Object Model (DOM) and its importance in web development.

- **Answer:**
    - The DOM is a programming interface for HTML and XML documents. It represents the structure of the document as a tree, where each part of the document (elements, text, attributes) is a node.
    - Importance: JavaScript uses the DOM to access and manipulate the content, structure, and style of a web page dynamically. This allows for creating interactive and dynamic web applications.
    - Example: JavaScript can use `document.getElementById()` to select an HTML element and then change its content, style, or attributes using the DOM.

4. Compare and contrast interpreted and compiled languages, and explain how this relates to Classic ASP and ASP.NET.

- **Answer:**
    - **Interpreted Languages:** Code is executed line by line at runtime. This can be slower but can make debugging easier.
        - Example: Classic ASP (VBScript) was interpreted.
    - **Compiled Languages:** Code is translated into machine code before execution. This results in faster performance but requires a compilation step.

        - Example: ASP.NET (C#, VB.NET) is compiled.
    - Classic ASP's interpreted nature made it slower than ASP.NET, which benefits from the performance of compiled code.

5. Describe the "code-behind" model introduced in ASP.NET and explain its advantages over the approach used in Classic ASP.

- **Answer:**
    - **Code-behind:** Separates the presentation (HTML/ASPX) from the application logic (C# or VB.NET code).
    - **Classic ASP:** Mixed HTML and script in the same file, leading to messy and hard-to-maintain code.
    - **Advantages of Code-behind:**
        - Improved code organization and readability.
        - Better separation of concerns.
        - Easier maintenance and collaboration between developers and designers.
        - Enhanced security.

6. Explain the concept of a web server and its role in the client-server architecture of the web.

- **Answer:**
    - A web server is a computer that stores website files and delivers them to users' web browsers.
    - Client-server architecture:
        - Client (browser) sends a request to the server.
        - Server processes the request (e.g., retrieves data from a database).
        - Server sends a response (e.g., HTML, CSS, JavaScript) back to the client.
    - The web server is a crucial component that enables communication between the client and the backend of a web application.

7. Describe three different ways to include CSS in an HTML document, and explain the advantages and disadvantages of each.

- **Answer:**
    - **Inline CSS:** Styles are applied directly within HTML elements using the `style` attribute.
        - Advantage: Quick for small, specific styling.
        - Disadvantage: Not reusable, makes HTML messy.
    - **Internal (Embedded) CSS:** Styles are defined within the `<style>` tag in the `<head>` section of the HTML document.
        - Advantage: Useful for styling a single page.
        - Disadvantage: Not reusable across multiple pages.
    - **External CSS:** Styles are defined in a separate `.css` file, linked to the HTML document using the `<link>` tag.

        - Advantage: Reusable across multiple pages, promotes better organization and maintainability.
        - Disadvantage: Requires an extra file to be loaded.

8. Explain what JavaScript frameworks and libraries are, and provide two examples of each, describing their common uses.

- **Answer:**
    - JavaScript frameworks and libraries are collections of pre-written JavaScript code that provide reusable components and functionalities to simplify web development.
    - **Libraries:** Provide specific functionalities.
        - jQuery: Simplifies DOM manipulation, AJAX, and event handling.
        - D3.js: Used for creating dynamic and interactive data visualizations.
    - **Frameworks:** Provide a complete application structure.
        - React: Used for building user interfaces, especially single-page applications.
        - Angular: A comprehensive framework for building complex web applications.
    - Frameworks offer more structure, while libraries offer specific tools.

9. Discuss the security considerations in both client-side and server-side programming, and give examples of common vulnerabilities in each.

- **Answer:**
    - **Client-side Security:** Focuses on protecting the user and the application within the browser.
        - Vulnerabilities: Cross-Site Scripting (XSS), where malicious scripts are injected into web pages; Clickjacking, where users are tricked into clicking hidden elements.
    - **Server-side Security:** Focuses on protecting the server, its data, and the application's logic.
        - Vulnerabilities: SQL Injection, where malicious SQL code is inserted into input fields to gain unauthorized access to the database; Cross-Site Request Forgery (CSRF), where users are tricked into performing unwanted actions on a web application in which they're currently authenticated.
    - Both sides require careful coding practices to prevent these and other security risks.

10. Describe the evolution of web development from the perspective of a developer moving from Classic ASP to ASP.NET, highlighting the key improvements and challenges encountered.

- **Answer:**
    - Moving from Classic ASP to ASP.NET was a significant shift.

- Improvements:
  - Compiled code led to much better performance.
  - Code-behind made development more organized.
  - .NET framework provided a rich set of libraries and OOP support.
  - Improved security features.
- Challenges:
  - Learning a new language (C# or VB.NET) instead of VBScript.
  - Adapting to the new framework and its concepts.
  - Migrating existing Classic ASP applications.
- Overall, the transition was a move towards a more robust, scalable, and modern development paradigm.

CHAPTER 2: INTRODUCTION TO ASP.NET FRAMEWORK

This chapter introduces the ASP.NET framework and its underlying architecture. ASP.NET is a powerful web development platform developed by Microsoft, built on the .NET framework. Understanding how ASP.NET fits into the .NET ecosystem is crucial to mastering web development using Microsoft technologies.

◆ Overview of .NET and .NET Core

.NET Framework and .NET Core are both software development platforms developed by Microsoft, providing a comprehensive ecosystem for building and running various types of applications and services. While they share a common lineage and many similarities, they also have key differences that have shaped the modern .NET landscape.

1. .NET Framework: The Original Microsoft Platform

- **What it is:** The .NET Framework is the foundational software development platform introduced by Microsoft in the early 2000s. It provides a managed execution environment called the Common Language Runtime (CLR) and a vast class library (Framework Class Library - FCL) that offers pre-built functionalities for common programming tasks.
- **Language Support:** It primarily supports languages like **C# (C Sharp)**, **VB.NET (Visual Basic .NET)**, and **F#**, allowing developers to choose the language that best suits their needs and preferences.
- **Key Features (as highlighted in your table):**
  - **Platform Support: Windows only:** The .NET Framework was initially designed and tightly integrated with the Windows operating system. Applications built with it typically run exclusively on Windows.
    - **Example:** A Windows Forms (WinForms) application for desktop development or a traditional ASP.NET Web Forms application requires the .NET Framework to be installed on the Windows machine where it's being executed.
  - **Application Types: Desktop, Web, etc.:** The .NET Framework supports a wide range of application types, including:
    - **Windows Forms (WinForms):** For building rich desktop applications with graphical user interfaces.
    - **Windows Presentation Foundation (WPF):** A more modern framework for building visually stunning and feature-rich desktop applications with support for XAML (Extensible Application Markup Language).
    - **ASP.NET (Web Forms, MVC):** For building dynamic web applications and web services.
    - **Windows Services:** For creating long-running background processes.
    - **Console Applications:** For creating command-line tools.

- **WCF (Windows Communication Foundation):** For building service-oriented applications.
- **Open Source: No:** The .NET Framework was a proprietary platform developed and maintained by Microsoft, with its source code not publicly available for modification or contribution.
- **Performance: Moderate:** While the .NET Framework offered significant performance improvements over earlier technologies, its performance was sometimes limited by its tight integration with Windows and its larger overall size.
- **Deployment: System-wide:** Typically, applications built with the .NET Framework required the specific version of the framework they targeted to be installed on the target Windows machine. This could sometimes lead to compatibility issues if different applications required different versions.

Example (Traditional ASP.NET Web Forms):

C#

```
// Code-behind file (e.g., MyPage.aspx.cs)
using System;
using System.Web.UI;

namespace MyWebApp
{
    public partial class MyPage : Page
    {
        protected void Page_Load(object sender, EventArgs e)
        {
            lblMessage.Text = "Hello from .NET Framework!";
        }

        protected void btnClick_Click(object sender, EventArgs e)
        {
            lblCounter.Text = (int.Parse(lblCounter.Text) + 1).ToString();
        }
    }
}
```

HTML

```
<%@ Page Language="C#" AutoEventWireup="true" CodeBehind="MyPage.aspx.cs"
Inherits="MyWebApp.MyPage" %>

<!DOCTYPE html>
<html>
<head>
    <title>.NET Framework Web Page</title>
</head>
<body>
    <form id="form1" runat="server">
        <div>
            <asp:Label ID="lblMessage" runat="server"></asp:Label><br />
            <asp:Label ID="lblCounter" runat="server"
Text="0"></asp:Label><br />
            <asp:Button ID="btnClick" runat="server" Text="Click Me"
OnClick="btnClick_Click" />
```

```
        </div>
    </form>
</body>
</html>
```

This example shows a simple ASP.NET Web Forms page built with the .NET Framework. It demonstrates the code-behind model (C# logic in `.aspx.cs` and the UI in `.aspx`). This application would typically be deployed to a Windows server with the .NET Framework installed.

2. .NET Core: The Cross-Platform, Modern Successor

- **What it is:** .NET Core was introduced by Microsoft as a modern, **cross-platform**, **high-performance**, and **open-source** evolution of the .NET Framework. It was designed to address the limitations of the .NET Framework, particularly its Windows-only nature, and to cater to the demands of modern application development, such as cloud-native applications, microservices, and cross-platform deployments.
- **Language Support:** Like the .NET Framework, .NET Core also primarily supports **C#**, **VB.NET**, and **F#**. This allows developers to leverage their existing .NET language skills while targeting a wider range of platforms.
- **Key Features (as highlighted in your table):**
    - **Platform Support: Windows, Linux, macOS:** A fundamental difference from the .NET Framework. .NET Core applications can run seamlessly on various operating systems, providing greater flexibility in deployment and development environments.
        - **Example:** As mentioned in your example, an ASP.NET Core web application can be developed on a Windows machine and then deployed to a Linux server, which is often a cost-effective and scalable option for web hosting.
    - **Application Types: Web, Console, Microservices:** While .NET Core can also build desktop applications (though initially less mature than .NET Framework in this area), it was primarily designed for:
        - **Modern Web Applications (ASP.NET Core):** Building high-performance, scalable web applications and APIs.
        - **Console Applications:** For creating command-line tools and utilities that can run on any supported platform.
        - **Microservices:** Architecting distributed applications as a collection of small, independent services that can be deployed and scaled independently.
        - **Cross-Platform Libraries:** Creating reusable code libraries that can be used in .NET Core applications across different operating systems.
    - **Open Source: Yes:** .NET Core is a significant shift towards open source. Its source code is available on GitHub, allowing the community to contribute, inspect, and extend the platform. This fosters innovation and transparency.
    - **Performance: High:** .NET Core was architected with performance in mind. It boasts significant performance improvements over the .NET Framework in many

scenarios, particularly for web applications and microservices. This is due to factors like a streamlined runtime and optimized libraries.

- **Deployment: Self-contained option:** While .NET Core applications can be deployed with the .NET Core runtime installed on the target machine (framework-dependent deployment), it also offers the option of **self-contained deployment**. This bundles the necessary parts of the .NET Core runtime and libraries directly with the application, ensuring it can run on a machine without .NET Core being pre-installed. This simplifies deployment and avoids dependency conflicts.

Example (ASP.NET Core Web API):

C#
```
// Startup.cs (Configuration)
public class Startup
{
    public void ConfigureServices(IServiceCollection services)
    {
        services.AddControllers();
    }

    public void Configure(IApplicationBuilder app, IWebHostEnvironment env)
    {
        if (env.IsDevelopment())
        {
            app.UseDeveloperExceptionPage();
        }

        app.UseRouting();

        app.UseEndpoints(endpoints =>
        {
            endpoints.MapControllers();
        });
    }
}

// Controller (e.g., ProductsController.cs)
using Microsoft.AspNetCore.Mvc;
using System.Collections.Generic;

[ApiController]
[Route("api/[controller]")]
public class ProductsController : ControllerBase
{
    private static readonly List<string> Products = new List<string> {
"Laptop", "Mouse", "Keyboard" };

    [HttpGet]
    public ActionResult<IEnumerable<string>> Get()
    {
        return Products;
    }
}
```

This example shows a simple ASP.NET Core Web API controller. It defines an endpoint (`/api/products`) that returns a list of product names as JSON. This application can be built and deployed to Windows, Linux, or macOS servers that have the .NET Core runtime installed, or it can be deployed as a self-contained application.

The Future: .NET (The Unification)

It's important to note that Microsoft has been working towards unifying the .NET ecosystem. Starting with **.NET 5** (released in 2020), the .NET Framework and .NET Core have been converging into a single .NET platform. Subsequent versions like .NET 6, .NET 7, and the upcoming .NET 8 continue this unification process.

The goal is to have one .NET that provides the best of both worlds: the broad capabilities of the .NET Framework and the cross-platform nature, performance, and open-source benefits of .NET Core. While the .NET Framework 4.x is still supported, **.NET (5 and later)** is the recommended platform for new application development.

◆ Role of CLR, CTS, and BCL in .NET

The .NET platform relies on a set of core components that enable developers to build and run applications efficiently and reliably. Among these fundamental elements are the **Common Language Runtime (CLR)**, the **Common Type System (CTS)**, and the **Base Class Library (BCL)**. They work in concert to provide a robust and consistent development experience across different .NET languages.

1. CLR (Common Language Runtime): The .NET Execution Engine

- **What it is:** The CLR is the heart of the .NET platform. It's the managed execution environment that acts as an intermediary between the operating system and the .NET application code. When you compile code written in a .NET language (like C#, VB.NET, or F#), it's not directly translated into machine code for a specific processor. Instead, it's compiled into an intermediate language called **Intermediate Language (IL)** or **Common Intermediate Language (CIL)**. The CLR then takes this IL and executes it.
- **Key Responsibilities (as highlighted in your text):**
    - **Memory Management:** The CLR automatically manages the allocation and deallocation of memory for your application's objects. Developers don't need to explicitly handle memory management tasks like in languages like C++. The CLR uses a **managed heap** to allocate memory and a **garbage collector** to reclaim memory occupied by objects that are no longer in use.
        - **Example:** When you create a new object in C# using the `new` keyword (e.g., `string myString = new string("Hello");`), the CLR allocates memory for this string on the managed heap. When `myString` is no longer referenced by any part of your program, the garbage collector will eventually identify it and reclaim the memory it occupies.
    - **Exception Handling:** The CLR provides a structured mechanism for handling runtime errors, known as **exceptions**. When an unexpected event occurs during

program execution (like trying to divide by zero or access a file that doesn't exist), the CLR raises an exception. Your code can then catch and handle these exceptions gracefully, preventing the application from crashing.

- **Example (as in your text):** If a program attempts to perform a division by zero (`int result = 10 / 0;`), the CLR will detect this illegal operation and throw a `DivideByZeroException`. If the code is enclosed in a `try-catch` block, the `catch` block can handle this exception, perhaps by logging an error message or displaying a user-friendly message.

C#

```
try
{
    int numerator = 10;
    int denominator = 0;
    int result = numerator / denominator; // This will throw a
DivideByZeroException
    Console.WriteLine($"Result: {result}");
}
catch (DivideByZeroException ex)
{
    Console.WriteLine($"Error: Cannot divide by zero. Details:
{ex.Message}");
    // Optionally log the error or take other recovery actions
}
```

- **Garbage Collection:** As mentioned in memory management, the CLR's garbage collector automatically reclaims memory occupied by objects that are no longer referenced by the application. This process runs in the background and helps prevent memory leaks, freeing developers from manual memory management. The garbage collector periodically identifies and removes "dead" objects, making the memory available for new allocations.
- **Security:** The CLR enforces security mechanisms to protect the system and other applications. This includes **code access security (CAS)** (though less emphasized in modern .NET) and ensuring that managed code operates within a controlled environment. The CLR verifies the type safety of the IL code and performs other checks to prevent malicious code from performing harmful actions.

2. CTS (Common Type System): Ensuring Language Interoperability

- **What it is:** The CTS is a fundamental part of the .NET framework that defines a standard set of data types that all .NET languages must adhere to. It acts as a unifying system for data types across different languages like C#, VB.NET, and F#. This ensures seamless interoperability, allowing code written in one .NET language to interact with code written in another without type compatibility issues.
- **Key Responsibility (as highlighted in your text):**
  - **Type Compatibility Across Languages:** The CTS defines a common set of value types (like integers, floating-point numbers, booleans), reference types (like

objects and strings), and interfaces. When a language implements these CTS types, it guarantees that a type in one language has a direct equivalent in another.

- **Example (as in your text):** The `int` keyword in C# and the `Integer` keyword in VB.NET both map to the same underlying CTS type: `System.Int32`. This means that a function written in C# that expects an `int` can seamlessly receive an `Integer` value passed from VB.NET code, and vice versa.

C#

```
// C# code
public class Calculator
{
    public int Add(int a, int b)
    {
        return a + b;
    }
}

// VB.NET code
Module MyModule
    Sub Main()
        Dim calc As New Calculator()
        Dim num1 As Integer = 5
        Dim num2 As Integer = 10
        Dim sum As Integer = calc.Add(num1, num2) ' Calling C#
method with VB.NET Integer
        Console.WriteLine($"The sum is: {sum}")
    End Sub
End Module
```

In this example, the VB.NET code uses the `Integer` type, which is compatible with the `int` type expected by the C# `Add` method due to the CTS.

3. BCL (Base Class Library): The Foundation of Functionality

- **What it is:** The BCL is a vast collection of pre-built classes, interfaces, structures, and delegates provided by the .NET framework. It offers a wide range of functionalities that developers can readily use in their applications, saving them from having to write common code from scratch. The BCL covers areas like input/output operations, networking, data access, collections, security, XML processing, and much more.
- **Key Responsibility (as highlighted in your text):**
    - **Providing Standard Libraries for Common Tasks:** The BCL encapsulates common programming tasks into reusable components. This promotes code reuse, reduces development time, and ensures a consistent way of performing standard operations across .NET applications.
        - **Example (as in your text):** The `System.IO` namespace within the BCL provides classes for working with files and directories. The `File.ReadAllText()` method (as used in your C# example) is part of the `System.IO` namespace and allows you to easily read the entire content of a

text file into a string. Similarly, the `System.IO.StreamReader` class can be used for reading data from a stream (like a file) line by line or in chunks.

C#

```
using System;
using System.IO;

class Example
{
    static void Main()
    {
        try
        {
            // Using File.ReadAllText to read the entire file
            string allText = File.ReadAllText("my_document.txt");
            Console.WriteLine($"Contents of the
file:\n{allText}");

            // Using StreamReader to read the file line by line
            using (StreamReader reader = new
StreamReader("another_file.txt"))
            {
                string line;
                Console.WriteLine("\nContents of another file
(line by line):");
                while ((line = reader.ReadLine()) != null)
                {
                    Console.WriteLine(line);
                }
            }
        }
        catch (FileNotFoundException)
        {
            Console.WriteLine("Error: One or more files not
found.");
        }
        catch (IOException ex)
        {
            Console.WriteLine($"An I/O error occurred:
{ex.Message}");
        }
    }
}
```

Other important namespaces within the BCL include:

- **`System.Net`:** For building network applications (e.g., making HTTP requests, working with sockets).
- **`System.Data` and `System.Data.SqlClient` (and other data providers):** For interacting with databases (e.g., executing SQL queries).

- **`System.Collections.Generic`:** For working with various data structures like lists, dictionaries, and sets.
- **`System.Linq`:** For performing powerful data querying and manipulation using Language Integrated Query (LINQ).
- **`System.Threading`:** For managing threads and performing asynchronous operations.
- **`System.Xml`:** For working with XML data.

◆ Components of ASP.NET: Building Modern Web Applications

ASP.NET is a powerful and versatile framework within the .NET ecosystem for building dynamic web applications, web services, and websites. Over its evolution, it has introduced various components and architectural patterns to cater to different development needs and preferences. The diagram you provided accurately represents the core components and their relationship. Let's explore each of these components in detail with examples:

1. ASP.NET Web Forms: Rapid UI Development with Event-Driven Model

- **What it is:** ASP.NET Web Forms was the original programming model for building web applications in ASP.NET. It utilizes an **event-driven model**, similar to desktop application development (like Windows Forms). Developers can design user interfaces by dragging and dropping server controls onto a visual designer, and then write code that executes in response to events triggered by user interactions (e.g., button clicks, form submissions).
- **Key Features:**
  - **Visual Designer:** Provides a drag-and-drop interface in Visual Studio for visually designing web pages by placing server controls (e.g., buttons, text boxes, grids).
  - **Server Controls:** Reusable UI components that are processed on the server and render HTML to the browser. They encapsulate both UI elements and server-side logic.
  - **Event Handling:** Developers write code within event handlers associated with server control events (e.g., `ButtonClick`, `TextChanged`).
  - **ViewState:** A mechanism to automatically persist the state of server controls between postbacks (when the page is submitted to the server).
  - **Page Lifecycle:** A well-defined sequence of events that occur during the processing of an ASP.NET Web Forms page.
- **Example:**

  `.aspx` (The View - UI Design):

  HTML

```
<%@ Page Language="C#" AutoEventWireup="true"
CodeBehind="WebForm1.aspx.cs" Inherits="YourWebApp.WebForm1" %>
```

```
<!DOCTYPE html>
<html>
<head>
    <title>Web Forms Example</title>
</head>
<body>
    <form id="form1" runat="server">
        <div>
            <asp:Label ID="lblMessage" runat="server" Text="Initial
Message"></asp:Label><br />
            <asp:TextBox ID="txtName" runat="server"></asp:TextBox><br
/>
            <asp:Button ID="btnSubmit" runat="server" Text="Submit"
OnClick="btnSubmit_Click" />
        </div>
    </form>
</body>
</html>
```

`.aspx.cs` (The Code-Behind - Logic):

C#

```
using System;
using System.Web.UI;
using System.Web.UI.WebControls;

namespace YourWebApp
{
    public partial class WebForm1 : Page
    {
        protected void Page_Load(object sender, EventArgs e)
        {
            if (!IsPostBack)
            {
                lblMessage.Text = "Welcome to Web Forms!";
            }
        }

        protected void btnSubmit_Click(object sender, EventArgs e)
        {
            lblMessage.Text = "Hello, " + txtName.Text + "!";
        }
    }
}
```

In this example, the `.aspx` file defines the UI with a label, textbox, and button (server controls). The `runat="server"` attribute indicates that these controls are processed on the server. The `OnClick` attribute of the button links it to the `btnSubmit_Click` event handler in the `.aspx.cs` file. The code-behind handles the logic when the button is clicked, updating the label's text based on the textbox input.

- **Use Cases:** Rapid development of data-driven web applications, intranet sites, and applications where a visual designer and event-driven model are preferred.

2. ASP.NET MVC: Separation of Concerns with Model-View-Controller

- **What it is:** ASP.NET MVC (Model-View-Controller) is a framework that implements the **MVC architectural pattern**. This pattern promotes a clear separation of concerns into three interconnected parts:
  - **Model:** Represents the application's data and business logic.
  - **View:** Responsible for displaying the data to the user (the UI).
  - **Controller:** Acts as an intermediary, handling user input, updating the model, and selecting the view to display.
- **Key Features:**
  - **Separation of Concerns:** Improves code organization, testability, and maintainability.
  - **URL Routing:** Provides a clean and SEO-friendly way to map URLs to controller actions.
  - **Testability:** The decoupled nature of MVC makes it easier to write unit tests for individual components.
  - **Full Control over HTML:** Developers have more direct control over the rendered HTML compared to Web Forms.
  - **Lightweight:** Generally results in smaller page sizes and better performance compared to Web Forms for complex applications.
- **Example:**

  Model (`Models/GreetingModel.cs`):

  C#

```
namespace YourWebApp.Models
{
    public class GreetingModel
    {
        public string Message { get; set; }
    }
}
```

  View (`Views/Home/Index.cshtml`):

  Razor CSHTML

```
@model YourWebApp.Models.GreetingModel
@{
    ViewBag.Title = "Home Page";
}

<h1>@Model.Message</h1>
<p>Welcome to ASP.NET MVC!</p>
```

Controller (`Controllers/HomeController.cs`):

C#

```
using Microsoft.AspNetCore.Mvc;
using YourWebApp.Models;

namespace YourWebApp.Controllers
{
    public class HomeController : Controller
    {
        public IActionResult Index()
        {
            var model = new GreetingModel { Message = "Hello from the
Controller!" };
            return View(model);
        }
    }
}
```

In this example, the `HomeController`'s `Index` action creates a `GreetingModel` and passes it to the `Index.cshtml` view. The view then uses the `@Model` directive to access and display the `Message` property. The URL routing is configured to map a specific URL (e.g., `/Home/Index` or just `/`) to the `Index` action of the `HomeController`.

- **Use Cases:** Building modern, scalable, and testable web applications with a clear separation of concerns, often favored for complex UIs and APIs.

3. ASP.NET Web API: Building RESTful Services

- **What it is:** ASP.NET Web API is a framework specifically designed for building **RESTful (Representational State Transfer)** services that can be consumed by a wide range of clients, including web browsers, mobile apps, and other applications. It focuses on building APIs over HTTP using conventions like verbs (GET, POST, PUT, DELETE) and status codes.
- **Key Features:**
    - **RESTful Principles:** Adheres to the principles of REST architecture for stateless and resource-based communication.
    - **HTTP Verbs:** Utilizes standard HTTP methods to represent actions on resources.
    - **Content Negotiation:** Supports different data formats for request and response (e.g., JSON, XML).
    - **Routing:** Configurable routing system to map URLs to API controller actions.
    - **Integration with ASP.NET MVC:** Can be integrated within an ASP.NET MVC application or built as a standalone service.
- **Example:**

Controller (`Controllers/ProductsController.cs`):

C#

```
using Microsoft.AspNetCore.Mvc;
using System.Collections.Generic;

[ApiController]
[Route("api/[controller]")]
public class ProductsController : ControllerBase
{
    private static readonly List<string> _products = new List<string> {
"Laptop", "Mouse", "Keyboard" };

    [HttpGet]
    public ActionResult<IEnumerable<string>> Get()
    {
        return _products;
    }

    [HttpGet("{id}")]
    public ActionResult<string> Get(int id)
    {
        if (id >= 0 && id < _products.Count)
        {
            return _products[id];
        }
        return NotFound();
    }

    [HttpPost]
    public ActionResult<string> Post([FromBody] string newProduct)
    {
        _products.Add(newProduct);
        return CreatedAtAction(nameof(Get), new { id = _products.Count
- 1 }, newProduct);
    }
}
```

This Web API controller defines endpoints for retrieving all products (`GET /api/products`), retrieving a specific product by ID (`GET /api/products/{id}`), and adding a new product (`POST /api/products`). It uses attributes like `[ApiController]`, `[Route]`, `[HttpGet]`, and `[HttpPost]` to define the API behavior. The responses are typically formatted as JSON.

- **Use Cases:** Building backend APIs for single-page applications (SPAs), mobile applications, and microservices.

4. ASP.NET Core: The Unified, Cross-Platform Future

- **What it is:** ASP.NET Core is a **re-architected and unified platform** that combines the features of ASP.NET MVC and ASP.NET Web API into a single framework. It is designed to be **cross-platform**, **high-performance**, and **open-source**, making it suitable for modern cloud-based applications and microservices that need to run on Windows, Linux, and macOS.
- **Key Features:**

- **Unified MVC and Web API:** No longer a distinction between building web UIs and web APIs; both are built using the same controller and routing concepts.
  - **Cross-Platform:** Can be developed and deployed on Windows, Linux, and macOS.
  - **High Performance:** Optimized for speed and scalability.
  - **Open Source:** Developed with community involvement on GitHub.
  - **Dependency Injection:** Built-in support for dependency injection, promoting better testability and maintainability.
  - **Middleware Pipeline:** A flexible pipeline for handling HTTP requests and responses.
  - **Kestrel:** A cross-platform web server built into ASP.NET Core.
  - **Self-Hosting:** Applications can be run independently without relying on IIS (Internet Information Services) on Windows.
- **Example:** The MVC and Web API examples shown above are actually written using ASP.NET Core conventions. The `ApiController` attribute and the unified routing system are key features of ASP.NET Core.
- **Use Cases:** Building modern web applications, RESTful APIs, microservices, cloud-native applications, and cross-platform solutions. It is the recommended platform for new .NET web development.

5. ASP.NET Razor Pages: Lightweight Approach for Page-Focused Development

- **What it is:** ASP.NET Razor Pages is a simplified, page-focused programming model that makes coding page-centric scenarios easier and more productive. It's built on top of ASP.NET Core and provides a more streamlined way to handle requests directly within a Razor file (which combines HTML and C#).
- **Key Features:**
  - **Page-Focused:** Each Razor Page (`.cshtml` file) has an associated code-behind file (`.cshtml.cs`) that handles the page's logic.
  - **Simplified Structure:** Reduces the complexity compared to traditional MVC for simpler page-driven applications.
  - **Direct Event Handling:** Handlers for HTTP GET and POST requests are defined directly in the code-behind.
  - **Data Binding:** Simplifies the process of binding form data to page model properties.
  - **Built on ASP.NET Core:** Inherits all the benefits of ASP.NET Core (cross-platform, performance, etc.).
- **Example:**

  `.cshtml` (The View - UI and Directives):

  Razor CSHTML

```
@page
@model MyWebApp.Pages.GreetingModel
@{
    ViewData["Title"] = "Greeting";
```

```
}

<h1>@Model.Message</h1>

<form method="post">
    <label for="Name">Your Name:</label>
    <input type="text" asp-for="Name" />
    <button type="submit">Greet Me</button>
</form>
```

`.cshtml.cs` (The Page Model - Logic):

C#

```
using Microsoft.AspNetCore.Mvc.RazorPages;

namespace MyWebApp.Pages
{
    public class GreetingModel : PageModel
    {
        public string Message { get; set; }
        public string Name { get; set; }

        public void OnGet()
        {
            Message = "Enter your name:";
        }

        public void OnPost()
        {
            Message = $"Hello, {Name}!";
        }
    }
}
```

In this example, the `GreetingModel` class handles both the GET request (initial page load, setting the initial `Message`) and the POST request (when the form is submitted, updating the `Message` with the entered `Name`). The `@page` directive makes this a Razor Page, and `@model` links it to the `GreetingModel` class. `asp-for` tag helpers simplify form binding.

- **Use Cases:** Building simpler, page-centric web applications, prototypes, and applications where the full MVC separation might be overkill.

◆ Features and Advantages of ASP.NET: Building Robust Web Solutions

ASP.NET, as a comprehensive web development framework within the .NET ecosystem, offers a multitude of features and advantages that make it a popular choice for building a wide range of web applications, from simple websites to complex enterprise-level solutions. Let's delve into each of the listed features and advantages with detailed explanations and examples.

1. Rich Toolbox in Visual Studio: Enhanced Developer Productivity

- **Drag-and-Drop Controls:** Visual Studio, the primary Integrated Development Environment (IDE) for .NET development, provides a powerful visual designer for ASP.NET Web Forms. Developers can visually construct user interfaces by dragging and dropping pre-built server controls (like buttons, text boxes, grids, labels) onto the design surface. Visual Studio automatically generates the corresponding HTML markup, significantly speeding up UI development, especially for data-driven applications.
    - **Example:** To add a button to a Web Forms page, a developer can simply drag the "Button" control from the Toolbox onto the design view and position it as desired. Visual Studio will generate the `<asp:Button>` tag with default attributes.
- **IntelliSense Support:** Visual Studio offers excellent IntelliSense (code completion and suggestion) for ASP.NET development. As developers type HTML, CSS, C#, VB.NET, or JavaScript within ASP.NET files, IntelliSense provides context-aware suggestions for tags, attributes, properties, methods, and keywords. This reduces typing errors, helps developers discover available options, and accelerates the coding process.
    - **Example:** When typing `<asp:`, IntelliSense will pop up a list of available ASP.NET server controls. When typing the name of a server control (e.g., `Label1.`), IntelliSense will display a list of its available properties and methods (e.g., `Text`, `ForeColor`).

2. Security: Built-in Mechanisms for Protection

- **Built-in Windows Authentication and Role-Based Access Control:** ASP.NET provides robust built-in support for integrating with Windows authentication. This allows web applications to leverage the existing user accounts and security policies managed by the Windows operating system or Active Directory. Additionally, ASP.NET facilitates the implementation of Role-Based Access Control (RBAC), where permissions and access to different parts of the application are granted based on the roles assigned to users.
    - **Example (Web.config configuration for Windows Authentication):**

      XML

```xml
<configuration>
  <system.web>
    <authentication mode="Windows" />
    <authorization>
      <deny users="?" /> <allow roles="Administrators" /> <deny
users="*" /> </authorization>
  </system.web>
</configuration>
```

This configuration in the `web.config` file configures the application to use Windows authentication, denies access to anonymous users, allows users in the "Administrators" role, and denies all other authenticated users.

- **Other Security Features:** ASP.NET also includes built-in features and mechanisms to protect against common web vulnerabilities, such as:
    - **Cross-Site Scripting (XSS) Prevention:** Features like request validation help prevent the injection of malicious scripts into the application.
    - **SQL Injection Prevention:** While developers need to write secure database queries, ASP.NET encourages the use of parameterized queries and provides tools to help prevent SQL injection attacks.
    - **Cross-Site Request Forgery (CSRF) Protection:** ASP.NET provides mechanisms like Anti-Forgery Tokens (`@Html.AntiForgeryToken()`) to help prevent CSRF attacks.
    - **Authentication and Authorization Frameworks (ASP.NET Identity):** A comprehensive system for managing user accounts, logins, roles, and claims.

3. State Management: Handling User-Specific Data Across Requests

- **Techniques like Session, ViewState, and Cookies:** HTTP is a stateless protocol, meaning each request from a browser to the server is treated independently. ASP.NET provides various techniques to manage user-specific data across multiple requests within the same user session:
    - **Session State:** Stores user-specific data on the server for the duration of a user's session. It's identified by a unique session ID sent to the client (usually via a cookie).
        - **Example:** Storing a user's shopping cart contents or login status in the session.

C#

```
// Setting a session variable in C#
Session["UserID"] = 123;

// Retrieving a session variable
int userId = (int)Session["UserID"];
```

-
    - **ViewState (Web Forms):** Automatically persists the state of server controls on a page between postbacks. The state is encoded and embedded in the HTML of the page.
        - **Example:** When a user enters text into a textbox, ViewState ensures that the text remains in the textbox after the form is submitted and the page reloads (postback), without the developer needing to explicitly handle it.
    - **Cookies:** Small text files stored on the user's browser that can be used to store user preferences or session identifiers.
        - **Example:** Remembering a user's preferred website theme or storing an authentication token.

C#

```
// Setting a cookie
HttpCookie myCookie = new HttpCookie("Theme", "Dark");
Response.Cookies.Add(myCookie);

// Retrieving a cookie
if (Request.Cookies["Theme"] != null)
{
    string theme = Request.Cookies["Theme"].Value;
}
```

- **Other Techniques:** ASP.NET also supports other state management options like Application State (shared by all users), Query Strings, and Hidden Fields.

4. Performance Optimization: Building Fast and Efficient Applications

- **Caching:** ASP.NET offers various caching mechanisms to improve application performance by storing frequently accessed data in memory. This reduces the need to repeatedly fetch data from slower sources like databases or file systems.
  - **Example:** Caching the results of a frequently executed database query or storing rendered HTML fragments.
  - **Types of Caching:** Output Caching (caching the entire rendered page), Data Caching (caching specific data objects), Distributed Caching (using external cache providers like Redis or Memcached).

- **Bundling and Minification:** These techniques are used to reduce the number of HTTP requests and the size of static assets (CSS and JavaScript files) sent to the browser.
  - **Bundling:** Combines multiple CSS or JavaScript files into a single file.
  - **Minification:** Removes unnecessary characters (whitespace, comments) from CSS and JavaScript files, reducing their size.
  - **Example (ASP.NET Core configuration for bundling and minification):**

C#

```
public void ConfigureServices(IServiceCollection services)
{
    services.AddWebOptimizer(pipeline =>
    {
        pipeline.AddCssBundle("/css/bundle.css", "css/site.css",
"css/theme.css");
        pipeline.AddJavaScriptBundle("/js/bundle.js",
"js/script1.js", "js/script2.js");
    });
}

public void Configure(IApplicationBuilder app,
IWebHostEnvironment env)
```

```
{
    app.UseWebOptimizer();
    // ... other middleware
}
```

This configuration in ASP.NET Core uses a middleware to bundle `site.css` and `theme.css` into `/css/bundle.css` and `script1.js` and `script2.js` into `/js/bundle.js`.

- **Asynchronous Programming:** ASP.NET supports asynchronous operations (using `async` and `await` keywords in C#) to improve the responsiveness and scalability of applications by freeing up server threads while waiting for I/O-bound operations (like database calls or network requests) to complete.

5. Scalability and Reliability: Handling Growth and Ensuring Uptime

- **Supports Large-Scale Enterprise Applications:** ASP.NET is designed to build robust and scalable applications that can handle a large number of concurrent users and significant data volumes. Its architecture, along with features like caching, asynchronous programming, and support for distributed sessions, enables applications to scale horizontally (by adding more servers) and vertically (by increasing the resources of a single server).
- **Reliability Features:** The .NET runtime (CLR) provides features like managed memory, exception handling, and garbage collection, which contribute to the stability and reliability of ASP.NET applications, reducing the likelihood of crashes and memory leaks. ASP.NET also integrates well with infrastructure components like load balancers and failover systems to ensure high availability.

6. Language Interoperability: Flexibility in Language Choice

- **Use multiple .NET languages like C#, VB.NET in a single application:** The .NET platform's Common Language Runtime (CLR) and Common Type System (CTS) enable seamless interoperability between different .NET languages. Developers can write different parts of the same application using C#, VB.NET, and F# (and other .NET languages) without significant compatibility issues. This allows teams to leverage the specific strengths of different languages and the existing skills of their developers.
    - **Example:** A web application's user interface might be built using C# and ASP.NET MVC, while a separate business logic component could be written in F# for its functional programming capabilities. These components can interact with each other within the same application.

7. Cross-Platform Development (ASP.NET Core): Reach a Wider Audience

- **Develop applications for multiple platforms with the same codebase:** ASP.NET Core, the modern evolution of ASP.NET, provides true cross-platform capabilities. Developers can build web applications, APIs, and console applications that can run on Windows, Linux, and macOS without requiring significant code changes. This significantly expands the deployment options and allows organizations to choose the operating system that best suits their infrastructure and cost requirements.

   - **Example:** A development team can build an ASP.NET Core Web API on their Windows development machines and then deploy it to a cost-effective Linux server in the cloud.

Example of a Simple ASP.NET Web Page (Web Forms):

HTML
```
<%@ Page Language="C#" AutoEventWireup="true" CodeBehind="Default.aspx.cs"
Inherits="WebApp.Default" %>
<html>
<head>
    <title>Hello ASP.NET</title>
</head>
<body>
    <form runat="server">
        <asp:Label ID="Label1" runat="server" Text="Welcome to
ASP.NET!"></asp:Label>
    </form>
</body>
</html>
```

This simple Web Forms page demonstrates the use of a server control (`<asp:Label>`) and the `runat="server"` attribute, indicating that the form and label are processed on the server. The `CodeBehind` and `Inherits` attributes link this page to its associated C# code-behind file (though not shown here, it could dynamically set the `Text` property of the `Label1`).

📌*Summary:*

- .NET and .NET Core provide the foundation for ASP.NET.
- CLR manages execution; CTS provides type safety; BCL provides common functionality.
- ASP.NET has various modules suited for different development needs.
- Key features make ASP.NET a preferred choice for enterprise web applications.

10 PRACTICAL EXAMPLES WITH SOLUTION

1. Simple Cross-Platform Console Application (.NET Core)

- **Problem:** Create a basic console application that prints "Hello, .NET Core!" and can run on Windows and Linux.
- **Solution (C#):**

  C#

```
// Program.cs
using System;

namespace HelloCore
{
    class Program
    {
        static void Main(string[] args)
        {
            Console.WriteLine("Hello, .NET Core!");
        }
    }
}
```

  - **Execution:** Compile and run this application using the .NET CLI (`dotnet run`) on both Windows and a Linux distribution to demonstrate cross-platform capability.
  - **Learning Outcome:** Understanding the basic structure of a .NET Core application and its platform independence.

2. Examining CLR Exception Handling

- **Problem:** Write a C# .NET Framework console application that intentionally throws an exception and demonstrate how the CLR handles it using a `try-catch` block.
- **Solution (C# .NET Framework):**

  C#

```
using System;

namespace ExceptionHandlingDemo
{
    class Program
    {
        static void Main(string[] args)
        {
            try
            {
                int result = 10 / int.Parse("zero"); // This will throw
a FormatException
                Console.WriteLine($"Result: {result}");
```

```
            }
            catch (FormatException ex)
            {
                Console.WriteLine($"Caught a FormatException: 
{ex.Message}");
                Console.WriteLine("The CLR gracefully handled the 
error.");
            }
            Console.WriteLine("Application continues after the 
exception.");
        }
    }
}
```

- **Execution:** Run this application to see how the CLR throws the exception, and the `catch` block handles it, allowing the program to continue.
- **Learning Outcome:** Understanding the CLR's role in exception management and the use of `try-catch`.

3. Demonstrating CTS Type Interoperability (Conceptual)

- **Problem:** Explain how a C# `int` and a VB.NET `Integer` are compatible within the .NET ecosystem.
- **Solution (Explanation):**
  - The Common Type System (CTS) defines a common set of data types that all .NET languages adhere to. Both C#'s `int` and VB.NET's `Integer` are mapped to the same underlying CTS type: `System.Int32`. This ensures that methods written in C# can accept arguments of type `Integer` from VB.NET code and vice versa without explicit conversion.
  - **Conceptual Example:** Imagine a C# library with a function `Add(int a, int b)`. A VB.NET application can call this function passing `Integer` variables as arguments because the CTS ensures their compatibility at the .NET level.
  - **Learning Outcome:** Grasping the role of CTS in enabling language interoperability through a unified type system.

4. Using BCL for File Input/Output (.NET Core)

- **Problem:** Write a .NET Core console application to read the content of a text file using the `System.IO` namespace from the BCL.
- **Solution (C# .NET Core):**

C#

```
using System;
using System.IO;

namespace FileIODemo
{
    class Program
    {
```

```
        static void Main(string[] args)
        {
            try
            {
                string filePath = "sample.txt";
                if (File.Exists(filePath))
                {
                    string content = File.ReadAllText(filePath);
                    Console.WriteLine($"Content of
{filePath}:\n{content}");
                }
                else
                {
                    Console.WriteLine($"{filePath} not found.");
                }
            }
            catch (IOException ex)
            {
                Console.WriteLine($"An error occurred: {ex.Message}");
            }
        }
    }
}
```

  - **Execution:** Create a `sample.txt` file in the application's directory and run the application.
  - **Learning Outcome:** Understanding how to leverage the BCL (`System.IO`) for common tasks like file reading.

5. Simple ASP.NET Web Forms Page with a Server Control

- **Problem:** Create a basic ASP.NET Web Forms page that displays a greeting using a `Label` server control.
- **Solution (`Default.aspx` and `Default.aspx.cs`):**
  - **`Default.aspx`:**

    HTML

```
<%@ Page Language="C#" AutoEventWireup="true"
CodeBehind="Default.aspx.cs" Inherits="WebApp.Default" %>

<!DOCTYPE html>
<html>
<head>
    <title>Web Forms Greeting</title>
</head>
<body>
    <form id="form1" runat="server">
        <div>
            <asp:Label ID="GreetingLabel" runat="server"
Text="Hello from Web Forms!"></asp:Label>
        </div>
    </form>
```

```
</body>
</html>
```

- o **`Default.aspx.cs`:**

C#

```
using System;
using System.Web.UI;

namespace WebApp
{
    public partial class Default : Page
    {
        protected void Page_Load(object sender, EventArgs e)
        {
            // You can dynamically set the text here if needed
            // GreetingLabel.Text = "Welcome!";
        }
    }
}
```

- o **Execution:** Run this in Visual Studio or a web server configured for ASP.NET.
- o **Learning Outcome:** Understanding the basic structure of an ASP.NET Web Forms page and the use of server controls.

6. Basic ASP.NET MVC Application Displaying Data

- **Problem:** Create a simple ASP.NET MVC application that displays a message from a model in a view.
- **Solution (Model, View, Controller):**
  - o **Model (`Models/MessageModel.cs`):**

C#

```
namespace SimpleMVC.Models
{
    public class MessageModel
    {
        public string Greeting { get; set; }
    }
}
```

  - o **View (`Views/Home/Index.cshtml`):**

Razor CSHTML

```
@model SimpleMVC.Models.MessageModel
@{
    ViewData["Title"] = "Home Page";
}
```

```
<h1>@Model.Greeting</h1>
```

- **Controller (`Controllers/HomeController.cs`):**

  C#

```
using Microsoft.AspNetCore.Mvc;
using SimpleMVC.Models;

namespace SimpleMVC.Controllers
{
    public class HomeController : Controller
    {
        public IActionResult Index()
        {
            var model = new MessageModel { Greeting = "Hello from
MVC!" };
            return View(model);
        }
    }
}
```

- **Execution:** Run this in Visual Studio.
- **Learning Outcome:** Understanding the basic MVC architecture and how data flows from the controller to the view.

7. Simple ASP.NET Core Web API Endpoint

- **Problem:** Create a minimal ASP.NET Core Web API endpoint that returns a JSON response.
- **Solution (`Program.cs` and a simple controller):**
  - **`Program.cs` (Minimal Hosting Model):**

    C#

```
var builder = WebApplication.CreateBuilder(args);
builder.Services.AddControllers();
var app = builder.Build();
app.MapControllers();
app.Run();
```

  - **Controller[1] (`Controllers/HelloApiController.cs`):**

    C#

```
using Microsoft.AspNetCore.Mvc;

[ApiController]
[Route("api/[controller]")]
public class HelloApiController : ControllerBase
```

```
{
    [HttpGet]
    public ActionResult<object> Get()
    {
        return new { Message = "Hello from ASP.NET Core Web API!"
};
    }
}
```

Execution: Run this application and access the `/api/HelloApi` endpoint using a browser or a tool like Postman.

- **Learning Outcome:** Understanding the basics of building RESTful APIs with ASP.NET Core.

8. Demonstrating ASP.NET Core Cross-Platform Deployment (Conceptual)

- **Problem:** Explain the steps involved in deploying an ASP.NET Core application to a Linux server.
- **Solution (Explanation):**
  1. **Publish the Application:** Use the `dotnet publish -c Release -r linux-x64` command (or a similar RID) to publish a self-contained or framework-dependent deployment package for Linux.
  2. **Transfer Files:** Transfer the published output to the Linux server using tools like SCP or SFTP.
  3. **Install .NET Runtime (if framework-dependent):** If not self-contained, ensure the appropriate .NET runtime is installed on the Linux server.
  4. **Configure a Web Server (e.g., Nginx, Apache):** Set up a reverse proxy like Nginx or Apache to forward incoming HTTP requests to the Kestrel server that hosts the ASP.NET Core application.
  5. **Run the Application:** Execute the application's entry point (the compiled DLL) using `dotnet YourAppName.dll`. You might use a process manager like `systemd` to manage the application as a service.

  - **Learning Outcome:** Understanding the general process of cross-platform deployment with ASP.NET Core.

9. Exploring ASP.NET State Management (Session)

- **Problem:** Create a simple ASP.NET Core application that demonstrates the use of Session to store and retrieve user-specific data.
- **Solution (`Program.cs`, Controller, View):**
  - **`Program.cs`:**

C#

```
var builder = WebApplication.CreateBuilder(args);
builder.Services.AddControllersWithViews();
```

```
builder.Services.AddSession();
var app = builder.Build();
app.UseSession();
app.MapDefaultControllerRoute();
app.Run();
```

- **Controller** (**`Controllers/SessionDemoController.cs`**):

  C#

```
using Microsoft.AspNetCore.Mvc;
using Microsoft.AspNetCore.Http;

public class SessionDemoController : Controller
{
    public IActionResult Index()
    {
        return View();
    }

    [HttpPost]
    public IActionResult SetName(string name)
    {
        HttpContext.Session.SetString("UserName", name);
        return RedirectToAction("ShowName");
    }

    public IActionResult ShowName()
    {
        string userName =
HttpContext.Session.GetString("UserName");
        ViewBag.UserName = userName;
        return View();
    }
}
```

- **Views** (**`Views/SessionDemo/Index.cshtml`, `Views/SessionDemo/ShowName.cshtml`**):
  - **`Index.cshtml`:**

    Razor CSHTML

```
<form method="post" asp-action="SetName">
    <label for="name">Enter your name:</label>
    <input type="text" id="name" name="name" />
    <button type="submit">Submit</button>
</form>
```

  - **`ShowName.cshtml`:**

    Razor CSHTML

```
<h1>Hello, @ViewBag.UserName!</h1>
```

- **Execution:** Run the application, enter a name on the index page, and see it displayed on the `ShowName` page using Session.
- **Learning Outcome:** Understanding how to use Session for managing user-specific data in ASP.NET Core.

10. Investigating ASP.NET Performance Optimization (Conceptual)

- **Problem:** Explain the concepts of caching and bundling/minification in the context of improving ASP.NET application performance.
- **Solution (Explanation):**
  - **Caching:** Storing frequently accessed data (e.g., database query results, rendered HTML) in memory to reduce the load on the server and improve response times for subsequent requests. ASP.NET offers various caching levels (in-memory, distributed).
  - **Bundling and Minification:** Optimizing static assets (CSS, JavaScript) by combining multiple files into fewer requests (bundling) and reducing their file size by removing unnecessary characters (minification). This reduces the number of round trips between the browser and the server and speeds up page load times.
  - **Conceptual Example:** Imagine a website displaying a list of product categories. Caching the results of the database query that fetches these categories can significantly speed up page load times for all users. Bundling and minifying the CSS and JavaScript files reduces the total size of resources the browser needs to download.
  - **Learning Outcome:** Understanding key performance optimization techniques in ASP.NET.

- ## 30 multiple-choice questions with answers
- **1. Which company developed .NET?** a) Oracle b) Google c) Microsoft d) Apple *Answer: c) Microsoft*
- **2. What is the primary purpose of the .NET Framework?** a) To design databases b) To build and run applications c) To create operating systems d) To manage networks *Answer: b) To build and run applications*
- **3. Which of the following is a cross-platform .NET implementation?** a) .NET Framework b) .NET Core c) ASP.NET Web Forms d) WPF *Answer: b) .NET Core*
- **4. Which operating system is primarily targeted by the .NET Framework?** a) Linux b) macOS c) Windows d) Android *Answer: c) Windows*
- **5. Which of the following is NOT a supported language in .NET?** a) C# b) VB.NET c) F# d) Java *Answer: d) Java*
- **6. What does CLR stand for?** a) Common Language Runtime b) Common Language Reader c) Common Logic Runtime d) Compiled Language Runtime *Answer: a) Common Language Runtime*
- **7. Which of the following is the execution engine of the .NET framework?** a) BCL b) CTS c) CLR d) ASP.NET *Answer: c) CLR*

- **8. Which of the following is NOT a responsibility of the CLR?** a) Memory management b) Garbage collection c) Database access d) Exception handling *Answer: c) Database access*
- **9. What does CTS stand for?** a) Common Type System b) Common Transfer System c) Compiled Type System d) Common Text Standard *Answer: a) Common Type System*
- **10. What is the primary purpose of the CTS?** a) To manage memory b) To ensure type compatibility across .NET languages c) To handle exceptions d) To provide standard libraries *Answer: b) To ensure type compatibility across .NET languages*
- **11. Which of the following ensures that an `int` in C# is the same as an `Integer` in VB.NET?** a) CLR b) BCL c) CTS d) ASP.NET *Answer: c) CTS*
- **12. What does BCL stand for?** a) Base Class Library b) Basic Class Library c) Best Class Library d) Binary Code Library *Answer: a) Base Class Library*
- **13. Which of the following provides standard libraries for input/output, networking, and data access in .NET?** a) CLR b) CTS c) BCL d) ASP.NET *Answer: c) BCL*
- **14. Which namespace in the BCL is used for file input/output operations?** a) System.Net b) System.Data c) System.IO d) System.Web *Answer: c) System.IO*
- **15. Which component of ASP.NET is an event-driven model for rapid UI design?** a) ASP.NET MVC b) ASP.NET Web API c) ASP.NET Web Forms d) ASP.NET Core *Answer: c) ASP.NET Web Forms*
- **16. Which component of ASP.NET implements the Model-View-Controller architecture?** a) ASP.NET Web Forms b) ASP.NET Web API c) ASP.NET MVC d) ASP.NET Core *Answer: c) ASP.NET MVC*
- **17. Which component of ASP.NET is used for building RESTful services?** a) ASP.NET Web Forms b) ASP.NET MVC c) ASP.NET Web API d) ASP.NET Core *Answer: c) ASP.NET Web API*
- **18. Which component of ASP.NET is a cross-platform framework?** a) ASP.NET Web Forms b) ASP.NET MVC c) ASP.NET Web API d) ASP.NET Core *Answer: d) ASP.NET Core*
- **19. Which component of ASP.NET uses a lightweight syntax for building dynamic web pages using C#?** a) ASP.NET Web Forms b) ASP.NET MVC c) ASP.NET Web API d) ASP.NET Razor Pages *Answer: d) ASP.NET Razor Pages*
- **20. Which ASP.NET component is best suited for building traditional, data-driven web applications with a visual designer?** a) ASP.NET MVC b) ASP.NET Web API c) ASP.NET Web Forms d) ASP.NET Core *Answer: c) ASP.NET Web Forms*
- **21. Which ASP.NET component promotes a clear separation of concerns and is often preferred for complex web applications?** a) ASP.NET Web Forms b) ASP.NET Web API c) ASP.NET MVC d) ASP.NET Core *Answer: c) ASP.NET MVC*
- **22. Which ASP.NET component is ideal for creating backend services that can be consumed by various clients (e.g., mobile apps, SPAs)?** a) ASP.NET Web Forms b) ASP.NET MVC c) ASP.NET Web API d) ASP.NET Core *Answer: c) ASP.NET Web API*
- **23. Which of the following is a feature of Visual Studio's toolbox for ASP.NET development?** a) Database management b) Drag-and-drop controls c) Server administration d) Network configuration *Answer: b) Drag-and-drop controls*
- **24. What does IntelliSense provide in Visual Studio?** a) Database connectivity b) Code completion and suggestions c) Server monitoring d) Version control *Answer: b) Code completion and suggestions*

- **25. Which of the following is a built-in security feature in ASP.NET?** a) Client-side validation b) Windows authentication c) CSS styling d) JavaScript framework *Answer: b) Windows authentication*
- **26. Which of the following is NOT an ASP.NET state management technique?** a) Session b) ViewState c) Cookies d) LocalStorage *Answer: d) LocalStorage*
- **27. Which of the following techniques can improve ASP.NET application performance?** a) Using HTML tables for layout b) Caching c) Client-side scripting only d) Inline CSS *Answer: b) Caching*
- **28. Which of the following helps reduce the number of HTTP requests in ASP.NET?** a) Server-side rendering b) Bundling c) Database normalization d) Client-side routing *Answer: b) Bundling*
- **29. Which of the following is a benefit of ASP.NET supporting multiple .NET languages?** a) Reduced code complexity b) Improved client-side performance c) Language interoperability d) Simplified database access *Answer: c) Language interoperability*
- **30. Which of the following ASP.NET versions allows for cross-platform development?** a) ASP.NET Web Forms b) ASP.NET MVC c) ASP.NET Web API d) ASP.NET Core *Answer: d) ASP.NET Core*

9 medium-sized questions with answers covering the Overview of .NET and .NET Core, the roles of CLR, CTS, and BCL, the components of ASP.NET, and the features and advantages of ASP.NET:

1. Briefly explain the key differences between .NET Framework and .NET Core, highlighting the primary reasons for the introduction of .NET Core.

- **Answer:** .NET Framework was the original Windows-centric .NET platform. .NET Core was introduced as a cross-platform, open-source, and high-performance successor. The primary reasons for .NET Core's introduction were to enable .NET development and deployment on non-Windows operating systems (Linux, macOS), to improve performance and scalability for modern web applications and microservices, and to embrace the open-source development model.

2. Describe the role of the Common Language Runtime (CLR) in the .NET ecosystem. Explain how it manages the execution of .NET applications, including memory management and exception handling.

- **Answer:** The CLR is the managed execution environment for .NET applications. It takes Intermediate Language (IL) code and executes it. Its key roles include:
    - **Memory Management:** The CLR automatically manages memory allocation on the managed heap and reclaims memory using garbage collection, relieving developers from manual memory management.
    - **Exception Handling:** The CLR provides a structured mechanism for handling runtime errors (exceptions). When an exception occurs, the CLR allows developers to catch and handle these errors gracefully using `try-catch` blocks, preventing application crashes.

3. Explain the significance of the Common Type System (CTS) in .NET. How does it contribute to language interoperability within the .NET platform? Provide a simple example.

- **Answer:** The CTS defines a standard set of data types that all .NET languages must adhere to. This ensures that a type in one .NET language has a corresponding equivalent in another. This type compatibility is crucial for language interoperability, allowing code written in different .NET languages (like C# and VB.NET) to seamlessly interact and exchange data without type conversion issues. For example, the C# `int` and the VB.NET `Integer` both map to the `System.Int32` type in the CTS, making them directly compatible.

4. Describe the purpose and provide examples of the Base Class Library (BCL) in .NET. How does the BCL contribute to developer productivity?

- **Answer:** The BCL is a vast collection of pre-built classes, interfaces, structures, and delegates that provide reusable functionalities for common programming tasks. Examples include `System.IO` for file operations, `System.Net` for networking, `System.Data` for database access, and `System.Collections.Generic` for working with data structures. The BCL significantly enhances developer productivity by providing ready-to-use components, reducing the need to write fundamental code from scratch and promoting code reuse and consistency.

5. Compare and contrast ASP.NET Web Forms and ASP.NET MVC in terms of their architectural patterns, control over HTML, and suitability for different types of applications.

- **Answer:**
    - **ASP.NET Web Forms:** Uses an event-driven model with server controls, providing a visual designer and abstracting away some HTML details. It's suitable for rapid development of data-centric applications and intranet sites. However, it offers less control over HTML and can be harder to test.
    - **ASP.NET MVC:** Implements the Model-View-Controller pattern, offering a clear separation of concerns and more control over HTML. It's better suited for complex web applications, APIs, and scenarios where testability and SEO-friendly URLs are important.

6. Explain the primary purpose of ASP.NET Web API. How does it differ from building traditional web applications using ASP.NET MVC or Web Forms?

- **Answer:** The primary purpose of ASP.NET Web API is to build RESTful services over HTTP that can be consumed by a wide range of clients (web browsers, mobile apps, other services). Unlike traditional web applications built with MVC or Web Forms that primarily focus on rendering HTML for browser-based UIs, Web API focuses on exposing data and functionality as services using standard HTTP verbs (GET, POST, PUT, DELETE) and formats like JSON or XML for data exchange.

7. Describe the key features and benefits of ASP.NET Core. How does it address some of the limitations of the .NET Framework for modern web development?

- **Answer:** Key features of ASP.NET Core include cross-platform support (Windows, Linux, macOS), high performance, open-source nature, a unified MVC and Web API framework, built-in dependency injection, and a flexible middleware pipeline. It addresses the .NET Framework's Windows-only limitation, offers significant performance improvements for modern workloads, embraces community-driven development through open source, and provides a more streamlined and modular architecture suitable for cloud-native applications and microservices.

8. Explain the concept of "State Management" in ASP.NET. Describe two common techniques (e.g., Session, ViewState) and their use cases, advantages, and disadvantages.

- **Answer:** State management in ASP.NET refers to techniques used to maintain user-specific data across multiple HTTP requests in a stateless environment.
  - **Session:** Stores user-specific data on the server for the duration of a user's session.
    - **Use Case:** Storing shopping cart contents, user login status.
    - **Advantages:** Server-side storage, more secure for sensitive data.
    - **Disadvantages:** Can consume server resources, requires session ID management.
  - **ViewState (Web Forms):** Persists the state of server controls on a page between postbacks by embedding it in the HTML.
    - **Use Case:** Maintaining the values of form fields after a postback.
    - **Advantages:** Automatic management, data travels with the page.
    - **Disadvantages:** Can increase page size, potential security risks if not handled carefully.

9. Discuss three key advantages of using ASP.NET for web development, providing a brief explanation for each.

- **Answer:**
  - **Rich Tooling (Visual Studio):** Provides a productive development environment with features like drag-and-drop controls, IntelliSense, and debugging tools, accelerating development.
  - **Security Features:** Offers built-in mechanisms for authentication (Windows, ASP.NET Identity), authorization (roles), and protection against common web vulnerabilities (XSS, CSRF), helping developers build secure applications.
  - **Performance and Scalability:** ASP.NET (especially Core) is designed for high performance and provides features like caching, asynchronous programming, and support for distributed environments, enabling the development of scalable and responsive applications.

📌 1. Installing Visual Studio and .NET SDK: Setting Up Your Development Environment

To embark on the journey of developing ASP.NET applications, the first crucial step is to set up your development environment. This primarily involves installing two essential components provided by Microsoft: **Visual Studio**, a powerful Integrated Development Environment (IDE), and the **.NET SDK (Software Development Kit)**. These tools work in tandem to provide you with everything you need to write, build, debug, and run ASP.NET applications.

Let's break down the installation process in detail, following the steps you've outlined, and explain the significance of each step.

A. Installing Visual Studio: Your Comprehensive Development IDE

Visual Studio is a feature-rich IDE that provides a wide array of tools and features designed to enhance developer productivity. It supports various programming languages and development platforms, including ASP.NET.

Step 1: Navigating to the Visual Studio Download Page

- **Action:** Open your web browser (e.g., Chrome, Firefox, Edge) and go to the official Visual Studio website: `https://visualstudio.microsoft.com`.
- **Explanation:** This URL is the central hub for all Visual Studio downloads and related information. Microsoft offers different editions of Visual Studio tailored for various needs.

Step 2: Downloading Visual Studio Community Edition

- **Action:** On the Visual Studio website, you will typically see options for different editions like Professional, Enterprise, and Community. Locate the **"Community"** edition and click the **"Download"** button associated with it.
- **Explanation:**
  - **Visual Studio Community Edition:** This is a **free**, fully-featured IDE designed for students, individual developers, open-source contributors, and small teams. It provides the core functionalities needed for ASP.NET development without any licensing costs for eligible users. The Professional and Enterprise editions offer additional features geared towards larger teams and enterprise-level development, but the Community edition is usually sufficient for learning and many practical projects.
  - The website will likely detect your operating system and offer the appropriate installer.

Step 3: Selecting the "ASP.NET and web development" Workload During Installation

- **Action:** Once the installer (`.exe` file on Windows) is downloaded, run it. The Visual Studio Installer will launch. This installer allows you to customize your Visual Studio installation by selecting specific **workloads**, individual components, and language packs. During the installation process, you will see a screen with various workload options. **Make sure to check the box next to "ASP.NET and web development."** You can also select other workloads you might be interested in (e.g., ".NET desktop development" for WinForms or WPF, "Azure development" for cloud applications), but the "ASP.NET and web development" workload is essential for ASP.NET projects.
- **Explanation:**
    - **Workloads:** Workloads are pre-configured sets of tools and components tailored for specific development tasks. By selecting the "ASP.NET and web development" workload, you ensure that the installer includes all the necessary components for building ASP.NET applications, such as:
        - **.NET SDK (often included with this workload):** The core development kit for building .NET applications.
        - **ASP.NET and Web Tools:** Specific tools and templates for creating ASP.NET Web Forms, ASP.NET MVC, ASP.NET Core, and other web projects.
        - **IIS Support (Internet Information Services):** Components for running and debugging web applications locally on Windows.
        - **HTML, CSS, and JavaScript editing support:** Essential tools for frontend development within ASP.NET projects.
        - **SQL Server Express LocalDB (optional but often included):** A lightweight version of SQL Server for local database development.
    - **Individual Components:** You can also select or deselect individual components within each workload or in the "Individual components" tab for more granular control over the installation. However, for beginners, sticking with the recommended components within the "ASP.NET and web development" workload is usually the best approach.

Step 4: Clicking on "Install"

- **Action:** After selecting the "ASP.NET and web development" workload (and any other desired workloads or individual components), click the **"Install"** button.
- **Explanation:** The Visual Studio Installer will now download and install the selected components onto your computer. The installation process can take some time depending on your internet speed and the number of components selected. You can monitor the progress within the installer window. You might be prompted to restart your computer after the installation is complete.

B. Installing .NET SDK: The Core Development Kit (If Not Included)

- **Action:** The "ASP.NET and web development" workload in Visual Studio often includes the .NET SDK. However, if for some reason it wasn't included or if you want to install a specific version separately, you can download it from `https://dotnet.microsoft.com/download`.

- **Explanation:**
    - **.NET SDK (Software Development Kit):** This is a crucial set of tools, libraries, and documentation needed to develop, build, run, and publish .NET applications (including ASP.NET). It includes:
        - **.NET CLI (Command-Line Interface):** A powerful command-line tool (`dotnet`) for creating projects, building code, running applications, managing NuGet packages, and more.
        - **.NET Runtime:** The environment in which your .NET applications execute.
        - **.NET Libraries:** The core set of classes and APIs that provide fundamental functionalities.
        - **Compilers (e.g., C# compiler - `csc.exe`):** Tools for translating your .NET language code into Intermediate Language (IL).
        - **Build Tools (MSBuild):** A platform for building .NET applications.
    - **Download Options:** On the .NET download page, you will typically see options for different versions of the .NET SDK (e.g., .NET 8.0, .NET 7.0) and for different operating systems (Windows, Linux, macOS). Choose the latest stable version recommended for development and the installer appropriate for your operating system.
    - **Installation Process:** Run the downloaded installer and follow the on-screen instructions. The installation process is usually straightforward.

Verifying Installation: Ensuring Everything is Set Up Correctly

After installing Visual Studio and (potentially) the .NET SDK, it's essential to verify that the installation was successful and that the necessary tools are accessible. You can do this using the Command Prompt (on Windows) or Terminal (on macOS and Linux).

1. Checking the Installed .NET Version (`dotnet --version`)

- **Action:**
    1. Open **Command Prompt** (on Windows): Press `Win + R`, type `cmd`, and press Enter.
    2. Open **Terminal** (on macOS/Linux): You can usually find it in your Applications/Utilities folder or use a keyboard shortcut.
    3. In the Command Prompt or Terminal, type the following command and press Enter:

       Bash

       ```
       dotnet --version
       ```

- **Expected Output:** If the .NET SDK is installed correctly and its path is configured in your system's environment variables, this command should return the version number of the installed .NET SDK (e.g., `8.0.100`, `7.0.300`). If you see an error message like "`dotnet` is not recognized as an internal or external command...", it indicates that the

.NET CLI is not properly installed or its path is not set up correctly. In this case, you might need to reinstall the .NET SDK or check your system's environment variables.

- **Significance:** This command confirms that the .NET CLI, a fundamental tool for .NET development, is installed and accessible from your command line. The version number helps you know which .NET runtime and features are available.

2. Listing Project Templates (`dotnet new`)

- **Action:** In the same Command Prompt or Terminal, type the following command and press Enter:

  Bash

  ```
  dotnet new
  ```

- **Expected Output:** This command will display a list of available project templates that you can use to create new .NET projects. You should see templates related to ASP.NET Core (e.g., `webapi`, `mvc`, `razorpage`), console applications (`console`), class libraries (`classlib`), and more.
- **Significance:** This confirms that the .NET SDK is properly configured and that you can use the `.NET CLI` to create new .NET projects, including various types of ASP.NET applications. The presence of ASP.NET Core templates indicates that the necessary components for web development are installed.

Example Workflow: Creating a Simple ASP.NET Core Web API Project (After Installation)

Once you have successfully installed Visual Studio and the .NET SDK, you can create your first ASP.NET Core project using either Visual Studio or the .NET CLI.

Using Visual Studio:

1. Open Visual Studio.
2. Click on "Create a new project."
3. In the "Create a new project" window, search for "ASP.NET Core Web API" [1] (or "ASP.NET Core Empty" if you want a minimal starting point).
4. Select the template and click "Next."
5. Configure the project name, location, and other options, then click "Create."
6. Visual Studio will scaffold a basic ASP.NET Core Web API project with necessary files and folders.

Using .NET CLI:

1. Open Command Prompt or Terminal.
2. Navigate to the directory where you want to create your project using the `cd` command.
3. Run the following command to create a new ASP.NET Core Web API project:

Bash

```
dotnet new webapi -o MyWebApp
```

(This will create a new folder named `MyWebApp` containing the project files.)

4. Navigate into the project directory:

   Bash

   ```
   cd MyWebApp
   ```

5. You can then build and run the application using:

   Bash

   ```
   dotnet build
   dotnet run
   ```

   This will typically start a development web server, and you can access the API endpoints in your web browser or with tools like Postman.

By successfully installing Visual Studio and the .NET SDK and verifying the installation, you have laid the foundation for your ASP.NET development journey. You now have the necessary tools to start building powerful and dynamic web applications. Remember to keep your tools updated to benefit from the latest features, performance improvements, and security patches.

📌 2. Creating Your First ASP.NET Project: A Step-by-Step Guide with Example

After successfully installing Visual Studio and the .NET SDK, you're ready to create your first ASP.NET project. This guide will walk you through the process of creating a basic ASP.NET Core Web App using the Model-View-Controller (MVC) architectural pattern within Visual Studio. MVC is a popular and well-structured approach for building web applications, promoting separation of concerns and maintainability.

A. Steps to Create Your First ASP.NET Project in Visual Studio:

Step 1: Open Visual Studio and Initiate Project Creation

- **Action:** Launch the Visual Studio application on your computer. Once it opens, you will typically see the Visual Studio start window. On this window, click on the option **"Create a new project."**

Step 2: Select the ASP.NET Core Web App (Model-View-Controller) Template

- **Action:** In the "Create a new project" window, you will see a list of various project templates for different languages and platforms. In the search bar at the top, type **"ASP.NET Core Web App (Model-View-Controller)"**. Select this template from the search results.
- **Explanation:**
  - **ASP.NET Core:** As discussed earlier, ASP.NET Core is the modern, cross-platform framework for building web applications and APIs with .NET.
  - **Web App (Model-View-Controller):** This template provides the basic structure for an ASP.NET Core web application that follows the MVC architectural pattern. Choosing this template sets up the necessary folders, files, and configurations to get started with MVC development.

Step 3: Name Your Project

- **Action:** After selecting the template, click the **"Next"** button. You will be prompted to configure your new project. In the "Project name" field, enter a descriptive name for your project. For this example, let's use **"FirstAspNetApp"**. You can also choose a location to save your project files in the "Location" field.
- **Explanation:** The project name will be used as the name of the project folder and the default namespace for your code. Choosing a clear and meaningful name helps in organizing your projects.

Step 4: Choose the .NET Version

- **Action:** On the next screen, you will be asked to choose the **target framework**. This dropdown list will display the different versions of the .NET SDK that are installed on your system. It's generally recommended to select the **latest LTS (Long-Term Support)** version available. LTS versions receive critical security updates and support for a longer period, making them a stable choice for most projects.
- **Explanation:**
  - **.NET Version:** This specifies the specific version of the .NET runtime and libraries that your application will target. Choosing a newer version often gives you access to the latest features and performance improvements.
  - **LTS (Long-Term Support):** Microsoft designates certain .NET versions as LTS, providing support and updates for several years. For learning and many production applications, using an LTS version is a good practice for stability.

Step 5: Click "Create"

- **Action:** After selecting the .NET version, click the **"Create"** button.
- **Explanation:** Visual Studio will now use the selected "ASP.NET Core Web App (Model-View-Controller)" template to generate the basic structure and files for your "FirstAspNetApp" project. This process might take a few moments.

Visual Studio Generated Template ASP.NET MVC Project:

Once the project is created, Visual Studio's Solution Explorer will display the generated file and folder structure. Here are some of the key components you'll find in a typical ASP.NET Core MVC project:

- **Solution (`FirstAspNetApp.sln`):** A container that can hold one or more projects.
- **Project (`FirstAspNetApp`):** Contains all the source code, configuration files, and other assets for your web application.
  - **Dependencies:** Manages external libraries (NuGet packages) that your project relies on.
  - **Properties:** Contains project settings, such as launch profiles.
  - **appsettings.json:** Stores application configuration settings (e.g., connection strings, logging levels).
  - **wwwroot:** Contains static web assets like HTML, CSS, JavaScript, and images.
  - **Controllers:** This folder will contain your **Controllers** (e.g., `HomeController.cs`). Controllers handle user input, interact with the model, and determine which view to display.
  - **Models:** This folder is intended to contain your **Models**, which represent the data and business logic of your application.
  - **Views:** This folder contains your **Views** (e.g., `Views/Home/Index.cshtml`). Views are responsible for rendering the user interface using HTML and displaying data passed from the controller.
  - **Program.cs:** The entry point of your application. It configures the web host and the application startup process.
  - **Startup.cs:** Configures services that the application will use (like MVC, routing) and sets up the request processing pipeline (middleware).

Example Project Components:

- **Controller: `HomeController.cs`**

  C#

```
using Microsoft.AspNetCore.Mvc;
using System.Diagnostics;

namespace FirstAspNetApp.Controllers
{
    public class HomeController : Controller
    {
        private readonly ILogger<HomeController> _logger;

        public HomeController(ILogger<HomeController> logger)
        {
            _logger = logger;
        }

        public IActionResult Index()
```

```
        {
            return View(); // Returns the View located at
Views/Home/Index.cshtml
        }

        public IActionResult Privacy()
        {
            return View(); // Returns the View located at
Views/Home/Privacy.cshtml
        }

        [ResponseCache(Duration = 0, Location =
ResponseCacheLocation.None, NoStore = true)]
        public IActionResult Error()
        {
            return View(new ErrorViewModel { RequestId =
Activity.Current?.Id ?? HttpContext.TraceIdentifier });
        }
    }
}
```

 - **Explanation:** This is a basic controller named `HomeController`. It has actions (methods) like `Index()`, `Privacy()`, and `Error()`. The `Index()` action, in this default template, simply returns a View. By convention, it looks for a View named `Index.cshtml` within the `Views/Home/` folder.

- **Views: `Views/Home/Index.cshtml`**

  Razor CSHTML

```
@{
    ViewData["Title"] = "Home Page";
}

<div class="text-center">
    <h1 class="display-4">Welcome</h1>
    <p>Learn about <a
href="https://docs.microsoft.com/aspnet/core">building Web apps with
ASP.NET Core</a>.</p>
</div>
```

 - **Explanation:** This is the default View associated with the `Index()` action of the `HomeController`. It uses Razor syntax (`@`) to embed C# code within HTML. Here, it sets the page title and displays a welcome message with a link to the ASP.NET Core documentation.

Running the Project:

- **Action:** To run your newly created "FirstAspNetApp" project, you can click the green "Play" button (often labeled with the project name or "IIS Express") in the Visual Studio toolbar. Alternatively, you can press `Ctrl + F5` (Start Without Debugging) or `F5` (Start Debugging).

- **Expected Output:** Visual Studio will build your project and launch a development web server (usually IIS Express). Your default web browser will automatically open, and you should see a basic homepage displayed. This homepage is rendered by the `Views/Home/Index.cshtml` view, served by the `HomeController`'s `Index()` action.
- **Significance:** Successfully running the default template confirms that your development environment is set up correctly and that you can create and execute basic ASP.NET Core MVC applications.

📌 3. Understanding ASP.NET Project Structure: A Detailed Exploration

When you create a new ASP.NET project (especially using the MVC or Razor Pages templates in ASP.NET Core), Visual Studio generates a well-defined folder and file structure. Understanding this structure is crucial for organizing your code, managing assets, and following the conventions of ASP.NET development. Let's explore the key folders and files you typically encounter:

1. Controllers Folder:

- **Description (as in your table):** Contains C# classes that handle incoming HTTP requests and return responses to the client (usually a web browser). Controllers act as the intermediary between the Model and the View in the MVC pattern. They receive user input, interact with the data layer (Models), and then select and pass data to the appropriate View to be rendered as HTML.
- **Detailed Explanation:**
  - **Naming Convention:** Controller class names typically end with the suffix "Controller" (e.g., `HomeController`, `ProductController`, `UserController`). This convention helps in identifying their role within the application.
  - **Actions:** Within a controller class, public methods are called "action methods" (e.g., `Index()`, `Details()`, `Create()`). These actions are invoked based on the incoming URL route.
  - **Return Types:** Controller actions often return an `IActionResult` object (or a derived type like `ViewResult`, `JsonResult`, `RedirectResult`). This result determines the type of response sent back to the client (e.g., an HTML page, a JSON object, a redirect to another URL).
- **Example (as in your table):**

  C#

```csharp
using Microsoft.AspNetCore.Mvc; // Namespace for Controller base class

public class HomeController : Controller
{
    // Action method to display the homepage
```

```
    public IActionResult Index()
    {
        // Typically, you might fetch data from a Model here
        // and pass it to the View using ViewBag or ViewData.
        return View(); // Returns the View named "Index" (by
convention, looks in Views/Home/Index.cshtml)
    }

    // Action method to display details of a product
    public IActionResult Details(int id)
    {
        // Logic to retrieve product details based on the 'id'
        var product = GetProductById(id); // Assume this method
retrieves a product

        if (product == null)
        {
            return NotFound(); // Returns a 404 Not Found response
        }

        return View(product); // Returns the View named "Details",
passing the 'product' data
    }

    private Product GetProductById(int id)
    {
        // Implementation to fetch product from a data source
        return new Product { Id = id, Name = "Sample Product" };
    }
}

// Assume a simple Model class
public class Product
{
    public int Id { get; set; }
    public string Name { get; set; }
}
```

In this example, `HomeController` handles requests related to the homepage and product details. The `Index()` action returns the default homepage view, and the `Details()` action retrieves product information and passes it to the "Details" view.

2. Views Folder:

- **Description (as in your table):** Contains Razor files (`.cshtml` extension), which are used to define the user interface (UI) of your web application. Razor is a templating engine that allows you to embed C# code directly within your HTML markup to dynamically generate content.
- **Detailed Explanation:**
    - **Structure:** Views are typically organized in subfolders that correspond to the names of your controllers (e.g., `Views/Home/`, `Views/Product/`, `Views/User/`). There's also a `Views/Shared/` folder for views that are used across multiple controllers (like layouts and error pages).

- **Razor Syntax:** Razor uses `@` symbols to switch between HTML and C# code. You can use C# expressions, control flow statements (like `if`, `foreach`), and access data passed from the controller.
- **Layouts:** Layout views (`_Layout.cshtml` in `Views/Shared/`) provide a consistent structure for your application's pages (e.g., header, navigation, footer). Individual content views are rendered within this layout.
- **Partial Views:** Reusable view components that can be embedded within other views (`_PartialView.cshtml`).
- **ViewBag and ViewData:** Mechanisms for passing data from the controller to the view. Model binding allows you to pass strongly-typed model objects to the view.

- **Example (as in your table): `Views/Home/Index.cshtml`:**

  Razor CSHTML

```
@{
    ViewData["Title"] = "Home Page"; // Setting the page title
}

<h1>Welcome to My First ASP.NET App</h1>

<p>This is the homepage of our application.</p>

@if (DateTime.Now.DayOfWeek == DayOfWeek.Friday)
{
    <p>Happy Friday!</p>
}
else
{
    <p>Enjoy your day!</p>
}

<ul>
    @foreach (var item in ViewBag.MessageList) // Accessing data passed
from the controller
    {
        <li>@item</li>
    }
</ul>
```

  This `Index.cshtml` view displays a welcome message and dynamically renders content based on the current day of the week. It also iterates through a list of messages passed from the controller using `ViewBag`.

3. `wwwroot` Folder:

- **Description (as in your table):** This folder is the designated root for all static files that are served directly to the client's browser. These files are not processed by the ASP.NET engine; the web server (like Kestrel or IIS) directly serves them.
- **Detailed Explanation:**
  - **Content:** Typically contains folders for:

        - **css:** Cascading Style Sheets for styling the application's appearance.
        - **js:** JavaScript files for client-side interactivity and logic.
        - **images:** Image files used in the application.
        - **lib:** Client-side libraries (like jQuery, Bootstrap) often managed using tools like LibMan or npm/yarn.
        - **Other static assets:** Fonts, favicons, etc.
    - **Directly Accessible:** Files within `wwwroot` are directly accessible via the application's base URL followed by the file path. For example, if you have an image named `logo.png` in `wwwroot/images/`, you can access it in your HTML using `<img src="/images/logo.png" alt="Logo">`. The leading `/` refers to the root of the `wwwroot` folder.
- **Example:**
    - **wwwroot/css/site.css:**

      CSS

```css
body {
    font-family: sans-serif;
    background-color: #f0f0f0;
}

h1 {
    color: blue;
    text-align: center;
}
```

    - **wwwroot/js/script.js:**

      JavaScript

```javascript
document.addEventListener('DOMContentLoaded', function() {
    alert('Page loaded!');
});
```

- These static files are linked in your Razor views using `<link>` tags for CSS and `<script>` tags for JavaScript, with paths relative to the `wwwroot` folder.

4. `appsettings.json` File:

- **Description (as in your table):** This is the primary configuration file used to store application-wide settings in a JSON (JavaScript Object Notation) format. It's commonly used for storing sensitive information like database connection strings, API keys, logging levels, and custom application-specific settings.
- **Detailed Explanation:**
    - **Hierarchical Structure:** JSON allows for a hierarchical structure, making it easy to organize configuration settings into sections.
    - **Environment-Specific Configurations:** You can have environment-specific configuration files (e.g., `appsettings.Development.json`,

appsettings.Production.json) that override or extend the base appsettings.json based on the current environment.
    - **Accessing Configuration:** ASP.NET Core provides mechanisms (using the IConfiguration interface) to easily read and access these configuration settings in your code.
- **Example:**

JSON

```
{
  "Logging": {
    "LogLevel": {
      "Default": "Information",
      "Microsoft": "Warning",
      "Microsoft.Hosting.Lifetime": "Information"
    }
  },
  "ConnectionStrings": {
    "DefaultConnection":
"Server=(localdb)\\mssqllocaldb;Database=MyWebAppDb;Trusted_Connection=
True;MultipleActiveResultSets=true"
  },
  "ApiSettings": {
    "ApiKey": "your_api_key_here",
    "ApiUrl": "https://api.example.com"
  },
  "AllowedHosts": "*"
}
```

In your C# code, you can access these settings like this:

C#

```
public class MyService
{
    private readonly IConfiguration _configuration;

    public MyService(IConfiguration configuration)
    {
        _configuration = configuration;
    }

    public string GetConnectionString()
    {
        return _configuration.GetConnectionString("DefaultConnection");
    }

    public string GetApiKey()
    {
        return _configuration["ApiSettings:ApiKey"];
    }

    public string GetApiUrl()
```

```
    {
        return _configuration["ApiSettings:ApiUrl"];
    }
}
```

5. `Startup.cs` or `Program.cs` Files:

- **Description (as in your table):** These files (in modern .NET 6+ projects, much of this logic is consolidated in `Program.cs` with a minimal hosting model) are crucial for configuring the services that your application will use and setting up the **middleware pipeline** that handles incoming HTTP requests.
- **Detailed Explanation:**
    - **`Program.cs` (or `Startup.cs` and `Program.cs` in older versions):**
        - **Web Host Builder:** Sets up the web server (typically Kestrel).
        - **Service Configuration (`ConfigureServices` method in `Startup.cs`):** Registers services that will be used by your application (e.g., MVC, Razor Pages, database contexts, custom services) with the dependency injection container.
        - **Middleware Pipeline Configuration (`Configure` method in `Startup.cs`):** Defines the sequence of middleware components that will process each incoming HTTP request. Middleware can handle tasks like routing, authentication, authorization, logging, exception handling, serving static files, and more.
- **Example (`Program.cs` - Minimal Hosting Model in .NET 6+):**

C#

```csharp
var builder = WebApplication.CreateBuilder(args);

// Add services to the container.
builder.Services.AddControllersWithViews(); // For MVC
// builder.Services.AddRazorPages(); // For Razor Pages

var app = builder.Build();

// Configure the HTTP request pipeline.
if (app.Environment.IsDevelopment())
{
    app.UseDeveloperExceptionPage();
}
else
{
    app.UseExceptionHandler("/Home/Error");
    app.UseHsts();
}

app.UseHttpsRedirection();
app.UseStaticFiles(); // To serve files from wwwroot

app.UseRouting();
```

```
app.UseAuthorization(); // For authentication and authorization

app.MapControllerRoute(
    name: "default",
    pattern: "{controller=Home}/{action=Index}/{id?}");

// app.MapRazorPages(); // If using Razor Pages

app.Run();
```

This `Program.cs` file configures essential services like MVC, sets up middleware for error handling, static file serving, routing, and authorization, and defines the default URL routing pattern.

6. Models Folder:

- **Description (as in your table):** Contains C# classes that represent the data structures and business entities of your application. Models are responsible for holding and managing the application's data. They often interact with the data storage layer (e.g., databases).
- **Detailed Explanation:**
  - **Plain Old CLR Objects (POCOs):** Models are typically simple C# classes with properties that represent the data attributes of an entity.
  - **Data Annotations:** You can use data annotations (from the `System.ComponentModel.DataAnnotations` namespace) to define validation rules, display names, and other metadata for your model properties.
  - **Interaction with Data Access:** Models might contain logic for interacting with databases or other data sources, or this logic might be handled in separate service or repository layers that the controllers interact with.
- **Example:**

C#

```
namespace FirstAspNetApp.Models
{
    public class Product
    {
        public int ProductId { get; set; }
        public string Name { get; set; }
        public string Description { get; set; }
        public decimal Price { get; set; }
    }

    public class Customer
    {
        public int CustomerId { get; set; }
        public string FirstName { get; set; }
        public string LastName { get; set; }
        public string Email { get; set; }
    }
}
```

These are simple model classes representing a `Product` and a `Customer` with their respective properties. Controllers would typically create instances of these models to pass data to views or to receive data from user input.

Understanding this fundamental project structure in ASP.NET is the first step towards building well-organized and maintainable web applications. As your projects grow in complexity, adhering to these conventions will become increasingly important for managing your codebase effectively.

📌 4. Running and Debugging ASP.NET Applications: Bringing Your Code to Life and Troubleshooting

Once you've created your ASP.NET application, the next crucial steps are running it to see it in action and debugging it to identify and fix any issues or unexpected behavior. Visual Studio provides excellent tools for both these processes.

A. Running the App: Launching Your Web Application

Running your ASP.NET application in Visual Studio is straightforward and allows you to see the user interface and functionality you've built in a web browser.

Step 1: Initiating the Run Process

- **Action:** There are a couple of primary ways to run your ASP.NET application from within Visual Studio:
  - **Press F5:** This is the most common method and will start the application in debug mode (allowing you to set breakpoints and step through your code).
  - **Click the Green Play Button:** Located in the Visual Studio toolbar (usually near the "Debug" dropdown), this button will also start your application. The label on the button might vary slightly depending on your project type (e.g., it might show the project name or "IIS Express").
- **Explanation:**
  - **Debug Mode (F5):** When you run in debug mode, Visual Studio attaches a debugger to the running process. This enables you to pause the execution of your code at specific points (breakpoints), inspect variable values, step through the code line by line, and analyze the application's behavior in detail.
  - **Without Debugging (Ctrl + F5):** This option runs your application without attaching the debugger. It's faster for simply viewing the application's output without needing to step through the code. However, you won't be able to use debugging features like breakpoints.
  - **IIS Express:** By default, ASP.NET Core projects in Visual Studio often use IIS Express, a lightweight version of IIS (Internet Information Services), as the

development web server. Visual Studio manages the configuration and launching of IIS Express for your project.

Step 2: Observing the Browser Output

- **Action:** Once you initiate the run process, Visual Studio will build your project (if necessary) and then launch your default web browser. The browser will navigate to the URL configured for your application (typically `https://localhost:portnumber`, where `portnumber` is a dynamically assigned port).
- **Expected Output:** You should see the homepage of your ASP.NET application displayed in the browser. This is usually the view associated with the default controller's default action (often `HomeController`'s `Index()` action). The content you see is the HTML generated by your Razor views and any client-side scripts.
- **Significance:** This step allows you to visually verify that your application is running and that the basic UI elements are rendering as expected. It's the first tangible output of your development efforts.

B. Debugging the App: Finding and Fixing Issues

Debugging is a critical skill in software development. Visual Studio provides a powerful set of debugging tools to help you understand the flow of your ASP.NET application and identify the root causes of bugs.

Step 1: Setting Breakpoints

- **Action:** To pause the execution of your code at a specific line, you need to set a **breakpoint**. You can do this in the Visual Studio code editor in several ways:
  - **Click in the Margin:** Click in the gray margin to the left of the line number where you want to set a breakpoint. A red circle will appear, indicating a breakpoint.
  - **Press F9:** Place your cursor on the line of code where you want to break and press the `F9` key.
  - **Right-Click and Select "Breakpoint" -> "Insert Breakpoint":** Right-click on the line of code and choose this option from the context menu.
- **Explanation:** When you run your application in debug mode (F5), the execution will pause when it reaches a line of code where a breakpoint is set. This allows you to examine the current state of your application.
- **Example (as in your table):**

  C#

```csharp
public IActionResult About()
{
    string message = "This is the About Page"; // Set breakpoint here
    return View();
}
```

Setting a breakpoint on the `string message = ...;` line will cause the application to pause execution right before this line is executed when the `/Home/About` URL is accessed.

Step 2: Using the Immediate Window to Inspect Variables

- **Action:** When your application is paused at a breakpoint, the **Immediate Window** allows you to inspect and even modify the values of variables, evaluate expressions, and execute single lines of code within the current context. To open the Immediate Window, go to **Debug -> Windows -> Immediate**.
- **Explanation:**
  - **Inspecting Variables:** In the Immediate Window, you can type the name of a variable and press Enter to see its current value.
  - **Evaluating Expressions:** You can type and evaluate C# expressions (e.g., `1 + 2`, `myList.Count()`).
  - **Modifying Variables (Use with Caution):** You can also assign new values to variables directly in the Immediate Window (e.g., `message = "New Message";`). Be cautious when doing this as it can alter the application's state during debugging.
- **Example (Continuing from the "About" action with a breakpoint):**

  0. Run the application in debug mode (F5) and navigate to the `/Home/About` URL in your browser. The execution will pause at the breakpoint.
  1. Open the Immediate Window (**Debug -> Windows -> Immediate**).
  2. In the Immediate Window, type `message` and press Enter. You will see the current value of the `message` variable: `"This is the About Page"`.
  3. You could also type `message = "Updated About Text";` and press Enter to change the value of the `message` variable for the remainder of the current execution.

Step 3: Hovering Over Variables During Runtime

- **Action:** When your application is paused at a breakpoint, you can simply hover your mouse cursor over a variable in the code editor. A small tooltip will appear, displaying the current value of that variable.
- **Explanation:** This is a quick and convenient way to inspect the values of variables without having to type their names in the Immediate Window. It's especially useful for checking the values of multiple variables as you step through your code.
- **Example (Continuing from the "About" action with a breakpoint):**
  1. Run the application in debug mode (F5) and navigate to `/Home/About`. The execution will pause.
  2. In the code editor, hover your mouse cursor over the `message` variable on the line where the breakpoint is set. A tooltip will pop up showing the value `"This is the About Page"`.

Additional Debugging Features in Visual Studio:

- **Stepping Through Code:** Visual Studio allows you to execute your code line by line to follow its flow:
  - **Step Over (F10):** Executes the current line and moves to the next line of code within the current method, without stepping into function calls.
  - **Step Into (F11):** Executes the current line and, if it's a function call, steps into the code of that function.
  - **Step Out (Shift + F11):** Executes the remaining code in the current function and returns to the calling function.
- **Watch Window:** Allows you to define variables or expressions that you want to monitor continuously during debugging. Go to **Debug -> Windows -> Watch** (and choose Watch 1, Watch 2, etc.).
- **Locals Window:** Automatically displays the variables that are in the current scope during debugging. Go to **Debug -> Windows -> Locals**.
- **Call Stack Window:** Shows the sequence of method calls that led to the current point of execution. This is helpful for understanding the flow of your application and identifying where a problem might have originated. Go to **Debug -> Windows -> Call Stack**.
- **Breakpoints Window:** Allows you to manage all the breakpoints you have set in your project (enable/disable, delete, set conditions). Go to **Debug -> Windows -> Breakpoints**.

By mastering the techniques of running and debugging your ASP.NET applications in Visual Studio, you gain the ability to not only see your creations come to life but also to effectively diagnose and resolve any issues that arise during development. This iterative process of coding, running, and debugging is fundamental to building robust and reliable web applications.

Summary:

- Visual Studio + .NET SDK form the backbone of ASP.NET development.
- Understanding project structure is key to effective coding.
- Running and debugging tools in Visual Studio make development easier.

10 PRACTICAL EXAMPLES WITH SOLUTION'

1. Verifying .NET SDK Installation on Different OS

- **Problem:** Demonstrate how to verify the .NET SDK installation on both a Windows machine and a Linux machine (if accessible).
- **Solution (Windows):**
    1. Open Command Prompt (type `cmd` in the Start Menu).
    2. Type `dotnet --version` and press Enter. Observe the output.
    3. Type `dotnet new` and press Enter. Observe the list of templates.
- **Solution (Linux - Assuming .NET SDK is installed):**
    1. Open the Terminal.
    2. Type `dotnet --version` and press Enter. Observe the output.
    3. Type `dotnet new` and press Enter. Observe the list of templates.
- **Learning Outcome:** Understanding how to confirm a successful .NET SDK installation across different operating systems using the command line.

2. Creating a Basic ASP.NET Core Empty Project

- **Problem:** Create a minimal ASP.NET Core web application without pre-configured MVC or Razor Pages.
- **Solution (Visual Studio):**
    1. Open Visual Studio -> Create a new project.
    2. Search for and select "ASP.NET Core Empty".
    3. Name the project (e.g., `MinimalWebApp`).
    4. Choose a .NET version and click "Create".
    5. Observe the very basic project structure in Solution Explorer (Program.cs, Properties).
- **Solution (.NET CLI):**
    1. Open Command Prompt or Terminal.
    2. Navigate to your desired project directory (`cd Projects`).
    3. Type `dotnet new web -o MinimalWebApp` and press Enter.
    4. Navigate into the project directory (`cd MinimalWebApp`).
    5. Examine the generated files (`Program.cs`, `MinimalWebApp.csproj`).
- **Learning Outcome:** Understanding the foundational structure of a bare-bones ASP.NET Core application.

3. Exploring `wwwroot` and Serving Static Files

- **Problem:** Add a simple HTML file and an image to the `wwwroot` folder of an existing ASP.NET Core project and access them through the browser.
- **Solution:**
    1. In your `FirstAspNetApp` project (or a new one), navigate to the `wwwroot` folder in Solution Explorer.
    2. Create a new HTML file named `static.html` with some basic content (e.g., `<h1>Static Content</h1><img src="image.jpg" alt="Test Image">`).

3. Add a sample image file named `image.jpg` inside the `wwwroot` folder (or a subfolder like `wwwroot/images/` and adjust the `src` attribute accordingly).
4. Run the application (F5).
5. In the browser, navigate to `https://localhost:yourport/static.html` (adjust the port if needed). If you placed the image in a subfolder, access it via `https://localhost:yourport/images/image.jpg`.

- **Learning Outcome:** Understanding the role of the `wwwroot` folder for serving static content directly to the client.

4. Examining `appsettings.json` and Accessing Configuration

- **Problem:** Add a custom configuration setting to `appsettings.json` and access it in your `HomeController`.
- **Solution:**
  1. Open `appsettings.json` in your `FirstAspNetApp` project.
  2. Add a new section:

     JSON

     ```
     {
       "Logging": { ... },
       "AllowedHosts": "*",
       "MyCustomSettings": {
         "Greeting": "Hello from Configuration!"
       }
     }
     ```

  3. Open `HomeController.cs`.
  4. Inject the `IConfiguration` service in the constructor:

private readonly IConfiguration _configuration; private readonly ILogger<HomeController> _logger;

```
    public HomeController(ILogger<HomeController> logger, IConfiguration
configuration)
    {
        _logger = logger;
        _configuration = configuration;
    }
    ```

5. In the `Index` action, read the configuration and pass it to the view:
    ```csharp
    public IActionResult Index()
    {
        ViewBag.CustomGreeting = _configuration["MyCustomSettings:Greeting"];
        return View();
    }
    ```

6. Modify `Views/Home/Index.cshtml` to display the value:
    ```cshtml
    @{
```

```
    ViewData["Title"] = "Home Page";
}

<div class="text-center">
    <h1 class="display-4">Welcome</h1>
    <p>@ViewBag.CustomGreeting</p>
</div>
```

7. Run the application (F5) and observe the output on the homepage.

- **Learning Outcome:** Understanding how to configure application settings in `appsettings.json` and access them in your code.

5. Setting and Inspecting Breakpoints in a Controller Action

- **Problem:** Set a breakpoint in a controller action, run the application in debug mode, and inspect the values of variables.
- **Solution:**
    1. Open `HomeController.cs` and set a breakpoint on a line within the `Index` action (e.g., `ViewBag.CustomGreeting = ...;`).
    2. Run the application by pressing F5. The browser will open the homepage, and the execution will pause at your breakpoint in Visual Studio.
    3. Hover your mouse over `_configuration` and `ViewBag` to see their values.
    4. Open the "Locals" window (Debug -> Windows -> Locals) to see all variables in the current scope.
    5. Step over the code using F10 to see the next line being executed.
    6. Continue execution by pressing F5 or clicking "Continue".
- **Learning Outcome:** Learning how to use breakpoints and the "Locals" window for basic debugging.

6. Using the Immediate Window to Evaluate Expressions

- **Problem:** While debugging, use the Immediate Window to evaluate a simple expression.
- **Solution:**
    1. Set a breakpoint in the `Index` action of `HomeController.cs` (as in the previous example).
    2. Run the application in debug mode (F5) and let it hit the breakpoint.
    3. Open the "Immediate Window" (Debug -> Windows -> Immediate).
    4. Type `DateTime.Now.DayOfWeek` in the Immediate Window and press Enter. Observe the output (the current day of the week).
    5. Type `1 + 1` and press Enter. Observe the result.
- **Learning Outcome:** Understanding how to use the Immediate Window to dynamically evaluate expressions during debugging.

7. Exploring the `Views` Folder and Passing Data

- **Problem:** Modify the `HomeController` to pass a list of strings to the `Index` view and display them using a `foreach` loop in the view.

- **Solution (`HomeController.cs`):**

  C#

```
public IActionResult Index()
{
    ViewBag.MessageList = new List<string> { "Message 1", "Message 2",
"Message 3" };
    return View();
}
```

- **Solution (`Views/Home/Index.cshtml`):**

  Razor CSHTML

```
@{
    ViewData["Title"] = "Home Page";
}

<div class="text-center">
    <h1 class="display-4">Welcome</h1>
    <ul>
        @foreach (var message in ViewBag.MessageList)
        {
            <li>@message</li>
        }
    </ul>
</div>
```

- **Execution:** Run the application (F5) and observe the list of messages on the homepage.
- **Learning Outcome:** Understanding the role of the `Views` folder and how to pass data from the controller to the view using `ViewBag`.

8. Understanding `Startup.cs` (or `Program.cs` in minimal hosting)

- **Problem:** Identify and briefly explain the purpose of key lines in the `Startup.cs` (or `Program.cs`) file related to adding MVC services and configuring the HTTP request pipeline.
- **Solution (Explanation - Refer to the generated `Startup.cs` or `Program.cs`):**
  - **`builder.Services.AddControllersWithViews();` (or similar):** This line registers the services required for using MVC (Controllers and Views) within the application's dependency injection container.
  - **`app.UseRouting();`:** This middleware component is responsible for matching incoming HTTP requests to route handlers (like controller actions).
  - **`app.UseEndpoints(endpoints => { ... });`:** This middleware defines how routes are mapped to executable code. The default route `"{controller=Home}/{action=Index}/{id?}"` specifies how URLs are translated into controller and action names.

  - **`app.UseStaticFiles();`**: This middleware enables the serving of static files from the `wwwroot` folder.
- **Learning Outcome:** Gaining a basic understanding of the configuration and request pipeline setup in the application's startup file.

9. Debugging with Step Into (F11)

- **Problem:** Create a simple helper method in your controller and use "Step Into" to trace its execution during debugging.
- **Solution (`HomeController.cs`):**

C#

```
public IActionResult Index()
{
    string greeting = GetGreeting();
    ViewBag.Greeting = greeting;
    return View();
}

private string GetGreeting()
{
    string message = "Hello from the helper!";
    return message.ToUpper();
}
```

- **Solution (`Views/Home/Index.cshtml`):**

Razor CSHTML

```
<h1>@ViewBag.Greeting</h1>
```

- **Execution:**
  1. Set a breakpoint on the `string greeting = GetGreeting();` line in `HomeController.cs`.
  2. Run the application in debug mode (F5).
  3. When the breakpoint is hit, press F11 ("Step Into"). You will be taken inside the `GetGreeting()` method.
  4. Step through the lines within `GetGreeting()` using F10 (Step Over).
  5. Press Shift + F11 ("Step Out") to return to the `Index()` action.
- **Learning Outcome:** Understanding how to use "Step Into" to debug the execution flow of methods.

10. Exploring Different Project Templates

- **Problem:** Create a new ASP.NET Core project using a different template (e.g., "Razor Pages") and compare its basic project structure with the MVC project.
- **Solution:**

1. Open Visual Studio -> Create a new project.
2. Search for and select "ASP.NET Core Web App".
3. On the next screen, choose "Razor Pages" from the "Authentication type" dropdown (or select the standalone "ASP.NET Core Web App (Razor Pages)" template if available).
4. Name the project (e.g., `RazorWebApp`) and click "Create".
5. Observe the project structure in Solution Explorer. Notice the "Pages" folder instead of "Controllers" and "Views/Home". Examine the `.cshtml` and `.cshtml.cs` files within the "Pages" folder (e.g., `Pages/Index.cshtml`, `Pages/Index.cshtml.cs`).

- **Learning Outcome:** Understanding the basic structure of a Razor Pages project and how it differs from the MVC structure.

30 multiple-choice questions with answers covering the topics you requested:

1. Which company provides Visual Studio? a) Google b) Apple c) Microsoft d) Oracle *Answer: c) Microsoft*

2. Which Visual Studio edition is free for students and individual developers? a) Professional b) Enterprise c) Community d) Code *Answer: c) Community*

3. What should you select during Visual Studio installation for ASP.NET development? a) .NET desktop development b) ASP.NET and web development c) Mobile development with .NET d) Universal Windows Platform development *Answer: b) ASP.NET and web development*

4. Where can you download the .NET SDK? a) visualstudio.com b) dotnet.microsoft.com c) microsoft.com d) nuget.org *Answer: b) dotnet.microsoft.com*

5. Which command is used to check the installed .NET version in the command line? a) dotnet version b) .net version c) dotnet --version d) .net --version *Answer: c) dotnet --version*

6. Which command lists available .NET project templates? a) dotnet list b) dotnet templates c) dotnet new d) dotnet create *Answer: c) dotnet new*

7. What is the first step in creating a new ASP.NET project in Visual Studio? a) Select a .NET version b) Name the project c) Open Visual Studio d) Choose a project location *Answer: c) Open Visual Studio*

8. Which project template is commonly used for building web applications with the Model-View-Controller pattern? a) ASP.NET Core Empty b) ASP.NET Core Web App (Model-View-Controller) c) Console Application d) Class Library *Answer: b) ASP.NET Core Web App (Model-View-Controller)*

9. What is the default name given to the primary controller in a new ASP.NET MVC project? a) MainController b) DefaultController c) HomeController d) AppController *Answer: c) HomeController*

10. Which file extension is used for Razor view files? a) .html b) .aspx c) .cshtml d) .razor *Answer: c) .cshtml*

11. Which folder in an ASP.NET project typically contains C# classes that handle requests? a) Views b) Models c) Controllers d) wwwroot *Answer: c) Controllers*

12. Which folder contains Razor files in an ASP.NET MVC project? a) Models b) Controllers c) wwwroot d) Views *Answer: d) Views*

13. Which folder is used to store static files like CSS, JavaScript, and images? a) Content b) Assets c) wwwroot d) StaticFiles *Answer: c) wwwroot*

14. Which file is the primary configuration file for ASP.NET applications? a) web.config b) config.json c) appsettings.json d) settings.xml *Answer: c) appsettings.json*

15. Which file is responsible for configuring services and middleware in ASP.NET Core? a) Global.asax b) Web.config c) Startup.cs (or Program.cs in minimal hosting) d) RouteConfig.cs *Answer: c) Startup.cs (or Program.cs in minimal hosting)*

16. Which folder is used to store data classes or business entities? a) Data b) Entities c) Models d) Classes *Answer: c) Models*

17. What does the `HomeController` class typically inherit from? a) ControllerBase b) ModelBase c) ViewBase d) ServiceBase *Answer: a) ControllerBase*

18. What is the purpose of the `Index()` method in a `HomeController`? a) To create a new record b) To delete a record c) To display the homepage d) To update a record *Answer: c) To display the homepage*

19. What is the primary function of a Razor view? a) To handle HTTP requests b) To define data models c) To generate HTML output d) To manage database connections *Answer: c) To generate HTML output*

20. How do you run an ASP.NET application in Visual Studio? a) Press Ctrl + R b) Press F10 c) Press F5 d) Press Shift + F5 *Answer: c) Press F5*

21. What happens when you press F5 in Visual Studio while working on an ASP.NET project? a) It builds the project only b) It opens the project settings c) It runs the application in debug mode d) It closes the project *Answer: c) It runs the application in debug mode*

22. What is the purpose of setting a breakpoint in your code? a) To mark the end of a function b) To pause code execution for inspection c) To optimize performance d) To define code comments *Answer: b) To pause code execution for inspection*

23. Where do you typically set a breakpoint in Visual Studio? a) In the Solution Explorer b) In the Output window c) In the code editor margin d) In the Properties window *Answer: c) In the code editor margin*

24. Which window in Visual Studio allows you to inspect variable values and evaluate expressions during debugging? a) Output Window b) Error List Window c) Immediate Window d) Properties Window *Answer: c) Immediate Window*

25. What is the purpose of hovering over a variable during debugging? a) To rename the variable b) To delete the variable c) To check the variable's data type d) To view the variable's current value *Answer: d) To view the variable's current value*

26. Which key is used to "Step Over" in Visual Studio debugging? a) F11 b) F10 c) F9 d) F5 *Answer: b) F10*

27. Which key is used to "Step Into" in Visual Studio debugging? a) F10 b) F9 c) F11 d) F5 *Answer: c) F11*

28. Which window displays the sequence of method calls during debugging? a) Locals Window b) Watch Window c) Call Stack Window d) Breakpoints Window *Answer: c) Call Stack Window*

29. What is the purpose of the "Locals" window during debugging? a) To display all variables in the project b) To display variables in the current scope c) To display global variables d) To display static variables *Answer: b) To display variables in the current scope*

30. Which button in Visual Studio starts the application without debugging? a) The green "Play" button b) Ctrl + F5 c) F5 d) Shift + F5 *Answer: b) Ctrl + F5*

9 medium-sized questions with answers covering the installation of Visual Studio and .NET SDK, creating a first ASP.NET project, understanding its structure, and running/debugging:

1. Describe the process of installing Visual Studio for ASP.NET development. What are the key considerations during the installation, and why is selecting the "ASP.NET and web development" workload crucial?

- **Answer:** The installation involves downloading the Visual Studio Installer from the official Microsoft website (`visualstudio.microsoft.com`). Key considerations include choosing the appropriate edition (Community for students/individuals), ensuring sufficient disk space and internet connectivity, and carefully selecting the workloads. The "ASP.NET and web development" workload is crucial because it bundles all the necessary components for building ASP.NET applications, including the .NET SDK (often), ASP.NET and Web Tools, IIS support, and frontend development essentials, streamlining the setup process and ensuring all required dependencies are installed together.

2. Explain the role of the .NET SDK in ASP.NET development. How can you verify its successful installation after downloading and running the installer?

- **Answer:** The .NET SDK (Software Development Kit) is a fundamental set of tools, libraries, and documentation required to develop, build, run, and publish .NET applications, including ASP.NET. It includes the .NET CLI (`dotnet`), the .NET runtime, compilers, and build tools. You can verify its successful installation by opening Command Prompt (Windows) or Terminal (macOS/Linux) and running the command `dotnet --version`. This should return the installed SDK version. Additionally, running `dotnet new` should list available project templates, confirming the CLI is functional and can access the project scaffolding tools.

3. Outline the steps involved in creating a new ASP.NET Core Web App (Model-View-Controller) project in Visual Studio. Briefly describe the purpose of selecting the MVC template.

- **Answer:** The steps are: 1. Open Visual Studio and click "Create a new project." 2. Search for and select the "ASP.NET Core Web App (Model-View-Controller)" template. 3. Provide a name and location for the project. 4. Choose the target .NET version (ideally the latest LTS). 5. Click "Create." Selecting the MVC template is crucial as it sets up the basic folder structure (`Controllers`, `Models`, `Views`), necessary configurations, and pre-configured dependencies that follow the Model-View-Controller architectural pattern, which promotes separation of concerns and is widely used for building well-structured web applications.

4. Describe the fundamental purpose of the `Controllers`, `Views`, and `Models` folders in an ASP.NET MVC project. How do these components interact with each other to handle a user request and generate a response?

- **Answer:**
    - **Controllers:** Handle incoming HTTP requests, interact with the `Models` to retrieve or manipulate data, and then select a `View` to display the response.
    - **Views:** Are responsible for rendering the user interface (HTML) and displaying data passed to them by the `Controllers`. They use Razor syntax to embed C# code for dynamic content generation.
    - **Models:** Represent the application's data and business logic. They encapsulate data structures and may contain rules for data manipulation.
- **Interaction:** When a user makes a request, the routing mechanism directs it to a specific action in a `Controller`. The `Controller` may interact with `Models` to fetch or update

data. Finally, the `Controller` selects a `View`, passes data to it (often via `ViewBag`, `ViewData`, or Model binding), and the `View` renders the HTML response sent back to the user's browser.

5. Explain the significance of the `wwwroot` folder in an ASP.NET Core project. What types of files are typically stored here, and how are they served to the client's browser?

- **Answer:** The `wwwroot` folder is the designated root directory for all static files that are served directly to the client's browser without being processed by the ASP.NET engine. Typically, it stores client-side assets such as HTML files (though primary views are in the `Views` folder), CSS stylesheets, JavaScript files, images, fonts, and client-side libraries. These files are served directly by the web server (like Kestrel or IIS) based on the URL path requested by the browser, where the path is relative to the `wwwroot` folder. For example, `/css/style.css` would map to the `style.css` file within the `wwwroot/css/` directory.

6. Describe the purpose and common contents of the `appsettings.json` file in an ASP.NET Core project. How can you access the configuration settings stored in this file within your application's code?

- **Answer:** The `appsettings.json` file is the primary configuration file for ASP.NET Core applications, storing application-wide settings in JSON format. Common contents include logging configurations, database connection strings, API keys, and custom application-specific settings. You can access these settings in your code by injecting the `IConfiguration` interface into your classes (e.g., controllers, services). The `IConfiguration` object provides methods and indexers to retrieve configuration values based on their key hierarchy (e.g., `_configuration["Logging:LogLevel:Default"]` or `_configuration.GetConnectionString("DefaultConnection")`).

7. Explain the role of the `Startup.cs` (or `Program.cs` in minimal hosting) file in an ASP.NET Core application. What are the key tasks performed within this file during application initialization?

- **Answer:** The `Startup.cs` (or `Program.cs` in minimal hosting) file is the entry point for configuring the application's services and the HTTP request processing pipeline. Key tasks performed include:
  - **Registering Services:** Using `builder.Services.Add...()` methods to add services that the application will use (e.g., MVC, Razor Pages, database contexts, custom services) to the dependency injection container.
  - **Configuring Middleware:** Using `app.Use...()` methods to define the sequence of middleware components that will handle incoming HTTP requests. Middleware can handle tasks like routing, authentication, static file serving, exception handling, and more.
  - **Defining Endpoints/Routes:** Configuring how incoming URLs are mapped to executable code (e.g., controller actions or Razor Pages).

8. Outline the basic steps to run an ASP.NET application in Visual Studio. What is the difference between running with debugging (F5) and without debugging (Ctrl + F5)?

- **Answer:** The basic steps to run an ASP.NET application in Visual Studio are to either press the `F5` key or click the green "Play" button in the toolbar.
    - **Running with debugging (F5):** Starts the application and attaches the Visual Studio debugger to the running process. This allows you to set breakpoints, step through code, inspect variables, and analyze the application's runtime behavior.
    - **Running without debugging (Ctrl + F5):** Starts the application without attaching the debugger. It's faster for simply viewing the application's output but doesn't allow for interactive debugging features like breakpoints or stepping through code.

9. Describe how to set and use breakpoints in Visual Studio to debug an ASP.NET application. Explain the purpose of the "Locals" window and the "Immediate Window" during a debugging session.

- **Answer:** To set a breakpoint, click in the gray margin to the left of the line number in the code editor or press `F9` on the desired line. When the application runs in debug mode (F5) and reaches a breakpoint, execution pauses.
    - **Locals Window:** Displays the variables that are currently in scope (i.e., accessible in the current method) along with their current values. It automatically updates as you step through the code.
    - **Immediate Window:** Allows you to evaluate expressions, inspect and modify variable values, and execute single lines of code within the current execution context. You can type the name of a variable or an expression and press Enter to see its value.

ASP.NET Web Forms is a part of the ASP.NET framework that allows developers to build dynamic web pages using a rich set of server-side controls and event-driven programming. This chapter introduces you to the core concepts of Web Forms.

📌 1. ASPX Pages and Code-Behind: The Foundation of ASP.NET Web Forms

In the ASP.NET Web Forms framework, the architecture of a web page is fundamentally structured around the concept of **separation of presentation (UI) and logic (code)**. This is achieved through the pairing of two distinct files for each web page: the **ASPX Page** and its associated **Code-Behind File**. This model, reminiscent of desktop application development, aims to make web development more intuitive for developers familiar with event-driven programming.

Let's delve into each of these components in detail with the example you provided:

1. ASPX Page: The HTML Markup and UI Controls

- **What it is:** The ASPX page is the file with the `.aspx` extension. It primarily contains the **HTML markup** that defines the structure and content of the web page. Crucially, it also includes **server-side UI controls** provided by the ASP.NET framework. These controls are special HTML-like elements that are processed on the server before being rendered as standard HTML to the user's browser.
- **Key Characteristics:**
    - **HTML Structure:** It forms the basic skeleton of the web page using standard HTML tags (`<html>`, `<body>`, `<div>`, etc.).
    - **Server-Side Controls:** ASP.NET Web Forms provides a rich set of pre-built server controls (e.g., `<asp:Button>`, `<asp:Label>`, `<asp:TextBox>`, `<asp:GridView>`). These controls have properties, methods, and events that can be manipulated on the server-side. The `runat="server"` attribute is essential for these controls, indicating that they should be processed by the ASP.NET engine on the server.
    - **Declarative UI Design:** Developers can visually design the user interface by arranging these server controls within the HTML markup. Visual Studio's design view provides a drag-and-drop interface for this purpose.
    - **Directives:** ASPX pages often start with directives enclosed in `<%@ ... %>`. These directives provide instructions to the ASP.NET page parser. Common directives include:
        - **`<%@ Page ... %>`:** Defines page-specific attributes like the programming language (`Language`), whether events should be automatically wired up

(`AutoEventWireup`), the path to the code-behind file (`CodeFile`), and the class that the page inherits from (`Inherits`).
    - **`<%@ Control ... %>`:** Used for creating user controls (reusable UI components).
    - **`<%@ Register ... %>`:** Used for registering custom controls or namespaces.
  - **Event Handling Attributes:** Server controls can have attributes that link UI events (like a button click) to specific event handler methods in the code-behind file (e.g., `OnClick="btnClick_Click"`).
- **Example Breakdown (from `Default.aspx`):**

  HTML

```
<%@ Page Language="C#" AutoEventWireup="true"
CodeFile="Default.aspx.cs" Inherits="Default" %>
<html>
<body>
    <form id="form1" runat="server">
        <asp:Button ID="btnClick" runat="server" Text="Click Me"
OnClick="btnClick_Click" />
        <asp:Label ID="lblMessage" runat="server" Text=""></asp:Label>
    </form>
</body>
</html>
```

  - **`<%@ Page Language="C#" AutoEventWireup="true" CodeFile="Default.aspx.cs" Inherits="Default" %>`:**
    - **`Language="C#"`:** Specifies that the server-side code for this page will be written in C#.
    - **`AutoEventWireup="true"`:** Automatically connects standard events of server controls (like `Click` for a button) to methods in the code-behind file with matching names (e.g., `btnClick_Click`). While convenient for simpler scenarios, it can sometimes lead to less explicit control and is often set to `false` in more complex applications for better control over the page lifecycle.
    - **`CodeFile="Default.aspx.cs"`:** Specifies the path to the associated code-behind file containing the server-side logic for this ASPX page.
    - **`Inherits="Default"`:** Indicates that the ASPX page's class in the compiled assembly will inherit from the `Default` class defined in the `Default.aspx.cs` file.
  - **`<form id="form1" runat="server">`:**
    - **`<form>`:** A standard HTML form element.
    - **`runat="server"`:** This crucial attribute makes the HTML form a server-side control. This allows you to access and manipulate the form and its child controls on the server.
  - **`<asp:Button ID="btnClick" runat="server" Text="Click Me" OnClick="btnClick_Click" />`:**

        - **<asp:Button>:** This is an ASP.NET server-side Button control. It will be rendered as a standard HTML `<input type="submit">` button in the browser.
        - **ID="btnClick":** A unique identifier for this control within the ASPX page, allowing you to reference it in the code-behind file.
        - **runat="server":** Indicates that this control is processed on the server.
        - **Text="Click Me":** Sets the text displayed on the button.
        - **OnClick="btnClick_Click":** This attribute links the button's `Click` event (when the user clicks the button) to a method named `btnClick_Click` in the associated code-behind file (`Default.aspx.cs`).
    - **<asp:Label ID="lblMessage" runat="server" Text=""></asp:Label>:**
        - **<asp:Label>:** An ASP.NET server-side Label control. It will be rendered as a standard HTML `<span>` element (by default) in the browser.
        - **ID="lblMessage":** A unique identifier for this label control.
        - **runat="server":** Indicates server-side processing.
        - **Text="":** Sets the initial text content of the label to an empty string. This text will be dynamically updated from the code-behind.

2. Code-Behind File: Containing the Server-Side Logic

- **What it is:** The code-behind file is a separate file (e.g., `Default.aspx.cs` for `Default.aspx`) that contains the server-side logic for the corresponding ASPX page. It is typically written in C# (as in the example) or VB.NET, as specified in the `<%@ Page %>` directive.
- **Key Characteristics:**
    - **Class Definition:** The code-behind file defines a class that inherits from the `System.Web.UI.Page` class (or a custom base page class). The `Inherits` attribute in the ASPX page directive links the ASPX markup to this code-behind class.
    - **Event Handlers:** It contains methods that act as event handlers for events raised by the server controls on the ASPX page (e.g., `btnClick_Click` for the `Click` event of the `btnClick` button). These methods execute on the server when the corresponding event occurs.
    - **Business Logic:** This is where you write the C# (or VB.NET) code that implements the application's logic, data manipulation, and interactions with other parts of your application (e.g., databases, services).
    - **Control Manipulation:** Within the code-behind, you can access and manipulate the properties of the server controls defined in the ASPX page using their `ID`s (e.g., `lblMessage.Text = "..."`).
    - **Page Lifecycle Events:** The `System.Web.UI.Page` class exposes a series of events that occur during the processing of an ASPX page (e.g., `Page_Init`, `Page_Load`, `Page_PreRender`, `Page_Unload`). You can write event handlers for these events to execute code at specific stages of the page lifecycle.
- **Example Breakdown (from `Default.aspx.cs`):**

  C#

```
using System;
using System.Web.UI;
using System.Web.UI.WebControls; // Namespace for server controls like
Label and Button

public partial class Default : Page // Inherits from System.Web.UI.Page
{
    protected void Page_Load(object sender, EventArgs e)
    {
        // This event is raised every time the page is loaded.
        // You might put initialization code here, but be mindful of
postbacks.
        if (!IsPostBack)
        {
            // Code to execute only on the initial page load (not on
postbacks)
        }
    }

    protected void btnClick_Click(object sender, EventArgs e)
    {
        // This event handler is executed when the btnClick button is
clicked.
        lblMessage.Text = "Hello, Web Forms!"; // Accessing and setting
the Text property of the lblMessage control.
    }
}
```

- **`using System; using System.Web.UI; using System.Web.UI.WebControls;`:** These lines import necessary namespaces that provide access to core .NET classes and ASP.NET Web Forms specific classes, including the `Page` class and server control classes like `Label` and `Button`.
- **`public partial class Default : Page`:** This defines a class named `Default` that inherits from the `System.Web.UI.Page` class. The `partial` keyword allows the class definition to be split between the ASPX markup (which is also compiled into the same class) and this code-behind file. The `Inherits="Default"` attribute in the ASPX page links them.
- **`protected void Page_Load(object sender, EventArgs e)`:** This is an event handler for the `Load` event of the `Page` lifecycle. It is executed every time the page is loaded, including the initial request and any subsequent postbacks (when the form is submitted). The `IsPostBack` property is often checked to execute code only on the initial load.
- **`protected void btnClick_Click(object sender, EventArgs e)`:** This is the event handler method that is executed when the `Click` event of the `btnClick` button occurs (due to the `OnClick="btnClick_Click"` attribute in the ASPX).
  - **`object sender`:** Represents the control that raised the event (in this case, the `btnClick` button).
  - **`EventArgs e`:** Provides event-specific data (though often empty for simple click events).
  - **`lblMessage.Text = "Hello, Web Forms!";`:** This line demonstrates how to access and manipulate a server control from the code-behind. It

sets the `Text` property of the `lblMessage` (the Label control defined in the ASPX page) to the string "Hello, Web Forms!". This change will be reflected in the HTML rendered to the browser after the button click event is processed on the server.

Benefits of ASPX Pages and Code-Behind:

- **Separation of Concerns:** Clearly separates the UI design (ASPX) from the application logic (Code-Behind), making the code more organized, maintainable, and easier to understand. Designers can focus on the UI without directly modifying the business logic, and developers can work on the code without altering the visual layout.
- **Event-Driven Model:** Provides a familiar event-driven programming model for developers accustomed to desktop application development. UI interactions trigger events that are handled by specific methods in the code-behind.
- **Visual Studio Integration:** Visual Studio provides excellent support for ASPX pages and code-behind files, including a visual designer for the ASPX page and seamless navigation between the two linked files.
- **State Management:** ASP.NET Web Forms provides built-in mechanisms for managing the state of server controls and the page across multiple requests (e.g., ViewState), simplifying the development of interactive applications.

📌 2. Page Life Cycle in ASP.NET Web Forms: A Detailed Journey from Request to Response

The ASP.NET Web Forms Page Life Cycle is a sequence of events that occur from the moment a user requests a page until the server sends the rendered HTML back to the browser. Understanding this lifecycle is crucial for ASP.NET Web Forms developers as it dictates when and how you can interact with page elements, manage state, and execute your code effectively.

Let's break down each stage of the Page Life Cycle in detail with explanations and examples:

1. Page Request:

- **Description (as in your table):** The process begins when a user initiates a request for an ASPX page from the web server. This can happen by:
  - **Entering a URL directly into the browser's address bar.** (HTTP GET request for the initial page load)
  - **Clicking a hyperlink (`<a href="...">`) that points to an ASPX page.** (HTTP GET request)
  - **Submitting a form (`<form method="post" runat="server">`) on an ASPX page.** (HTTP POST request for a postback)
- **Detailed Explanation:** At this stage, the browser sends an HTTP request to the web server hosting the ASP.NET application. The server's ASP.NET ISAPI extension (for

IIS) or the ASP.NET Development Server intercepts this request and starts the process of handling the requested ASPX page.

2. Start:

- **Description (as in your table):** During the Start stage, the ASP.NET runtime does some initial setup for the page. Key actions include:
  - **Creating an instance of the `Page` class:** A new instance of the class associated with the requested ASPX page (defined in the code-behind) is created.
  - **Setting initial page properties:** Properties of the `Page` object are initialized, such as `IsPostBack`, `Request`, `Response`, `Session`, `User`, and `ViewState`.
    - **`IsPostBack`:** A boolean property that indicates whether the current request is the initial request for the page (`false`) or a subsequent request resulting from a form submission back to the same page (`true`). This is a very important property for controlling code execution.
    - **`Request`:** Provides access to the incoming HTTP request data (e.g., query string parameters, form data, cookies).
    - **`Response`:** Provides access to the outgoing HTTP response that will be sent to the browser.
    - **`Session`:** Provides access to the session state for the current user.
    - **`User`:** Provides information about the authenticated user (if authentication is enabled).
    - **`ViewState`:** A dictionary used to store the state of server controls between postbacks.

3. Initialization (Init):

- **Description (as in your table):** In the Initialization stage, the server controls on the ASPX page are created and initialized.
- **Detailed Explanation:**
  - **Control Tree Creation:** ASP.NET parses the ASPX markup and creates a tree of server control objects.
  - **Unique Control IDs:** Each server control's `ID` property is assigned, ensuring unique identification within the page's control hierarchy.
  - **Theme and Skin Application (if applicable):** If themes or skins are being used, they are applied to the controls during this stage.
  - **`OnInit` Event:** The `OnInit` event of the `Page` and the `OnInit` events of individual controls are raised. You can handle these events in your code-behind to perform early initialization tasks that need to occur before ViewState is loaded. It's often used to dynamically create controls or set initial properties that shouldn't be overwritten by ViewState.

4. Load:

- **Description (as in your table):** During the Load stage, the page loads values from the ViewState and the posted form data (if it's a postback).

- **Detailed Explanation:**
  - **ViewState Loading:** If the request is a postback (`IsPostBack` is `true`), ASP.NET loads the saved state of the server controls from the ViewState. This allows controls to retain their values and properties across postbacks.
  - **Form Data Loading:** If the request is a postback due to a form submission, the values entered by the user in the form controls are loaded into the corresponding server control properties. For example, if a user typed "John Doe" into a `<asp:TextBox>` with `ID="txtName"`, the `Text` property of the `txtName` control will be set to "John Doe" during this stage.
  - **`OnLoad` Event:** The `OnLoad` event of the `Page` and the `OnLoad` events of individual controls are raised. This is a common place to perform actions that depend on the control values being loaded from ViewState or form data. The example you provided demonstrates using the `Page_Load` event handler.

Example with `Page_Load` Event (as in your table):

C#
```
protected void Page_Load(object sender, EventArgs e)
{
    if (!IsPostBack)
    {
        // Runs only on first load
        lblMessage.Text = "Welcome!";
        // You might also load initial data from a database here.
    }
    else
    {
        // Runs on every postback (when the form is submitted)
        // You might process form data or update the UI based on user input
here.
    }
}
```

In this example, the code inside the `if (!IsPostBack)` block will execute only when the page is loaded for the very first time (e.g., when the user navigates to the page via a link). On subsequent postbacks (when the user submits the form), this code will be skipped. This is a common pattern for initializing controls with default values or loading data that should only occur once per session on that page.

5. Postback Event Handling:

- **Description (as in your table):** This stage occurs *only* when the request is a postback (i.e., the page is being loaded as a result of a form submission back to itself). Events like `Button_Click`, `TextChanged`, `SelectedIndexChanged`, etc., are triggered and their corresponding event handlers in the code-behind are executed.
- **Detailed Explanation:**
  - **Identifying the Event Source:** ASP.NET determines which control caused the postback (e.g., which button was clicked). This information is typically stored in hidden form fields (`__EVENTTARGET` and `__EVENTARGUMENT`).

- **Raising the Event:** The appropriate event of the control that caused the postback is raised.
- **Executing Event Handlers:** The event handler method associated with the raised event (e.g., the `btnClick_Click` method linked to a button's `Click` event via the `OnClick` attribute in the ASPX) is executed. This is where you implement the logic to respond to user interactions.
- **Control-Specific Events:** Different server controls have different sets of events (e.g., a `Button` has a `Click` event, a `TextBox` has a `TextChanged` event, a `DropDownList` has a `SelectedIndexChanged` event).

Example with `btnClick_Click` Event (from the previous explanation):

C#
```
protected void btnClick_Click(object sender, EventArgs e)
{
    lblMessage.Text = "Hello, Web Forms!";
    // You might perform other actions here, like saving data to a database
    // or updating other controls based on the button click.
}
```

When the user clicks the button defined in the `Default.aspx` example, the `btnClick_Click` method in the `Default.aspx.cs` code-behind will be executed during the Postback Event Handling stage. This method then updates the `Text` property of the `lblMessage` Label control.

6. Rendering:

- **Description (as in your table):** In the Rendering stage, ASP.NET generates the HTML markup that will be sent to the client's browser.
- **Detailed Explanation:**
    - **Control State Preservation:** Before rendering, the current state of the server controls (e.g., the text in a `TextBox`, the selected item in a `DropDownList`) is saved into the ViewState if necessary. This ViewState is then embedded as a hidden field (`__VIEWSTATE`) in the HTML form.
    - **HTML Generation:** The ASP.NET runtime traverses the control tree and calls the `Render` method of each control. Each control's `Render` method generates the appropriate HTML markup based on its current properties and state.
    - **Response Stream:** The generated HTML is written to the `Response` object's output stream.
    - **`OnPreRender` Event:** The `OnPreRender` event of the `Page` and the `OnPreRender` events of individual controls are raised just before rendering occurs. This is the last opportunity to make changes to the controls or the page that will be reflected in the rendered HTML.

7. Unload:

- **Description (as in your table):** The Unload stage is the final stage of the Page Life Cycle. It's where cleanup operations are performed before the response is sent to the client.
- **Detailed Explanation:**
    - **Resource Cleanup:** ASP.NET performs final cleanup tasks, such as closing database connections, releasing file handles, and disposing of any unmanaged resources used by the page and its controls.
    - **`OnUnload` Event:** The `OnUnload` event of the `Page` and the `OnUnload` events of individual controls are raised. You can handle these events to perform any last-minute cleanup or logging. However, it's important to note that during the `Unload` stage, the response has already been sent to the client, so you cannot make changes to the rendered HTML.
    - **Page Disposal:** The `Page` object and its associated resources are released from memory.

📌 3. AutoPostBack and ViewState in ASP.NET Web Forms: Enhancing Interactivity and Preserving State

AutoPostBack:

AutoPostBack is a powerful feature in ASP.NET Web Forms that allows specific server controls to automatically trigger a postback to the server when a certain event occurs. Instead of the user having to explicitly submit a form (by clicking a button), an AutoPostBack control will send the current page data back to the server as soon as the relevant event is fired. This enables more interactive and dynamic user experiences without full page submissions for every small interaction.

How it Works:

When the `AutoPostBack` property of a server control is set to `true`, ASP.NET injects JavaScript code into the rendered HTML. This JavaScript code is associated with the control's specific event (e.g., `SelectedIndexChanged` for a `DropDownList`, `TextChanged` for a `TextBox` when the control loses focus). When this event occurs on the client-side, the JavaScript code automatically submits the form containing the control back to the server.

Example Breakdown (from your provided code):

HTML
```
<asp:DropDownList ID="ddlColors" runat="server" AutoPostBack="true"
OnSelectedIndexChanged="ddlColors_SelectedIndexChanged">
    <asp:ListItem Text="Red" />
    <asp:ListItem Text="Green" />
</asp:DropDownList>
<asp:Label ID="lblColor" runat="server" />
```

C#

```
protected void ddlColors_SelectedIndexChanged(object sender, EventArgs e)
{
    lblColor.Text = "You selected: " + ddlColors.SelectedItem.Text;
}
```

- **`<asp:DropDownList ID="ddlColors" runat="server" AutoPostBack="true" OnSelectedIndexChanged="ddlColors_SelectedIndexChanged">`:**
  - **`AutoPostBack="true"`:** This is the key attribute that enables the automatic postback behavior for this `DropDownList`.
  - **`OnSelectedIndexChanged="ddlColors_SelectedIndexChanged"`:** This attribute links the `SelectedIndexChanged` event of the `DropDownList` to the `ddlColors_SelectedIndexChanged` method in the code-behind. The `SelectedIndexChanged` event is fired when the user selects a different item in the dropdown list.
- **`<asp:Label ID="lblColor" runat="server" />`:** A simple Label control to display the selected color.
- **`protected void ddlColors_SelectedIndexChanged(object sender, EventArgs e)`:**
  - This is the event handler method in the code-behind that is executed on the server when the `SelectedIndexChanged` event of the `ddlColors DropDownList` occurs due to the AutoPostBack.
  - **`ddlColors.SelectedItem.Text`:** This accesses the `SelectedItem` property of the `DropDownList` (the currently selected `ListItem`) and retrieves its `Text` value (e.g., "Red" or "Green").
  - **`lblColor.Text = "You selected: " + ddlColors.SelectedItem.Text;`:** This line updates the `Text` property of the `lblColor` Label control to display the user's selection.

Workflow of the Example:

1. The user initially loads the page containing the `DropDownList` and the `Label`.
2. The user interacts with the `DropDownList` and selects a different color (e.g., changes from "Red" to "Green").
3. Because `AutoPostBack` is set to `true`, this action triggers a postback to the server *immediately* without the user having to click a separate submit button.
4. The page data, including the selected value in the `DropDownList`, is sent to the server.
5. The ASP.NET Page Life Cycle begins on the server.
6. During the Postback Event Handling stage, the `ddlColors_SelectedIndexChanged` event handler is executed.
7. Inside the event handler, the `lblColor.Text` is updated with the selected color.
8. The page is re-rendered on the server, including the updated `lblColor`.
9. The new HTML is sent back to the browser, and the page is reloaded, now displaying "You selected: Green" (or whichever color was chosen).

Common Use Cases for AutoPostBack:

- **Cascading DropDownLists:** Updating the items in one `DropDownList` based on the selection in another.
- **Real-time Filtering:** Dynamically filtering data in a GridView or other data-bound control as the user types in a `TextBox` or selects an option.
- **Immediate UI Updates:** Changing the visibility or properties of other controls based on the selection in a control.
- **Interactive Forms:** Creating more responsive forms where changes in one field immediately affect others.

Considerations for AutoPostBack:

- **Increased Server Load:** Each AutoPostBack results in a round trip to the server, which can increase server load and potentially slow down the application if overused on controls with frequent user interactions.
- **Potential for Flicker:** The page reloads after each AutoPostBack, which can sometimes cause a brief flicker in the user interface. Techniques like AJAX (Asynchronous JavaScript and XML) in more modern ASP.NET development (like ASP.NET AJAX in older Web Forms or ASP.NET Core) are often preferred for smoother, partial-page updates.
- **User Experience:** While it can enhance interactivity, excessive AutoPostBacks can be disruptive if they occur too frequently for minor interactions.

ViewState:

ViewState is a mechanism in ASP.NET Web Forms used to **preserve the state of the page and its server controls between postbacks**. Because HTTP is a stateless protocol, the server doesn't inherently remember the values of controls from one request to the next. ViewState solves this by storing the state of controls on the client-side and sending it back to the server with each postback.

How it Works:

When an ASP.NET Web Forms page is rendered, the ASP.NET engine automatically tracks the values of server control properties that need to be persisted across postbacks. This information is then serialized (converted into a string) and embedded into the rendered HTML as a hidden form field named `__VIEWSTATE`.

When the user submits the form (either through a standard submit or an AutoPostBack), this `__VIEWSTATE` hidden field is sent back to the server along with other form data. During the Page Life Cycle on the server (specifically in the Load stage), ASP.NET deserializes the `__VIEWSTATE` data and automatically restores the properties of the server controls to their previous state.

Example Breakdown (from your provided code):

C#
```
ViewState["Clicks"] = 5; // Store
int clicks = (int)ViewState["Clicks"]; // Retrieve
```

- **`ViewState["Clicks"] = 5;`:** This line in the code-behind demonstrates how to store a value (in this case, the integer `5`) in the ViewState. The `ViewState` property of the `Page` object is a dictionary (a collection of key-value pairs). Here, "Clicks" is the key, and `5` is the value being stored. This value will be persisted across subsequent postbacks for this page.
- **`int clicks = (int)ViewState["Clicks"];`:** This line shows how to retrieve a value from the ViewState. You access the `ViewState` dictionary using the same key ("Clicks"). Since `ViewState` stores values as objects, you need to explicitly cast the retrieved value back to its original type (in this case, `int`). If a value with the given key doesn't exist in ViewState, it will return `null`, so it's often good practice to check for `null` before casting.

What is Stored in ViewState?

ViewState typically stores:

- The values of input controls (e.g., `Text` of `TextBox`, `SelectedValue` of `DropDownList`).
- The state of UI controls (e.g., the current page index in a `GridView`, the expanded/collapsed state of a `TreeView`).
- Any custom data explicitly saved into the `ViewState` dictionary by the developer.

Benefits of ViewState:

- **Automatic State Preservation:** It automatically handles the persistence of control values between postbacks, reducing the need for developers to manually manage this state.
- **Simplified Development:** For many common scenarios, ViewState simplifies development by making web forms behave more like stateful desktop applications.

Drawbacks and Considerations for ViewState:

- **Increased Page Size:** The `__VIEWSTATE` data is embedded in the HTML of the page. Storing large amounts of data in ViewState can significantly increase the page size, leading to longer download times and increased bandwidth usage.
- **Security Concerns (if not handled carefully):** Although ViewState data is encoded (and can be optionally encrypted and MAC-protected), sensitive information should generally not be stored directly in ViewState.
- **Performance Impact:** Larger ViewState can also slightly impact the server's processing time during postbacks as it needs to be serialized and deserialized.
- **Not Suitable for All Scenarios:** For applications with heavy reliance on client-side interactions or when minimizing page size is critical, alternative state management techniques (like Session, Cookies, or server-side databases) might be more appropriate.

Best Practices for Using ViewState:

- **Use it judiciously:** Only store the necessary information required to maintain the state of controls across postbacks.

- **Avoid storing large datasets:** For large amounts of data, consider using server-side storage (e.g., Session, database).
- **Be mindful of sensitive data:** Avoid storing sensitive information directly in ViewState. Consider encryption or alternative storage.
- **Disable ViewState for controls that don't need it:** You can disable ViewState for individual controls by setting their `EnableViewState` property to `false`. This can help reduce the overall page size.

📌 4. Writing Event-Driven Code in ASP.NET Web Forms: Creating Interactive Applications

ASP.NET Web Forms embraces an **event-driven programming model**, a paradigm where the flow of the program is determined by events – actions or occurrences that happen, such as user interactions (like clicking a button, changing a dropdown selection, or typing in a text box) or system-generated notifications. This model is very similar to the event-driven nature of Windows Forms development, making it familiar to developers with a desktop application background.

In Web Forms, you define server-side controls in your ASPX markup, and then you write code in the associated code-behind file to respond to specific events that these controls raise. This allows you to build interactive web applications with server-side logic triggered by user actions, often minimizing the need for extensive client-side JavaScript.

Core Concepts of Event-Driven Programming in Web Forms:

1. **Server Controls:** ASP.NET provides a rich set of server-side UI controls (e.g., `Button`, `TextBox`, `DropDownList`, `CheckBox`). These controls are rendered as standard HTML in the browser but have server-side counterparts that can raise events.
2. **Events:** Server controls have various events associated with them that occur in response to user interactions or changes in their state. Examples include `Click` for a `Button`, `SelectedIndexChanged` for a `DropDownList`, `TextChanged` for a `TextBox`, and `CheckedChanged` for a `CheckBox`.
3. **Event Handlers:** In the code-behind file, you write methods called **event handlers** that contain the code to be executed when a specific event is raised by a particular server control.
4. **Event Wiring:** You need to establish a connection (or "wire up") between a control's event and the corresponding event handler method in your code-behind. This is typically done declaratively in the ASPX markup using attributes like `OnClick`, `OnSelectedIndexChanged`, `OnTextChanged`, etc.

Example with Button Click (as in your provided code):

HTML

```
<asp:Button ID="btnSubmit" runat="server" Text="Submit"
OnClick="btnSubmit_Click" />
<asp:Label ID="lblResult" runat="server" />
```

C#

```
protected void btnSubmit_Click(object sender, EventArgs e)
{
    lblResult.Text = "Button clicked at: " + DateTime.Now.ToString();
}
```

Breakdown of the Button Click Example:

- **`<asp:Button ID="btnSubmit" runat="server" Text="Submit" OnClick="btnSubmit_Click" />`:**
    - **`<asp:Button>`:** This defines a server-side Button control.
    - **`ID="btnSubmit"`:** A unique identifier for the button.
    - **`runat="server"`:** Indicates that this control is processed on the server.
    - **`Text="Submit"`:** Sets the text displayed on the button.
    - **`OnClick="btnSubmit_Click"`:** This is the crucial part for event handling. It tells ASP.NET that when the `Click` event occurs on this `btnSubmit` control in the browser (when the user clicks it), the `btnSubmit_Click` method in the associated code-behind file should be executed on the server during the Postback Event Handling stage of the Page Life Cycle.
- **`<asp:Label ID="lblResult" runat="server" />`:** A Label control to display the result of the button click.
- **`protected void btnSubmit_Click(object sender, EventArgs e)`:**
    - This is the event handler method in the `Page` class (in the code-behind file) that is executed when the `Click` event of the `btnSubmit` button fires.
    - **`protected void`:** The method is typically declared as `protected` to be accessible within the class.
    - **`btnSubmit_Click`:** The name of the method must match the value specified in the `OnClick` attribute of the `Button` control. The naming convention is usually `controlID_eventName`.
    - **`(object sender, EventArgs e)`:** These are the standard parameters for most ASP.NET event handlers:
        - **`object sender`:** A reference to the control that raised the event (in this case, the `btnSubmit` Button object).
        - **`EventArgs e`:** An object that contains event-specific data. For a simple `Click` event, this object is often empty or contains base event information. For other events (like `SelectedIndexChanged`), it might contain information about the event (e.g., the old and new index).
    - **`lblResult.Text = "Button clicked at: " + DateTime.Now.ToString();`:** This line of code accesses the `lblResult` Label control (using its `ID`) and sets its `Text` property to a string indicating that the button was clicked and the current date and time on the server. This updated text will be rendered back to the browser on the subsequent page reload (postback).

Common Events You Might Handle (as listed in your example):

- **`Click`:** Raised when a user clicks on a button (`<asp:Button>`, `LinkButton`, `ImageButton`). The example above demonstrates this.
- **`SelectedIndexChanged`:** Raised when the selected item in a data-bound control like a `DropDownList`, `ListBox`, or `RadioButtonList` changes. The AutoPostBack example in the previous section illustrated this event.

  HTML

```
<asp:DropDownList ID="ddlOptions" runat="server" AutoPostBack="true"
OnSelectedIndexChanged="ddlOptions_SelectedIndexChanged">
    <asp:ListItem Text="Option A" Value="A" />
    <asp:ListItem Text="Option B" Value="B" />
</asp:DropDownList>
<asp:Label ID="lblSelection" runat="server" />
```

  C#

```
protected void ddlOptions_SelectedIndexChanged(object sender, EventArgs
e)
{
    lblSelection.Text = "You selected: " + ddlOptions.SelectedItem.Text
+ " (Value: " + ddlOptions.SelectedValue + ")";
}
```

- **`TextChanged`:** Raised when the text in a `TextBox` control has been changed and the control loses focus (if `AutoPostBack="true"` is set) or when a form containing the `TextBox` is submitted.

  HTML

```
<asp:TextBox ID="txtInput" runat="server" AutoPostBack="true"
OnTextChanged="txtInput_TextChanged" />
<asp:Label ID="lblInput" runat="server" />
```

  C#

```
protected void txtInput_TextChanged(object sender, EventArgs e)
{
    lblInput.Text = "You entered: " + txtInput.Text;
}
```

- **`CheckedChanged`:** Raised when the state of a `CheckBox` or `RadioButton` control is changed (checked or unchecked). Often used with `AutoPostBack="true"` for immediate server-side actions.

  HTML

```
<asp:CheckBox ID="chkAgree" runat="server" AutoPostBack="true"
OnCheckedChanged="chkAgree_CheckedChanged" Text="I agree" />
<asp:Label ID="lblAgreement" runat="server" />
```

C#

```
protected void chkAgree_CheckedChanged(object sender, EventArgs e)
{
    lblAgreement.Text = chkAgree.Checked ? "You agreed." : "You
disagreed.";
}
```

Benefits of the Event-Driven Model in Web Forms:

- **Familiarity for Desktop Developers:** Developers with experience in Windows Forms or other GUI frameworks find this model intuitive.
- **Server-Side Processing:** Logic is executed on the server, which can be beneficial for security, data access, and complex operations.
- **Reduced Client-Side Scripting (in some cases):** For many common interactions, you can achieve dynamic behavior with minimal or no custom JavaScript, relying on the server control events and AutoPostBack.
- **Simplified State Management (with ViewState):** The framework handles much of the state preservation across postbacks associated with these events through ViewState.
- **Rich Control Set:** ASP.NET provides a wide variety of server controls, each with its own set of events that you can handle.

Limitations:

- **Postbacks for Every Interaction (with AutoPostBack):** As discussed in the AutoPostBack section, frequent postbacks can lead to a less smooth user experience and increased server load.
- **Page Reloads:** The inherent nature of postbacks involves a full or partial page reload, which can sometimes cause flicker.

Modern Approaches:

While the event-driven model with postbacks is a core part of ASP.NET Web Forms, modern web development often favors more client-side interaction and asynchronous communication with the server (using technologies like AJAX) for a richer and more responsive user experience. However, the event-driven paradigm within the server-side code remains relevant for handling user actions and processing data.

Summary:

- Web Forms use ASPX + code-behind structure.
- The page life cycle is crucial for understanding events and rendering.
- `AutoPostBack` allows real-time server interaction.
- `ViewState` helps maintain control values.
- Writing event-driven code is central to Web Forms.

10 PRACTICAL EXAMPLES WITH SOLUTION

1. Displaying a Welcome Message on Initial Page Load

- **Problem:** Display a "Welcome!" message in a Label control only when the page is loaded for the first time.
- **Solution (`Default.aspx`):**

  HTML

```
<%@ Page Language="C#" AutoEventWireup="true"
CodeFile="Default.aspx.cs" Inherits="Default" %>
<!DOCTYPE html>
<html>
<head>
    <title>Welcome Page</title>
</head>
<body>
    <form id="form1" runat="server">
        <asp:Label ID="lblWelcome" runat="server" Text=""></asp:Label>
    </form>
</body>
</html>
```

- **Solution (`Default.aspx.cs`):**

  C#

```
using System;

public partial class Default : System.Web.UI.Page
{
    protected void Page_Load(object sender, EventArgs e)
    {
        if (!IsPostBack)
        {
            lblWelcome.Text = "Welcome!";
        }
    }
}
```

- **Learning Outcome:** Understanding `Page_Load` and `IsPostBack` to execute code only on the initial page load.

2. Handling a Button Click to Display a Dynamic Message

- **Problem:** Display a message in a Label control when a button is clicked, including the current date and time.
- **Solution (`ClickButton.aspx`):**

  HTML

```
<%@ Page Language="C#" AutoEventWireup="true"
CodeFile="ClickButton.aspx.cs" Inherits="ClickButton" %>
<!DOCTYPE html>
<html>
<head>
    <title>Button Click Example</title>
</head>
<body>
    <form id="form1" runat="server">
        <asp:Button ID="btnClick" runat="server" Text="Click Me"
OnClick="btnClick_Click" />
        <asp:Label ID="lblMessage" runat="server" Text=""></asp:Label>
    </form>
</body>
</html>
```

- **Solution (`ClickButton.aspx.cs`):**

C#

```
using System;

public partial class ClickButton : System.Web.UI.Page
{
    protected void btnClick_Click(object sender, EventArgs e)
    {
        lblMessage.Text = "Button clicked at: " +
DateTime.Now.ToString();
    }
}
```

- **Learning Outcome:** Implementing event handling for button clicks and accessing control properties.

3. Preserving Textbox Input Using ViewState

- **Problem:** Create a TextBox and a Label. Display the text entered in the TextBox in the Label, persisting the text across postbacks.
- **Solution (`TextBoxViewState.aspx`):**

HTML

```
<%@ Page Language="C#" AutoEventWireup="true"
CodeFile="TextBoxViewState.aspx.cs" Inherits="TextBoxViewState" %>
<!DOCTYPE html>
<html>
<head>
    <title>TextBox ViewState</title>
</head>
<body>
    <form id="form1" runat="server">
        <asp:TextBox ID="txtInput" runat="server"></asp:TextBox><br />
```

```
        <asp:Button ID="btnDisplay" runat="server" Text="Display"
OnClick="btnDisplay_Click" /><br />
        <asp:Label ID="lblOutput" runat="server" Text=""></asp:Label>
    </form>
</body>
</html>
```

- **Solution (`TextBoxViewState.aspx.cs`):**

  C#

```
using System;

public partial class TextBoxViewState : System.Web.UI.Page
{
    protected void Page_Load(object sender, EventArgs e)
    {
        if (IsPostBack && ViewState["InputText"] != null)
        {
            lblOutput.Text = (string)ViewState["InputText"];
        }
    }

    protected void btnDisplay_Click(object sender, EventArgs e)
    {
        ViewState["InputText"] = txtInput.Text;
        lblOutput.Text = "You entered: " + txtInput.Text;
    }
}
```

- **Learning Outcome:** Understanding ViewState for preserving control values between postbacks.

4. Using AutoPostBack with a DropDownList

- **Problem:** Create a DropDownList and a Label. When the user selects an item, immediately display the selected item's text in the Label without a separate button click.
- **Solution (`DropdownAutoPostBack.aspx`):**

  HTML

```
<%@ Page Language="C#" AutoEventWireup="true"
CodeFile="DropdownAutoPostBack.aspx.cs" Inherits="DropdownAutoPostBack"
%>
<!DOCTYPE html>
<html>
<head>
    <title>DropDownList AutoPostBack</title>
</head>
<body>
    <form id="form1" runat="server">
```

```
        <asp:DropDownList ID="ddlOptions" runat="server"
AutoPostBack="true"
OnSelectedIndexChanged="ddlOptions_SelectedIndexChanged">
            <asp:ListItem Text="Option 1" Value="1" />
            <asp:ListItem Text="Option 2" Value="2" />
            <asp:ListItem Text="Option 3" Value="3" />
        </asp:DropDownList><br />
        <asp:Label ID="lblSelection" runat="server"
Text=""></asp:Label>
    </form>
</body>
</html>
```

- **Solution (`DropdownAutoPostBack.aspx.cs`):**

  C#

```
using System;

public partial class DropdownAutoPostBack : System.Web.UI.Page
{
    protected void Page_Load(object sender, EventArgs e)
    {
        if (!IsPostBack)
        {
            lblSelection.Text = "Please select an option.";
        }
    }
    protected void ddlOptions_SelectedIndexChanged(object sender,
EventArgs e)
    {
        lblSelection.Text = "You selected: " +
ddlOptions.SelectedItem.Text;
    }
}
```

- **Learning Outcome:** Implementing AutoPostBack to trigger server-side events immediately upon control interaction.

5. Dynamically Changing Label Text on CheckBox Change

- **Problem:** Create a CheckBox and a Label. When the CheckBox is checked or unchecked, update the Label's text to reflect the CheckBox's state.
- **Solution (`CheckBoxAutoPostBack.aspx`):**

  HTML

```
<%@ Page Language="C#" AutoEventWireup="true"
CodeFile="CheckBoxAutoPostBack.aspx.cs" Inherits="CheckBoxAutoPostBack"
%>
<!DOCTYPE html>
<html>
<head>
```

```
    <title>CheckBox AutoPostBack</title>
</head>
<body>
    <form id="form1" runat="server">
        <asp:CheckBox ID="chkAgree" runat="server" AutoPostBack="true"
OnCheckedChanged="chkAgree_CheckedChanged" Text="I Agree" /><br />
        <asp:Label ID="lblAgreement" runat="server"
Text=""></asp:Label>
    </form>
</body>
</html>
```

- **Solution (`CheckBoxAutoPostBack.aspx.cs`):**

  C#

```
using System;

public partial class CheckBoxAutoPostBack : System.Web.UI.Page
{
    protected void Page_Load(object sender, EventArgs e)
    {
        if (!IsPostBack)
        {
            lblAgreement.Text = "Please indicate your agreement.";
        }
    }
    protected void chkAgree_CheckedChanged(object sender, EventArgs e)
    {
        lblAgreement.Text = chkAgree.Checked ? "You Agreed." : "You
Disagreed.";
    }
}
```

- **Learning Outcome:** Handling the `CheckedChanged` event and using AutoPostBack for real-time updates.

6. Understanding the Page Lifecycle with Trace

- **Problem:** Display messages at different stages of the page lifecycle to understand the order of events.
- **Solution (`PageLifeCycleTrace.aspx`):**

  HTML

```
<%@ Page Language="C#" AutoEventWireup="true"
CodeFile="PageLifeCycleTrace.aspx.cs" Inherits="PageLifeCycleTrace"
Trace="true" %>
<!DOCTYPE html>
<html>
<head>
    <title>Page Life Cycle Trace</title>
</head>
```

```
<body>
    <form id="form1" runat="server">
        <asp:Label ID="lblMessage" runat="server"
Text=""></asp:Label><br/>
        <asp:Button ID="btnPostBack" runat="server" Text="PostBack"
OnClick="btnPostBack_Click" />
    </form>
</body>
</html>
```

- **Solution (`PageLifeCycleTrace.aspx.cs`):**

C#

```
using System;

public partial class PageLifeCycleTrace : System.Web.UI.Page
{
    protected void Page_PreInit(object sender, EventArgs e)
    {
        Trace.Write("Page_PreInit", "PreInit stage");
    }

    protected void Page_Init(object sender, EventArgs e)
    {
        Trace.Write("Page_Init", "Init stage");
    }

    protected void Page_Load(object sender, EventArgs e)
    {
        Trace.Write("Page_Load", "Load stage. IsPostBack: " +
IsPostBack);
        if (!IsPostBack)
        {
            lblMessage.Text = "Page Loaded Initially";
        }
        else
        {
            lblMessage.Text = "Page PostBack";
        }
    }

     protected void btnPostBack_Click(object sender, EventArgs e)
    {
        Trace.Write("btnPostBack_Click", "Button Clicked");
    }

    protected void Page_PreRender(object sender, EventArgs e)
    {
        Trace.Write("Page_PreRender", "PreRender stage");
    }

    protected void Page_Render(object sender, EventArgs e)
    {
         Trace.Write("Page_Render", "Render stage");
    }
```

```
    protected void Page_Unload(object sender, EventArgs e)
    {
        Trace.Write("Page_Unload", "Unload stage");
    }
}
```

- **Learning Outcome:** Using `Trace` to understand the sequence of page lifecycle events.

7. Storing and Retrieving Data from ViewState

- **Problem:** Store a counter in ViewState and increment it on each button click, displaying the current count in a Label.
- **Solution (`ViewStateCounter.aspx`):**

  HTML

```
<%@ Page Language="C#" AutoEventWireup="true"
CodeFile="ViewStateCounter.aspx.cs" Inherits="ViewStateCounter" %>
<!DOCTYPE html>
<html>
<head>
    <title>ViewState Counter</title>
</head>
<body>
    <form id="form1" runat="server">
        <asp:Button ID="btnIncrement" runat="server" Text="Increment"
OnClick="btnIncrement_Click" /><br />
        <asp:Label ID="lblCount" runat="server" Text=""></asp:Label>
    </form>
</body>
</html>
```

- **Solution (`ViewStateCounter.aspx.cs`):**

  C#

```
using System;

public partial class ViewStateCounter : System.Web.UI.Page
{
    protected void Page_Load(object sender, EventArgs e)
    {
        if (!IsPostBack)
        {
            ViewState["ClickCount"] = 0;
            lblCount.Text = "Clicks: 0";
        }
    }

    protected void btnIncrement_Click(object sender, EventArgs e)
    {
        int count = (int)ViewState["ClickCount"];
```

```
            count++;
            ViewState["ClickCount"] = count;
            lblCount.Text = "Clicks: " + count.ToString();
        }
    }
```

- **Learning Outcome:** Storing and retrieving integer data from ViewState across multiple postbacks.

8. Accessing Control Values on Postback

- **Problem:** Create a TextBox and a Button. When the button is clicked, retrieve the text from the TextBox and display it in a Label.
- **Solution (`AccessControlValue.aspx`):**

  HTML

```
<%@ Page Language="C#" AutoEventWireup="true"
CodeFile="AccessControlValue.aspx.cs" Inherits="AccessControlValue" %>
<!DOCTYPE html>
<html>
<head>
    <title>Access Control Value</title>
</head>
<body>
    <form id="form1" runat="server">
        Enter text: <asp:TextBox ID="txtInput"
runat="server"></asp:TextBox><br />
        <asp:Button ID="btnSubmit" runat="server" Text="Submit"
OnClick="btnSubmit_Click" /><br />
        <asp:Label ID="lblOutput" runat="server" Text=""></asp:Label>
    </form>
</body>
</html>
```

- **Solution (`AccessControlValue.aspx.cs`):**

  C#

```
using System;

public partial class AccessControlValue : System.Web.UI.Page
{
    protected void btnSubmit_Click(object sender, EventArgs e)
    {
        string inputText = txtInput.Text;
        lblOutput.Text = "You entered: " + inputText;
    }
}
```

- **Learning Outcome:** Accessing the value of a server-side control (TextBox) in the code-behind during a postback.

9. Handling RadioButtonList Selection

- **Problem:** Create a RadioButtonList and a Label. When a radio button is selected, display the selected value in the Label.
- **Solution (`RadioButtonListSelection.aspx`):**

  HTML

```
<%@ Page Language="C#" AutoEventWireup="true"
CodeFile="RadioButtonListSelection.aspx.cs"
Inherits="RadioButtonListSelection" %>
<!DOCTYPE html>
<html>
<head>
    <title>RadioButtonList Selection</title>
</head>
<body>
    <form id="form1" runat="server">
        <asp:RadioButtonList ID="rblOptions" runat="server"
OnSelectedIndexChanged="rblOptions_SelectedIndexChanged"
AutoPostBack="true">
            <asp:ListItem Text="Option A" Value="A" />
            <asp:ListItem Text="Option B" Value="B" />
            <asp:ListItem Text="Option C" Value="C" />
        </asp:RadioButtonList><br />
        <asp:Label ID="lblSelection" runat="server"
Text=""></asp:Label>
    </form>
</body>
</html>
```

- **Solution (`RadioButtonListSelection.aspx.cs`):**

  C#

```
using System;

public partial class RadioButtonListSelection : System.Web.UI.Page
{
    protected void Page_Load(object sender, EventArgs e)
    {
        if (!IsPostBack)
        {
            lblSelection.Text = "Select an option.";
        }
    }
    protected void rblOptions_SelectedIndexChanged(object sender,
EventArgs e)
    {
        lblSelection.Text = "You selected: " +
rblOptions.SelectedItem.Text + " (Value: " + rblOptions.SelectedValue +
")";
    }
}
```

- **Learning Outcome:** Handling the `SelectedIndexChanged` event for a RadioButtonList.

10. Simple Validation and Display

- **Problem:** Create a TextBox, a Button, and a Label. When the button is clicked, check if the TextBox is empty. If it's empty, display an error message; otherwise, display the entered text.
- **Solution (`SimpleValidation.aspx`):**

  HTML

```html
<%@ Page Language="C#" AutoEventWireup="true"
CodeFile="SimpleValidation.aspx.cs" Inherits="SimpleValidation" %>
<!DOCTYPE html>
<html>
<head>
    <title>Simple Validation</title>
</head>
<body>
    <form id="form1" runat="server">
        Enter text: <asp:TextBox ID="txtInput"
runat="server"></asp:TextBox><br />
        <asp:Button ID="btnValidate" runat="server" Text="Validate"
OnClick="btnValidate_Click" /><br />
        <asp:Label ID="lblMessage" runat="server" Text=""></asp:Label>
    </form>
</body>
</html>
```

- **Solution (`SimpleValidation.aspx.cs`):**

  C#

```csharp
using System;

public partial class SimpleValidation : System.Web.UI.Page
{
    protected void btnValidate_Click(object sender, EventArgs e)
    {
        if (string.IsNullOrEmpty(txtInput.Text))
        {
            lblMessage.Text = "Please enter some text!";
        }
        else
        {
            lblMessage.Text = "You entered: " + txtInput.Text;
        }
    }
}
```

- **Learning Outcome:** Performing basic input validation and displaying messages based on the validation result.

- 30 multiple-choice questions with answers covering ASPX Pages and Code-Behind, Page Life Cycle, AutoPostBack and ViewState, and Writing Event-Driven Code in ASP.NET Web Forms:
- **1. What is the file extension for an ASP.NET Web Forms page?** a) .html b) .aspx c) .ascx d) .cs *Answer: b) .aspx*
- **2. Which file contains the HTML markup and server-side controls in ASP.NET Web Forms?** a) Code-Behind file b) ASPX page c) Web.config d) Global.asax *Answer: b) ASPX page*
- **3. Which file contains the C# or VB.NET code for an ASP.NET Web Forms page?** a) ASPX page b) Code-Behind file c) Web.config d) Global.asax *Answer: b) Code-Behind file*
- **4. What is the primary purpose of the `runat="server"` attribute in an ASP.NET server control?** a) To specify the client-side scripting language b) To indicate that the control is processed on the server c) To define the control's style d) To set the control's initial value *Answer: b) To indicate that the control is processed on the server*
- **5. Which directive is used at the top of an ASPX page to define page-specific attributes?** a) <%@ Control %> b) <%@ Register %> c) <%@ Page %> d) <%@ Application %> *Answer: c) <%@ Page %>*
- **6. Which property in the Page class indicates whether the page is being loaded for the first time or as a result of a postback?** a) IsNew b) IsInitial c) IsPostBack d) IsLoaded *Answer: c) IsPostBack*
- **7. In which stage of the Page Life Cycle are server controls initialized?** a) Load b) Init c) PreRender d) Unload *Answer: b) Init*
- **8. In which stage of the Page Life Cycle are control values loaded from ViewState?** a) Init b) Load c) PreRender d) Render *Answer: b) Load*
- **9. In which stage of the Page Life Cycle are control events like Button_Click handled?** a) Init b) Load c) Postback Event Handling d) Render *Answer: c) Postback Event Handling*
- **10. In which stage of the Page Life Cycle is the HTML markup generated and sent to the client?** a) Load b) Init c) Render d) Unload *Answer: c) Render*
- **11. In which stage of the Page Life Cycle are resources like database connections closed?** a) Load b) PreRender c) Render d) Unload *Answer: d) Unload*
- **12. What does AutoPostBack do?** a) Automatically updates the client-side UI b) Automatically sends data to the server and reloads the page c) Automatically validates user input d) Automatically saves data to a database *Answer: b) Automatically sends data to the server and reloads the page*
- **13. Which property of a server control enables AutoPostBack?** a) PostBack b) AutoSubmit c) AutoPostBack d) EnablePostBack *Answer: c) AutoPostBack*
- **14. Which of the following controls can be set to AutoPostBack?** a) Label b) Literal c) Button d) Panel *Answer: c) Button*
- **15. What is the primary purpose of ViewState?** a) To store application settings b) To store user session data c) To preserve page and control values between postbacks d) To store static files *Answer: c) To preserve page and control values between postbacks*
- **16. Where is ViewState data stored?** a) On the server's hard drive b) In the browser's cookies c) In a hidden field in the HTML of the page d) In the server's memory *Answer: c) In a hidden field in the HTML of the page*

- **17. Which hidden form field is used to store ViewState data?** a) __SESSIONSTATE b) __VIEWSTATE c) __POSTBACK d) __CONTROLSTATE *Answer: b) __VIEWSTATE*
- **18. What is a potential drawback of using ViewState?** a) It can increase server load b) It can increase page size c) It can cause security vulnerabilities d) It can only store strings *Answer: b) It can increase page size*
- **19. Which programming model is ASP.NET Web Forms based on?** a) Procedural programming b) Object-oriented programming c) Event-driven programming d) Functional programming *Answer: c) Event-driven programming*
- **20. What is an event handler?** a) A client-side JavaScript function b) A server-side method that executes in response to an event c) A database stored procedure d) A CSS style definition *Answer: b) A server-side method that executes in response to an event*
- **21. Which attribute is used to associate a server control event with an event handler method in the code-behind?** a) OnEvent b) EventName c) HandleEvent d) OnClick (or OnSelectedIndexChanged, etc.) *Answer: d) OnClick (or OnSelectedIndexChanged, etc.)*
- **22. Which event is raised when a user clicks a Button control?** a) Clicked b) MouseClick c) Click d) Action *Answer: c) Click*
- **23. Which event is raised when the selected item in a DropDownList control changes?** a) SelectedChange b) SelectedIndexChange c) SelectedValueChanged d) SelectedIndexChanged *Answer: d) SelectedIndexChanged*
- **24. Which event is raised when the text in a TextBox control is changed?** a) TextChange b) TextChanged c) ChangeText d) InputChanged *Answer: b) TextChanged*
- **25. Which event is raised when the state of a CheckBox control changes?** a) CheckStateChanged b) CheckedChange c) CheckChanged d) StateChanged *Answer: c) CheckChanged*
- **26. In the `Page_Load` event, what is the purpose of checking `!IsPostBack`?** a) To execute code on every page load, including postbacks b) To execute code only on the initial page load c) To execute code only on postbacks d) To prevent the page from loading *Answer: b) To execute code only on the initial page load*
- **27. Which of the following is NOT a valid Page Life Cycle event?** a) Page_Init b) Page_Load c) Page_Rendered d) Page_Unload *Answer: c) Page_Rendered*
- **28. If AutoPostBack is set to `true` for a control, what happens when the control's event occurs?** a) The page is refreshed on the client-side using JavaScript b) The page sends data to the server and reloads c) The control's value is saved to a cookie d) The control's value is stored in Session state *Answer: b) The page sends data to the server and reloads*
- **29. Which of the following is a security concern related to ViewState?** a) It can be easily modified by the server b) It stores data on the server c) It can be tampered with on the client-side (if not properly protected) d) It is not encrypted *Answer: c) It can be tampered with on the client-side (if not properly protected)*
- **30. Which of the following is a benefit of the event-driven model in Web Forms?** a) It requires extensive client-side scripting b) It allows for server-side processing of user interactions c) It is stateless d) It is difficult to learn *Answer: b) It allows for server-side processing of user interactions*

10 medium-sized questions with detailed answers, covering the ASP.NET Web Forms topics you requested:

1. Explain the relationship between an ASPX page and its code-behind file. How are they connected, and what are the primary responsibilities of each file?

- **Answer:** An ASPX page and its code-behind file work together to define a single web page in ASP.NET Web Forms. They are connected primarily through the `<%@ Page %>` directive in the ASPX page, specifically the `CodeFile` and `Inherits` attributes. The `CodeFile` attribute specifies the path to the code-behind file (e.g., `Default.aspx.cs`), while the `Inherits` attribute specifies the class in the code-behind that the ASPX page's dynamically generated class inherits from.
  - **ASPX Page Responsibilities:**
    - Defines the structure and presentation of the web page using HTML markup.
    - Contains server-side ASP.NET controls, marked with `runat="server"`.
    - Declares event-handling attributes (e.g., `OnClick`) that link UI events to methods in the code-behind.
  - **Code-Behind File Responsibilities:**
    - Contains the server-side logic for the page, written in C# or VB.NET.
    - Defines a class that inherits from `System.Web.UI.Page`.
    - Implements event handlers for control events and page lifecycle events.
    - Manipulates server controls, interacts with data sources, and handles business logic.
  - In essence, the ASPX page handles the UI, and the code-behind handles the behavior.

2. Describe the ASP.NET Web Forms Page Life Cycle. Explain the purpose of at least five key stages, and provide a scenario where understanding a specific stage is crucial for correct application behavior.

- **Answer:** The ASP.NET Web Forms Page Life Cycle is the sequence of events that occur when a page is requested, processed, and rendered. Five key stages are:
  - **Page Request:** The initial request for the ASPX page from the server.
  - **Init:** Server controls are initialized, and their properties are set.
  - **Load:** The page loads values from ViewState and form data.
  - **Postback Event Handling:** Control events (e.g., Button clicks) are processed.
  - **Render:** HTML is generated and sent to the client.
  - **Unload:** Cleanup operations are performed.
  - **Crucial Scenario (Page_Load):** Understanding `Page_Load` is vital. If you load data from a database in `Page_Load` *without* checking `IsPostBack`, the data will be reloaded on *every* postback, potentially causing performance issues or overwriting user input. You typically use `if (!IsPostBack)` to load data only on the initial page load.

3. Explain the concept of ViewState in ASP.NET Web Forms. How does it work, what problem does it solve, and what are its limitations?

- **Answer:** ViewState is a mechanism to preserve the state of a web page and its server controls across HTTP requests. HTTP is stateless, meaning the server doesn't remember control values between requests. ViewState solves this.
    - **How it works:** ASP.NET serializes the state of controls into a string, stores it in a hidden form field (`__VIEWSTATE`), and sends it to the browser. On postback, this data is sent back to the server, and ASP.NET uses it to restore the control values.
    - **Problem solved:** Preserves user input and control settings (e.g., text in a textbox, selected dropdown item) across postbacks, making web forms behave more like stateful applications.
    - **Limitations:**
        - Increases page size, impacting performance.
        - Can be a security concern if not handled carefully (though encoding/encryption is available).
        - Not suitable for storing large amounts of data.

4. Describe the AutoPostBack feature in ASP.NET Web Forms. How does it enhance user interaction, and what are the potential drawbacks of its use?

- **Answer:** AutoPostBack allows certain server controls to automatically trigger a postback to the server when a specific event occurs (e.g., `SelectedIndexChanged` in a `DropDownList`).
    - **Enhances user interaction:** Makes the page more dynamic and responsive by triggering server-side actions without requiring a full form submission. For example, updating a second dropdown based on the first dropdown's selection.
    - **Potential drawbacks:**
        - Increases server load, as each AutoPostBack is a round trip to the server.
        - Can cause page flicker due to the page reload.
        - If overused, can lead to a less-than-ideal user experience due to frequent small reloads.

5. Explain how event handling works in ASP.NET Web Forms. Provide an example of how to handle a button click event, and describe the role of the `sender` and `EventArgs` parameters in an event handler method.

- **Answer:** ASP.NET Web Forms uses an event-driven model. Server controls raise events in response to user actions, and developers write event handlers to execute code when those events occur.
    - **Example:** (From a previous answer)

      HTML

      ```
      <asp:Button ID="btnSubmit" runat="server" Text="Submit"
      OnClick="btnSubmit_Click" />
      ```csharp
      ```
      ```

```
protected void btnSubmit_Click(object sender, EventArgs e)
{
    lblResult.Text = "Button clicked!";
}
```

- **`sender` parameter:** A reference to the control that raised the event (e.g., the `btnSubmit` Button). You can use this to access the properties of the control that triggered the event.
- **`EventArgs e` parameter:** Provides event-specific data. For a simple `Click` event, this is often empty or contains base event information. Other events may have more specific data (e.g., `SelectedIndexChangedEventArgs` for a dropdown).

6. Compare and contrast client-side scripting (JavaScript) and server-side code (C# in code-behind) in ASP.NET Web Forms. When would you typically use each approach?

- **Answer:**
  - **Client-side scripting (JavaScript):**
    - Executes in the user's browser.
    - Used for enhancing UI interactivity, validating input before sending to the server, and making asynchronous requests (AJAX).
    - Provides a more responsive user experience (no full page reloads for some actions).
  - **Server-side code (C# in code-behind):**
    - Executes on the web server.
    - Used for accessing databases, handling business logic, manipulating server controls, and generating dynamic HTML.
    - More secure for sensitive operations.
  - **When to use each:**
    - Use JavaScript for UI enhancements, immediate feedback, and reducing server load.
    - Use C# for data access, complex logic, security-sensitive operations, and server-side control over the UI.

7. Explain the purpose of the `IsPostBack` property of the `Page` class. Provide an example of how it is used in the `Page_Load` event to prevent code from executing on every request.

- **Answer:** The `IsPostBack` property indicates whether the page is being loaded for the first time (`false`) or as a result of a form submission back to the same page (`true`).
  - **Purpose:** To allow developers to write code that executes only on the initial page load, and different code for subsequent requests (postbacks).
  - **Example:** (From a previous answer)

    C#

```
protected void Page_Load(object sender, EventArgs e)
{
```

```
    if (!IsPostBack)
    {
        // Code here runs only the first time the page loads.
        // e.g., Loading initial data, setting default values.
        lblMessage.Text = "Welcome!";
    }
    // Code outside the if block runs on every load, including
postbacks.
}
```

- This prevents unnecessary re-execution of initialization code on every request.

8. Describe how to access and manipulate server controls from the code-behind file in ASP.NET Web Forms. Provide an example of setting the text of a Label control and getting the value of a TextBox control.

- **Answer:** Server controls are accessed in the code-behind using their `ID` property, which you set in the ASPX markup.
  - **Setting Label text:**

    C#

    ```
    lblMessage.Text = "Hello, User!"; // lblMessage is the ID of the
    Label control.
    ```

  - **Getting TextBox value:**

    C#

    ```
    string userText = txtInput.Text;  // txtInput is the ID of the
    TextBox control.
    ```

  - The `runat="server"` attribute in the ASPX markup makes the controls accessible in the code-behind.

9. Explain the concept of event wiring in ASP.NET Web Forms. How is an event handler method associated with a server control event, and provide an example using the `OnClick` attribute?

- **Answer:** Event wiring is the process of connecting a server control's event to a method in the code-behind that will handle that event.
  - **Method:** This is typically done declaratively in the ASPX markup using an event-handling attribute. The attribute name usually starts with "On" followed by the event name (e.g., `OnClick`, `OnSelectedIndexChanged`).
  - **Example:** (From a previous answer)

    HTML

```
<asp:Button ID="btnSubmit" runat="server" Text="Submit"
OnClick="btnSubmit_Click" />
```

        - The `OnClick="btnSubmit_Click"` attribute tells ASP.NET to execute the `btnSubmit_Click` method in the code-behind when the `Click` event of the `btnSubmit` button occurs. The method signature in the code-behind must match the expected event handler delegate.

10. Discuss the trade-offs between using ViewState and other state management techniques in ASP.NET Web Forms, such as Session or Cookies. When might you choose one over the others?

- **Answer:**
    - **ViewState:**
        - Stores data on the client-side (in a hidden field).
        - Automatic, control-level state persistence.
        - Pros: Easy to use for simple control state.
        - Cons: Increases page size, less secure for sensitive data.
        - Use for: Small amounts of control-specific data that need to be preserved across postbacks for a single page.
    - **Session:**
        - Stores data on the server, associated with a user's session.
        - Pros: More secure, can store larger amounts of data.
        - Cons: Consumes server resources, less scalable for high-traffic sites.
        - Use for: User-specific data that needs to be available across multiple pages within a session (e.g., shopping cart data, login information).
    - **Cookies:**
        - Stores data on the client's computer in small text files.
        - Pros: Can persist data across browser sessions.
        - Cons: Limited size, security risks, user can disable them.
        - Use for: Small amounts of non-sensitive data, user preferences (e.g., theme settings), "remember me" functionality.
    - **Other options:** Application state (data shared by all users), database storage.

ASP.NET Web Forms provides a wide variety of server controls to build dynamic and interactive web pages. These controls help developers design forms with minimal effort, as they abstract a lot of underlying HTML, JavaScript, and postback behavior.

📌 1. Fundamental ASP.NET Server Controls: Label, TextBox, Button, CheckBox, RadioButton - A Detailed Exploration

ASP.NET Web Forms offers a variety of server-side controls that simplify the creation of dynamic web interfaces. These controls are rendered as standard HTML in the browser but are managed on the server, providing a rich set of properties, methods, and events that you can interact with in your code-behind. Let's explore the core controls you've mentioned in detail:

◆ Label Control (`<asp:Label>`)

- **Description:** As you correctly stated, the `Label` control is primarily used to display **static or dynamic text** on a web page. It acts as a container for text that is typically read-only from the user's perspective.
- **Detailed Explanation:**
    - The `asp:Label` control renders as an HTML `<span>` element by default. This is a lightweight inline container, making it suitable for displaying short pieces of text.
    - It's a server-side control, meaning its properties can be manipulated in the code-behind. This allows you to dynamically change the text displayed based on user actions, data retrieval, or application logic.
- **Key Properties (Beyond the Basics):**
    - **`ID`:** The unique identifier that allows you to reference the control in your C# or VB.NET code.
    - **`runat="server"`:** Essential for indicating that the control should be processed on the server.
    - **`Text`:** The string value that is displayed by the label. This is the primary property you'll interact with.
    - **`CssClass`:** Allows you to apply CSS styles defined in your stylesheets to the label, controlling its appearance (font, color, size, etc.).
    - **`ForeColor`:** Sets the color of the text.
    - **`BackColor`:** Sets the background color of the label.
    - **`Font`:** Provides access to font-related properties like `Bold`, `Italic`, `Size`, and `Name`.
    - **`Visible`:** A boolean property that determines whether the label is displayed on the page. You can hide or show labels dynamically.
    - **`AssociatedControlID`:** This property is crucial for accessibility. You can link a label to another control (like a `TextBox`) by setting this property to the `ID` of the target control. This helps screen readers understand the purpose of the input field.

- **Example (as provided):**

  HTML

```
<asp:Label ID="lblMessage" runat="server" Text="Hello,
ASP.NET!"></asp:Label>
```

- **Dynamic Example (Code-Behind):**

  C#

```
protected void Page_Load(object sender, EventArgs e)
{
    lblMessage.Text = "The current date and time is: " +
DateTime.Now.ToString();
}
```

  This code, placed in the `Page_Load` event handler, will update the `lblMessage` label with the current server time each time the page loads.

◆ TextBox Control (`<asp:TextBox>`)

- **Description:** As you mentioned, the `TextBox` control allows users to **input text**. It's the fundamental control for collecting textual data from users.
- **Detailed Explanation:**
  - The `asp:TextBox` control renders as an HTML `<input type="text">` element by default, creating a single-line text input field. However, its behavior can be modified using the `TextMode` property.
  - It's a server-side control, allowing you to access and manipulate the entered text in the code-behind.
- **Key Properties (Beyond the Basics):**
  - **`ID`:** The unique identifier.
  - **`runat="server"`:** Indicates server-side processing.
  - **`Text`:** The string value entered by the user or set programmatically. This is the primary property for getting and setting the text.
  - **`TextMode`:** This powerful property determines the type of text box rendered:
    - `SingleLine` (default): A standard single-line text input.
    - `MultiLine`: Creates a multi-line text area (`<textarea>` in HTML). You can control the number of visible rows and columns using the `Rows` and `Columns` properties.
    - `Password`: Renders a password input field where the entered characters are masked (typically with asterisks).
    - HTML5 Input Types (browser support may vary): `Email`, `Number`, `Url`, `Date`, `Time`, `DateTimeLocal`, `Range`, `Color`, `Search`, `Tel`. These provide built-in browser features and validation.
  - **`MaxLength`:** Specifies the maximum number of characters the user can enter into the text box. This helps with client-side validation.
  - **`ReadOnly`:** A boolean property. If set to `true`, the user cannot edit the text in the box.

- **Enabled:** A boolean property. If set to `false`, the text box is grayed out and cannot be interacted with.
- **CssClass, ForeColor, BackColor, Font, Visible:** For styling and visibility.
- **AutoPostBack:** If set to `true`, a postback to the server occurs automatically when the `TextChanged` event fires (typically when the control loses focus).
- **OnTextChanged:** An event that fires when the text in the text box has changed and the control loses focus (if `AutoPostBack` is `true`) or when the form is submitted. You can handle this event in the code-behind.

- **Example (as provided):**

  HTML

```
<asp:TextBox ID="txtName" runat="server"></asp:TextBox>
```

- **Multi-line Example:**

  HTML

```
<asp:TextBox ID="txtAddress" runat="server" TextMode="MultiLine"
Rows="5" Columns="40"></asp:TextBox>
```

- **Password Input:**

  HTML

```
<asp:TextBox ID="txtPassword" runat="server"
TextMode="Password"></asp:TextBox>
```

- **Handling Text Changed Event (Code-Behind):**

  C#

```
protected void txtName_TextChanged(object sender, EventArgs e)
{
    lblMessage.Text = "You are typing: " + txtName.Text;
}
```

This event handler would execute on the server each time the text in `txtName` changes and the control loses focus (if `AutoPostBack="true"` is set on the `txtName` TextBox).

◆ Button Control (`<asp:Button>`)

- **Description:** As you correctly stated, the `Button` control is used to **trigger events**, most commonly a form submission or other server-side actions.
- **Detailed Explanation:**
  - The `asp:Button` control renders as an HTML `<input type="submit">` element by default within a `<form runat="server">`. Clicking it typically causes a postback to the server, sending the form data.

    - It's a crucial control for initiating server-side processing based on user interaction.
- **Key Properties (Beyond the Basics):**
    - **`ID`:** The unique identifier.
    - **`runat="server"`:** Indicates server-side processing.
    - **`Text`:** The text displayed on the button.
    - **`OnClick`:** The primary event for handling button clicks. You assign the name of a method in the code-behind to this attribute. This method is executed on the server when the button is clicked.
    - **`CommandName`:** An optional property that allows you to assign a logical command name to the button. This is useful when you have multiple buttons in a form and want to differentiate their actions in a single event handler (using the `Command` event of the `Page` or a container control).
    - **`CommandArgument`:** An optional property that allows you to pass additional string data along with the command when the button is clicked.
    - **`UseSubmitBehavior`:** A boolean property (default is `true`). If `true`, the button performs a standard HTML form submission. If `false`, it performs a postback without the default submit behavior (often used with client-side scripting or specific server-side handling).
    - **`CausesValidation`:** A boolean property (default is `true`). If `true`, clicking the button will trigger any associated validation controls on the page. Set to `false` if you want the button to perform an action without triggering validation.
    - **`CssClass`, `ForeColor`, `BackColor`, `Font`, `Visible`, `Enabled`:** For styling and control state.
- **Example (as provided):**

  HTML

```
<asp:Button ID="btnSubmit" runat="server" Text="Submit"
OnClick="btnSubmit_Click" />
```

- **Handling the Click Event (Code-Behind - as provided):**

  C#

```
protected void btnSubmit_Click(object sender, EventArgs e)
{
    lblMessage.Text = "Welcome, " + txtName.Text;
    // Perform other server-side actions here (e.g., save to database).
}
```

- **Using `CommandName` and `CommandArgument`:**

  HTML

```
<asp:Button ID="btnSave" runat="server" Text="Save"
CommandName="DataAction" CommandArgument="SaveData"
OnCommand="HandleButtonClick" />
```

```
<asp:Button ID="btnDelete" runat="server" Text="Delete"
CommandName="DataAction" CommandArgument="DeleteRecord"
OnCommand="HandleButtonClick" />
<asp:Label ID="lblAction" runat="server"></asp:Label>
```

C#

```
protected void HandleButtonClick(object sender, CommandEventArgs e)
{
    if (e.CommandName == "DataAction")
    {
        if (e.CommandArgument.ToString() == "SaveData")
        {
            lblAction.Text = "Saving data...";
            // Save data logic
        }
        else if (e.CommandArgument.ToString() == "DeleteRecord")
        {
            lblAction.Text = "Deleting record...";
            // Delete record logic
        }
    }
}
```

◆ CheckBox Control (`<asp:CheckBox>`)

- **Description:** As you stated, the `CheckBox` control allows users to make **multiple selections** from a set of independent options.
- **Detailed Explanation:**
  - The `asp:CheckBox` control renders as an HTML `<input type="checkbox">` element along with an associated label (defined by its `Text` property).
  - Users can toggle the checked state of each checkbox independently.
- **Key Properties (Beyond the Basics):**
  - **`ID`:** The unique identifier.
  - **`runat="server"`:** Indicates server-side processing.
  - **`Text`:** The label displayed next to the checkbox.
  - **`Checked`:** A boolean property that gets or sets the checked state of the checkbox.
  - **`AutoPostBack`:** If `true`, changing the checked state will trigger a postback.
  - **`OnCheckedChanged`:** An event that fires when the `Checked` state changes (and a postback occurs if `AutoPostBack` is `true`).
  - **`GroupName`:** While primarily used for `RadioButton` controls to enforce single selection, setting a `GroupName` on a `CheckBox` doesn't create a mutually exclusive group. It's generally not used for `CheckBox` in the same way.
  - **`TextAlign`:** Specifies the alignment of the text relative to the checkbox (`Left` or `Right`).
  - **`CssClass`, `ForeColor`, `BackColor`, `Font`, `Visible`, `Enabled`:** For styling and control state.
- **Example (as provided):**

HTML

```
<asp:CheckBox ID="chkAgree" runat="server" Text="I agree to the terms"
/>
```

- **Checking the State (Code-Behind):**

C#

```
protected void btnSubmit_Click(object sender, EventArgs e)
{
    if (chkAgree.Checked)
    {
        lblMessage.Text = "You have agreed.";
    }
    else
    {
        lblMessage.Text = "You have not agreed.";
    }
}
```

- **Handling `CheckedChanged` with AutoPostBack:**

HTML

```
<asp:CheckBox ID="chkOption1" runat="server" Text="Option 1"
AutoPostBack="true" OnCheckedChanged="chkOption1_CheckedChanged" />
<asp:Label ID="lblOption1Status" runat="server"></asp:Label>
```

C#

```
protected void chkOption1_CheckedChanged(object sender, EventArgs e)
{
    lblOption1Status.Text = chkOption1.Checked ? "Option 1 is
selected." : "Option 1 is not selected.";
}
```

◆ RadioButton Control (`<asp:RadioButton>`)

- **Description:** As you correctly pointed out, `RadioButton` controls allow users to make a **single selection from a group of mutually exclusive options.**
- **Detailed Explanation:**
  - The `asp:RadioButton` control renders as an HTML `<input type="radio">` element along with a label.
  - The key to enforcing single selection is the **`GroupName` property**. All radio buttons within the same `GroupName` on a single page will behave as a group where only one can be selected at a time.
- **Key Properties (Beyond the Basics):**
  - **`ID`:** The unique identifier for each radio button in the group.
  - **`runat="server"`:** Indicates server-side processing.
  - **`Text`:** The label displayed next to the radio button.

- **`GroupName`:** A string that logically links radio buttons together for single selection. **All radio buttons that should be part of the same selection group must have the same `GroupName`.**
- **`Checked`:** A boolean property that gets or sets whether the radio button is currently selected. When one radio button in a group is checked, all others in the same group are automatically unchecked.
- **`AutoPostBack`:** If `true`, changing the selected radio button will trigger a postback.
- **`OnCheckedChanged`:** Event fired when the `Checked` state changes (with AutoPostBack).
- **`TextAlign`:** Specifies the alignment of the text relative to the radio button (`Left` or `Right`).
- **`CssClass`, `ForeColor`, `BackColor`, `Font`, `Visible`, `Enabled`:** For styling and control state.

- **Example (as provided):**

HTML

```
<asp:RadioButton ID="rdoMale" runat="server" GroupName="Gender"
Text="Male" />
<asp:RadioButton ID="rdoFemale" runat="server" GroupName="Gender"
Text="Female" />
```

- **Getting the Selected Radio Button (Code-Behind):**

C#

```
protected void btnSubmit_Click(object sender, EventArgs e)
{
    string gender = "";
    if (rdoMale.Checked)
    {
        gender = "Male";
    }
    else if (rdoFemale.Checked)
    {
        gender = "Female";
    }

    if (!string.IsNullOrEmpty(gender))
    {
        lblMessage.Text += "<br/>You selected gender: " + gender;
    }
    else
    {
        lblMessage.Text += "<br/>Please select a gender.";
    }
}
```

- **Handling `CheckedChanged` with AutoPostBack:**

HTML

```
<asp:RadioButton ID="rdoOptionA" runat="server" GroupName="Choice"
Text="Option A" AutoPostBack="true"
OnCheckedChanged="rdoChoice_CheckedChanged" />
<asp:RadioButton ID="rdoOptionB" runat="server" GroupName="Choice"
Text="Option B" AutoPostBack="true"
OnCheckedChanged="rdoChoice_CheckedChanged" />
<asp:Label ID="lblChoice" runat="server"></asp:Label>
```

C#

```
protected void rdoChoice_CheckedChanged(object sender, EventArgs e)
{
    RadioButton selectedRadioButton = (RadioButton)sender;
    if (selectedRadioButton.Checked)
    {
        lblChoice.Text = "You selected: " + selectedRadioButton.Text;
    }
}
```

These fundamental server controls are the building blocks for creating interactive web forms in ASP.NET. By understanding their properties and how to handle their events in the code-behind, you can create rich and dynamic user experiences. Remember to utilize the `ID` and `runat="server"` attributes consistently to interact with these controls programmatically.

📌 2. Essential ASP.NET Server Controls for Navigation and Display: DropDownList, ListBox, HyperLink, Image - A Detailed Exploration

Building interactive web applications often involves presenting lists of options, providing navigation, and displaying visual content. ASP.NET Web Forms offers server controls specifically designed for these purposes. Let's delve into the details of **DropDownList**, **ListBox**, **HyperLink**, and **Image** controls with comprehensive explanations and examples.

◆ DropDownList Control (`<asp:DropDownList>`)

- **Description (as in your table):** The `DropDownList` control displays a list of items in a **dropdown menu**. This is a space-efficient way to present a limited number of choices to the user, where only the selected item is visible by default.
- **Detailed Explanation:**
    - The `asp:DropDownList` control renders as an HTML `<select>` element. The list items within the `DropDownList` are defined using the `<asp:ListItem>` child elements, which correspond to the `<option>` tags in HTML.
    - It's a server-side control, allowing you to dynamically populate the list, retrieve the user's selection, and respond to changes in the selection.
- **Key Properties (Beyond the Basics):**

- **ID:** The unique identifier for the control.
- **runat="server":** Indicates server-side processing.
- **Items:** A collection of `ListItem` objects that represent the options in the dropdown list. You can add, remove, and manipulate these items programmatically in the code-behind.
- **<asp:ListItem>:** Child elements used to define each option in the dropdown. Each `ListItem` has the following key properties:
  - **Text:** The text displayed to the user in the dropdown.
  - **Value:** The value associated with the item, which is submitted to the server when the form is posted. It's good practice to have distinct values even if the text is the same.
  - **Selected:** A boolean property that determines if this item is initially selected. Only one item can be selected by default.
- **SelectedIndex:** An integer representing the zero-based index of the currently selected item.
- **SelectedItem:** A `ListItem` object representing the currently selected item. This provides access to the `Text` and `Value` of the selected item.
- **SelectedValue:** A string representing the `Value` of the currently selected `ListItem`.
- **AutoPostBack:** If set to `true`, a postback occurs automatically when the user selects a different item in the dropdown, triggering the `SelectedIndexChanged` event.
- **OnSelectedIndexChanged:** An event that fires when the selected index in the dropdown changes (and a postback occurs if `AutoPostBack` is `true`).
- **CssClass, ForeColor, BackColor, Font, Visible, Enabled:** For styling and control state.

- **Example (as provided):**

HTML

```
<asp:DropDownList ID="ddlCity" runat="server">
    <asp:ListItem Text="Select City" Value="" />
    <asp:ListItem Text="Delhi" Value="Delhi" />
    <asp:ListItem Text="Mumbai" Value="Mumbai" />
</asp:DropDownList>
```

- **Dynamic Population (Code-Behind):**

C#

```
protected void Page_Load(object sender, EventArgs e)
{
    if (!IsPostBack)
    {
        ddlCity.Items.Clear(); // Clear any existing items
        ddlCity.Items.Add(new ListItem("Select City", ""));
        ddlCity.Items.Add(new ListItem("Kolkata", "Kolkata"));
        ddlCity.Items.Add(new ListItem("Chennai", "Chennai"));
    }
}

protected void ddlCity_SelectedIndexChanged(object sender, EventArgs e)
```

```
{
    if (ddlCity.SelectedValue != "")
    {
        lblMessage.Text = "You selected: " + ddlCity.SelectedItem.Text
+ " (Value: " + ddlCity.SelectedValue + ")";
    }
    else
    {
        lblMessage.Text = "Please select a city.";
    }
}
```

This code dynamically adds cities to the dropdown on the initial page load and handles the `SelectedIndexChanged` event (assuming `AutoPostBack="true"` is set on `ddlCity`).

◆ ListBox Control (`<asp:ListBox>`)

- **Description (as in your table):** The `ListBox` control displays a **list of items** and, as you correctly noted, supports **multiple selections** when the `SelectionMode` property is set accordingly.
- **Detailed Explanation:**
    - The `asp:ListBox` control renders as an HTML `<select>` element with the `multiple` attribute if `SelectionMode="Multiple"`. Like `DropDownList`, its options are defined using `<asp:ListItem>` child elements.
    - It's useful when you need to present a larger number of options or when the user needs to select more than one item simultaneously.
- **Key Properties (Beyond the Basics):**
    - **`ID`:** The unique identifier.
    - **`runat="server"`:** Indicates server-side processing.
    - **`Items`:** A collection of `ListItem` objects, similar to `DropDownList`.
    - **`<asp:ListItem>`:** Child elements defining the options, with `Text`, `Value`, and `Selected` properties.
    - **`SelectedIndex`:** For single-selection mode, the zero-based index of the selected item. For multiple selection, it returns the index of the first selected item (if any).
    - **`SelectedItem`:** For single-selection, the selected `ListItem`.
    - **`SelectedValue`:** For single-selection, the `Value` of the selected `ListItem`.
    - **`SelectedIndexes`:** A collection of integers representing the zero-based indices of all selected items (in multiple selection mode).
    - **`SelectedItems`:** A collection of `ListItem` objects representing all selected items (in multiple selection mode).
    - **`SelectedValues`:** A collection of strings representing the `Value` of all selected `ListItem` objects (in multiple selection mode).
    - **`SelectionMode`:** Determines whether the user can select one or multiple items. Possible values are `Single` (default) and `Multiple`.
    - **`Rows`:** Specifies the number of rows to display in the list box. If the number of items exceeds this, a scrollbar will appear.
    - **`AutoPostBack`:** If `true`, a postback occurs when the selection changes (even for multiple selections), triggering the `SelectedIndexChanged` event.

- **OnSelectedIndexChanged:** An event that fires when the selection in the list box changes (and a postback occurs if `AutoPostBack` is `true`).
- **CssClass, ForeColor, BackColor, Font, Visible, Enabled:** For styling and control state.

- **Example (as provided):**

HTML

```
<asp:ListBox ID="lstLanguages" runat="server" SelectionMode="Multiple">
    <asp:ListItem Text="C#" />
    <asp:ListItem Text="Java" />
    <asp:ListItem Text="Python" />
    <asp:ListItem Text="JavaScript" />
</asp:ListBox>
```

- **Accessing Selected Items (Code-Behind):**

C#

```
protected void btnSubmit_Click(object sender, EventArgs e)
{
    string selectedLanguages = "You selected: ";
    foreach (ListItem item in lstLanguages.SelectedItems)
    {
        selectedLanguages += item.Text + ", ";
    }
    if (selectedLanguages.EndsWith(", "))
    {
        selectedLanguages = selectedLanguages.Substring(0,
selectedLanguages.Length - 2);
    }
    lblMessage.Text = selectedLanguages;
}
```

This code iterates through the `SelectedItems` collection of the `lstLanguages` ListBox to get the text of all selected languages.

◆ HyperLink Control (`<asp:HyperLink>`)

- **Description (as in your table):** The `HyperLink` control creates a standard **hyperlink** that allows users to navigate to another web page or resource.
- **Detailed Explanation:**
  - The `asp:HyperLink` control renders as an HTML `<a>` (anchor) tag. It provides a server-side way to define and manage hyperlinks.
- **Key Properties (Beyond the Basics):**
  - **ID:** The unique identifier.
  - **runat="server":** Indicates server-side processing.
  - **NavigateUrl:** The most important property, specifying the URL or path that the hyperlink points to. This is equivalent to the `href` attribute in HTML. It can be an

absolute URL (e.g., `https://www.google.com`) or a relative URL within your application (`~/Default.aspx`). The ~ represents the application's root directory.
    - **`Text`:** The text that is displayed as the hyperlink to the user. This is the content within the `<a>` tag.
    - **`ImageUrl`:** If you want to display an image as the hyperlink instead of text, you can set this property to the URL of the image. If both `Text` and `ImageUrl` are set, the image will typically take precedence or be displayed instead of the text, depending on browser rendering.
    - **`Target`:** Specifies where to open the linked document. Common values include `_blank` (new window or tab), `_self` (current window), `_parent`, and `_top`. This corresponds directly to the `target` attribute in HTML.
    - **`ToolTip`:** Provides a tooltip that appears when the user hovers the mouse over the hyperlink (corresponds to the `title` attribute in HTML).
    - **`CssClass`, `ForeColor`, `BackColor`, `Font`, `Visible`, `Enabled`:** For styling and control state.
- **Example (as provided):**

  HTML

  ```
  <asp:HyperLink ID="lnkGoogle" runat="server"
  NavigateUrl="https://www.google.com" Text="Visit Google" />
  ```

  This creates a hyperlink with the text "Visit Google" that will navigate the user to `https://www.google.com` when clicked.

- **Using `ImageUrl`:**

  HTML

  ```
  <asp:HyperLink ID="lnkHome" runat="server" NavigateUrl="~/Default.aspx"
  ImageUrl="~/images/home.png" AlternateText="Home" />
  ```

  This creates a hyperlink that displays an image (`home.png`) and navigates to the `Default.aspx` page when clicked. The `AlternateText` provides alternative text for accessibility if the image cannot be loaded.

- **Setting the Target:**

  HTML

  ```
  <asp:HyperLink ID="lnkNewWindow" runat="server"
  NavigateUrl="https://www.example.com" Text="Open in New Window"
  Target="_blank" />
  ```

  This hyperlink will open `https://www.example.com` in a new browser window or tab.

◆ Image Control (`<asp:Image>`)

- **Description (as in your table):** The `Image` control is used to **display an image** on the web page.
- **Detailed Explanation:**
  - The `asp:Image` control renders as an HTML `<img>` tag. It provides a server-side way to specify the image source and other image-related attributes.
- **Key Properties (Beyond the Basics):**
  - **`ID`:** The unique identifier.
  - **`runat="server"`:** Indicates server-side processing.
  - **`ImageUrl`:** The URL or path to the image file that you want to display. This is equivalent to the `src` attribute in HTML. You can use relative paths (`~/images/logo.png`) or absolute URLs.
  - **`AlternateText`:** Essential for accessibility. This text is displayed if the image cannot be loaded and is also read by screen readers. It corresponds to the `alt` attribute in HTML.
  - **`Width`:** Sets the width of the image (can be in pixels or percentages).
  - **`Height`:** Sets the height of the image (can be in pixels or percentages).
  - **`ImageAlign`:** Specifies the alignment of the image with surrounding text (e.g., `Top`, `Bottom`, `Left`, `Right`, `Middle`). Corresponds to the `align` attribute (though CSS is generally preferred for layout).
  - **`CssClass`, `Visible`, `Enabled`:** For styling and control state.
- **Example (as provided):**

  HTML

```
<asp:Image ID="imgLogo" runat="server" ImageUrl="~/images/logo.png"
AlternateText="Site Logo" />
```

  This displays the image located at the `~/images/logo.png` path. If the image cannot be displayed, "Site Logo" will be shown as alternative text.

- **Setting Dimensions:**

  HTML

```
<asp:Image ID="imgBanner" runat="server" ImageUrl="~/images/banner.jpg"
AlternateText="Website Banner" Width="500px" Height="100px" />
```

  This sets the width of the banner image to 500 pixels and the height to 100 pixels.

- **Dynamic Image Source (Code-Behind):**

  C#

```
protected void Page_Load(object sender, EventArgs e)
{
    if (User.IsInRole("Admin"))
    {
        imgLogo.ImageUrl = "~/images/admin_logo.png";
    }
```

```
        else
        {
            imgLogo.ImageUrl = "~/images/user_logo.png";
        }
    }
```

This code dynamically sets the `ImageUrl` of the `imgLogo` based on the user's role.

These controls – `DropDownList`, `ListBox`, `HyperLink`, and `Image` – are fundamental for creating interactive and visually appealing web applications in ASP.NET Web Forms. Understanding their properties and how to manipulate them both in the ASPX markup and the code-behind allows you to build a wide range of user interface elements for navigation, data selection, and content display. Remember to consider accessibility best practices when using the `HyperLink` and `Image` controls (using `Text` and `AlternateText` appropriately).

📌 3. Advanced ASP.NET Server Controls for User Interaction and Content Display: Calendar, FileUpload, AdRotator - A Detailed Exploration

ASP.NET Web Forms provides more specialized server controls to handle specific user interactions and dynamic content display. Let's explore the **Calendar**, **FileUpload**, and **AdRotator** controls in detail with comprehensive explanations and examples.

◆ Calendar Control (`<asp:Calendar>`)

- **Description (as in your table):** The `Calendar` control provides a user-friendly interface for **selecting dates**. It displays a visual calendar that users can navigate through to choose a specific date or a range of dates.
- **Detailed Explanation:**
    - The `asp:Calendar` control renders as a dynamic HTML table representing a calendar. Users can click on days to select them, and it provides built-in navigation to move between months and years.
    - It's a server-side control, offering various properties and events to customize its appearance and handle date selections.
- **Key Properties (Beyond the Basics):**
    - **`ID`:** The unique identifier for the control.
    - **`runat="server"`:** Indicates server-side processing.
    - **`SelectedDate`:** A `DateTime` object representing the currently selected date. You can get or set this value in the code-behind.
    - **`SelectedDates`:** A `SelectedDatesCollection` that allows you to manage multiple selected dates (if `SelectionMode` is set to `DayWeekMonth` or `DayWeekMonth`).
    - **`SelectionMode`:** Determines how users can select dates:
        - `Day` (default): Allows selection of a single day.

        - `DayWeek`: Allows selection of a day or an entire week by clicking on the day header.
        - `DayWeekMonth`: Allows selection of a day, a week, or an entire month by clicking on the day header or month header.
    - **`FirstDayOfWeek`:** Specifies the day to display as the first day of the week (e.g., `Sunday`, `Monday`).
    - **`ShowToday`:** A boolean property that determines whether a "Today" link is displayed.
    - **`TodayDayStyle`, `WeekendDayStyle`, `OtherMonthDayStyle`, `SelectedDayStyle`:** Properties that allow you to customize the appearance of different types of days using CSS styles.
    - **`NextPrevFormat`:** Controls the appearance of the next and previous month navigation elements (e.g., `LinkButton`, `CustomText`).
    - **`TitleFormat`:** Controls the format of the month and year displayed in the title (e.g., `MonthYear`, `Month`).
    - **`VisibleDate`:** A `DateTime` object that determines the month and year currently displayed in the calendar. You can programmatically navigate the calendar by setting this property.
    - **`AutoPostBack`:** If set to `true`, a postback occurs automatically when the user selects a date, triggering the `SelectionChanged` event.
    - **`OnSelectionChanged`:** An event that fires when the user selects a date (and a postback occurs if `AutoPostBack` is `true`).
    - **`OnDayRender`:** A powerful event that fires for each day rendered in the calendar, allowing you to dynamically customize the appearance and behavior of individual days based on your logic (e.g., disable certain dates).
- **Example (as provided):**

  HTML

  ```
  <asp:Calendar ID="calDate" runat="server"></asp:Calendar>
  ```

- **Basic Date Selection Handling (Code-Behind):**

  C#

  ```
  protected void calDate_SelectionChanged(object sender, EventArgs e)
  {
      lblMessage.Text = "You selected the date: " +
  calDate.SelectedDate.ToShortDateString();
  }
  ```

  To make this event fire automatically upon selection, you would need to set `AutoPostBack="true"` on the `Calendar` control in the ASPX.

- **Disabling Future Dates (using `OnDayRender`):**

  C#

  ```
  protected void calDate_DayRender(object sender, DayRenderEventArgs e)
  ```

```
{
    if (e.Day.Date > DateTime.Now.Date)
    {
        e.Day.IsSelectable = false;
        e.Cell.ForeColor = System.Drawing.Color.Gray; // Optionally
style the disabled dates
    }
}
```

You would need to wire this event in the ASPX:

HTML

```html
<asp:Calendar ID="calDate" runat="server"
OnDayRender="calDate_DayRender"></asp:Calendar>
```

◆ FileUpload Control (`<asp:FileUpload>`)

- **Description (as in your table):** The `FileUpload` control enables users to **select and upload files** from their local computer to the web server.
- **Detailed Explanation:**
  - The `asp:FileUpload` control renders as an HTML `<input type="file">` element in the browser. This allows the user to browse their file system and choose a file.
  - It's a server-side control that provides properties and methods to access the selected file on the server during a postback.
- **Key Properties (Beyond the Basics):**
  - **`ID`:** The unique identifier.
  - **`runat="server"`:** Indicates server-side processing.
  - **`HasFile`:** A boolean property that indicates whether the user has selected a file for upload. You should always check this before attempting to access the file.
  - **`FileName`:** A string representing the name of the selected file (including the extension) on the client's computer.
  - **`PostedFile`:** An `HttpPostedFile` object that provides access to the contents and properties of the uploaded file (e.g., `ContentLength` - size in bytes, `ContentType` - MIME type, `InputStream` - a stream to read the file content).
  - **`AllowMultiple`:** An HTML5 attribute (browser support may vary) that, when set to `true`, allows the user to select multiple files for upload in a single control. You'll need to iterate through the `PostedFiles` collection in the code-behind to handle multiple uploads.
  - **`CssClass`, `Visible`, `Enabled`:** For styling and control state.
- **Example (as provided):**

HTML

```html
<asp:FileUpload ID="fileUpload" runat="server" />
<asp:Button ID="btnUpload" runat="server" Text="Upload"
OnClick="btnUpload_Click" />
```

- **Code-Behind for Single File Upload (as provided):**

C#

```
protected void btnUpload_Click(object sender, EventArgs e)
{
    if (fileUpload.HasFile)
    {
        try
        {
            string filePath = Server.MapPath("~/Uploads/") +
fileUpload.FileName;
            fileUpload.SaveAs(filePath);
            lblMessage.Text = "File uploaded successfully to: " +
filePath;
        }
        catch (Exception ex)
        {
            lblMessage.Text = "Error uploading file: " + ex.Message;
        }
    }
    else
    {
        lblMessage.Text = "Please select a file to upload.";
    }
}
```

- **Code-Behind for Multiple File Upload (if `AllowMultiple="true"`):**

C#

```
protected void btnUpload_Click(object sender, EventArgs e)
{
    if (fileUpload.HasFile) // For browsers that don't fully support
AllowMultiple
    {
        try
        {
            string filePath = Server.MapPath("~/Uploads/") +
fileUpload.FileName;
            fileUpload.SaveAs(filePath);
            lblMessage.Text += "File uploaded: " + filePath + "<br/>";
        }
        catch (Exception ex)
        {
            lblMessage.Text += "Error uploading file: " + ex.Message +
"<br/>";
        }
    }

    if (fileUpload.PostedFiles != null && fileUpload.PostedFiles.Count
> 0)
    {
        foreach (HttpPostedFile uploadedFile in fileUpload.PostedFiles)
        {
            try
            {
```

```
                string filePath = Server.MapPath("~/Uploads/") +
System.IO.Path.GetFileName(uploadedFile.FileName);
                uploadedFile.SaveAs(filePath);
                lblMessage.Text += "File uploaded: " + filePath +
"<br/>";
            }
            catch (Exception ex)
            {
                lblMessage.Text += "Error uploading file: " +
System.IO.Path.GetFileName(uploadedFile.FileName) + ": " + ex.Message +
"<br/>";
            }
        }
    }

    if (string.IsNullOrEmpty(lblMessage.Text))
    {
        lblMessage.Text = "Please select files to upload.";
    }
}
```

Important Security Considerations for File Uploads:

- **File Size Limits:** Always enforce maximum file size limits to prevent denial-of-service attacks. You can configure this in your `web.config` file.
- **File Type Validation:** Validate the file extension and MIME type on the server-side to ensure users are uploading expected file types and prevent execution of malicious scripts.
- **Directory Permissions:** Ensure the upload directory on the server has appropriate permissions to prevent unauthorized access or modification.
- **Unique File Names:** Consider renaming uploaded files to prevent overwriting existing files and potential security risks. Use timestamps or GUIDs to generate unique names.
- **Scanning for Malware:** For sensitive applications, consider integrating with anti-malware scanning tools.

◆ AdRotator Control (`<asp:AdRotator>`)

- **Description (as in your table):** The `AdRotator` control displays **rotating banner advertisements** on your web page. It allows you to manage a set of ads and display them randomly or based on a weighting system.
- **Detailed Explanation:**
    - The `asp:AdRotator` control doesn't directly contain the ad content. Instead, it reads information about the advertisements from an **XML file** (specified by the `AdvertisementFile` property). This XML file defines the image URL, navigation URL, alternate text, and optionally, impression weights for each ad.
    - The `AdRotator` then dynamically selects and renders one of these ads each time the page is loaded or refreshed (or on a postback).
- **Key Properties (Beyond the Basics):**
    - **`ID`:** The unique identifier.
    - **`runat="server"`:** Indicates server-side processing.

- **AdvertisementFile:** The path to the XML file that contains the advertisement definitions. The path can be absolute or relative to the application root (~).
  - **ImageUrlField:** The name of the XML element that specifies the image URL for each ad (default is `ImageUrl`).
  - **NavigateUrlField:** The name of the XML element that specifies the URL to navigate to when the ad is clicked (default is `NavigateUrl`).
  - **AlternateTextField:** The name of the XML element that provides the alternate text for the image (default is `AlternateText`).
  - **Target:** Specifies the target window or frame for the hyperlink when the ad is clicked (e.g., `_blank`).
  - **ImpressionsField:** The name of the XML element that specifies the weight or number of impressions for each ad (default is `Impressions`). Ads with higher impression values are displayed more frequently.
  - **DataMember:** If your XML file has a root element and then a child element containing the list of ads, you can specify the name of that child element here.
  - **OnAdCreated:** An event that fires after the `AdRotator` has selected an ad and is about to render it. This allows you to further customize the ad's properties programmatically before it's displayed.

- **Example (as provided):**

  HTML

```html
<asp:AdRotator ID="AdRotator1" runat="server"
AdvertisementFile="~/Ads.xml" />
```

- **`Ads.xml` Example (as provided):**

  XML

```xml
<Advertisements>
  <Ad>
    <ImageUrl>~/images/ad1.jpg</ImageUrl>
    <NavigateUrl>https://www.example.com</NavigateUrl>
    <AlternateText>Ad 1</AlternateText>
    <Impressions>80</Impressions>
  </Ad>
  <Ad>
    <ImageUrl>~/images/ad2.jpg</ImageUrl>
    <NavigateUrl>https://www.anotherexample.com</NavigateUrl>
    <AlternateText>Ad 2</AlternateText>
    <Impressions>20</Impressions>
  </Ad>
</Advertisements>
```

  In this example, `ad1.jpg` will be displayed more frequently than `ad2.jpg` due to its higher `Impressions` value.

- **Handling the `OnAdCreated` Event (Code-Behind):**

C#

```
protected void AdRotator1_AdCreated(object sender, AdCreatedEventArgs
e)
{
    // You can access the properties of the selected ad here
    // e.AdProperties["ImageUrl"], e.AdProperties["NavigateUrl"], etc.
    // You could modify these properties if needed.
    // For example, adding a custom query string parameter to the
NavigateUrl.
    e.NavigateUrl += "?source=adrotator";
}
```

You would need to wire this event in the ASPX:

HTML

```
<asp:AdRotator ID="AdRotator1" runat="server"
AdvertisementFile="~/Ads.xml" OnAdCreated="AdRotator1_AdCreated" />
```

These more advanced server controls – `Calendar`, `FileUpload`, and `AdRotator` – extend the capabilities of ASP.NET Web Forms, allowing you to implement sophisticated user interactions for date selection, file uploading, and dynamic advertisement display. Understanding their specific properties, events, and underlying mechanisms is crucial for building feature-rich web applications. Remember to consider security implications, especially with file uploads, and to structure your advertisement data correctly for the `AdRotator` control.

📌 4. Structuring and Dynamically Managing Controls: Using Panels and PlaceHolders in ASP.NET Web Forms - A Detailed Exploration

ASP.NET Web Forms provides server controls that go beyond basic input and output. **Panel** and **PlaceHolder** are container controls that offer powerful ways to organize your UI and dynamically manage the controls displayed on your web pages. Let's explore these controls in detail with comprehensive explanations and examples.

◆ Panel Control (`<asp:Panel>`)

- **Description (as in your table):** The `Panel` control acts as a **container for grouping other controls**. It allows you to treat a set of controls as a single unit for purposes like visibility, styling, and scrolling.
- **Detailed Explanation:**

- The `asp:Panel` control renders as an HTML `<div>` element by default. You can place other server controls (like `Label`, `TextBox`, `Button`, etc.) within the opening and closing tags of the `Panel` in your ASPX markup.
  - By manipulating the properties of the `Panel`, you can affect all the controls it contains. This is particularly useful for showing or hiding entire sections of your UI or applying consistent styling.
- **Key Properties (Beyond the Basics):**
  - **`ID`:** The unique identifier for the control.
  - **`runat="server"`:** Indicates server-side processing.
  - **`Visible`:** A boolean property that determines whether the panel and all its contained controls are displayed on the page. Setting this to `false` effectively hides the entire group.
  - **`CssClass`:** Allows you to apply CSS styles to the `<div>` element that represents the panel, controlling its layout, background, borders, etc.
  - **`BackColor`, `ForeColor`, `BorderColor`, `BorderStyle`, `BorderWidth`:** Properties for directly setting the background, text color, and border styles of the panel.
  - **`Width`, `Height`:** Set the dimensions of the panel.
  - **`ScrollBars`:** Controls the display of scrollbars if the content within the panel exceeds its dimensions. Possible values include `None`, `Horizontal`, `Vertical`, and `Both`.
  - **`GroupingText`:** Adds a `<fieldset>` and `<legend>` element around the panel, providing a visual grouping with a title.
  - **`DefaultButton`:** Specifies the `ID` of a button within the panel that should be treated as the default button when the user presses the Enter key while focus is within the panel.
- **Example (as provided):**

  HTML

```
<asp:Panel ID="pnlLogin" runat="server" Visible="true">
    <asp:Label ID="lblUser" runat="server"
Text="Username:"></asp:Label>
    <asp:TextBox ID="txtUser" runat="server"></asp:TextBox><br />
    <asp:Label ID="lblPass" runat="server"
Text="Password:"></asp:Label>
    <asp:TextBox ID="txtPass" runat="server"
TextMode="Password"></asp:TextBox><br />
    <asp:Button ID="btnLogin" runat="server" Text="Login"
OnClick="btnLogin_Click" />
</asp:Panel>
```

  This creates a panel named `pnlLogin` that initially is visible and contains labels, text boxes for username and password, and a login button.

- **Dynamic Visibility (Code-Behind):**

  C#

```
protected void btnShowHide_Click(object sender, EventArgs e)
{
```

```
    pnlLogin.Visible = !pnlLogin.Visible;
    if (pnlLogin.Visible)
    {
        btnShowHide.Text = "Hide Login";
    }
    else
    {
        btnShowHide.Text = "Show Login";
    }
}
```

You would need a button (`btnShowHide`) on the page to trigger this code. Clicking it would toggle the visibility of the entire `pnlLogin` panel.

- **Using `GroupingText`:**

  HTML

```
<asp:Panel ID="pnlAddress" runat="server" GroupingText="Address
Information">
    <asp:Label ID="lblStreet" runat="server"
Text="Street:"></asp:Label>
    <asp:TextBox ID="txtStreet" runat="server"></asp:TextBox><br />
    <asp:Label ID="lblCity" runat="server" Text="City:"></asp:Label>
    <asp:TextBox ID="txtCity" runat="server"></asp:TextBox>
</asp:Panel>
```

  This would render the address fields within a bordered box with the title "Address Information".

◆ PlaceHolder Control (`<asp:PlaceHolder>`)

- **Description (as in your table):** The `PlaceHolder` control serves as a **container where you can dynamically add controls at runtime** from your code-behind. Unlike the `Panel`, it doesn't render any visible HTML element itself (it essentially acts as an empty tag).
- **Detailed Explanation:**
  - The `asp:PlaceHolder` control is a lightweight container that reserves a spot in your ASPX markup where you can programmatically insert other server controls.
  - It's extremely useful for scenarios where the number or type of controls you need to display depends on data, user actions, or application logic that can only be determined during the page's execution.
- **Key Properties (Beyond the Basics):**
  - **`ID`:** The unique identifier for the control.
  - **`runat="server"`:** Indicates server-side processing.
  - **`Controls`:** A collection property that allows you to add, remove, and access the child controls within the `PlaceHolder` programmatically in the code-behind. This is the primary way you interact with the `PlaceHolder`.

- **Visible, CssClass, etc.:** Standard control properties, although the `PlaceHolder` itself doesn't have a visual representation unless you style it indirectly through its parent or the controls you add to it.

- **Example (as provided):**

  HTML

```
<asp:PlaceHolder ID="phControls" runat="server"></asp:PlaceHolder>
```

- **Code-Behind for Dynamic Control Addition (as provided):**

  C#

```
protected void Page_Load(object sender, EventArgs e)
{
    TextBox txtDynamic = new TextBox();
    txtDynamic.ID = "txtDynamic";
    phControls.Controls.Add(txtDynamic);

    Label lblDynamic = new Label();
    lblDynamic.ID = "lblDynamic";
    lblDynamic.Text = "This label was added dynamically.";
    phControls.Controls.Add(lblDynamic);

    Button btnDynamic = new Button();
    btnDynamic.ID = "btnDynamic";
    btnDynamic.Text = "Click Me Dynamically";
    btnDynamic.Click += BtnDynamic_Click; // Attach an event handler
    phControls.Controls.Add(btnDynamic);
}

protected void BtnDynamic_Click(object sender, EventArgs e)
{
    lblMessage.Text = "Dynamic button clicked!";
}
```

In this example, during the `Page_Load` event, a `TextBox`, a `Label`, and a `Button` are created programmatically and added to the `Controls` collection of the `phControls` PlaceHolder. These controls will then be rendered within the location of the `PlaceHolder` in the ASPX. An event handler is also attached to the dynamically created button.

- **Dynamically Adding Controls Based on Data:**

  C#

```
protected void Page_Load(object sender, EventArgs e)
{
    if (!IsPostBack)
    {
        string[] items = { "Apple", "Banana", "Cherry" };
```

```
        foreach (string item in items)
        {
            CheckBox chkItem = new CheckBox();
            chkItem.ID = "chk" + item;
            chkItem.Text = item;
            phControls.Controls.Add(chkItem);
            phControls.Controls.Add(new LiteralControl("<br />")); //
Add a line break
        }
    }
}
```

This code dynamically creates a `CheckBox` for each item in the `items` array and adds them to the `phControls` PlaceHolder, along with line breaks for formatting.

Key Differences Between Panel and PlaceHolder:

Feature	Panel (`<asp:Panel>`)	PlaceHolder (`<asp:PlaceHolder>`)
Renders as	HTML `<div>` (or `<fieldset>` with `GroupingText`)	No visible HTML element by default
Purpose	Grouping and managing existing controls	Container for dynamically adding controls
Visibility	Can be shown/hidden as a unit	Primarily controlled by the visibility of its child controls
Styling	Can be directly styled (background, border, etc.)	Styling is applied to the controls within it
Use Cases	Organizing form sections, showing/hiding logical groups of controls, applying consistent styling	Dynamically generating forms or UI elements based on data or logic

---

Summary:

- **Standard controls** are crucial for user interaction and data collection.
- Each control supports various properties like ID, Text, Value, Visible, etc.
- Code-behind allows processing input data and generating output dynamically.

10 PRACTICAL EXAMPLES WITH SOLUTION

1. Simple Calculator (Label, TextBox, Button)

- **Problem:** Create a basic calculator with two text boxes for input, buttons for addition, subtraction, multiplication, and division, and a label to display the result.
- **Solution (`Calculator.aspx`):**

  HTML

```
<%@ Page Language="C#" AutoEventWireup="true"
CodeFile="Calculator.aspx.cs" Inherits="Calculator" %>
<!DOCTYPE html>
<html>
<head>
    <title>Simple Calculator</title>
</head>
<body>
    <form id="form1" runat="server">
        <asp:Label ID="lblNum1" runat="server" Text="Number
1:"></asp:Label>
        <asp:TextBox ID="txtNum1" runat="server"></asp:TextBox><br />
        <asp:Label ID="lblNum2" runat="server" Text="Number
2:"></asp:Label>
        <asp:TextBox ID="txtNum2" runat="server"></asp:TextBox><br />
        <asp:Button ID="btnAdd" runat="server" Text="+"
OnClick="btnAdd_Click" />
        <asp:Button ID="btnSub" runat="server" Text="-"
OnClick="btnSub_Click" />
        <asp:Button ID="btnMul" runat="server" Text="*"
OnClick="btnMul_Click" />
        <asp:Button ID="btnDiv" runat="server" Text="/"
OnClick="btnDiv_Click" /><br />
        <asp:Label ID="lblResult" runat="server"
Text="Result:"></asp:Label>
    </form>
</body>
</html>
```

- **Solution (`Calculator.aspx.cs`):**

  C#

```
using System;

public partial class Calculator : System.Web.UI.Page
{
    protected void Page_Load(object sender, EventArgs e)
    {
        if (!IsPostBack)
        {
            lblResult.Text = "Result:";
        }
```

```
}
protected void btnAdd_Click(object sender, EventArgs e)
{
    try
    {
        double num1 = double.Parse(txtNum1.Text);
        double num2 = double.Parse(txtNum2.Text);
        lblResult.Text = "Result: " + (num1 + num2).ToString();
    }
    catch (Exception ex)
    {
        lblResult.Text = "Error: " + ex.Message;
    }
}

protected void btnSub_Click(object sender, EventArgs e)
{
    // Similar logic for subtraction, multiplication, and division
     try
    {
        double num1 = double.Parse(txtNum1.Text);
        double num2 = double.Parse(txtNum2.Text);
        lblResult.Text = "Result: " + (num1 - num2).ToString();
    }
    catch (Exception ex)
    {
        lblResult.Text = "Error: " + ex.Message;
    }
}

protected void btnMul_Click(object sender, EventArgs e)
{
     try
    {
        double num1 = double.Parse(txtNum1.Text);
        double num2 = double.Parse(txtNum2.Text);
        lblResult.Text = "Result: " + (num1 * num2).ToString();
    }
    catch (Exception ex)
    {
        lblResult.Text = "Error: " + ex.Message;
    }
}

protected void btnDiv_Click(object sender, EventArgs e)
{
     try
    {
        double num1 = double.Parse(txtNum1.Text);
        double num2 = double.Parse(txtNum2.Text);
        if (num2 == 0)
        {
            lblResult.Text = "Error: Cannot divide by zero.";
        }
        else
        {
            lblResult.Text = "Result: " + (num1 / num2).ToString();
```

```
            }
        }
        catch (Exception ex)
        {
            lblResult.Text = "Error: " + ex.Message;
        }
    }
}
```

- **Learning Outcome:** Handling multiple button events, parsing input, performing calculations, and displaying results.

2. Simple Survey (Label, TextBox, RadioButton, CheckBox, Button)

- **Problem:** Create a simple survey form to collect user information, including name, gender, and favorite programming languages.
- **Solution (`SurveyForm.aspx`):**

  HTML

```
<%@ Page Language="C#" AutoEventWireup="true"
CodeFile="SurveyForm.aspx.cs" Inherits="SurveyForm" %>
<!DOCTYPE html>
<html>
<head>
    <title>Survey Form</title>
</head>
<body>
    <form id="form1" runat="server">
        <asp:Label ID="lblName" runat="server"
Text="Name:"></asp:Label>
        <asp:TextBox ID="txtName" runat="server"></asp:TextBox><br />
        <asp:Label ID="lblGender" runat="server"
Text="Gender:"></asp:Label><br />
        <asp:RadioButton ID="rdoMale" runat="server" GroupName="Gender"
Text="Male" />
        <asp:RadioButton ID="rdoFemale" runat="server"
GroupName="Gender" Text="Female" /><br />
        <asp:Label ID="lblLanguages" runat="server" Text="Favorite
Languages:"></asp:Label><br />
        <asp:CheckBox ID="chkCSharp" runat="server" Text="C#" />
        <asp:CheckBox ID="chkJava" runat="server" Text="Java" />
        <asp:CheckBox ID="chkPython" runat="server" Text="Python" /><br
/>
        <asp:Button ID="btnSubmit" runat="server" Text="Submit"
OnClick="btnSubmit_Click" />
        <asp:Label ID="lblResult" runat="server" Text=""></asp:Label>
    </form>
</body>
</html>
```

- **Solution (`SurveyForm.aspx.cs`):**

C#

```
using System;

public partial class SurveyForm : System.Web.UI.Page
{
    protected void btnSubmit_Click(object sender, EventArgs e)
    {
        string name = txtName.Text;
        string gender = rdoMale.Checked ? "Male" : (rdoFemale.Checked ?
"Female" : "Not Selected");
        string languages = "";
        if (chkCSharp.Checked) languages += "C#, ";
        if (chkJava.Checked) languages += "Java, ";
        if (chkPython.Checked) languages += "Python, ";
        if (languages.EndsWith(", ")) languages =
languages.Substring(0, languages.Length - 2);
        if (string.IsNullOrEmpty(languages)) languages = "None";

        lblResult.Text = "Name: " + name + "<br/>" +
                         "Gender: " + gender + "<br/>" +
                         "Favorite Languages: " + languages;
    }
}
```

- **Learning Outcome:** Collecting user input from various controls and combining it into a meaningful result.

3. City Selection (DropDownList, Label)

- **Problem:** Create a dropdown list of cities and display the selected city in a label.
- **Solution (`CitySelection.aspx`):**

HTML

```
<%@ Page Language="C#" AutoEventWireup="true"
CodeFile="CitySelection.aspx.cs" Inherits="CitySelection" %>
<!DOCTYPE html>
<html>
<head>
    <title>City Selection</title>
</head>
<body>
    <form id="form1" runat="server">
        <asp:DropDownList ID="ddlCity" runat="server"
AutoPostBack="true"
OnSelectedIndexChanged="ddlCity_SelectedIndexChanged">
            <asp:ListItem Text="Select City" Value="" />
            <asp:ListItem Text="Delhi" Value="Delhi" />
            <asp:ListItem Text="Mumbai" Value="Mumbai" />
            <asp:ListItem Text="Kolkata" Value="Kolkata" />
            <asp:ListItem Text="Chennai" Value="Chennai" />
        </asp:DropDownList><br />
```

```
        <asp:Label ID="lblSelectedCity" runat="server"
Text=""></asp:Label>
    </form>
</body>
</html>
```

- **Solution (`CitySelection.aspx.cs`):**

  C#

```
using System;

public partial class CitySelection : System.Web.UI.Page
{
    protected void Page_Load(object sender, EventArgs e)
    {
        if (!IsPostBack)
        {
            lblSelectedCity.Text = "Please select a city.";
        }
    }
    protected void ddlCity_SelectedIndexChanged(object sender,
EventArgs e)
    {
        if (ddlCity.SelectedValue != "")
        {
            lblSelectedCity.Text = "You selected: " +
ddlCity.SelectedItem.Text;
        }
        else
        {
             lblSelectedCity.Text = "Please select a city.";
        }
    }
}
```

- **Learning Outcome:** Using `DropDownList` and handling the `SelectedIndexChanged` event with `AutoPostBack`.

4. Language Selection (ListBox, Label)

- **Problem:** Create a list box of programming languages and display the selected languages in a label.
- **Solution (`LanguageSelection.aspx`):**

  HTML

```
<%@ Page Language="C#" AutoEventWireup="true"
CodeFile="LanguageSelection.aspx.cs" Inherits="LanguageSelection" %>
<!DOCTYPE html>
<html>
<head>
    <title>Language Selection</title>
```

```
</head>
<body>
    <form id="form1" runat="server">
        <asp:ListBox ID="lstLanguages" runat="server"
SelectionMode="Multiple">
            <asp:ListItem Text="C#" />
            <asp:ListItem Text="Java" />
            <asp:ListItem Text="Python" />
            <asp:ListItem Text="JavaScript" />
            <asp:ListItem Text="C++" />
        </asp:ListBox><br />
        <asp:Button ID="btnShowLanguages" runat="server" Text="Show
Selected Languages" OnClick="btnShowLanguages_Click" />
        <asp:Label ID="lblSelectedLanguages" runat="server"
Text=""></asp:Label>
    </form>
</body>
</html>
```

- **Solution (`LanguageSelection.aspx.cs`):**

  C#

```
using System;
using System.Web.UI.WebControls;

public partial class LanguageSelection : System.Web.UI.Page
{
    protected void btnShowLanguages_Click(object sender, EventArgs e)
    {
        string selectedLanguages = "Selected Languages: ";
        if (lstLanguages.SelectedItems.Count == 0)
        {
            lblSelectedLanguages.Text = "No languages selected.";
        }
        else
        {
            foreach (ListItem item in lstLanguages.SelectedItems)
            {
                selectedLanguages += item.Text + ", ";
            }
            selectedLanguages = selectedLanguages.TrimEnd(',', ' '); //
Remove trailing comma and space
            lblSelectedLanguages.Text = selectedLanguages;
        }
    }
}
```

- **Learning Outcome:** Using `ListBox` with `SelectionMode="Multiple"` and iterating through the `SelectedItems` collection.

5. Navigation (HyperLink)

- **Problem:** Create hyperlinks to navigate to different websites or pages within the application.
- **Solution (`Navigation.aspx`):**

  HTML

```
<%@ Page Language="C#" AutoEventWireup="true"
CodeFile="Navigation.aspx.cs" Inherits="Navigation" %>
<!DOCTYPE html>
<html>
<head>
    <title>Navigation</title>
</head>
<body>
    <form id="form1" runat="server">
        <asp:HyperLink ID="lnkGoogle" runat="server"
NavigateUrl="https://www.google.com" Text="Visit Google"
Target="_blank" /><br />
        <asp:HyperLink ID="lnkAbout" runat="server"
NavigateUrl="~/About.aspx" Text="About This Site" /><br />
        <asp:HyperLink ID="lnkContact" runat="server"
NavigateUrl="Contact.aspx" Text="Contact Us" />
    </form>
</body>
</html>
```

- **Solution (`About.aspx`):**

  HTML

```
<%@ Page Language="C#" AutoEventWireup="true" CodeFile="About.aspx.cs"
Inherits="About" %>
<!DOCTYPE html>
<html xmlns="http://www.w3.org/1999/xhtml">
<head runat="server">
    <title>About Us</title>
</head>
<body>
    <form id="form1" runat="server">
        <div>
            <h1>About Us</h1>
            <p>This is the about us page.</p>
        </div>
    </form>
</body>
</html>
```

- **Learning Outcome:** Using the `HyperLink` control to create navigation links, including external URLs and internal pages, and setting the `Target` attribute.

6. Image Display (Image)

- **Problem:** Display an image on the web page.
- **Solution (`ImageDisplay.aspx`):**

HTML

```
<%@ Page Language="C#" AutoEventWireup="true"
CodeFile="ImageDisplay.aspx.cs" Inherits="ImageDisplay" %>
<!DOCTYPE html>
<html>
<head>
    <title>Image Display</title>
</head>
<body>
    <form id="form1" runat="server">
        <asp:Image ID="imgLogo" runat="server"
ImageUrl="~/images/logo.png" AlternateText="Company Logo" Width="200"
Height="100" />
    </form>
</body>
</html>
```

- **Learning Outcome:** Using the `Image` control to display images, setting the `ImageUrl`, `AlternateText`, and dimensions.

7. Date Selection (Calendar)

- **Problem:** Allow the user to select a date and display the selected date.
- **Solution (`DateSelection.aspx`):**

HTML

```
<%@ Page Language="C#" AutoEventWireup="true"
CodeFile="DateSelection.aspx.cs" Inherits="DateSelection" %>
<!DOCTYPE html>
<html>
<head>
    <title>Date Selection</title>
</head>
<body>
    <form id="form1" runat="server">
        <asp:Calendar ID="calDate" runat="server"
OnSelectionChanged="calDate_SelectionChanged"
AutoPostBack="true"></asp:Calendar><br />
        <asp:Label ID="lblSelectedDate" runat="server"
Text=""></asp:Label>
    </form>
</body>
</html>
```

- **Solution (`DateSelection.aspx.cs`):**

C#

```
using System;

public partial class DateSelection : System.Web.UI.Page
{
    protected void Page_Load(object sender, EventArgs e)
    {
        if (!IsPostBack)
        {
            lblSelectedDate.Text = "Please select a date.";
        }
    }
    protected void calDate_SelectionChanged(object sender, EventArgs e)
    {
        lblSelectedDate.Text = "You selected: " +
calDate.SelectedDate.ToShortDateString();
    }
}
```

- **Learning Outcome:** Using the `Calendar` control to allow date selection and handling the `SelectionChanged` event.

8. File Upload (FileUpload)

- **Problem:** Allow the user to upload a file and save it to the server.
- **Solution (`FileUploadPage.aspx`):**

HTML

```
<%@ Page Language="C#" AutoEventWireup="true"
CodeFile="FileUploadPage.aspx.cs" Inherits="FileUploadPage" %>
<!DOCTYPE html>
<html>
<head>
    <title>File Upload</title>
</head>
<body>
    <form id="form1" runat="server" enctype="multipart/form-data">
        <asp:FileUpload ID="fileUpload" runat="server" /><br />
        <asp:Button ID="btnUpload" runat="server" Text="Upload"
OnClick="btnUpload_Click" /><br />
        <asp:Label ID="lblMessage" runat="server" Text=""></asp:Label>
    </form>
</body>
</html>
```

- **Solution (`FileUploadPage.aspx.cs`):**

C#

```
using System;
using System.IO;

public partial class FileUploadPage : System.Web.UI.Page
```

```
{
    protected void btnUpload_Click(object sender, EventArgs e)
    {
        if (fileUpload.HasFile)
        {
            try
            {
                string fileName =
Path.GetFileName(fileUpload.FileName);
                string filePath = Server.MapPath("~/Uploads/") +
fileName;
                fileUpload.SaveAs(filePath);
                lblMessage.Text = "File uploaded successfully to: " +
filePath;
            }
            catch (Exception ex)
            {
                lblMessage.Text = "Error: " + ex.Message;
            }
        }
        else
        {
            lblMessage.Text = "Please select a file to upload.";
        }
    }
}
```

- **Important:** Create an "Uploads" folder in your application's root directory and ensure the application has write permissions to that folder.

- **Learning Outcome:** Using the `FileUpload` control to upload files and handling the `SaveAs` method.

9. Advertisement Display (AdRotator)

- **Problem:** Display rotating advertisements on a page.
- **Solution (`AdRotatorPage.aspx`):**

HTML

```
<%@ Page Language="C#" AutoEventWireup="true"
CodeFile="AdRotatorPage.aspx.cs" Inherits="AdRotatorPage" %>
<!DOCTYPE html>
<html>
<head>
    <title>Ad Rotator</title>
</head>
<body>
    <form id="form1" runat="server">
        <asp:AdRotator ID="AdRotator1" runat="server"
AdvertisementFile="~/Ads.xml" />
    </form>
</body>
</html>
```

- **Solution (`Ads.xml`):**

  XML

```
<Advertisements>
    <Ad>
        <ImageUrl>~/images/ad1.jpg</ImageUrl>
        <NavigateUrl>https://www.example1.com</NavigateUrl>
        <AlternateText>Ad 1</AlternateText>
        <Impressions>70</Impressions>
    </Ad>
    <Ad>
        <ImageUrl>~/images/ad2.jpg</ImageUrl>
        <NavigateUrl>https://www.example2.com</NavigateUrl>
        <AlternateText>Ad 2</AlternateText>
        <Impressions>30</Impressions>
    </Ad>
     <Ad>
        <ImageUrl>~/images/ad3.jpg</ImageUrl>
        <NavigateUrl>https://www.example3.com</NavigateUrl>
        <AlternateText>Ad 3</AlternateText>
        <Impressions>50</Impressions>
    </Ad>
</Advertisements>
```

  - **Important:** Create an "images" folder in your application and place placeholder images (ad1.jpg, ad2.jpg, ad3.jpg) there, or modify the `ImageUrl` paths accordingly.
- **Learning Outcome:** Using the `AdRotator` control and configuring it with an XML file.

10. Dynamic Form (Panel, PlaceHolder)

- **Problem:** Create a form where the number of input fields is dynamically determined.
- **Solution (`DynamicForm.aspx`):**

  HTML

```
<%@ Page Language="C#" AutoEventWireup="true"
CodeFile="DynamicForm.aspx.cs" Inherits="DynamicForm" %>
<!DOCTYPE html>
<html>
<head>
    <title>Dynamic Form</title>
</head>
<body>
    <form id="form1" runat="server">
        <asp:Panel ID="pnlForm" runat="server">
            <asp:Label ID="lblCount" runat="server" Text="Enter number
of fields:"></asp:Label>
            <asp:TextBox ID="txtCount" runat="server"></asp:TextBox>
            <asp:Button ID="btnGenerate" runat="server" Text="Generate
Fields" OnClick="btnGenerate_Click" /><br />
```

```
            <asp:PlaceHolder ID="phFields"
runat="server"></asp:PlaceHolder><br />
            <asp:Button ID="btnSubmit" runat="server" Text="Submit"
OnClick="btnSubmit_Click" Visible="false" />
        </asp:Panel>
        <asp:Label ID="lblResult" runat="server" Text=""></asp:Label>
    </form>
</body>
</html>
```

- **Solution (`DynamicForm.aspx.cs`):**

C#

```
using System;
using System.Web.UI.WebControls;

public partial class DynamicForm : System.Web.UI.Page
{
    protected void Page_Load(object sender, EventArgs e)
    {
        //  phFields.Controls.Clear();  //Removed this line.
    }

    protected void btnGenerate_Click(object sender, EventArgs e)
    {
        phFields.Controls.Clear(); // Clear any previously generated
controls.
        int count = 0;
        if (int.TryParse(txtCount.Text, out count))
        {
            if (count > 0)
            {
                for (int i = 1; i <= count; i++)
                {
                    Label lbl = new Label();
                    lbl.Text = "Field " + i + ": ";
                    TextBox txt = new TextBox();
                    txt.ID = "txtField" + i;
                    phFields.Controls.Add(lbl);
                    phFields.Controls.Add(txt);
                    phFields.Controls.Add(new LiteralControl("<br
/>")); // Add a line break
                }
                btnSubmit.Visible = true; // Show the submit button
                lblResult.Text = "";
            }
            else
            {
                lblResult.Text = "Please enter a positive number.";
                btnSubmit.Visible = false;
            }
        }
        else
        {
            lblResult.Text = "Invalid input. Please enter a number.";
```

```
                btnSubmit.Visible = false;
            }
        }

        protected void btnSubmit_Click(object sender, EventArgs e)
        {
            string result = "You entered:<br/>";
            foreach (Control control in phFields.Controls)
            {
                if (control is TextBox)
                {
                    TextBox txt = (TextBox)control;
                    result += txt.ID + ": " + txt.Text + "<br/>";
                }
            }
            lblResult.Text = result;
        }
    }
```

- **Learning Outcome:** Using `Panel` to group controls, `PlaceHolder` to dynamically add controls, and accessing dynamically created controls in the code-behind.

30 MCQ QUESTION WITH ANSWER

1. Which control is used to display static or dynamic text? a) TextBox b) Label c) Literal d) Span *Answer: b) Label*

2. Which control allows users to enter text input? a) Label b) Button c) TextBox d) HyperLink *Answer: c) TextBox*

3. Which control triggers an event when clicked? a) Label b) TextBox c) Button d) CheckBox *Answer: c) Button*

4. Which control allows users to select multiple options? a) RadioButton b) DropDownList c) ListBox d) CheckBox *Answer: d) CheckBox*

5. Which control allows users to select a single option from a group? a) CheckBox b) ListBox c) RadioButton d) DropDownList *Answer: c) RadioButton*

6. What is the default HTML element rendered by the Label control? a) <div> b) <span> c) <p> d) <label> *Answer: b) <span>*

7. Which property of the TextBox control is used to get or set the text? a) Value b) Text c) InnerHTML d) Content *Answer: b) Text*

8. Which event is raised when a Button control is clicked? a) Clicked b) MouseClick c) Click d) Action *Answer: c) Click*

9. Which property of the CheckBox control indicates whether it is checked? a) IsChecked b) Selected c) Checked d) Value *Answer: c) Checked*

10. Which property is used to group RadioButton controls for single selection? a) Group b) GroupName c) RadioGroup d) SelectionGroup *Answer: b) GroupName*

11. Which control displays a list of items in a dropdown menu? a) ListBox b) RadioButtonList c) DropDownList d) CheckBoxList *Answer: c) DropDownList*

12. Which control displays a list of items and supports multiple selections? a) DropDownList b) ListBox c) RadioButtonList d) CheckBoxList *Answer: b) ListBox*

13. Which control is used to create a hyperlink? a) Link b) Hyperlink c) LinkButton d) HyperLink *Answer: d) HyperLink*

14. Which control is used to display an image? a) ImageControl b) Image c) Picture d) Img *Answer: b) Image*

15. Which property of the HyperLink control specifies the URL to navigate to? a) URL b) NavigateURL c) Href d) LinkURL *Answer: b) NavigateURL*

16. Which property of the Image control specifies the URL of the image? a) Source b) ImageURL c) URL d) ImageSource *Answer: b) ImageURL*

`17. What does the ~ symbol represent in the ImageUrl property?` a) The user's home directory b) The current directory c) The application's root directory d) The server's root directory *Answer: c) The application's root directory*

18. Which control allows users to select a date? a) DateTimePicker b) DatePicker c) Calendar d) DayPicker *Answer: c) Calendar*

19. Which control enables users to upload files? a) FileUploader b) FileUpload c) UploadControl d) InputFile *Answer: b) FileUpload*

20. Which control displays rotating banner advertisements? a) BannerRotator b) AdBanner c) AdRotator d) ImageRotator *Answer: c) AdRotator*

21. Which event of the Calendar control is raised when a date is selected? a) DateChanged b) SelectedDateChanged c) SelectionChanged d) DayClick *Answer: c) SelectionChanged*

22. Which property of the FileUpload control indicates whether a file has been selected? a) HasFile b) FileSelected c) IsFile d) FileAvailable *Answer: a) HasFile*

23. Which property of the AdRotator control specifies the XML file containing ad information? a) AdFile b) AdvertisementFile c) AdSource d) AdData *Answer: b) AdvertisementFile*

24. Which control is used to group other controls? a) GroupBox b) Container c) Panel d) Section *Answer: c) Panel*

25. Which control is used to dynamically add controls at runtime? a) DynamicPanel b) ControlContainer c) PlaceHolder d) AddControl *Answer: c) PlaceHolder*

26. What is the default HTML element rendered by the Panel control? a) <span> b) <div> c) <form> d) <table> *Answer: b) <div>*

27. Which property of the Panel control is used to set its visibility? a) Display b) Visible c) Show d) IsVisible *Answer: b) Visible*

28. Which collection of the PlaceHolder control is used to add dynamic controls? a) Controls b) Items c) Children d) Elements *Answer: a) Controls*

29. Can a Panel control contain other Panel controls? a) Yes b) No *Answer: a) Yes*

30. Does PlaceHolder control render any HTML element by itself? a) Yes b) No *Answer: b) No*

10 MID SIZE QUESTION WITH ANSWER

1. Explain the differences between the DropDownList and ListBox controls. When would you choose one over the other, and why?

- **Answer:**
  - `DropDownList`: Displays a single-selection dropdown menu. It's space-efficient when the list of options is moderately sized and you only need the user to choose one.
  - `ListBox`: Displays a list of items, and can be configured for single or multiple selection. It takes up more space but allows users to see more options at once.
  - **When to choose:**
    - Use `DropDownList` when space is limited, and the user only needs to select one option (e.g., selecting a country).
    - Use `ListBox` when you need to display more options directly, or when you want to allow users to select multiple options (e.g., selecting multiple interests).

2. Describe the purpose of the NavigateUrl and ImageUrl properties of the HyperLink control. Provide examples of how they are used.

- **Answer:**
  - `NavigateUrl`: Specifies the URL that the hyperlink points to. When the user clicks the link, the browser will navigate to this URL.

        - Example: `<asp:HyperLink ID="lnkGoogle" runat="server" NavigateUrl="https://www.google.com" Text="Go to Google" />`
    - `ImageUrl`: Instead of text, displays an image as the hyperlink. The user clicks the image to navigate.
        - Example: `<asp:HyperLink ID="lnkHome" runat="server" NavigateUrl="~/Default.aspx" ImageUrl="~/images/home.gif" AlternateText="Home" />`
    - If both are set, the ImageUrl is typically shown.

3. Explain how to dynamically populate a DropDownList from a data source (e.g., a database table). Provide a code example.

- **Answer:** You populate a `DropDownList` by setting its `DataSource` property and calling `DataBind()`.
- **Example:**

```
protected void Page_Load(object sender, EventArgs e)
{
    if (!IsPostBack)
    {
        string connectionString = "YourConnectionString";
        string query = "SELECT id, name FROM categories";
        using (SqlConnection conn = new SqlConnection(connectionString))
        {
            using (SqlCommand cmd = new SqlCommand(query, conn))
            {
                conn.Open();
                SqlDataReader reader = cmd.ExecuteReader();
                ddlCategories.DataSource = reader;
                ddlCategories.DataTextField = "name";  // Text to display
                ddlCategories.DataValueField = "id";    // Value on postback
                ddlCategories.DataBind();
                ddlCategories.Items.Insert(0, new ListItem("Select Category",
"")); // Add default
            }
        }
    }
}
```

4. Describe the purpose and key properties of the Calendar control. How can you handle date selection?

- **Answer:**
    - Purpose: Provides a user-friendly interface for selecting dates.
    - Key Properties:
        - `SelectedDate`: The currently selected date.
        - `SelectionMode`: `Day`, `DayWeek`, `DayWeekMonth`.
        - `VisibleDate`: The month displayed.
        - `FirstDayOfWeek`: Sets the first day (Sunday, Monday...)

- Handling Selection: Use the `SelectionChanged` event. Set `AutoPostBack="true"` to trigger it.
  - Example:

```
protected void calDate_SelectionChanged(object sender, EventArgs e)
{
    lblSelected.Text = calDate.SelectedDate.ToShortDateString();
}
```

5. Explain the process of uploading a file using the FileUpload control. What are the key security considerations?

- **Answer:**
  1. In ASPX: `<form runat="server" enctype="multipart/form-data">` is essential. Add `<asp:FileUpload>` and a `Button`.
  2. In Code-Behind:
     - Check `fileUpload.HasFile`.
     - Use `fileUpload.PostedFile.SaveAs(Server.MapPath("~/uploads/") + filename)`
  - Security:
    - Validate file type (extension, MIME).
    - Limit file size (in web.config).
    - Store files outside the web root if possible.
    - Generate unique filenames.
    - Check permissions on the upload directory.

6. Describe the purpose of the AdRotator control. How does it work, and what are the key components involved?

- **Answer:**
  - Purpose: Displays rotating banner advertisements.
  - How it works: Reads ad information from an XML file. Selects an ad based on weights (Impressions) or randomly.
  - Key components:
    - `AdRotator` control in ASPX.
    - XML file (specified by `AdvertisementFile`): Contains ad details.
    - XML structure: `<Advertisements><Ad><ImageUrl>`, `<NavigateUrl>`, `<AlternateText>`, `<Impressions></Ad></Advertisements>`
  - The `AdRotator` control reads the XML, selects an ad, and renders the HTML for the image and link.

7. Explain the purpose of the Panel control and provide a scenario where it would be useful.

- **Answer:**
  - Purpose: A container for grouping other controls. Treats them as a unit.

- Useful for:
  - Showing/hiding a section of a form (e.g., advanced options).
  - Applying consistent styling to a group of controls.
  - Implementing collapsible sections.
  - Managing scrollable areas.
- Example: A login form with a "Forgot Password" section that can be shown/hidden using a Panel.

8. Explain the purpose of the PlaceHolder control. How does it differ from a Panel, and when would you use it?

- **Answer:**
  - Purpose: A container where you can *dynamically* add controls at runtime.
  - Difference from Panel: Panel renders a `<div>`; PlaceHolder renders nothing itself.
  - When to use: When the controls you need to display are not known at design time, but are created based on data or user interaction.
  - Example: Dynamically generating a form with a variable number of input fields based on a user-selected value.

9. How do you access the selected value of a DropDownList or ListBox control in the code-behind? Provide examples.

- **Answer:**
  - `DropDownList`: Use `ddl.SelectedValue` (to get the *value*) or `ddl.SelectedItem.Text` (to get the displayed *text*).
    - Example: `string selectedValue = ddlCity.SelectedValue;`
  - `ListBox`:
    - Single Selection: `lst.SelectedValue`, `lst.SelectedItem.Text` (same as DropDownList).
    - Multiple Selection: Use `lst.SelectedValues` (returns a `string[]`) or iterate through `lst.Items` and check the `item.Selected` property.
    - Example:

```
foreach (ListItem item in lstLanguages.Items)
{
    if (item.Selected)
    {
        //  Do something with item.Text and item.Value
    }
}
```

10. Explain how to use the OnDayRender event of the Calendar control to customize the appearance or behavior of individual days.

- **Answer:** The `OnDayRender` event fires for each day in the calendar as it's being rendered. You can use it to:
  - Disable specific dates.
  - Change the style of certain days (e.g., highlight holidays).
  - Add custom content to a day's cell.

- Example:

```
protected void cal_DayRender(object sender, DayRenderEventArgs e)
{
    if (e.Day.Date < DateTime.Today)  // Disable past dates
    {
        e.Day.IsSelectable = false;
        e.Cell.ForeColor = System.Drawing.Color.Gray;
    }
    if (e.Day.Date.DayOfWeek == DayOfWeek.Sunday) // Highlight Sundays
    {
         e.Cell.BackColor = System.Drawing.Color.LightYellow;
    }
}
```

    - Remember to add `OnDayRender="cal_DayRender"` to your Calendar control in the ASPX.

CHAPTER 6: VALIDATION CONTROLS AND USER INPUT

User input validation is critical in web development to ensure that the data entered by the user meets the required standards before it is processed or stored. ASP.NET provides a rich set of server-side validation controls that simplify this task. These controls are easy to use and integrate seamlessly with Web Forms.

RequiredFieldValidator in ASP.NET Web Forms

The `RequiredFieldValidator` is one of the essential validation controls in ASP.NET Web Forms. It plays a crucial role in ensuring data integrity by preventing users from submitting forms with empty required fields.

Purpose

As you mentioned, the primary purpose of the `RequiredFieldValidator` is to:

- Ensure that a user does not skip a required input field.
- Enforce that a specific control (like a `TextBox`, `DropDownList`, etc.) contains a value before the form can be considered valid and processed.

How it Works

The `RequiredFieldValidator` works by checking if the associated input control has a value other than its default empty state. For a `TextBox`, this means checking if the `Text` property is not an empty string (""). For other controls, the definition of "empty" might vary slightly.

Key Properties (Beyond the Basics)

- **`ID`**: A unique identifier for the validator control. This is how you can reference it in your code-behind, though you rarely need to do so directly.
- **`runat="server"`**: Indicates that this is a server-side control, processed by ASP.NET.
- **`ControlToValidate`**: This is the most important property. It specifies the `ID` of the control that this validator is associated with. The validator checks the value of *this* control.
- **`ErrorMessage`**: The text that is displayed to the user when the validation fails (i.e., when the input control is empty).
- **`ForeColor`**: Sets the color of the `ErrorMessage`. Commonly set to "Red" to visually indicate an error.
- **`Display`**: Controls how the error message is displayed. Possible values:

    - `None`: The error message is not displayed inline. You would typically use a `ValidationSummary` control to display errors.
    - `Static`: Space is reserved in the page layout for the error message, even if the field is valid. This prevents the page from jumping when an error message appears.
    - `Dynamic`: Space is only allocated for the error message when the field is invalid. This can cause the page layout to shift.
- **`EnableClientScript`**: A boolean property (default is `true`). If `true`, the validation is performed on the client-side using JavaScript (if the browser supports it) *before* the form is submitted to the server. This provides a better user experience by giving immediate feedback. If `false`, validation is only performed on the server-side.
- **`ValidationGroup`**: Allows you to group validators. Controls within the same validation group are validated together. This is useful when you have multiple sections in a form (e.g., "Personal Information" and "Address") and want to validate them separately (e.g., only validate "Personal Information" when a "Save Personal Info" button is clicked).

Example (as provided)

```
<asp:TextBox ID="txtName" runat="server"></asp:TextBox>
<asp:RequiredFieldValidator ID="rfvName" runat="server"
ControlToValidate="txtName"
    ErrorMessage="Name is required."
ForeColor="Red"></asp:RequiredFieldValidator>
```

Explanation

- `<asp:TextBox ID="txtName" runat="server"></asp:TextBox>`: This creates a standard text box where the user is expected to enter their name.
- `<asp:RequiredFieldValidator ...>`: This creates a validator that ensures the user enters something into the `txtName` text box.
    - `ControlToValidate="txtName"`: This is the crucial link. It tells the validator to check the value of the control with the ID "txtName".
    - `ErrorMessage="Name is required."`: This is the message that will be displayed to the user if they leave the `txtName` text box empty and try to submit the form.
    - `ForeColor="Red"`: This sets the error message text color to red, making it visually prominent.

Complete Example with a Button

Here's a more complete example with a button to submit the form and see the validator in action:

```
<%@ Page Language="C#" AutoEventWireup="true" CodeFile="WebForm1.aspx.cs"
Inherits="WebForm1" %>
<!DOCTYPE html>
<html xmlns="http://www.w3.org/1999/xhtml">
<head runat="server">
```

```
    <title>Required Field Validation</title>
</head>
<body>
    <form id="form1" runat="server">
        <div>
            <asp:Label ID="lblName" runat="server" Text="Name:"></asp:Label>
            <asp:TextBox ID="txtName" runat="server"></asp:TextBox>
            <asp:RequiredFieldValidator ID="rfvName" runat="server"
ControlToValidate="txtName"
                ErrorMessage="Name is required." ForeColor="Red"
Display="Dynamic"></asp:RequiredFieldValidator>
            <br />
            <asp:Label ID="lblEmail" runat="server"
Text="Email:"></asp:Label>
            <asp:TextBox ID="txtEmail" runat="server"></asp:TextBox>
            <asp:RequiredFieldValidator ID="rfvEmail" runat="server"
ControlToValidate="txtEmail"
                ErrorMessage="Email is required." ForeColor="Red"
Display="Dynamic"></asp:RequiredFieldValidator>
            <br />
            <asp:Button ID="btnSubmit" runat="server" Text="Submit"
OnClick="btnSubmit_Click" />
            <asp:Label ID="lblMessage" runat="server" Text=""></asp:Label>
        </div>
    </form>
</body>
</html>
```

Code-Behind (WebForm1.aspx.cs)

```
using System;

public partial class WebForm1 : System.Web.UI.Page
{
    protected void Page_Load(object sender, EventArgs e)
    {
        // No code needed here for basic validation.
    }

    protected void btnSubmit_Click(object sender, EventArgs e)
    {
        // This code will *only* execute if all validators on the page are
valid.
        lblMessage.Text = "Form submitted successfully! Name: " +
txtName.Text + ", Email: " + txtEmail.Text;
    }
}
```

Explanation of the Complete Example

1. **ASPX Markup:**
    - We have two input fields: `txtName` and `txtEmail`, each with its own `RequiredFieldValidator` (`rfvName` and `rfvEmail`).

- The `ControlToValidate` property of each validator is set to the `ID` of the corresponding text box.
    - The `ErrorMessage` and `ForeColor` are set for each validator.
    - `Display="Dynamic"` is used, so the error messages only appear when the fields are invalid.
    - A `Button` (`btnSubmit`) is included to trigger the form submission.
    - A `Label` (`lblMessage`) is used to display a success message *after* the form is successfully submitted (i.e., when all validations pass).
2. **Code-Behind:**
    - `Page_Load`: In a simple validation scenario, you don't need any code in the `Page_Load` event. The validators handle the checking.
    - `btnSubmit_Click`: This is the key. The ASP.NET page framework *automatically* checks the validity of all validators on the page *before* this event handler is executed.
        - If *any* of the validators are invalid, this `btnSubmit_Click` event handler is *not* called.
        - If *all* the validators are valid, this event handler *is* called.
    - Therefore, the code inside `btnSubmit_Click` only runs when the data is valid, and you can safely process it (e.g., save to a database).

CompareValidator in ASP.NET Web Forms

The `CompareValidator` is a versatile validation control that allows you to compare the value entered in one control with either:

- The value in another control.
- A constant value that you specify.

This makes it useful for a variety of validation scenarios beyond simply checking for an empty field.

Purpose

As you pointed out, the `CompareValidator`'s core function is to:

- Compare the value in one control to another or a constant.

This enables you to enforce rules like:

- Confirming that two password fields match.
- Ensuring that a numeric value is within a specific range.
- Checking if a date is greater than or less than another date.

Key Properties (Beyond the Basics)

- **ID**: A unique identifier for the validator.
- **runat="server"**: Indicates server-side processing.
- **ControlToValidate**: Specifies the `ID` of the control whose value you want to validate. This is the control whose value is being *checked.*
- **ControlToCompare**: Specifies the `ID` of the control whose value you want to compare against. If you're comparing against a constant, you don't use this property.
- **ValueToCompare**: Specifies a constant value to compare against. If you're comparing against another control, you don't use this property.
- **Operator**: Specifies the comparison operator. Possible values:
  - `Equal` (default): Checks if the values are equal.
  - `NotEqual`: Checks if the values are not equal.
  - `GreaterThan`: Checks if the value in `ControlToValidate` is greater than the comparison value.
  - `GreaterThanEqual`: Checks if the value in `ControlToValidate` is greater than or equal to the comparison value.
  - `LessThan`: Checks if the value in `ControlToValidate` is less than the comparison value.
  - `LessThanEqual`: Checks if the value in `ControlToValidate` is less than or equal to the comparison value.
  - `DataTypeCheck`: Checks if the value in `ControlToValidate` can be converted to the data type specified by the `Type` property. This operator does not perform a comparison.
- **Type**: Specifies the data type of the values being compared. This is important for correct comparisons. Possible values:
  - `String` (default): Performs a string comparison.
  - `Integer`: Performs an integer comparison.
  - `Double`: Performs a double (floating-point) comparison.
  - `Date`: Performs a date comparison.
  - `Currency`: Performs a currency comparison.
- **ErrorMessage**: The message displayed to the user if the validation fails.
- **ForeColor**: Sets the color of the error message.
- **Display**: Controls how the error message is displayed (as explained for `RequiredFieldValidator`).
- **EnableClientScript**: Enables client-side validation.
- **ValidationGroup**: Allows you to group validators.

Example 1: Confirm Password (as provided)

```
<asp:TextBox ID="txtPassword" runat="server"
TextMode="Password"></asp:TextBox>
<asp:TextBox ID="txtConfirmPassword" runat="server"
TextMode="Password"></asp:TextBox>
<asp:CompareValidator ID="cvPassword" runat="server"
ControlToValidate="txtConfirmPassword"
```

```
    ControlToCompare="txtPassword" ErrorMessage="Passwords do not match."
ForeColor="Red" Display="Dynamic"></asp:CompareValidator>
```

Explanation

- Two `TextBox` controls (`txtPassword` and `txtConfirmPassword`) are used for entering and confirming a password. `TextMode="Password"` masks the input.
- The `CompareValidator` (`cvPassword`) is used to ensure that the value in `txtConfirmPassword` is the same as the value in `txtPassword`.
    - `ControlToValidate="txtConfirmPassword"`: The validator checks the value of the "Confirm Password" field.
    - `ControlToCompare="txtPassword"`: The validator compares the "Confirm Password" field's value against the "Password" field's value.
    - `ErrorMessage="Passwords do not match."`: The error message displayed if the values are different.
    - `ForeColor="Red"` and `Display="Dynamic"`: Styling for the error message.

Example 2: Numeric Comparison (as provided)

```
<asp:TextBox ID="txtAge" runat="server"></asp:TextBox>
<asp:CompareValidator ID="cvAge" runat="server" ControlToValidate="txtAge"
Operator="GreaterThanEqual"
    Type="Integer" ValueToCompare="18" ErrorMessage="Age must be 18 or
older." ForeColor="Red" Display="Dynamic"></asp:CompareValidator>
```

Explanation

- A `TextBox` (`txtAge`) is used for entering age.
- The `CompareValidator` (`cvAge`) ensures that the entered age is 18 or older.
    - `ControlToValidate="txtAge"`: The validator checks the value of the "Age" field.
    - `Operator="GreaterThanEqual"`: The comparison operator is set to "greater than or equal to".
    - `Type="Integer"`: The values are treated as integers for the comparison.
    - `ValueToCompare="18"`: The validator compares the age against the constant value 18.
    - `ErrorMessage="Age must be 18 or older."`: The error message.
    - `ForeColor="Red"` and `Display="Dynamic"`: Styling.

Complete Example with a Form

Here's a more complete example demonstrating both types of comparisons:

```
<%@ Page Language="C#" AutoEventWireup="true"
CodeFile="CompareValidatorExample.aspx.cs" Inherits="CompareValidatorExample"
%>
```

```
<!DOCTYPE html>
<html xmlns="http://www.w3.org/1999/xhtml">
<head runat="server">
    <title>CompareValidator Example</title>
</head>
<body>
    <form id="form1" runat="server">
        <div>
            <h2>Registration Form</h2>
            <asp:Label ID="lblName" runat="server" Text="Name:"></asp:Label>
            <asp:TextBox ID="txtName" runat="server"></asp:TextBox>
            <asp:RequiredFieldValidator ID="rfvName" runat="server"
ControlToValidate="txtName"
                ErrorMessage="Name is required." ForeColor="Red"
Display="Dynamic"></asp:RequiredFieldValidator>
            <br />
            <asp:Label ID="lblAge" runat="server" Text="Age:"></asp:Label>
            <asp:TextBox ID="txtAge" runat="server"></asp:TextBox>
            <asp:CompareValidator ID="cvAge" runat="server"
ControlToValidate="txtAge" Operator="GreaterThanEqual"
                Type="Integer" ValueToCompare="18" ErrorMessage="Age must be
18 or older." ForeColor="Red" Display="Dynamic"></asp:CompareValidator>
            <br />
            <asp:Label ID="lblPassword" runat="server"
Text="Password:"></asp:Label>
            <asp:TextBox ID="txtPassword" runat="server"
TextMode="Password"></asp:TextBox>
            <asp:RequiredFieldValidator ID="rfvPassword" runat="server"
ControlToValidate="txtPassword"
                ErrorMessage="Password is required" ForeColor="Red"
Display="Dynamic"></asp:RequiredFieldValidator>
            <br />
            <asp:Label ID="lblConfirmPassword" runat="server" Text="Confirm
Password:"></asp:Label>
            <asp:TextBox ID="txtConfirmPassword" runat="server"
TextMode="Password"></asp:TextBox>
            <asp:CompareValidator ID="cvPassword" runat="server"
ControlToValidate="txtConfirmPassword"
                ControlToCompare="txtPassword" ErrorMessage="Passwords do not
match." ForeColor="Red" Display="Dynamic"></asp:CompareValidator>
            <br />
            <asp:Button ID="btnRegister" runat="server" Text="Register"
OnClick="btnRegister_Click" />
            <asp:Label ID="lblMessage" runat="server" Text=""></asp:Label>
        </div>
    </form>
</body>
</html>
```

Code-Behind (CompareValidatorExample.aspx.cs)

```
using System;

public partial class CompareValidatorExample : System.Web.UI.Page
{
```

```
    protected void Page_Load(object sender, EventArgs e)
    {
        // No code needed here for basic validation.
    }

    protected void btnRegister_Click(object sender, EventArgs e)
    {
        // This code only runs if all validators are valid.
        lblMessage.Text = "Registration successful!  Name: " + txtName.Text +
", Age: " + txtAge.Text;
    }
}
```

This example demonstrates how to use `CompareValidator` for both comparing against another control (password confirmation) and comparing against a constant value (age validation), along with a `RequiredFieldValidator` to ensure name and password are not empty.

RangeValidator in ASP.NET Web Forms

The `RangeValidator` is used to ensure that the value entered by a user falls within a specified range. This is very useful for validating numerical data, dates, and even strings (lexicographical range).

Purpose

As you mentioned, the `RangeValidator`'s primary purpose is to:

- Ensure the user input falls within a specified range.

This allows you to enforce rules like:

- An age must be between 18 and 65.
- A date must be within a specific time period.
- A product quantity must be between a minimum and maximum value.

Key Properties (Beyond the Basics)

- **`ID`**: A unique identifier for the validator control.
- **`runat="server"`**: Indicates that this is a server-side control, processed by ASP.NET.
- **`ControlToValidate`**: Specifies the `ID` of the control whose value you want to validate.
- **`MinimumValue`**: Specifies the lower bound of the range.
- **`MaximumValue`**: Specifies the upper bound of the range.
- **`Type`**: Specifies the data type of the values being compared. Crucial for correct range checking. Possible values:
    - `String` (default): Performs a string comparison (lexicographical).

- `Integer`: Performs an integer comparison.
    - `Double`: Performs a double (floating-point) comparison.
    - `Date`: Performs a date comparison.
    - `Currency`: Performs a currency comparison.
- **`ErrorMessage`**: The message displayed to the user if the validation fails.
- **`ForeColor`**: Sets the color of the error message.
- **`Display`**: Controls how the error message is displayed (as explained for `RequiredFieldValidator`).
- **`EnableClientScript`**: Enables client-side validation using JavaScript.
- **`ValidationGroup`**: Allows you to group validators.

Example (Age Check) (as provided)

```
<asp:TextBox ID="txtAge" runat="server"></asp:TextBox>
<asp:RangeValidator ID="rvAge" runat="server" ControlToValidate="txtAge"
    MinimumValue="18" MaximumValue="60" Type="Integer"
    ErrorMessage="Age must be between 18 and 60." ForeColor="Red"
Display="Dynamic"></asp:RangeValidator>
```

Explanation

- `<asp:TextBox ID="txtAge" runat="server"></asp:TextBox>`: This creates a text box where the user enters their age.
- `<asp:RangeValidator ...>`: This creates a validator to check if the entered age is within the valid range.
    - `ControlToValidate="txtAge"`: Specifies that the validator checks the value of the `txtAge` control.
    - `MinimumValue="18"`: Sets the minimum allowed age to 18.
    - `MaximumValue="60"`: Sets the maximum allowed age to 60.
    - `Type="Integer"`: Specifies that the comparison should be done using integer values.
    - `ErrorMessage="Age must be between 18 and 60."`: The error message displayed if the age is outside the range.
    - `ForeColor="Red"` and `Display="Dynamic"`: Styling for the error message.

Complete Example with a Form

Here's a more complete example with a form and other controls:

```
<%@ Page Language="C#" AutoEventWireup="true"
CodeFile="RangeValidatorExample.aspx.cs" Inherits="RangeValidatorExample" %>

<!DOCTYPE html>
<html xmlns="http://www.w3.org/1999/xhtml">

<head runat="server">
    <title>RangeValidator Example</title>
```

```
</head>

<body>
    <form id="form1" runat="server">
        <div>
            <h2>Registration Form</h2>
            <asp:Label ID="lblName" runat="server" Text="Name:"></asp:Label>
            <asp:TextBox ID="txtName" runat="server"></asp:TextBox>
            <asp:RequiredFieldValidator ID="rfvName" runat="server"
ControlToValidate="txtName"
                ErrorMessage="Name is required." ForeColor="Red"
Display="Dynamic"></asp:RequiredFieldValidator>
            <br />
            <asp:Label ID="lblAge" runat="server" Text="Age:"></asp:Label>
            <asp:TextBox ID="txtAge" runat="server"></asp:TextBox>
            <asp:RangeValidator ID="rvAge" runat="server"
ControlToValidate="txtAge" MinimumValue="18"
                MaximumValue="60" Type="Integer" ErrorMessage="Age must be
between 18 and 60."
                ForeColor="Red" Display="Dynamic"></asp:RangeValidator>
            <br />
            <asp:Label ID="lblDate" runat="server" Text="Date of
Birth:"></asp:Label>
            <asp:TextBox ID="txtDOB" runat="server"></asp:TextBox>
            <asp:RangeValidator ID="rvDOB" runat="server"
ControlToValidate="txtDOB" MinimumValue="01/01/1950"
                MaximumValue="12/31/2005" Type="Date"
                ErrorMessage="Date of Birth must be between 01/01/1950 and
12/31/2005." ForeColor="Red"
                Display="Dynamic"></asp:RangeValidator>
            <br />
            <asp:Button ID="btnRegister" runat="server" Text="Register"
OnClick="btnRegister_Click" />
            <asp:Label ID="lblMessage" runat="server" Text=""></asp:Label>
        </div>
    </form>
</body>

</html>
```

Code-Behind (RangeValidatorExample.aspx.cs)

```
using System;

public partial class RangeValidatorExample : System.Web.UI.Page
{
    protected void Page_Load(object sender, EventArgs e)
    {
        // No code needed here for basic validation.
    }

    protected void btnRegister_Click(object sender, EventArgs e)
    {
        // This code only runs if all validators are valid.
```

```
        lblMessage.Text = "Registration successful!  Name: " + txtName.Text +
", Age: " + txtAge.Text +
                ", Date of Birth: " + txtDOB.Text;
    }
}
```

Explanation of the Complete Example

1. **ASPX Markup:**
   - We have three input fields: `txtName`, `txtAge`, and `txtDOB`.
   - `txtName` has a `RequiredFieldValidator` to ensure it's not empty.
   - `txtAge` has a `RangeValidator` (`rvAge`) to check the age range (18-60).
   - `txtDOB` has a `RangeValidator` (`rvDOB`) to check the date of birth range. Note that `Type="Date"` is used, and the `MinimumValue` and `MaximumValue` are date strings in a format that ASP.NET can understand (MM/DD/YYYY).
   - A `Button` (`btnRegister`) triggers the form submission.
   - A `Label` (`lblMessage`) displays a success message if all validations pass.
2. **Code-Behind:**
   - `Page_Load`: No code is needed here for basic validation.
   - `btnRegister_Click`: This code executes *only* if all validators on the page are valid. It displays a success message with the entered data.

RegularExpressionValidator in ASP.NET Web Forms

The `RegularExpressionValidator` is a powerful and flexible validation control that allows you to validate user input against a pattern defined by a regular expression. This enables you to enforce complex data formats and rules.

Purpose

As you mentioned, the primary purpose of the `RegularExpressionValidator` is to:

- Check the input against a regular expression pattern.

This is useful for validating a wide range of data formats, including:

- Email addresses
- Phone numbers
- ZIP codes
- Social Security numbers
- Dates in specific formats
- Custom formats

Key Properties (Beyond the Basics)

- **`ID`**: A unique identifier for the validator control.
- **`runat="server"`**: Indicates that this is a server-side control, processed by ASP.NET.
- **`ControlToValidate`**: Specifies the `ID` of the control whose value you want to validate.
- **`ValidationExpression`**: This is the most important property. It specifies the regular expression pattern that the input value must match.
- **`ErrorMessage`**: The message displayed to the user if the validation fails.
- **`ForeColor`**: Sets the color of the error message.
- **`Display`**: Controls how the error message is displayed (as explained for `RequiredFieldValidator`).
- **`EnableClientScript`**: Enables client-side validation using JavaScript.
- **`ValidationGroup`**: Allows you to group validators.

Example (Email Validation) (as provided)

```
<asp:TextBox ID="txtEmail" runat="server"></asp:TextBox>
<asp:RegularExpressionValidator ID="revEmail" runat="server"
ControlToValidate="txtEmail"
    ValidationExpression="\w+([-+.']\w+)*@\w+([-.]\w+)*\.\w+([-.]\w+)*"
    ErrorMessage="Enter a valid email address." ForeColor="Red"
Display="Dynamic"></asp:RegularExpressionValidator>
```

Explanation

- `<asp:TextBox ID="txtEmail" runat="server"></asp:TextBox>`: This creates a text box where the user enters their email address.
- `<asp:RegularExpressionValidator ...>`: This creates a validator to check if the entered email address is in a valid format.
  - `ControlToValidate="txtEmail"`: Specifies that the validator checks the value of the `txtEmail` control.
  - `ValidationExpression="\w+([-+.']\w+)*@\w+([-.]\w+)*\.\w+([-.]\w+)*"`: This is the regular expression pattern. It's a common (though not perfect) pattern for validating email addresses.
  - `ErrorMessage="Enter a valid email address."`: The error message displayed if the email address doesn't match the pattern.
  - `ForeColor="Red"` and `Display="Dynamic"`: Styling for the error message.

Understanding the Regular Expression (Email)

The regular expression used in the example is designed to match a typical email address format. Here's a breakdown:

- `\w+`: One or more word characters (letters, digits, underscore). (Part before the "@")

- `([-+.']\w+)*`: Zero or more occurrences of: a hyphen, plus sign, period, or apostrophe, followed by one or more word characters. (Allows for things like "user.name" or "user-name")
- `@`: The "@" symbol.
- `\w+`: One or more word characters. (Domain name part)
- `([-.]\w+)*`: Zero or more occurrences of: a hyphen or period, followed by one or more word characters. (Allows for subdomains)
- `\.`: A literal period (.).
- `\w+`: One or more word characters. (Top-level domain, e.g., "com", "org", "net")
- `([-.]\w+)*`: Zero or more occurrences of: a hyphen or period, followed by one or more word characters.

Important Notes on Email Validation Regex:

- This regex is a good starting point, but *perfectly* validating email addresses is extremely complex due to the many valid formats. More robust solutions often involve sending a confirmation email.
- For simpler validation, you might use a less strict regex, depending on your requirements.

More Examples

Here are some additional examples of using `RegularExpressionValidator` with different patterns:

1. Phone Number Validation (US Format)

```
<asp:TextBox ID="txtPhone" runat="server"></asp:TextBox>
<asp:RegularExpressionValidator ID="revPhone" runat="server"
ControlToValidate="txtPhone"
    ValidationExpression="^\(\d{3}\) \d{3}-\d{4}$"
    ErrorMessage="Enter phone number in (XXX) XXX-XXXX format."
ForeColor="Red" Display="Dynamic"></asp:RegularExpressionValidator>
```

- `^\(\d{3}\) \d{3}-\d{4}$`: This regex matches a phone number in the format (XXX) XXX-XXXX, where X is a digit.
    - `^`: Matches the beginning of the string.
    - `\(`: Matches a literal "("
    - `\d{3}`: Matches exactly three digits.
    - `\)`: Matches a literal ")"
    - : Matches a space
    - `-`: Matches a hyphen
    - `$`: Matches the end of the string.

2. ZIP Code Validation (US Format)

```
<asp:TextBox ID="txtZip" runat="server"></asp:TextBox>
```

```
<asp:RegularExpressionValidator ID="revZip" runat="server"
ControlToValidate="txtZip"
    ValidationExpression="^\d{5}(-\d{4})?$"
    ErrorMessage="Enter ZIP code in XXXXX or XXXXX-XXXX format."
ForeColor="Red" Display="Dynamic"></asp:RegularExpressionValidator>
```

- `^\d{5}(-\d{4})?$`: This regex matches a 5-digit ZIP code or a 5-digit ZIP code followed by a hyphen and 4 more digits.
    - `\d{5}`: Matches exactly five digits.
    - `(-\d{4})?`: Matches an optional group consisting of a hyphen and four digits. The `?` makes the group optional.

3. Date Validation (MM/DD/YYYY Format)

```
<asp:TextBox ID="txtDate" runat="server"></asp:TextBox>
<asp:RegularExpressionValidator ID="revDate" runat="server"
ControlToValidate="txtDate"
    ValidationExpression="^(0[1-9]|1[0-2])/(0[1-9]|[12][0-9]|3[01])/\d{4}$"
    ErrorMessage="Enter date in MM/DD/YYYY format." ForeColor="Red"
Display="Dynamic"></asp:RegularExpressionValidator>
```

- `^(0[1-9]|1[0-2])/(0[1-9]|[12][0-9]|3[01])/\d{4}$`: This regex matches a date in MM/DD/YYYY format.
    - `(0[1-9]|1[0-2])`: Matches months 01-09 or 10-12.
    - `(0[1-9]|[12][0-9]|3[01])`: Matches days 01-09, 10-29, or 30-31
    - `\d{4}`: Matches a four-digit year.

4. Custom Pattern (Username Validation)

```
<asp:TextBox ID="txtUsername" runat="server"></asp:TextBox>
<asp:RegularExpressionValidator ID="revUsername" runat="server"
ControlToValidate="txtUsername"
    ValidationExpression="^[a-zA-Z0-9_]{6,20}$"
    ErrorMessage="Username must be 6-20 characters, letters, numbers, or
underscore." ForeColor="Red"
Display="Dynamic"></asp:RegularExpressionValidator>
```

- `^[a-zA-Z0-9_]{6,20}$`: This regex matches a username that is 6 to 20 characters long and contains only letters, numbers, or underscores.
    - `^`: Start of string
    - `[a-zA-Z0-9_]`: Character class matching letters, numbers, or underscores.
    - `{6,20}`: Quantifier matching 6 to 20 occurrences of the preceding character class.
    - `$`: End of string

Complete Example with a Form

```
<%@ Page Language="C#" AutoEventWireup="true"
CodeFile="RegularExpressionValidatorExample.aspx.cs"
    Inherits="RegularExpressionValidatorExample" %>

<!DOCTYPE html>
<html xmlns="http://www.w3.org/1999/xhtml">

<head runat="server">
    <title>Regular Expression Validator</title>
</head>

<body>
    <form id="form1" runat="server">
        <div>
            <h2>Registration Form</h2>
            <asp:Label ID="lblName" runat="server" Text="Name:"></asp:Label>
            <asp:TextBox ID="txtName" runat="server"></asp:TextBox>
            <asp:RequiredFieldValidator ID="rfvName" runat="server"
ControlToValidate="txtName"
                ErrorMessage="Name is required." ForeColor="Red"
Display="Dynamic"></asp:RequiredFieldValidator>
            <br />
            <asp:Label ID="lblEmail" runat="server"
Text="Email:"></asp:Label>
            <asp:TextBox ID="txtEmail" runat="server"></asp:TextBox>
            <asp:RegularExpressionValidator ID="revEmail" runat="server"
ControlToValidate="txtEmail"
                ValidationExpression="\w+([-+.']\w+)*@\w+([-.]\w+)*\.\w+([-
.]\w+)*"
                ErrorMessage="Enter a valid email address." ForeColor="Red"
Display="Dynamic"></asp:RegularExpressionValidator>
            <br />
            <asp:Label ID="lblPhone" runat="server" Text="Phone (XXX) XXX-
XXXX:"></asp:Label>
            <asp:TextBox ID="txtPhone" runat="server"></asp:TextBox>
            <asp:RegularExpressionValidator ID="revPhone" runat="server"
                ControlToValidate="txtPhone" ValidationExpression="^\(\d{3}\)
\d{3}-\d{4}$"
                ErrorMessage="Enter phone number in (XXX) XXX-XXXX format."
ForeColor="Red"
                Display="Dynamic"></asp:RegularExpressionValidator>
            <br />
            <asp:Button ID="btnRegister" runat="server" Text="Register"
OnClick="btnRegister_Click" />
            <asp:Label ID="lblMessage" runat="server" Text=""></asp:Label>
        </div>
    </form>
</body>

</html>
```

Code-Behind (RegularExpressionValidatorExample.aspx.cs)

```
using System;
```

```
public partial class RegularExpressionValidatorExample : System.Web.UI.Page
{
    protected void Page_Load(object sender, EventArgs e)
    {
        // No code needed here for basic validation.
    }

    protected void btnRegister_Click(object sender, EventArgs e)
    {
        // This code only runs if all validators are valid.
        lblMessage.Text = "Registration successful!  Name: " + txtName.Text +
", Email: " + txtEmail.Text +
            ", Phone: " + txtPhone.Text;
    }
}
```

This example demonstrates how to use `RegularExpressionValidator` to validate email and phone number formats, along with a `RequiredFieldValidator` to ensure the name field is not empty.

CustomValidator in ASP.NET Web Forms

The `CustomValidator` is the most flexible of the ASP.NET validation controls. It allows you to implement your *own* validation logic, either on the server-side, the client-side (using JavaScript), or both. This is essential when the built-in validators (`RequiredFieldValidator`, `CompareValidator`, `RangeValidator`, `RegularExpressionValidator`) don't provide the specific validation rules you need.

Purpose

As you mentioned, the primary purpose of the `CustomValidator` is to:

- Allow for custom server-side or client-side validation logic.

This is necessary for scenarios such as:

- Checking if a username is unique in a database.
- Validating complex business rules that involve multiple fields.
- Performing cross-field validation that the other validators can't handle.
- Implementing sophisticated client-side validation for a better user experience.

Key Properties (Beyond the Basics)

- **`ID`**: A unique identifier for the validator control.
- **`runat="server"`**: Indicates that this is a server-side control, processed by ASP.NET.

- **ControlToValidate**: Specifies the ID of the control whose value you want to validate.
- **OnServerValidate**: Specifies the name of the server-side event handler method that will perform the validation.
- **ClientValidationFunction**: Specifies the name of the JavaScript function that will perform the client-side validation.
- **ErrorMessage**: The message displayed to the user if the validation fails.
- **ForeColor**: Sets the color of the error message.
- **Display**: Controls how the error message is displayed (as explained for RequiredFieldValidator).
- **ValidateEmptyText**: Boolean property. If set to true, the validator function will be called even if the validated control is empty. The default value is false.
- **ValidationGroup**: Allows you to group validators.

Example 1: Custom Server-Side Validation (as provided)

```
<asp:TextBox ID="txtUsername" runat="server"></asp:TextBox>
<asp:CustomValidator ID="cvUsername" runat="server"
ControlToValidate="txtUsername"
    OnServerValidate="cvUsername_ServerValidate" ErrorMessage="Invalid
username." ForeColor="Red" Display="Dynamic"></asp:CustomValidator>
```

Code-Behind (C#)

```
protected void cvUsername_ServerValidate(object source,
ServerValidateEventArgs args)
{
    if (args.Value.Length >= 6)
        args.IsValid = true;
    else
        args.IsValid = false;
}
```

Explanation

- `<asp:TextBox ID="txtUsername" runat="server"></asp:TextBox>`: This creates a text box where the user enters a username.
- `<asp:CustomValidator ...>`: This creates a validator to check if the username meets the custom validation rule.
    - ControlToValidate="txtUsername": Specifies that the validator checks the value of the txtUsername control.
    - OnServerValidate="cvUsername_ServerValidate": Specifies the name of the server-side method (cvUsername_ServerValidate) that will perform the validation.
    - ErrorMessage="Invalid username.": The error message displayed if the username is invalid.
    - ForeColor="Red" and Display="Dynamic": Styling.
- **Code-Behind:**

- cvUsername_ServerValidate(object source, ServerValidateEventArgs args):
    - This is the server-side event handler.
    - args.Value: Contains the value from the txtUsername control.
    - args.IsValid: You *must* set this property to true if the value is valid, and false if it's invalid.
    - In this example, the code checks if the username is at least 6 characters long.

Example 2: Custom Client-Side Validation

```
<asp:TextBox ID="txtPassword" runat="server"
TextMode="Password"></asp:TextBox>
<asp:CustomValidator ID="cvPasswordStrength" runat="server"
ControlToValidate="txtPassword"
    ClientValidationFunction="validatePasswordStrength"
OnServerValidate="cvPasswordStrength_ServerValidate"
    ErrorMessage="Password must be at least 8 characters with a number and a
symbol." ForeColor="Red" Display="Dynamic"></asp:CustomValidator>

<script type="text/javascript">
    function validatePasswordStrength(sender, args) {
        var password = document.getElementById("<%= txtPassword.ClientID
%>").value; //Get the value of the password
        var hasNumber = /\d/.test(password); //Check if the password has a
digit
        var hasSymbol = /[!@#$%^&*()_+\-
=\[\]{};':"\\|,.<>\/?]/.test(password); //Check if the password has a symbol

        args.IsValid = (password.length >= 8 && hasNumber && hasSymbol);
//Set the args is valid or not
    }
</script>
```

Code-Behind (C#)

```
protected void cvPasswordStrength_ServerValidate(object source,
ServerValidateEventArgs args)
{
    // Server-side check (same logic as client-side, for safety)
    string password = args.Value;
    bool hasNumber = System.Text.RegularExpressions.Regex.IsMatch(password,
@"\d");
    bool hasSymbol = System.Text.RegularExpressions.Regex.IsMatch(password,
@"[!@#$%^&*()_+\-=\[\]{};':""\\|,.<>\/?]");

    args.IsValid = (password.Length >= 8 && hasNumber && hasSymbol);
}
```

Explanation

- **ASPX Markup:**
    - `<asp:CustomValidator ...>`:
        - `ClientValidationFunction="validatePasswordStrength"`: Specifies the name of the JavaScript function (`validatePasswordStrength`) for client-side validation.
        - `OnServerValidate="cvPasswordStrength_ServerValidate"`: Specifies the server-side validation method.
- **`JavaScript (<script> block):`**
    - `validatePasswordStrength(sender, args)`:
        - This is the JavaScript function.
        - `sender`: The validator control.
        - `args`: An object with an `IsValid` property.
        - The code gets the password value from the `txtPassword` control using `document.getElementById("<%= txtPassword.ClientID %>").value;`. `<%= txtPassword.ClientID %>` is important; it renders the actual ID of the TextBox in the browser, which might be different from "txtPassword".
        - The code checks if the password is at least 8 characters long, contains a number, and contains a symbol, using regular expressions.
        - `args.IsValid = ...`: Sets the `IsValid` property to `true` or `false`.
- **Code-Behind (C#):**
    - `cvPasswordStrength_ServerValidate(object source, ServerValidateEventArgs args)`:
        - This is the server-side event handler.
        - It performs the *same* validation logic as the JavaScript function. **This is crucial!** Client-side validation can be bypassed, so you *must* always validate on the server as well.

Key Points

- **Server-Side is Mandatory:** Always include server-side validation with `CustomValidator`, even if you have client-side validation. Client-side validation is a convenience for the user, but it's not secure on its own.
- **`Client-Side with <%= Control.ClientID %>`:** In your JavaScript, use `<%= Control.ClientID %>` to get the actual ID of the control you're validating. This ensures your JavaScript works correctly, as ASP.NET might change the ID in the rendered HTML.
- **Same Logic:** Ideally, your client-side and server-side validation logic should be as similar as possible to ensure consistency.
- **`ValidateEmptyText`** Property: If you want your custom validation logic to execute even when the associated input control is empty, set the `ValidateEmptyText` property of the `CustomValidator` to `true`. By default, it's `false`, meaning the custom validation function won't be called for empty controls.

The `CustomValidator` provides the ultimate flexibility for validation in ASP.NET Web Forms. By combining server-side and client-side logic, you can create robust and user-friendly validation rules for your web applications.

ValidationSummary in ASP.NET Web Forms

The `ValidationSummary` control is used to provide a consolidated view of all validation errors on a web page. Instead of displaying error messages next to each individual control, you can use a `ValidationSummary` to gather all the error messages and display them in a single location. This can improve the user experience, especially in forms with many fields.

Purpose

As you mentioned, the primary purpose of the `ValidationSummary` is to:

- Display a summary of all validation errors on the page.

This allows you to:

- Provide a centralized location for error messages.
- Offer a clearer overview of all the validation issues.
- Customize how the error messages are presented.

Key Properties (Beyond the Basics)

- **`ID`**: A unique identifier for the control.
- **`runat="server"`**: Indicates server-side processing.
- **`HeaderText`**: A string that appears as the title of the summary.
- **`ForeColor`**: Sets the color of the text in the summary.
- **`ShowSummary`**: A boolean property (default is `true`) that determines whether the summary is displayed on the page.
- **`ShowMessageBox`**: A boolean property (default is `false`) that determines whether the summary is displayed in a client-side message box.
- **`DisplayMode`**: Controls how the summary is displayed. Possible values:
    - `List` (default): Displays the errors as a bulleted list.
    - `BulletList`: Same as List.
    - `SingleParagraph`: Displays the errors as a single paragraph, separated by line breaks.
    - `None`: Suppresses the display of the summary itself, but you can still use `ShowMessageBox`.

- **`ValidationGroup`**: If you're using validation groups, the `ValidationSummary` will only display errors for validators in the same group.

Example (as provided)

```
<asp:ValidationSummary ID="vsSummary" runat="server" HeaderText="Please fix
the following errors:"
    ForeColor="Red" ShowMessageBox="false" ShowSummary="true" />
```

Explanation

- `<asp:ValidationSummary ...>`: This creates a ValidationSummary control.
  - `ID="vsSummary"`: Sets the ID.
  - `runat="server"`: Indicates server-side processing.
  - `HeaderText="Please fix the following errors:"`: Sets the title of the summary.
  - `ForeColor="Red"`: Sets the text color to red.
  - `ShowMessageBox="false"`: Prevents the errors from being displayed in a message box.
  - `ShowSummary="true"`: Ensures that the summary is displayed on the page.

Complete Example with a Form

Here's a complete example demonstrating how to use `ValidationSummary` with other validation controls:

```
<%@ Page Language="C#" AutoEventWireup="true"
CodeFile="ValidationSummaryExample.aspx.cs"
    Inherits="ValidationSummaryExample" %>

<!DOCTYPE html>
<html xmlns="http://www.w3.org/1999/xhtml">

<head runat="server">
    <title>Validation Summary Example</title>
</head>

<body>
    <form id="form1" runat="server">
        <div>
            <h2>Registration Form</h2>
            <asp:Label ID="lblName" runat="server" Text="Name:"></asp:Label>
            <asp:TextBox ID="txtName" runat="server"></asp:TextBox>
            <asp:RequiredFieldValidator ID="rfvName" runat="server"
ControlToValidate="txtName"
                ErrorMessage="Name is required." ForeColor="Red"
Display="Dynamic"></asp:RequiredFieldValidator>
            <br />
            <asp:Label ID="lblEmail" runat="server"
Text="Email:"></asp:Label>
```

```
            <asp:TextBox ID="txtEmail" runat="server"></asp:TextBox>
            <asp:RegularExpressionValidator ID="revEmail" runat="server"
ControlToValidate="txtEmail"
                ValidationExpression="\w+([-+.']\w+)*@\w+([-.]\w+)*\.\w+([-
.]\w+)*"
                ErrorMessage="Enter a valid email address." ForeColor="Red"
Display="Dynamic"></asp:RegularExpressionValidator>
            <br />
            <asp:Label ID="lblAge" runat="server" Text="Age:"></asp:Label>
            <asp:TextBox ID="txtAge" runat="server"></asp:TextBox>
            <asp:RangeValidator ID="rvAge" runat="server"
ControlToValidate="txtAge" MinimumValue="18"
                MaximumValue="60" Type="Integer" ErrorMessage="Age must be
between 18 and 60."
                ForeColor="Red" Display="Dynamic"></asp:RangeValidator>
            <br />
            <asp:ValidationSummary ID="vsSummary" runat="server"
HeaderText="Please fix the following errors:"
                ForeColor="Red" ShowMessageBox="false" ShowSummary="true" />
            <br />
            <asp:Button ID="btnRegister" runat="server" Text="Register"
OnClick="btnRegister_Click" />
            <asp:Label ID="lblMessage" runat="server" Text=""></asp:Label>
        </div>
    </form>
</body>

</html>
```

Code-Behind (ValidationSummaryExample.aspx.cs)

```
using System;

public partial class ValidationSummaryExample : System.Web.UI.Page
{
    protected void Page_Load(object sender, EventArgs e)
    {
        // No code needed here for basic validation.
    }

    protected void btnRegister_Click(object sender, EventArgs e)
    {
        // This code only runs if all validators are valid.
        lblMessage.Text = "Registration successful!  Name: " + txtName.Text +
", Email: " + txtEmail.Text +
            ", Age: " + txtAge.Text;
    }
}
```

Explanation of the Complete Example

1. **ASPX Markup:**

- We have three input fields: `txtName`, `txtEmail`, and `txtAge`, each with its own validator (`RequiredFieldValidator`, `RegularExpressionValidator`, and `RangeValidator`, respectively).
- The `Display="Dynamic"` property is set for each of these validators. This is important when using a `ValidationSummary` because it prevents the individual error messages from cluttering the page when the fields are valid.
- The `ValidationSummary` control (`vsSummary`) is included to display the error summary.
- A `Button` (`btnRegister`) triggers the form submission.
- A `Label` (`lblMessage`) displays a success message if all validations pass.

2. **Code-Behind:**
   - `Page_Load`: No code is needed here for basic validation.
   - `btnRegister_Click`: This code executes *only* if all validators on the page are valid. It displays a success message with the entered data.

Key Points

- **Complementary to Individual Validators:** The `ValidationSummary` works in conjunction with the individual validator controls (`RequiredFieldValidator`, `CompareValidator`, etc.). You still need those validators to perform the actual validation checks. The `ValidationSummary` simply provides a way to display their error messages collectively.
- **`DisplayMode`** Options:
  - `List` (or `BulletList`): The most common and user-friendly option.
  - `SingleParagraph`: Useful for very simple forms with only a few potential errors.
  - `None`: Use this if you only want to display the errors in a message box (`ShowMessageBox="true"`).
- **`ShowMessageBox`**: Using `ShowMessageBox="true"` will display a client-side alert box with the error messages *in addition* to the summary on the page. This can be useful for drawing extra attention to the errors, but it can also be disruptive to the user experience. Use it sparingly.
- **`ValidationGroup`**: If you have multiple sections in your form and are using validation groups, make sure your `ValidationSummary` has the same `ValidationGroup` value as the validators you want it to summarize. Otherwise, it will display *all* errors on the page, regardless of the group.

Summary

ASP.NET validation controls provide an efficient way to enforce data integrity and improve user experience. With minimal coding, you can apply powerful validation logic and combine multiple validators to ensure that all data entered into your web forms is correct and secure.

These controls support both client-side and server-side validation, making them powerful tools for building robust ASP.NET applications.

30 MCQ QUESTION WITH ANSWER

1. Which validator ensures that a control is not left blank? a) CompareValidator b) RangeValidator c) RequiredFieldValidator d) RegularExpressionValidator *Answer: c) RequiredFieldValidator*

2. Which property of the RequiredFieldValidator specifies the control to validate? a) Control b) ValidateControl c) ControlToValidate d) TargetControl *Answer: c) ControlToValidate*

3. Which validator compares the value of one control to another or a constant? a) RangeValidator b) CompareValidator c) RegularExpressionValidator d) CustomValidator *Answer: b) CompareValidator*

4. Which property of the CompareValidator specifies the comparison operator? a) Comparison b) Operator c) CompareOperator d) Operation *Answer: b) Operator*

5. Which property of the CompareValidator is used to compare against a constant value? a) CompareValue b) ValueToCompare c) ConstantValue d) ToCompare *Answer: b) ValueToCompare*

6. Which validator checks if a value is within a specified range? a) CompareValidator b) RangeValidator c) RegularExpressionValidator d) CustomValidator *Answer: b) RangeValidator*

7. Which property of the RangeValidator specifies the minimum value of the range? a) MinValue b) Minimum c) MinimumValue d) LowerBound *Answer: c) MinimumValue*

8. Which property of the RangeValidator specifies the maximum value of the range? a) MaxValue b) Maximum c) MaximumValue d) UpperBound *Answer: c) MaximumValue*

9. Which property of the RangeValidator and CompareValidator specifies the data type of the values being compared? a) DataType b) ValueType c) Type d) Format *Answer: c) Type*

10. Which validator checks the input against a regular expression pattern? a) CompareValidator b) RangeValidator c) RegularExpressionValidator d) CustomValidator *Answer: c) RegularExpressionValidator*

11. Which property of the RegularExpressionValidator specifies the regular expression pattern? a) Pattern b) Expression c) ValidationPattern d) ValidationExpression *Answer: d) ValidationExpression*

12. Which validator allows you to define custom validation logic? a) CompareValidator b) RangeValidator c) RegularExpressionValidator d) CustomValidator *Answer: d) CustomValidator*

13. Which event of the CustomValidator is used for server-side validation? a) OnValidate b) ServerValidate c) OnServerValidate d) ValidateServer *Answer: c) OnServerValidate*

14. Which property of the CustomValidator specifies the JavaScript function for client-side validation? a) ClientFunction b) ClientValidation c) ClientValidationFunction d) JSFunction *Answer: c) ClientValidationFunction*

15. Which control displays a summary of all validation errors on the page? a) ErrorSummary b) ValidationList c) ValidationSummary d) PageErrors *Answer: c) ValidationSummary*

16. Which property of the ValidationSummary sets the title of the summary? a) Title b) Header c) HeaderText d) SummaryHeader *Answer: c) HeaderText*

17. Which property of the ValidationSummary controls whether the summary is displayed on the page? a) Show b) Display c) ShowSummary d) Visible *Answer: c) ShowSummary*

18. Which property of the ValidationSummary controls whether the errors are displayed in a message box? a) MessageBox b) ShowBox c) ShowMessage d) ShowMessageBox *Answer: d) ShowMessageBox*

19. What is the default value of the ShowMessageBox property of the ValidationSummary? a) true b) false *Answer: b) false*

20. What is the default value of the ShowSummary property of the ValidationSummary? a) true b) false *Answer: a) true*

21. Which value of the Display property of a validator control prevents the error message from taking up space when the input is valid? a) None b) Static c) Dynamic d) Hidden *Answer: c) Dynamic*

22. Which value of the Display property of a validator control reserves space for the error message, even when the input is valid? a) None b) Static c) Dynamic d) Visible *Answer: b) Static*

23. Which property is used to group validation controls? a) Group b) ValidationGroup c) ControlGroup d) GroupName *Answer: b) ValidationGroup*

24. If the Type property of a RangeValidator is set to "Date", what format should the MinimumValue and MaximumValue be in? a) Any format b) MM/DD/YYYY c) YYYY-MM-DD d) A format that ASP.NET can understand. *Answer: d) A format that ASP.NET can understand.*

25. Which of the following is NOT a valid value for the Operator property of the CompareValidator? a) Equal b) NotEqual c) Contains d) GreaterThan *Answer: c) Contains*

26. Which of the following is a valid value for the Type property of the CompareValidator and RangeValidator? a) Boolean b) String c) Array d) Object *Answer: b) String*

27. What happens if a validation control's ControlToValidate property is not set? a) The validator validates itself. b) The validator validates the form. c) The validator throws an error. d) The validator does nothing. *Answer: d) The validator does nothing.*

28. Can a ValidationSummary display errors from validators in different ValidationGroups? a) Yes b) No *Answer: b) No*

29. Which control is best suited for validating an email address format? a) CompareValidator b) RangeValidator c) RegularExpressionValidator d) CustomValidator *Answer: c) RegularExpressionValidator*

30. When should you use a CustomValidator? a) When you need to compare two values. b) When you need to check a range of values. c) When you need to validate against a regular expression. d) When you need to implement validation logic that the other validators don't provide. *Answer: d) When you need to implement validation logic that the other validators don't provide.*

10 MID SIZE QUESTION WITH ANSWER

1. Explain the purpose of the RequiredFieldValidator, and provide an example of how to use it in an ASP.NET Web Forms page. Include both the ASPX markup and a brief explanation.

- **Answer:**
    - The `RequiredFieldValidator` ensures that a user does not leave a form field empty. It forces the user to enter some value into the associated control before the form can be submitted.
    - **Example (ASPX):**

```
<asp:TextBox ID="txtName" runat="server"></asp:TextBox>
<asp:RequiredFieldValidator ID="rfvName" runat="server"
ControlToValidate="txtName"
    ErrorMessage="Please enter your name." ForeColor="Red"
Display="Dynamic"></asp:RequiredFieldValidator>
<asp:Button ID="btnSubmit" runat="server" Text="Submit" />

* **Explanation:**
    * The `ControlToValidate` property of the `RequiredFieldValidator` is set
to the `ID` of the `TextBox` (`txtName`).
    * If the user tries to submit the form without entering anything in the
`txtName` TextBox, the `RequiredFieldValidator` will display the error
message "Please enter your name." in red.
    * The `Display="Dynamic"` attribute ensures that the error message only
appears when the validation fails.
```

2. Describe the CompareValidator and its primary use cases. Provide an example of how to validate that two TextBox controls have the same value.

- **Answer:**
  - The `CompareValidator` compares the value of one control to the value of another control or to a constant value. It's used to ensure that two values match, or that a value meets a specific comparison criterion.
  - **Use Cases:**
    - Confirming password fields.
    - Comparing dates.
    - Checking if a number is greater than another number.
  - **Example (ASPX):**

```
<asp:TextBox ID="txtPassword" runat="server"
TextMode="Password"></asp:TextBox>
<asp:TextBox ID="txtConfirmPassword" runat="server"
TextMode="Password"></asp:TextBox>
<asp:CompareValidator ID="cvPassword" runat="server"
ControlToValidate="txtConfirmPassword"
    ControlToCompare="txtPassword" ErrorMessage="Passwords do not match."
ForeColor="Red" Display="Dynamic"></asp:CompareValidator>
```

* In this example, the `CompareValidator` checks if the value in the `txtConfirmPassword` TextBox is equal to the value in the `txtPassword` TextBox.

3. Explain the RangeValidator and its purpose. Provide an example of validating that a user's age is within a specific range.

- **Answer:**
  - The `RangeValidator` ensures that the value entered by a user falls within a specified range. This range can be numeric, alphabetic, or date-based.
  - **Example (ASPX):**

```
<asp:TextBox ID="txtAge" runat="server"></asp:TextBox>
<asp:RangeValidator ID="rvAge" runat="server" ControlToValidate="txtAge"
    MinimumValue="18" MaximumValue="65" Type="Integer"
    ErrorMessage="Age must be between 18 and 65." ForeColor="Red"
Display="Dynamic"></asp:RangeValidator>
```

* This example validates that the value entered in the `txtAge` TextBox is an integer between 18 and 65 (inclusive). The `Type` property is set to "Integer" to ensure a numeric comparison.

4. Describe the RegularExpressionValidator and its purpose. Provide an example of validating an email address.

- **Answer:**

- The `RegularExpressionValidator` validates user input against a pattern defined by a regular expression. This provides a very flexible way to enforce complex data formats.
- **Example (ASPX):**

```
<asp:TextBox ID="txtEmail" runat="server"></asp:TextBox>
<asp:RegularExpressionValidator ID="revEmail" runat="server"
ControlToValidate="txtEmail"
    ValidationExpression="\w+([-+.']\w+)*@\w+([-.]\w+)*\.\w+([-.]\w+)*"
    ErrorMessage="Invalid email address." ForeColor="Red"
Display="Dynamic"></asp:RegularExpressionValidator>

* The `ValidationExpression` property contains a regular expression that
defines a common email address format.  The validator checks if the value in
the `txtEmail` TextBox matches this pattern.
```

5. Explain the CustomValidator and its primary use case. Provide an example of server-side validation to check if a username is unique.

- **Answer:**
  - The `CustomValidator` allows you to define your own, application-specific validation logic, either on the server-side or the client-side. It's used when the built-in validators are not sufficient.
  - **Use Case:** Checking against a database, performing complex business rule checks, or cross-field validation.
  - **Example (ASPX):**

```
<asp:TextBox ID="txtUsername" runat="server"></asp:TextBox>
<asp:CustomValidator ID="cvUsername" runat="server"
ControlToValidate="txtUsername"
    OnServerValidate="cvUsername_ServerValidate" ErrorMessage="Username is
already taken."
    ForeColor="Red" Display="Dynamic"></asp:CustomValidator>

* **Code-Behind (C#):**

protected void cvUsername_ServerValidate(object source,
ServerValidateEventArgs args)
{
    // In a real application, you would check against a database here.
    string usernameToCheck = args.Value;
    bool isUnique = !CheckIfUsernameExists(usernameToCheck); // Assume this
method checks the database

    args.IsValid = isUnique;
}

private bool CheckIfUsernameExists(string username)
{
    //  Replace this with your actual database query.  This is just a
placeholder.
    //  Example (using System.Data.SqlClient):
```

```
    //  string connectionString = "YourConnectionString";
    //  string query = "SELECT COUNT(*) FROM Users WHERE Username =
@Username";
    //  using (SqlConnection conn = new SqlConnection(connectionString))
    //  {
    //      using (SqlCommand cmd = new SqlCommand(query, conn))
    //      {
    //          cmd.Parameters.AddWithValue("@Username", username);
    //          conn.Open();
    //          int count = (int)cmd.ExecuteScalar();
    //          return count > 0; // Returns true if the username exists
    //      }
    //  }
    if (username == "testuser")
        return true;
    else
        return false;
}
```

* The `OnServerValidate` property points to the `cvUsername_ServerValidate` method. This method is called on the server to perform the custom validation. The `args.Value` property contains the value from the `txtUsername` TextBox. The `args.IsValid` property *must* be set to `true` if the validation succeeds, and `false` if it fails.

6. Explain the purpose of the ValidationSummary control. How does it work with the other validation controls?

- **Answer:**
  - The `ValidationSummary` control displays a consolidated summary of all validation errors on the page. It gathers the error messages from all the individual validator controls (e.g., `RequiredFieldValidator`, `CompareValidator`) and displays them in a single location.
  - It does *not* perform the validation itself. It relies on the other validator controls to do the actual checking. If any of the other validators on the page are invalid, the `ValidationSummary` will display their error messages.
  - It improves user experience by providing a clear overview of all errors, rather than displaying them inline next to each input field.

7. Describe the key properties of the ValidationSummary control and explain how they affect its behavior.

- **Answer:**
  - `HeaderText`: Sets the title or heading of the summary (e.g., "Please correct the following errors:").
  - `ForeColor`: Sets the color of the text in the summary (e.g., "Red" for error messages).
  - `ShowSummary`: A boolean value that determines whether the summary is displayed on the page. The default is `true`.

- `ShowMessageBox`: A boolean value that determines whether the errors are also displayed in a client-side message box (using JavaScript's `alert()`). The default is `false`.
- `DisplayMode`: Sets how the errors are displayed, can be a `List`, `BulletList`, or `SingleParagraph`.

8. Explain the difference between client-side and server-side validation in ASP.NET Web Forms. Which validation controls support client-side validation, and what are the benefits and drawbacks of each approach?

- **Answer:**
  - **Client-Side Validation:** Validation is performed in the user's browser using JavaScript *before* the form is submitted to the server.
    - **Benefits:** Faster feedback to the user, reduced server load.
    - **Drawbacks:** Can be bypassed if JavaScript is disabled; less secure than server-side.
  - **Server-Side Validation:** Validation is performed on the web server *after* the form data has been submitted.
    - **Benefits:** More secure, cannot be bypassed.
    - **Drawbacks:** Slower feedback to the user (requires a round trip to the server), increased server load.
  - **Controls Supporting Client-Side:** `RequiredFieldValidator`, `CompareValidator`, `RangeValidator`, `RegularExpressionValidator`, and `CustomValidator` (if you provide a `ClientValidationFunction`).
  - **Important:** *Always* perform server-side validation, even if you have client-side validation. Client-side validation is a user convenience, but server-side validation is a security requirement.

9. Explain the purpose of the ValidationGroup property. Provide a scenario where it would be useful, and give a brief example.

- **Answer:**
  - The `ValidationGroup` property allows you to group validation controls. Validators within the same group are validated together. This is useful when you have multiple sections in a form that you want to validate independently.
  - **Scenario:** A multi-step registration form (e.g., "Personal Information", "Address", "Payment"). You might have a "Save Personal Information" button that only validates the fields in the "Personal Information" group.
  - **Example (ASPX):**

```
<h2>Personal Information</h2>
<asp:Label ID="lblName" runat="server" Text="Name:"></asp:Label>
<asp:TextBox ID="txtName" runat="server"></asp:TextBox>
<asp:RequiredFieldValidator ID="rfvName" runat="server"
ControlToValidate="txtName"
    ErrorMessage="Name is required." ForeColor="Red"
ValidationGroup="Personal"></asp:RequiredFieldValidator><br />
<asp:Label ID="lblEmail" runat="server" Text="Email:"></asp:Label>
```

```
<asp:TextBox ID="txtEmail" runat="server"></asp:TextBox>
<asp:RegularExpressionValidator ID="revEmail" runat="server"
ControlToValidate="txtEmail"
    ValidationExpression="\w+([-+.']\w+)*@\w+([-.]\w+)*\.\w+([-.]\w+)*"
    ErrorMessage="Invalid email address." ForeColor="Red"
ValidationGroup="Personal"></asp:RegularExpressionValidator><br />
<asp:Button ID="btnSavePersonal" runat="server" Text="Save Personal Info"
ValidationGroup="Personal" /><br/>

<h2>Address Information</h2>
<asp:Label ID="lblStreet" runat="server" Text="Street:"></asp:Label>
<asp:TextBox ID="txtStreet" runat="server"></asp:TextBox>
<asp:RequiredFieldValidator ID="rfvStreet" runat="server"
ControlToValidate="txtStreet"
    ErrorMessage="Street is required." ForeColor="Red"
ValidationGroup="Address"></asp:RequiredFieldValidator><br />
<asp:Label ID="lblCity" runat="server" Text="City:"></asp:Label>
<asp:TextBox ID="txtCity" runat="server"></asp:TextBox>
<asp:RequiredFieldValidator ID="rfvCity" runat="server"
ControlToValidate="txtCity"
    ErrorMessage="City is required." ForeColor="Red"
ValidationGroup="Address"></asp:RequiredFieldValidator><br />
<asp:Button ID="btnSaveAddress" runat="server" Text="Save Address"
ValidationGroup="Address" /><br/>

<asp:ValidationSummary ID="vsPersonal" runat="server" HeaderText="Personal
Info Errors" ValidationGroup="Personal" /><br/>
<asp:ValidationSummary ID="vsAddress" runat="server" HeaderText="Address Info
Errors" ValidationGroup="Address" />

* In this example, the `btnSavePersonal` button has
`ValidationGroup="Personal"`, so it will only trigger validation for the
`rfvName` and `revEmail` validators.  The `btnSaveAddress` button will only
trigger validation for `rfvStreet` and `rfvCity`.  The ValidationSummary
controls are also grouped, so `vsPersonal` will only show errors for the
"Personal" group, and `vsAddress` will only show errors for the "Address"
group.
```

10. Explain how to use the CustomValidator to perform both client-side and server-side validation. Why is it important to perform validation on both the client and the server?

- **Answer:**
  - To use `CustomValidator` for both:
    - Set the `ClientValidationFunction` property to the name of a JavaScript function.
    - Set the `OnServerValidate` property to the name of a server-side event handler.
  - **Example (See the CustomValidator examples in the previous response for detailed code).**
  - **Importance of Both:**
    - **Client-Side:** Provides immediate feedback to the user, improving the user experience and reducing server load.

- **Server-Side:** Essential for security. Client-side validation can be bypassed if the user disables JavaScript or uses a tool to manipulate the form data before submission. Server-side validation ensures that your application only processes valid data.

CHAPTER 7: MASTER PAGES AND THEMES

Creating a consistent layout and appearance across a website is essential for professional web development. ASP.NET provides Master Pages and Themes to achieve this. This chapter explores their purpose, usage, and implementation with examples.

The Concept of Master Pages: A Detailed Explanation with Example

The concept of Master Pages is a powerful feature in web development frameworks like ASP.NET Web Forms (as indicated by the provided code snippets) that allows developers to create a consistent look and feel across multiple web pages within an application. It essentially provides a template for your website's structure, separating the common layout elements from the specific content of individual pages.

Think of a Master Page as the blueprint of a house. It defines the common elements like the foundation, walls, roof, doors, and windows. Individual content pages are like the furniture and decorations you place inside that house. They fit within the predefined structure but have their own unique content.

Key Idea: Master Pages enable you to define the visual structure and common functionalities of your website in one central location. Any changes made to the Master Page are automatically reflected across all the content pages linked to it, ensuring consistency and simplifying maintenance.

Let's break down the core aspects:

1. Defining a Consistent Layout:

A Master Page (`.master` file in ASP.NET) contains the HTML markup for the elements that are shared across your website. This typically includes:

- **Header:** Website logo, navigation menu, search bar, etc.
- **Footer:** Copyright information, contact details, social media links, etc.
- **Sidebar:** Navigation links, advertisements, related content, etc.

- **Overall Page Structure:** The basic `<html>`, `<head>`, and `<body>` tags, along with structural `<div>` elements to organize the content.
- **CSS and JavaScript References:** Links to your stylesheet and script files that define the visual styling and interactive behavior of the website.

2. Content Placeholders (`<asp:ContentPlaceHolder>`):

The crucial element that makes Master Pages work is the `<asp:ContentPlaceHolder>` control. These are like designated slots or placeholders within the Master Page's layout where the specific content of individual pages will be injected.

- **Purpose:** They mark the regions within the Master Page where the content from the linked content pages will be rendered.
- **Naming:** Each `ContentPlaceHolder` is given a unique `ID` attribute, which is used by the content pages to identify which placeholder they are targeting.
- **Location:** You can have multiple `ContentPlaceHolder` controls in different parts of your Master Page (e.g., one for the page title in the `<head>`, one for the main body content, one for a sidebar, etc.).

3. Creating Content Pages and Linking:

Content pages (`.aspx` files in ASP.NET) are the individual web pages that display specific information. To utilize the layout defined in a Master Page, a content page needs to be explicitly linked to it. This is done using the `@ Page` directive at the top of the content page:

HTML

```
<%@ Page Title="My Specific Page" MasterPageFile="~/MyMaster.master"
Language="C#" AutoEventWireup="true" CodeBehind="MySpecificPage.aspx.cs"
Inherits="MyApp.MySpecificPage" %>
```

- **`MasterPageFile="~/MyMaster.master"`:** This attribute specifies the path to the Master Page file that this content page should use as its template. The ~ represents the root directory of the web application.

4. Providing Content for Placeholders (`<asp:Content>`):

Within the content page, you use `<asp:Content>` controls to define the specific content that should be placed into the `ContentPlaceHolder` controls defined in the Master Page.

- **`ContentPlaceHolderID`:** The `ContentPlaceHolderID` attribute of the `<asp:Content>` control must match the `ID` of the `ContentPlaceHolder` in the Master Page where this content should be rendered.
- **Multiple `<asp:Content>` Controls:** A content page can have multiple `<asp:Content>` controls, each targeting a different `ContentPlaceHolder` in the Master Page.

Example in Detail:

Let's consider a simple scenario for a website with a consistent header, navigation, main content area, and footer.

1. `Site.Master` (Master Page):

HTML

```
<%@ Master Language="C#" AutoEventWireup="true" CodeBehind="Site.master.cs"
Inherits="MyWebApp.SiteMaster" %>
<!DOCTYPE html>
<html lang="en">
<head>
    <meta charset="UTF-8">
    <meta name="viewport" content="width=device-width, initial-scale=1.0">
    <title><asp:ContentPlaceHolder ID="TitleContent" runat="server">My
Default Title</asp:ContentPlaceHolder></title>
    <link rel="stylesheet" href="styles.css">
</head>
<body>
    <div class="container">
        <header class="main-header">
            <div class="logo">My Awesome Website</div>
            <nav class="main-nav">
                <ul>
                    <li><a href="default.aspx">Home</a></li>
                    <li><a href="about.aspx">About Us</a></li>
                    <li><a href="contact.aspx">Contact</a></li>
                </ul>
            </nav>
        </header>

        <div class="content-wrapper">
            <aside class="sidebar">
                <h3>Quick Links</h3>
                <ul>
                    <li><a href="#">Link 1</a></li>
                    <li><a href="#">Link 2</a></li>
                </ul>
                <asp:ContentPlaceHolder ID="SidebarContent"
runat="server"></asp:ContentPlaceHolder>
            </aside>
            <main class="main-content">
                <asp:ContentPlaceHolder ID="MainContent"
runat="server"></asp:ContentPlaceHolder>
            </main>
        </div>

        <footer class="main-footer">
            <p>&copy; 2025 My Awesome Website. All rights reserved.</p>
        </footer>
    </div>
</body>
</html>
```

In this Master Page:

- We have defined the basic HTML structure, linked a CSS file (`styles.css`), and created a header with a logo and navigation.
- There's a `content-wrapper` div containing a `sidebar` and `main-content` area.
- We have three `ContentPlaceHolder` controls:
    - `TitleContent`: For the dynamic page title in the `<head>`. It has a default value "My Default Title" which will be used if a content page doesn't provide its own title.
    - `SidebarContent`: For adding specific content to the sidebar on certain pages.
    - `MainContent`: For the primary content of each page.

2. `HomePage.aspx` (Content Page):

HTML

```
<%@ Page Title="Home" MasterPageFile="~/Site.Master" Language="C#"
AutoEventWireup="true" CodeBehind="HomePage.aspx.cs"
Inherits="MyWebApp.HomePage" %>
<asp:Content ID="Content1" ContentPlaceHolderID="TitleContent"
runat="server">
    Home Page
</asp:Content>
<asp:Content ID="Content2" ContentPlaceHolderID="MainContent" runat="server">
    <h2>Welcome to Our Homepage!</h2>
    <p>This is the main content of the home page. You can add text, images,
and other elements here.</p>
    <ul>
        <li>Feature 1</li>
        <li>Feature 2</li>
        <li>Feature 3</li>
    </ul>
</asp:Content>
<asp:Content ID="Content3" ContentPlaceHolderID="SidebarContent"
runat="server">
    <h4>Special Announcement</h4>
    <p>Check out our latest offers!</p>
</asp:Content>
```

In this Content Page:

- The `@ Page` directive links it to `~/Site.Master`.
- We have three `<asp:Content>` controls:
    - `Content1` targets `TitleContent` and sets the page title to "Home Page".
    - `Content2` targets `MainContent` and provides the specific content for the homepage.
    - `Content3` targets `SidebarContent` and adds a special announcement to the sidebar on the homepage.

3. `AboutUs.aspx` (Another Content Page):

HTML

```
<%@ Page Title="About Us" MasterPageFile="~/Site.Master" Language="C#"
AutoEventWireup="true" CodeBehind="AboutUs.aspx.cs"
Inherits="MyWebApp.AboutUs" %>
```

```
<asp:Content ID="Content1" ContentPlaceHolderID="TitleContent"
runat="server">
    About Us
</asp:Content>
<asp:Content ID="Content2" ContentPlaceHolderID="MainContent" runat="server">
    <h2>About Our Company</h2>
    <p>Learn more about our history, mission, and team.</p>
    <img src="company_image.jpg" alt="Our Company">
</asp:Content>
```

In this Content Page:

- It also links to `~/Site.Master`.
- It provides specific content for the `TitleContent` ("About Us") and `MainContent` (information about the company).
- Notice that there's no `<asp:Content>` targeting `SidebarContent`. In this case, the sidebar will only display the default "Quick Links" from the Master Page.

Outcome:

When you browse to `HomePage.aspx`, the browser will render a page with:

- The header and navigation from `Site.Master`.
- The title "Home Page" in the browser tab (from the `TitleContent`).
- The main content "Welcome to Our Homepage!..." (from the `MainContent`).
- The "Quick Links" and the "Special Announcement" in the sidebar (combining default and content-specific elements).
- The footer from `Site.Master`.

When you browse to `AboutUs.aspx`, you will see:

- The same header and navigation from `Site.Master`.
- The title "About Us" in the browser tab.
- The "About Our Company..." content in the main area.
- Only the default "Quick Links" in the sidebar.
- The same footer from `Site.Master`.

Key Benefits Revisited:

- **Centralized Control over Layout:** Any changes to the header, footer, navigation, or overall structure in `Site.Master` are automatically applied to all linked content pages. For example, if you update the navigation menu in `Site.Master`, it will be updated across the entire website without needing to modify each individual page.
- **Easy Updates to Site Design:** Modifying the visual appearance (e.g., changing the header background color in the CSS linked in the Master Page) will instantly update the design across all pages.
- **Enhances Maintainability:** By separating the layout from the content, maintaining the website becomes much easier. You can focus on updating the content of individual pages without

worrying about breaking the overall design. Similarly, design changes can be made in one place (the Master Page) without affecting the content.

- **Reusability:** The defined layout in the Master Page is reused across multiple pages, reducing code duplication and ensuring consistency.

Applying Themes and Skins in ASP.NET: A Detailed Explanation with Example

Themes and Skins in ASP.NET provide a powerful mechanism to define and apply a consistent visual style across your web application. They allow you to centralize the definition of fonts, colors, control appearances, and other stylistic elements, making it easy to maintain a uniform look and feel and to change the entire website's appearance with minimal effort.

Understanding Themes:

A **Theme** is a collection of resources that define the visual styling of your web application. This collection typically includes:

- **Skin Files (`.skin`):** These files define the default property settings for individual ASP.NET server controls. You can specify properties like `BackColor`, `ForeColor`, `Font`, `BorderColor`, etc., for controls like `Button`, `Label`, `TextBox`, `GridView`, and more.
- **CSS Files (`.css`):** These standard cascading style sheets provide more advanced styling options that can be applied to HTML elements and server controls.
- **Images:** Themes can also include image files used for backgrounds, logos, or other visual elements.

The primary goal of themes is to separate the visual presentation of your web application from its functional logic (code-behind) and its structural layout (Master Pages and content pages). This separation enhances maintainability, reusability, and allows for easier customization of the website's appearance.

Understanding Skins:

Skins are an integral part of themes. A skin file (`.skin`) contains definitions for the appearance of one or more ASP.NET server controls. Each skin definition within a `.skin` file targets a specific control type (e.g., `<asp:Button>`) and optionally a specific skin ID for more granular control over individual control instances.

Key Concepts of Skins:

- **Default Skins:** If a skin definition in a `.skin` file does not have a `SkinID` attribute, it's considered the **default skin** for that control type within the theme. This default skin will be applied to all instances of that control on pages using the theme, unless a specific skin is explicitly applied to a control instance.

- **Named Skins:** You can create **named skins** by including the `SkinID` attribute in a control definition within a `.skin` file (e.g., `<asp:Button runat="server" SkinID="SpecialButton" BackColor="Red" />`). To apply a named skin to a specific control on a page, you set the control's `SkinID` property in the ASPX markup.

Steps to Add and Use Themes and Skins:

Let's elaborate on the steps provided with a more detailed example:

1. Create the `App_Themes` Folder:

- In your ASP.NET web application project in Visual Studio (or your preferred IDE), right-click on the project in the Solution Explorer.
- Select **Add** > **New Folder**.
- Name the new folder **`App_Themes`** (case-sensitive). ASP.NET recognizes this folder as the designated location for themes.

2. Add a Theme Folder Inside `App_Themes`:

- Right-click on the `App_Themes` folder.
- Select **Add** > **New Folder**.
- Give your theme a descriptive name (e.g., **`MyTheme`**, **`BlueTheme`**, **`CorporateTheme`**). This folder will contain all the resources for your theme.

3. Add `.skin` Files and Optionally CSS Files:

- **Adding Skin Files:**
  - Right-click on your theme folder (e.g., `MyTheme`).
  - Select **Add** > **New Item...**.
  - In the "Add New Item" dialog, select **Skin File**.
  - Give your skin file a meaningful name (e.g., **`ControlStyles.skin`**, **`Default.skin`**). It's common to have one or more `.skin` files within a theme to organize styles for different control types.
  - Click **Add**.
- **Adding CSS Files:**
  - Right-click on your theme folder (e.g., `MyTheme`).
  - Select **Add** > **New Item...**.
  - In the "Add New Item" dialog, select **Style Sheet**.
  - Give your CSS file a name (e.g., **`Style.css`**, **`ThemeStyles.css`**).
  - Click **Add**.

Example Skin File (`MyTheme/ControlStyles.skin`):

XML

```
<asp:Button runat="server" BackColor="LightBlue" ForeColor="White" Font-
Bold="true" BorderColor="Gray" BorderStyle="Solid" BorderWidth="1px" />
```

```
<asp:Label runat="server" ForeColor="DarkGreen" Font-Names="Verdana" Font-Size="Small" />

<asp:TextBox runat="server" BorderColor="Silver" BorderStyle="Dotted"
BorderWidth="1px" />

<asp:GridView runat="server" BackColor="White" BorderColor="#CCCCCC"
BorderStyle="None" BorderWidth="1px" CellPadding="3" GridLines="Both">
    <FooterStyle BackColor="White" ForeColor="#000066" />
    <PagerStyle BackColor="White" ForeColor="#000066" HorizontalAlign="Left"
/>
    <RowStyle ForeColor="#000066" />
    <SelectedRowStyle BackColor="#669999" Font-Bold="True" ForeColor="White"
/>
    <SortedAscendingCellStyle BackColor="#F1F1F1" />
    <SortedAscendingHeaderStyle BackColor="#DBDBDB" />
    <SortedDescendingCellStyle BackColor="#CAC9C8" />
    <SortedDescendingHeaderStyle BackColor="#B3B1B0" />
    <HeaderStyle BackColor="#000066" Font-Bold="True" ForeColor="White" />
</asp:GridView>
```

In this `ControlStyles.skin` file:

- We define the default appearance for all `<asp:Button>` controls within the `MyTheme`. They will have a light blue background, white text, bold font, a gray solid border of 1 pixel.
- We define the default appearance for all `<asp:Label>` controls to have dark green text, Verdana font, and a small font size.
- We define the default appearance for all `<asp:TextBox>` controls with a silver dotted border of 1 pixel.
- We also define the default styles for various parts of the `<asp:GridView>` control, such as header, row, footer, pager, etc.

Example CSS File (`MyTheme/Style.css`):

CSS

```
/* MyTheme/Style.css */
body {
    font-family: Arial, sans-serif;
    background-color: #f4f4f4;
    margin: 0;
    padding: 0;
}

.container {
    width: 960px;
    margin: 20px auto;
    background-color: #fff;
    padding: 20px;
    border: 1px solid #ccc;
}

h2 {
    color: #333;
```

```
}

.highlight {
    background-color: yellow;
    font-style: italic;
}
```

This CSS file provides general styling for HTML elements like `body`, `div` with class `container`, and `h2` elements, as well as a custom class `highlight`.

Applying Themes:

There are several ways to apply a theme to your ASP.NET web application:

1. Applying Theme to a Specific Page using the `@ Page` Directive:

You can apply a theme to an individual content page by adding the `Theme` attribute to the `@ Page` directive at the top of the `.aspx` file:

Code snippet

```
<%@ Page Language="C#" AutoEventWireup="true" CodeBehind="MyPage.aspx.cs"
Inherits="YourNamespace.MyPage" Theme="MyTheme" %>

<!DOCTYPE html>
<html xmlns="http://www.w3.org/1999/xhtml">
<head runat="server">
    <title>My Themed Page</title>
    <link href="App_Themes/MyTheme/Style.css" rel="stylesheet" />
</head>
<body>
    <form id="form1" runat="server">
        <asp:Label ID="Label1" runat="server" Text="This is a themed label."
CssClass="highlight"></asp:Label><br />
        <asp:Button ID="Button1" runat="server" Text="Themed Button" />
        <asp:TextBox ID="TextBox1" runat="server" Text="Themed
TextBox"></asp:TextBox>
        <asp:GridView ID="GridView1" runat="server"
AutoGenerateColumns="false">
            <Columns>
                <asp:BoundField DataField="ID" HeaderText="ID" />
                <asp:BoundField DataField="Name" HeaderText="Name" />
            </Columns>
            <asp:ListItemCollection>
                <asp:ListItem Text="Item 1" Value="1" />
                <asp:ListItem Text="Item 2" Value="2" />
            </asp:ListItemCollection>
        </asp:GridView>
    </form>
</body>
</html>
```

- **`Theme="MyTheme"`**: This attribute in the `@ Page` directive tells ASP.NET to apply the `MyTheme` to this specific page. The styles defined in `MyTheme/ControlStyles.skin` and `MyTheme/Style.css` will be applied to the controls on this page.
- **`<link href="App_Themes/MyTheme/Style.css" rel="stylesheet" />`**: You can explicitly link the CSS file within the `<head>` section of your content page or Master Page. ASP.NET will also automatically apply CSS files found within the theme folder.

2. Applying Theme Programmatically in the `Page_PreInit` Event:

You can dynamically apply a theme in the `Page_PreInit` event of your page lifecycle. This is useful if you want to allow users to select a theme or apply a theme based on certain conditions.

C#

```
// In your Page's code-behind (e.g., MyPage.aspx.cs)
protected void Page_PreInit(object sender, EventArgs e)
{
    Page.Theme = "MyTheme";
}
```

- The `Page_PreInit` event occurs early in the page lifecycle, before the controls are created and populated. Setting the `Page.Theme` property here ensures that the theme is applied before the page is rendered.

3. Applying Theme to the Entire Website in `web.config`:

You can set a default theme for your entire web application by configuring it in the `web.config` file.

XML

```
<configuration>
  <system.web>
    <pages theme="MyTheme">
      </pages>
  </system.web>
</configuration>
```

- The `<pages>` element within `<system.web>` has a `theme` attribute. Setting this attribute to your theme name (e.g., `"MyTheme"`) will apply this theme to all pages in your application by default. Individual pages can still override this default theme by specifying a different theme in their `@ Page` directive or programmatically.

How Themes and Skins are Applied:

When a page is requested and a theme is applied:

1. ASP.NET looks for the specified theme folder in the `App_Themes` directory.
2. It loads all the `.skin` files within that theme folder.

3. For each server control on the page, ASP.NET checks if there is a matching skin definition in the loaded `.skin` files:
    - First, it looks for a skin with a `SkinID` that matches the control's `SkinID` property (if set).
    - If no named skin is found, it looks for a default skin (without a `SkinID`) for that control type.
4. If a matching skin is found, the properties defined in the skin are applied to the control.
5. ASP.NET also automatically includes any CSS files found directly within the theme folder. You can also explicitly link CSS files from the theme folder in your Master Pages or content pages.

Benefits of Using Themes and Skins:

- **Consistency:** Ensures a uniform visual appearance across all pages of your website.
- **Centralized Styling:** All visual styles are defined in one place (the `App_Themes` folder), making it easier to manage and update the website's look and feel.
- **Easy Customization:** You can easily change the entire website's appearance by simply switching the applied theme.
- **Maintainability:** Separating presentation from content and logic makes the application easier to maintain and modify.
- **Reusability:** Themes can be reused across different projects, promoting code and design consistency.
- **Improved Development Workflow:** Designers can focus on creating themes, while developers focus on the application's functionality and structure.

By effectively utilizing themes and skins, you can create visually appealing, consistent, and easily maintainable ASP.NET web applications. Remember to organize your skin files and CSS effectively within your theme folders for better management.

Achieving Global Styling and Consistency in ASP.NET: A Detailed Explanation with Example

The combination of **Master Pages** for defining the structural layout and **Themes** (including Skins and CSS) for applying visual styles is a cornerstone of building scalable and maintainable ASP.NET web applications with a consistent user experience. This powerful synergy allows you to decouple design from content, promote reusability, and streamline updates across your entire website.

The Power of Combining Master Pages and Themes:

- **Design Decoupled from Content:** Master Pages handle the structural elements (header, footer, navigation, content placeholders), while Themes manage the visual presentation (fonts, colors, control appearances). This separation means that designers can work on the visual aspects without needing to modify the content or the underlying code, and developers can focus on the application's logic and content structure without worrying about the intricate design details.

- **Reusability of Layout and Look:** Once a Master Page and a Theme are created, they can be applied to numerous content pages. This eliminates the need toRedefine the basic layout and styling for each new page, saving significant development time and ensuring a consistent user interface across hundreds or even thousands of pages.
- **Centralized Updates for Reduced Effort and Improved Scalability:** When you need to make changes to the global layout (e.g., update the navigation menu) or the overall style (e.g., change the website's color scheme), you only need to modify the Master Page or the Theme files. These changes are automatically reflected on all the content pages that utilize them. This centralized control drastically reduces the effort required for updates and makes it much easier to scale your website while maintaining a consistent brand identity.

Detailed Example:

Let's build upon the previous examples to illustrate how Master Pages and Themes work together to achieve global styling and consistency.

Scenario: We want to create a website with a consistent header, navigation, footer, and a unified visual style (using a theme called "CorporateTheme").

1. `Site.Master` (Master Page - Defines Global Layout):

HTML

```
<%@ Master Language="C#" AutoEventWireup="true" CodeBehind="Site.master.cs"
Inherits="MyWebApp.SiteMaster" %>
<!DOCTYPE html>
<html lang="en">
<head>
    <meta charset="UTF-8">
    <meta name="viewport" content="width=device-width, initial-scale=1.0">
    <title><asp:ContentPlaceHolder ID="TitleContent" runat="server">My
Corporate Website</asp:ContentPlaceHolder></title>
    <link href="App_Themes/CorporateTheme/Style.css" rel="stylesheet" />
</head>
<body>
    <div class="page-container">
        <header class="main-header">
            <div class="logo">Corporate Logo</div>
            <nav class="main-nav">
                <ul>
                    <li><a href="default.aspx">Home</a></li>
                    <li><a href="products.aspx">Products</a></li>
                    <li><a href="services.aspx">Services</a></li>
                    <li><a href="contact.aspx">Contact Us</a></li>
                </ul>
            </nav>
        </header>
```

```
        <div class="main-content">
            <asp:ContentPlaceHolder ID="MainContent" 
runat="server"></asp:ContentPlaceHolder>
        </div>

        <footer class="main-footer">
            <p>&copy; 2025 Corporate Website. All rights reserved.</p>
        </footer>
    </div>
</body>
</html>
```

- This Master Page defines the basic HTML structure (`<html>`, `<head>`, `<body>`), a header with a logo and navigation, a `MainContent` placeholder, and a footer.
- It links to the `Style.css` file within the `CorporateTheme`.

2. `App_Themes/CorporateTheme/ControlStyles.skin` (Theme - Defines Control Styles):

XML

```
<asp:Button runat="server" BackColor="#007bff" ForeColor="White" Font-
Bold="true" BorderColor="#0056b3" BorderStyle="Solid" BorderWidth="1px" 
CssClass="button-primary" />

<asp:Label runat="server" ForeColor="#343a40" Font-Names="Segoe UI, Tahoma, 
sans-serif" Font-Size="Medium" />

<asp:TextBox runat="server" BorderColor="#ced4da" BorderStyle="Solid" 
BorderWidth="1px" Padding="5px" CssClass="form-control" />

<asp:HyperLink runat="server" ForeColor="#007bff" Font-Underline="true" />
```

- This skin file defines the default styles for `Button`, `Label`, `TextBox`, and `HyperLink` controls within the `CorporateTheme`. It sets background colors, text colors, fonts, borders, and even assigns CSS classes for further styling in the CSS file.

3. `App_Themes/CorporateTheme/Style.css` (Theme - Defines Global CSS Styles):

CSS

```
/* App_Themes/CorporateTheme/Style.css */
body {
    font-family: "Segoe UI", Tahoma, sans-serif;
    background-color: #f8f9fa;
    margin: 0;
    padding: 0;
    color: #343a40;
}

.page-container {
    width: 960px;
    margin: 20px auto;
    background-color: #fff;
    padding: 20px;
```

```
    border: 1px solid #dee2e6;
    box-shadow: 0 0 10px rgba(0, 0, 0, 0.1);
}

.main-header {
    background-color: #e9ecef;
    padding: 15px;
    border-bottom: 1px solid #ced4da;
    display: flex;
    justify-content: space-between;
    align-items: center;
}

.logo {
    font-size: 1.5em;
    font-weight: bold;
    color: #007bff;
}

.main-nav ul {
    list-style: none;
    padding: 0;
    margin: 0;
    display: flex;
}

.main-nav li {
    margin-left: 20px;
}

.main-nav a {
    text-decoration: none;
    color: #343a40;
    font-weight: 500;
}

.main-content {
    padding: 20px;
}

.main-footer {
    background-color: #f8f9fa;
    padding: 10px;
    text-align: center;
    border-top: 1px solid #ced4da;
    color: #6c757d;
    font-size: 0.9em;
}

h1 {
    color: #007bff;
}

p {
    line-height: 1.6;
}
```

```
.button-primary { /* Applied via Skin */
    padding: 10px 15px;
    border-radius: 5px;
    cursor: pointer;
    transition: background-color 0.3s ease;
}

.button-primary:hover {
    background-color: #0056b3;
}

.form-control { /* Applied via Skin */
    width: 100%;
    padding: 8px;
    margin-bottom: 10px;
    border-radius: 4px;
    box-sizing: border-box;
}
```

- This CSS file provides global styling for HTML elements (`body`, `div`, `h1`, `p`) and defines styles for the layout components (header, navigation, footer).
- It also includes styles for CSS classes (`button-primary`, `form-control`) that are applied to the server controls through the skin file.

4. `HomePage.aspx` (Content Page - Uses Master Page and Theme):

HTML

```
<%@ Page Title="Home" MasterPageFile="~/Site.Master" Language="C#"
AutoEventWireup="true" CodeBehind="HomePage.aspx.cs"
Inherits="MyWebApp.HomePage" Theme="CorporateTheme" %>
<asp:Content ID="Content1" ContentPlaceHolderID="MainContent" runat="server">
    <h1>Welcome to Our Corporate Website</h1>
    <p>This is the main content of the home page. We offer a range of
products and services to meet your business needs.</p>
    <asp:Button ID="CallToAction" runat="server" Text="Learn More" />
    <asp:Label ID="GreetingLabel" runat="server" Text="Hello User!" />
    <asp:TextBox ID="EmailTextBox" runat="server" placeholder="Enter your
email"></asp:TextBox>
    <asp:HyperLink ID="ProductsLink" runat="server"
NavigateUrl="~/products.aspx" Text="View our products"></asp:HyperLink>
</asp:Content>
```

- The `@ Page` directive specifies both the `MasterPageFile` (`~/Site.Master`) and the `Theme` (`CorporateTheme`).
- The content within the `<asp:Content>` tag will be rendered within the `MainContent` placeholder of the `Site.Master`.
- The `Button`, `Label`, `TextBox`, and `HyperLink` controls on this page will automatically inherit the styles defined in the `CorporateTheme/ControlStyles.skin` file and the `CorporateTheme/Style.css` file (through the assigned CSS classes).

Outcome:

When you browse to `HomePage.aspx`, you will see a page with:

- The consistent header, navigation, and footer defined in `Site.Master`.
- The visual styling (fonts, colors, background) applied by the `CorporateTheme/Style.css`.
- The `Button`, `Label`, `TextBox`, and `HyperLink` controls will have the default appearance as defined in `CorporateTheme/ControlStyles.skin`. For example, the button will be blue with white bold text, the label will be dark gray with Segoe UI font, and the textbox will have a light gray border.
- The specific content "Welcome to Our Corporate Website..." from `HomePage.aspx` rendered in the main content area.

If you create other content pages (e.g., `Products.aspx`, `Services.aspx`) and link them to `Site.Master` with the `CorporateTheme` applied, they will automatically inherit the same global layout and visual style, ensuring a consistent user experience across the entire website.

Best Practices for Global Styling and Consistency:

- **Use One Master Page for Global Layout and Nested Master Pages for Section-Specific Designs:** For websites with distinct sections that require different layouts (e.g., a public-facing area vs. an admin dashboard), you can use nested Master Pages. A root Master Page defines the overall global structure, and nested Master Pages inherit from it but can define section-specific layout variations.
- **Define Common Control Skins in `.skin` Files:** Utilize `.skin` files within your themes to set default appearances for frequently used server controls. This ensures consistency in how buttons, labels, textboxes, grids, etc., look across the application. Use CSS classes within the skins for more complex styling that is defined in your CSS files.
- **Maintain Responsive Design Using CSS Frameworks like Bootstrap Alongside ASP.NET Themes:** While ASP.NET Themes handle the visual styling of server controls and basic HTML elements, for creating responsive layouts that adapt to different screen sizes, integrate CSS frameworks like Bootstrap or Foundation. You can include the framework's CSS files in your Master Page or within your theme's CSS. You can also leverage Bootstrap's CSS classes within your skin files (as shown in the `button-primary` and `form-control` examples) to apply pre-defined responsive styles to your server controls.

✅ Summary:

- **Master Pages** = Layout consistency.
- **Themes & Skins** = Style consistency.
- Together, they enforce branding and improve user experience.

---

10 PRACTICAL EXAMPLES WITH SOLUTION

1. Consistent Navigation Menu:

- **Problem:** Create a website with a consistent navigation menu (Home, Products, Services, Contact) across all pages.
- **Solution:**
    - Create a Master Page (`Site.Master`) with the HTML for the navigation menu within the header section.
    - Add a `<asp:ContentPlaceHolder>` in the Master Page where the main page content will be displayed.
    - Create individual content pages (`Home.aspx`, `Products.aspx`, etc.) and link them to the Master Page.
    - In each content page, use `<asp:Content>` to provide the specific content for that page.

2. Website Footer with Copyright and Contact Info:

- **Problem:** Implement a consistent footer across all pages, displaying copyright information and contact details.
- **Solution:**
    - In the `Site.Master` page, add the HTML for the footer section, including the copyright notice and contact information.
    - Ensure that the content pages are linked to this Master Page; the footer will automatically appear on all of them.

3. Applying a Corporate Theme:

- **Problem:** Apply a consistent corporate theme (colors, fonts) to all pages of a website.
- **Solution:**
    - Create a theme in the `App_Themes` folder (e.g., `CorporateTheme`).
    - Create a CSS file (`Style.css`) within the theme folder to define the corporate colors, fonts, and styles for various HTML elements.
    - Create a skin file (`ControlStyles.skin`) to define the styles for ASP.NET server controls (e.g., set the button color, font, and border).
    - Apply the theme to the Master Page or individual content pages using the `@ Page` directive or in the `Page_PreInit` event.

4. Styling Buttons Consistently:

- **Problem:** Ensure that all buttons on a website have a uniform style (e.g., background color, font, hover effect).
- **Solution:**
    - Create a skin file (`ControlStyles.skin`) within the active theme.
    - Add a style definition for the `<asp:Button>` control in the skin file, specifying the desired properties.

- Optionally, use CSS classes in the skin file and define the actual styles in a CSS file within the theme for more advanced styling (e.g., hover effects).

5. Responsive Design with Master Pages and Bootstrap:

- **Problem:** Create a website with a responsive layout (adapts to different screen sizes) and a consistent look.
- **Solution:**
  - Include the Bootstrap CSS and JavaScript files in the Master Page.
  - Use Bootstrap's grid system (e.g., `container`, `row`, `col-md-`, etc.) in the Master Page to structure the layout.
  - Apply a theme to control the color scheme and font.
  - Content pages will inherit the responsive layout from the Master Page and the styles from the theme.

6. Dynamic Title for Each Page:

- **Problem:** Set a unique and dynamic title for each page in the browser tab.
- **Solution:**
  - Add a `<asp:ContentPlaceHolder>` control in the `<head>` section of the Master Page for the title.
  - In each content page, use an `<asp:Content>` control to specify the title for that page.

7. Implementing a Breadcrumb Navigation:

- **Problem:** Implement a breadcrumb navigation system to show the user's current location within the website.
- **Solution:**
  - Create a user control for the breadcrumb navigation.
  - Add the user control to the Master Page.
  - In each content page, dynamically set the breadcrumb path by adding the appropriate links.

8. Different Layout for Admin Section:

- **Problem:** Create a different layout for the admin section of a website while maintaining the global styles.
- **Solution:**
  - Create a separate Master Page (e.g., `Admin.Master`) for the admin section.
  - The `Admin.Master` can have a different layout (e.g., a sidebar for admin navigation) but can still use the same theme for consistent styling.
  - Create content pages for the admin section and link them to `Admin.Master`.

9. Theme Switching Functionality:

- **Problem:** Allow users to switch between different themes (e.g., light and dark mode).
- **Solution:**
    - Create multiple themes in the `App_Themes` folder (e.g., `LightTheme`, `DarkTheme`).
    - Add a dropdown list or buttons to a Master Page or a common control to allow the user to select a theme.
    - In the `Page_PreInit` event of the content pages, dynamically set the `Page.Theme` property based on the user's selection (stored in a session variable or cookie).

10. Consistent Error Page Styling:

- **Problem:** Ensure that error pages (e.g., 404, 500) have the same look and feel as the rest of the website.
- **Solution:**
    - Create a custom error page (e.g., `ErrorPage.aspx`).
    - Set the `MasterPageFile` property of the error page to the main Master Page (`Site.Master`).
    - Apply the website's theme to the error page.
    - Configure the `web.config` file to redirect to the custom error page for specific error codes.

30 Multiple Choice Questions (MCQs) on the Concept of Master Pages, Creating and Using Master Pages, Applying Themes and Skins, and Global Styling and Consistency in ASP.NET:

Concept of Master Pages

1. What is the primary purpose of a Master Page in ASP.NET?
    - a) To define the content of a specific page
    - b) To define the layout and structure of multiple pages
    - c) To define the styling of individual controls
    - d) To manage database connections
    - **Answer:** b) To define the layout and structure of multiple pages
2. Which file extension is typically used for Master Pages in ASP.NET?
    - a) .aspx
    - b) .html
    - c) .master
    - d) .css
    - **Answer:** c) .master
3. What control is used within a Master Page to define a region where content from other pages can be displayed?
    - a) `<asp:Panel>`
    - b) `<asp:Content>`
    - c) `<asp:ContentPlaceHolder>`
    - d) `<asp:Placeholder>`
    - **Answer:** c) `<asp:ContentPlaceHolder>`

4. A Master Page provides a way to achieve ________ across multiple pages.
    - a) Data consistency
    - b) Style consistency
    - c) Layout consistency
    - d) Both b and c
    - **Answer:** d) Both b and c
5. Which of the following is NOT a benefit of using Master Pages?
    - a) Centralized control over layout
    - b) Easier updates to site design
    - c) Improved maintainability
    - d) Increased code redundancy
    - **Answer:** d) Increased code redundancy

Creating and Using Master Pages

6. Which directive is used in a content page to link it to a Master Page?
    - a) `<%@ MasterPage %>`
    - b) `<%@ Page %>`
    - c) `<%@ Control %>`
    - d) `<%@ Theme %>`
    - **Answer:** b) `<%@ Page %>`
7. In a content page, which attribute of the `@ Page` directive specifies the Master Page to use?
    - a) `MasterPageName`
    - b) `Master`
    - c) `MasterPageFile`
    - d) `Template`
    - **Answer:** c) `MasterPageFile`
8. Content from a content page is placed into the Master Page using which control?
    - a) `<asp:Placeholder>`
    - b) `<asp:Content>`
    - c) `<asp:ContentHolder>`
    - d) `<asp:Panel>`
    - **Answer:** b) `<asp:Content>`
9. The `ContentPlaceHolderID` property of the `<asp:Content>` control in a content page must match the ________ of the corresponding control in the Master Page.
    - a) ID
    - b) Name
    - c) ClientID
    - d) UniqueID
    - **Answer:** a) ID
10. Can a content page have multiple `<asp:Content>` controls?
    - a) Yes
    - b) No
    - **Answer:** a) Yes

Applying Themes and Skins

11. What is a Theme in ASP.NET?
    - a) A collection of CSS files
    - b) A collection of images
    - c) A collection of resources that define the look and feel of a web application
    - d) A database schema
    - **Answer:** c) A collection of resources that define the look and feel of a web application
12. Which folder is used to store themes in ASP.NET?
    - a) Themes
    - b) App_Themes
    - c) Styles
    - d) Resources
    - **Answer:** b) App_Themes
13. What are Skins in ASP.NET?
    - a) CSS files
    - b) Images
    - c) Settings that define the appearance of individual server controls
    - d) JavaScript files
    - **Answer:** c) Settings that define the appearance of individual server controls
14. Skin files have which file extension?
    - a) .css
    - b) .skin
    - c) .theme
    - d) .xml
    - **Answer:** b) .skin
15. If a skin definition in a `.skin` file does not have a `SkinID`, it is called a ________ skin.
    - a) Named
    - b) Default
    - c) Global
    - d) Base
    - **Answer:** b) Default
16. How do you apply a theme to a specific page?
    - a) In the `web.config` file
    - b) In the Global.asax file
    - c) Using the `@ Page` directive
    - d) By adding a control to the page
    - **Answer:** c) Using the `@ Page` directive
17. Which property of the `Page` class is used to apply a theme programmatically?
    - a) `PageStyle`
    - b) `Theme`
    - c) `StyleSheet`
    - d) `Appearance`
    - **Answer:** b) `Theme`
18. Can a theme contain CSS files?

- a) Yes
- b) No
- **Answer:** a) Yes

19. Named skins are applied to a control by setting its ________ property. * a) ID * b) SkinID * c) CssClass * d) ControlStyle * **Answer:** b) SkinID
20. Themes are applied ________ Skins. * a) Before * b) After * c) Instead of * d) Simultaneously with * **Answer**: d) Simultaneously with

Global Styling and Consistency

21. Combining Master Pages and Themes helps to achieve ________.
    - a) Database consistency
    - b) Code consistency
    - c) Global styling and consistency
    - d) Network consistency
    - **Answer:** c) Global styling and consistency
22. Using Master Pages and Themes, the design of a website is ________ from its content.
    - a) Integrated with
    - b) Dependent on
    - c) Decoupled from
    - d) Controlled by
    - **Answer:** c) Decoupled from
23. Centralized updates in Master Pages and Themes ________ effort and improve scalability. * a) Increase * b) Reduce * c) Do not affect * d) Complicate * **Answer**: b) Reduce
24. For section-specific designs, it is a best practice to use ________. * a) Multiple themes * b) Nested master pages * c) Multiple content pages * d) Inline styles * **Answer:** b) Nested master pages
25. Common control styles should be defined in ________ files within a theme. * a) .css * b) .aspx * c) .skin * d) .html * **Answer:** c) .skin
26. To maintain responsive design, it is recommended to use ________ alongside ASP.NET themes. * a) JavaScript * b) CSS frameworks * c) ViewState * d) Cookies * **Answer:** b) CSS frameworks
27. Which of the following is NOT a part of Global Styling and Consistency? * a) Master Pages * b) Themes * c) Skins * d) ViewState * **Answer**: d) ViewState
28. A website has a consistent header and footer across all pages. This is most likely achieved using: * a) CSS * b) Master Pages * c) Themes * d) JavaScript * **Answer**: b) Master Pages
29. Which of the following helps in applying a uniform look and feel to all Button controls in a web application? * a) CSS * b) Master Pages * c) Skins * d) JavaScript * **Answer**: c) Skins
30. By combining Master Pages and Themes, developers can reuse the same ________ across many pages. * a) Data and content * b) Layout and look * c) Functionality and logic * d) Security and performance * **Answer**: b) Layout and look

10 MID SIZE QUESTION WITH ANSWER

1. **Explain the concept of a Master Page and its role in ASP.NET web development.**
   - **Answer:** A Master Page in ASP.NET is a template that provides a consistent layout and structure for multiple pages within a web application. It defines the common elements, such as headers, footers, and navigation menus, that are shared across different pages. Content pages then inherit this layout and insert their unique content into specific regions defined within the Master Page. This approach promotes code reuse, simplifies website maintenance, and ensures a uniform user experience.
2. **Describe the process of creating a Master Page and a content page in ASP.NET.**
   - **Answer:**
     - **Creating a Master Page:** In Visual Studio, you create a Master Page by adding a new item to your project and selecting "Master Page". This creates a file with the `.master` extension. You then design the layout using HTML and ASP.NET server controls, and define content placeholder regions using the `<asp:ContentPlaceHolder>` control.
     - **Creating a Content Page:** To create a content page, you add a new ASP.NET Web Form to your project. In the `@ Page` directive of the content page, you specify the `MasterPageFile` attribute to link it to the desired Master Page. You then use `<asp:Content>` controls to define the content that will be displayed in the corresponding `<asp:ContentPlaceHolder>` regions of the Master Page.
3. **How do you access and manipulate controls defined in a Master Page from a content page?**
   - **Answer:** To access controls in a Master Page from a content page, you can use the `Master` property of the `Page` object. There are a couple of ways to do this:
     - **`Using FindControl`:** You can use the `FindControl` method of the `Master` property to locate a specific control by its ID. However, this requires casting the returned object to the correct control type.
     - **`Using the @MasterType directive`:** A better approach is to use the `@MasterType` directive in the content page. This directive specifies the type of the Master Page, allowing you to access its public properties and methods directly through a strongly-typed `Master` property.
4. **What are ASP.NET Themes and how do they differ from CSS?**
   - **Answer:**
     - **ASP.NET Themes:** Themes are a collection of resources that define the overall look and feel of an ASP.NET web application. They include not only style information but also other visual properties, such as control skins, images, and CSS files. Themes allow you to apply a consistent appearance across multiple pages and controls.
     - **Difference from CSS:** While CSS focuses primarily on styling HTML elements, Themes provide a more comprehensive way to manage the visual aspects of a web application. Themes can define properties beyond

those available in CSS, such as control-specific settings. Also, Themes can include default and named skins.

5. **Explain the concept of Skins in ASP.NET and their relationship with Themes.**
   - **Answer:** Skins are a component of ASP.NET Themes that define the appearance of individual server controls. A skin defines the visual properties of a control, such as its font, color, and border.
     - **Relationship with Themes:** Themes can contain multiple skin files, each defining skins for different controls. Skins allow you to customize the look of controls within a Theme. A Theme can have a default skin for a control type and also named skins, which can be applied selectively to specific control instances.
6. **How do you apply a Theme to an ASP.NET web application, and what are the different ways to apply it?**
   - **Answer:** You can apply a Theme to an ASP.NET web application in the following ways:
     - **Page-level:** Apply the Theme to a specific page using the `Theme` attribute in the `@ Page` directive.
     - **Application-level:** Apply the Theme to all pages in the application by specifying it in the `<pages>` section of the `web.config` file.
     - **Programmatically:** You can apply a theme in the code-behind by setting the `Page.Theme` property.
7. **What is the difference between a Default Skin and a Named Skin in ASP.NET?**
   - **Answer:**
     - **Default Skin:** A default skin is a skin definition for a control type within a Theme that applies automatically to all instances of that control on any page where the Theme is applied. A default skin does not have a `SkinID` property defined.
     - **Named Skin:** A named skin is a skin definition that has a `SkinID` property. It does not apply automatically. Instead, you must explicitly assign the skin to a control by setting the control's `SkinID` property to match the name of the skin. Named skins allow you to apply different styles to different instances of the same control type within the same Theme.
8. **Discuss the benefits of using Master Pages, Themes, and Skins together in ASP.NET development.**
   - **Answer:** Using Master Pages, Themes, and Skins together provides several benefits:
     - **Consistency:** They ensure a consistent layout and visual style across the entire web application.
     - **Maintainability:** They simplify updates and modifications to the website's design.
     - **Code Reuse:** Master Pages promote code reuse by centralizing common layout elements, while Themes and Skins promote reuse of visual styles.
     - **Separation of Concerns:** They separate the presentation layer from the content, making the code more organized and easier to manage.

        - **Faster Development:** They speed up the development process by providing pre-defined layouts and styles.

9. **Explain how Master Pages and Themes contribute to global styling and consistency in a web application.**
    - **Answer:**
        - **Master Pages:** Ensure that the fundamental layout and structure of all pages are consistent. This includes elements like headers, footers, navigation, and the overall page structure.
        - **Themes:** Provide a consistent visual style for the application, including colors, fonts, and control appearances.
        - By combining Master Pages and Themes, developers can create a unified and professional look and feel for the entire web application, enhancing the user experience and reinforcing the brand identity.
10. **What are some best practices for using Master Pages, Themes, and Skins to create maintainable and scalable web applications?**
    - **Answer:** Here are some best practices:
        - **Use Master Pages for layout, Themes for look and feel:** Use Master Pages to define the structure of your pages (header, footer, etc.) and Themes/Skins to control the visual styling.
        - **Apply Themes at the application level:** For consistent styling, apply Themes at the application level in the web.config file.
        - **Use CSS Frameworks with Themes:** Integrate CSS frameworks like Bootstrap with ASP.NET Themes for responsive designs and better control over styling.
        - **Keep Master Pages simple:** Avoid adding too much content or logic to Master Pages. They should primarily define the layout.
        - **Use Content Placeholders effectively:** Define meaningful Content Placeholders in your Master Pages to provide flexibility for content pages.
        - **Organize Themes:** Organize Theme files (CSS, skins, images) in a logical folder structure within the `App_Themes` directory.

CHAPTER 8: INTRODUCTION TO ADO.NET

ADO.NET is a data access technology from the Microsoft .NET Framework, providing communication between relational and non-relational systems through a common set of components. ASP.NET applications frequently use ADO.NET to connect to databases, retrieve and manipulate data.

ADO.NET Architecture Explained

ADO.NET (ActiveX Data Objects for .NET) is Microsoft's framework for accessing data from various data sources within the .NET environment. It provides a set of classes and components that allow developers to connect to databases, execute commands, retrieve data, and manage data.

ADO.NET works with two main models of data access:

1. Connected Model

- The connected model provides a direct, real-time connection to the data source.
- It is suitable for scenarios where you need to retrieve data quickly and efficiently, and where you don't need to manipulate the data extensively or store it for a long time.
- **Key classes:** `SqlConnection`, `SqlCommand`, and `SqlDataReader` (for SQL Server). Other providers have similar classes (e.g., `OdbcConnection`, `OdbcCommand`, `OdbcDataReader`).

Components in Connected Model:

- **Connection Object:**
    - Manages the connection to a database.
    - Provides properties like connection string, connection state, and methods like `Open()` and `Close()`.
    - Example (C# with SQL Server):
    - `using System.Data.SqlClient; // Import the namespace`
    -

```
string connectionString = "Data Source=yourServer;Initial
Catalog=yourDatabase;Integrated Security=True;";
using (SqlConnection connection = new
SqlConnection(connectionString))
{
    connection.Open();
    Console.WriteLine("Connection opened!");
    // Perform database operations here
    connection.Close(); //explicitly close
    Console.WriteLine("Connection closed!");
} // Connection is automatically closed and disposed, when using
using
```

- **Command Object:**
    - Represents a SQL query or a stored procedure to be executed against the database.
    - Provides properties like `CommandText` (the query itself), `CommandType` (text, stored procedure, etc.), and methods like `ExecuteReader()`, `ExecuteNonQuery()`, and `ExecuteScalar()`.
    - Example (C# with SQL Server):

```
using System.Data.SqlClient;

string connectionString = "Data Source=yourServer;Initial
Catalog=yourDatabase;Integrated Security=True;";
string selectCommandText = "SELECT * FROM Products WHERE
CategoryID = @CategoryID";

using (SqlConnection connection = new
SqlConnection(connectionString))
{
    SqlCommand command = new SqlCommand(selectCommandText,
connection);
    command.Parameters.AddWithValue("@CategoryID", 1); // Use
parameters to prevent SQL Injection
    connection.Open();

    SqlDataReader reader = command.ExecuteReader();
    while (reader.Read())
    {
        Console.WriteLine($"{reader["ProductID"]} -
{reader["ProductName"]}");
    }
    reader.Close();
}
```

- **DataReader Object:**
    - Provides a fast, forward-only, read-only stream of data from the database.
    - Optimized for quickly retrieving large amounts of data.
    - Requires the Connection to remain open while reading data.
    - Example (C# with SQL Server):
        - See the `SqlDataReader` example in the `SqlCommand` section above. The `ExecuteReader()` method of the `SqlCommand` returns a `SqlDataReader`.

2. Disconnected Model

- The disconnected model retrieves a chunk of data from the data source and stores it locally in memory. The connection to the database is closed, allowing other users to access the database.
- It is useful for scenarios where you need to manipulate data, display data in a user interface, or transfer data between different layers of an application.
- **Key classes:** `DataSet` and `DataAdapter`.

Components in Disconnected Model:

- **DataSet Object:**
  - Represents an in-memory cache of data.
  - Can contain multiple `DataTable` objects, which are like tables in a database.
  - Provides features for navigating, filtering, sorting, and modifying data.
  - Supports relationships and constraints between tables.
  - Example (C# with SQL Server):

```
using System.Data;
using System.Data.SqlClient;

string connectionString = "Data Source=yourServer;Initial Catalog=yourDatabase;Integrated Security=True;";
string selectCommandText = "SELECT * FROM Customers";

using (SqlConnection connection = new SqlConnection(connectionString))
{
    SqlDataAdapter adapter = new SqlDataAdapter(selectCommandText, connection);
    DataSet dataSet = new DataSet();
    adapter.Fill(dataSet, "Customers"); // Fills the DataSet with data from the Customers table

    //connection is closed automatically by the DataAdapter

    // Now you can work with the data in the DataSet without an active connection
    foreach (DataRow row in dataSet.Tables["Customers"].Rows)
    {
        Console.WriteLine($"{row["CustomerID"]} - {row["ContactName"]}");
    }
}
```

- **DataAdapter Object:**
  - Acts as a bridge between a `DataSet` and a data source.
  - Uses `Command` objects to retrieve data from and update data in the database.
  - Provides the `Fill()` method to populate a `DataSet` with data, and the `Update()` method to save changes from the `DataSet` back to the database.

- Holds `SelectCommand`, `InsertCommand`, `UpdateCommand`, and `DeleteCommand` objects to manage data transfer and updates.
- Example (C# with SQL Server):
  - See the `SqlDataAdapter` example in the `DataSet` section above for how to fill the DataSet. Here's an example of updating the database:

```
using System.Data;
using System.Data.SqlClient;

string connectionString = "Data Source=yourServer;Initial Catalog=yourDatabase;Integrated Security=True;";
string selectCommandText = "SELECT * FROM Products";

using (SqlConnection connection = new SqlConnection(connectionString))
{
    SqlDataAdapter adapter = new SqlDataAdapter(selectCommandText, connection);
    //important:  set up the commands
    adapter.UpdateCommand = new SqlCommand("UPDATE Products SET ProductName = @ProductName WHERE ProductID = @ProductID", connection);
    adapter.UpdateCommand.Parameters.Add("@ProductName", SqlDbType.NVarChar, 50, "ProductName"); //SourceColumn
    adapter.UpdateCommand.Parameters.Add("@ProductID", SqlDbType.Int, 0, "ProductID");

    DataSet dataSet = new DataSet();
    adapter.Fill(dataSet, "Products");

    // Modify data in the DataSet
    DataRow productRow = dataSet.Tables["Products"].Rows.Find(1); // Find a product with ID = 1
    if (productRow != null)
    {
        productRow["ProductName"] = "New Product Name";
    }

    // Send changes back to the database
    adapter.Update(dataSet, "Products");
}
```

SqlConnection, SqlCommand, and SqlDataReader in Detail

These three classes are fundamental to the connected model of ADO.NET, specifically for working with SQL Server databases. They reside in the `System.Data.SqlClient` namespace.

SqlConnection

- **Purpose:** The `SqlConnection` class is used to establish a connection to a SQL Server database. It acts as the conduit through which your application communicates with the database server.
- **Key Properties and Methods:**
  - `ConnectionString`: A string that specifies how to connect to the database. It includes information like the server name, database name, authentication details, and other options.
  - `Open()`: Opens the database connection.
  - `Close()`: Closes the database connection. It's crucial to close connections to release database resources.
  - `State`: Gets the current state of the connection (e.g., Open, Closed, Connecting).
  - `BeginTransaction()`: Starts a database transaction.
- **Connection String Details:**
  - A connection string is a semicolon-separated string that contains the information needed to connect to a data source. Here are some common parts:
    - `Data Source` or `Server`: The name or address of the SQL Server instance. Can be `.` or `(local)` for the local server.
    - `Initial Catalog` or `Database`: The name of the database to connect to.
    - `Integrated Security` or `Trusted_Connection`: Specifies how the connection should be authenticated. `True` or `yes` indicates Windows Authentication (the current user's Windows credentials are used). `False` or `no` indicates SQL Server Authentication, in which case you need to provide `User ID` and `Password`.
    - `User ID`: The username to use when connecting to the SQL Server.
    - `Password`: The password to use when connecting to the SQL Server.
  - Example Connection Strings:
    - Windows Authentication:
    - `"Server=myServer;Database=myDatabase;Integrated Security=True;"`
    - `"Data Source=.;Initial Catalog=myDatabase;Trusted_Connection=yes;" // . or (local)`

    - SQL Server Authentication:
    - `"Server=myServer;Database=myDatabase;User ID=myUser;Password=myPassword;"`
    - `"Data Source=.;Initial Catalog=myDatabase;User ID=sa;Password=myPassword;"`

- **Example:**

```
using System.Data.SqlClient;

string connectionString = "Data Source=.;Initial Catalog=TestDB;Integrated Security=True;";

// Use the using statement to ensure the connection is properly closed and disposed.
```

```
using (SqlConnection connection = new SqlConnection(connectionString))
{
    try
    {
        connection.Open();
        Console.WriteLine("Connection to database established successfully.");

        // Perform database operations here...

        connection.Close(); // Although using closes it, it's good practice to explicitly close it in complex scenarios
        Console.WriteLine("Connection closed.");
    }
    catch (SqlException ex)
    {
        Console.WriteLine("Error connecting to database:");
        Console.WriteLine(ex.Message);
    }
    // The connection is automatically closed and disposed of here, even if an exception occurs.
}
```

SqlCommand

- **Purpose:** The `SqlCommand` class represents a SQL statement or a stored procedure that you want to execute against the SQL Server database.
- **Key Properties and Methods:**
  - `CommandText`: A string that contains the SQL statement or the name of the stored procedure.
  - `Connection`: The `SqlConnection` object that the command will use to execute the query.
  - `CommandType`: Specifies whether the `CommandText` is a SQL statement (Text), a stored procedure (StoredProcedure), or a table name (TableDirect). The default is `Text`.
  - `Parameters`: A collection of `SqlParameter` objects that allow you to pass values to parameterized SQL statements or stored procedures. This is crucial for security (to prevent SQL injection) and for code reusability.
  - `ExecuteReader()`: Executes the command and returns a `SqlDataReader` object, which you can use to read the results of a SELECT query.
  - `ExecuteNonQuery()`: Executes the command and returns the number of rows affected. Used for INSERT, UPDATE, and DELETE statements, and for executing DDL (Data Definition Language) statements.
  - `ExecuteScalar()`: Executes the command and returns the first column of the first row of the result set. Useful for retrieving a single value.
- **Parameters:**

- Parameterized queries are essential for security and efficiency. Instead of embedding values directly into the SQL string, you use placeholders (e.g., `@parameterName`) and then provide the actual values using `SqlParameter` objects.
- Example of adding parameters:
- `command.Parameters.AddWithValue("@ProductID", productID); // Simplest way`
- `command.Parameters.Add("@ProductName", SqlDbType.NVarChar, 50); //add with type and size`
- `command.Parameters["@ProductName"].Value = productName;`

- **Example:**

```csharp
using System.Data.SqlClient;

string connectionString = "Data Source=.;Initial Catalog=TestDB;Integrated Security=True;";
string selectCommandText = "SELECT ProductID, ProductName, Price FROM Products WHERE CategoryID = @CategoryID";

using (SqlConnection connection = new SqlConnection(connectionString))
{
    try
    {
        connection.Open();

        SqlCommand command = new SqlCommand(selectCommandText, connection);
        command.Parameters.AddWithValue("@CategoryID", 1); // Add parameter

        SqlDataReader reader = command.ExecuteReader();
        Console.WriteLine("Products:");
        while (reader.Read())
        {
            Console.WriteLine($"ID: {reader["ProductID"]}, Name: {reader["ProductName"]}, Price: {reader["Price"]}");
        }
        reader.Close();

        string insertCommandText = "INSERT INTO Orders (CustomerID, OrderDate) VALUES (@CustomerID, @OrderDate)";
        SqlCommand insertCommand = new SqlCommand(insertCommandText, connection);
        insertCommand.Parameters.AddWithValue("@CustomerID", "CUST001");
        insertCommand.Parameters.AddWithValue("@OrderDate", DateTime.Now);
        int rowsAffected = insertCommand.ExecuteNonQuery();
        Console.WriteLine($"{rowsAffected} row(s) inserted into Orders.");
```

```
        string countCommandText = "SELECT COUNT(*) FROM Products";
        SqlCommand countCommand = new SqlCommand(countCommandText, connection);
        int productCount = (int)countCommand.ExecuteScalar();
        Console.WriteLine($"Number of products: {productCount}");


    }
    catch (SqlException ex)
    {
        Console.WriteLine("Error executing command:");
        Console.WriteLine(ex.Message);
    }
}
```

SqlDataReader

- **Purpose:** The `SqlDataReader` provides a way to read data from a SQL Server database in a fast, forward-only, read-only manner. It's optimized for performance when you need to quickly iterate through the results of a query.
- **Key Characteristics:**
  - **Forward-only:** You can only read data sequentially, moving from one row to the next. You cannot go back to a previous row.
  - **Read-only:** You cannot use the `SqlDataReader` to modify data.
  - **Connected:** The `SqlDataReader` requires the `SqlConnection` to remain open while you are reading data. This is a key difference from the `DataSet`, which works in a disconnected manner.
  - **Fast:** It provides very efficient data retrieval because it reads data directly from the database stream without buffering the entire result set in memory.
- **Key Methods:**
  - `Read()`: Advances the reader to the next row. Returns `true` if there are more rows, `false` if you've reached the end of the result set.
  - `GetValue(int i)`: Gets the value of the column at the specified zero-based index.
  - `this[string columnName]` or `this[int columnIndex]`: Provides convenient access to column values using the column name or index.
  - `Close()`: Closes the `SqlDataReader` and releases any associated resources. You should always close the `DataReader` when you're finished with it, and closing the associated `SqlConnection` also closes the `DataReader`.
- **Example:**

```
using System.Data.SqlClient;

string connectionString = "Data Source=.;Initial Catalog=TestDB;Integrated Security=True;";
```

```
string selectCommandText = "SELECT EmployeeID, Name, Department FROM Employees";

using (SqlConnection connection = new SqlConnection(connectionString))
{
    try
    {
        connection.Open();
        SqlCommand command = new SqlCommand(selectCommandText, connection);
        SqlDataReader reader = command.ExecuteReader();

        Console.WriteLine("Employee Data:");
        while (reader.Read())
        {
            // Access data by column name or index
            int employeeId = (int)reader["EmployeeID"];
            string name = reader["Name"].ToString();
            string department = reader["Department"].ToString();
            Console.WriteLine($"ID: {employeeId}, Name: {name}, Department: {department}");
        }
        reader.Close(); // Important: Close the reader
    }
    catch (SqlException ex)
    {
        Console.WriteLine("Error reading data:");
        Console.WriteLine(ex.Message);
    }
}
```

SqlDataAdapter and DataSet in Detail

The `SqlDataAdapter` and `DataSet` are crucial components of the disconnected data access model in ADO.NET. They work together to allow you to retrieve data from a database, cache it in memory, manipulate it, and then update the database with any changes.

SqlDataAdapter

- **Purpose:** The `SqlDataAdapter` acts as a bridge between a `DataSet` and a data source (in this case, a SQL Server database, so we're using `SqlDataAdapter`). It's responsible for:
    - **Filling** the `DataSet` with data from the database.
    - **Updating** the database with changes made to the data in the `DataSet`.
- **Key Properties and Methods:**
    - `SelectCommand`: A `SqlCommand` object that specifies the SQL `SELECT` statement used to retrieve data from the database.
    - `InsertCommand`: A `SqlCommand` object used to insert new rows into the database.

- UpdateCommand: A SqlCommand object used to modify existing rows in the database.
- DeleteCommand: A SqlCommand object used to delete rows from the database.
- Fill(DataSet dataSet): Populates the specified DataSet with data from the database using the SelectCommand.
- Update(DataSet dataSet): Updates the database with changes made to the data in the specified DataSet. It uses the InsertCommand, UpdateCommand, and DeleteCommand properties to determine how to apply the changes.

- **Important Notes:**
  - When using a SqlDataAdapter to update the database, you must configure its InsertCommand, UpdateCommand, and DeleteCommand properties. These commands specify how to translate the changes made in the DataSet back to the database.
  - The DataAdapter uses the SelectCommand to retrieve the initial data.
- **Example (Filling a DataSet):**

```
using System.Data;
using System.Data.SqlClient;

string connectionString = "Data Source=.;Initial Catalog=TestDB;Integrated Security=True;";
string selectCommandText = "SELECT ProductID, ProductName, Price, CategoryID FROM Products";

using (SqlConnection connection = new SqlConnection(connectionString))
{
    SqlDataAdapter dataAdapter = new SqlDataAdapter(selectCommandText, connection);
    DataSet productDataSet = new DataSet();
    dataAdapter.Fill(productDataSet, "Products"); // "Products" is the name of the DataTable in the DataSet

    // The connection is implicitly opened and closed by the DataAdapter

    // Now the productDataSet contains the data from the Products table
    Console.WriteLine("Products in DataSet:");
    foreach (DataRow row in productDataSet.Tables["Products"].Rows)
    {
        Console.WriteLine($"ID: {row["ProductID"]}, Name: {row["ProductName"]}, Price: {row["Price"]}, Category: {row["CategoryID"]}");
    }
}
```

DataSet

- **Purpose:** The `DataSet` represents an in-memory cache of data. It's a disconnected data store, meaning that once the data is retrieved from the database and loaded into the `DataSet`, the connection to the database is no longer needed.
- **Key Features:**
  - **Disconnected:** Data is stored in memory, allowing you to work with it without maintaining an active connection to the database.
  - **Multiple Tables:** A `DataSet` can contain multiple `DataTable` objects, each representing a table of data.
  - **Relationships and Constraints:** You can define relationships and constraints between the tables in a `DataSet`, similar to how they are defined in a relational database.
  - **Data Manipulation:** You can add, modify, and delete rows in the `DataTable` objects within a `DataSet`.
  - **XML Support:** A `DataSet` can be serialized to and from XML, making it easy to transport data between different systems.
- **Key Classes:**
  - `DataTable`: Represents a single table of data within a `DataSet`. It consists of rows and columns.
  - `DataRow`: Represents a single row in a `DataTable`.
  - `DataColumn`: Represents a single column in a `DataTable`.
  - `DataRelation`: Represents a relationship between two `DataTable` objects.
- **Example (Working with a DataSet):**

```
using System.Data;
using System.Data.SqlClient;

string connectionString = "Data Source=.;Initial Catalog=TestDB;Integrated Security=True;";
string selectCommandText = "SELECT CustomerID, ContactName, City FROM Customers";

// Get data into a DataSet
DataSet customerDataSet = new DataSet();
using (SqlConnection connection = new SqlConnection(connectionString))
{
    SqlDataAdapter dataAdapter = new SqlDataAdapter(selectCommandText, connection);
    dataAdapter.Fill(customerDataSet, "Customers");
}

// Work with the data in the DataSet
DataTable customersTable = customerDataSet.Tables["Customers"];

// 1. Iterate through the rows
Console.WriteLine("Customers:");
foreach (DataRow row in customersTable.Rows)
{
    Console.WriteLine($"ID: {row["CustomerID"]}, Name: {row["ContactName"]}, City: {row["City"]}");
```

```
}

// 2. Add a new row
DataRow newRow = customersTable.NewRow();
newRow["CustomerID"] = "CUST006";
newRow["ContactName"] = "New Customer";
newRow["City"] = "New York";
customersTable.Rows.Add(newRow);
Console.WriteLine("\nAdded a new customer.");

// 3. Modify an existing row
DataRow rowToUpdate = customersTable.Rows.Find("CUST001"); // Requires a Primary Key
if (rowToUpdate != null)
{
    rowToUpdate["ContactName"] = "Updated Contact Name";
    Console.WriteLine("Updated customer name.");
}

// 4. Delete a row
DataRow rowToDelete = customersTable.Rows[0]; // Delete the first row
rowToDelete.Delete();
Console.WriteLine("Deleted a customer.");

//5.  check the state of the rows.
foreach (DataRow row in customersTable.Rows)
{
     Console.WriteLine($"Row State: {row.RowState}");
}

// 5. Update the database with the changes (explained in the next example)
```

Performing CRUD Operations with SQL Server

CRUD stands for **C**reate, **R**ead, **U**pdate, and **D**elete. These are the four basic operations that you can perform on data in a database. Here's how to perform CRUD operations in C# using ADO.NET with SQL Server.

Important: These examples use the `System.Data.SqlClient` namespace. Always use parameterized queries to prevent SQL injection.

1. Create (Insert)

- **Purpose:** To add new data to a table in the database.

- **Method:** Use the `SqlCommand` object with an `INSERT` SQL statement. It's best to use parameters to pass the values to be inserted. Execute the command using `ExecuteNonQuery()`.
- **Example:**

```
using System.Data.SqlClient;

string connectionString = "Data Source=.;Initial
Catalog=TestDB;Integrated Security=True;";
string insertCommandText = "INSERT INTO Employees (Name, Age,
Department) VALUES (@Name, @Age, @Department)";

using (SqlConnection connection = new SqlConnection(connectionString))
{
    try
    {
        connection.Open();
        SqlCommand insertCommand = new SqlCommand(insertCommandText,
connection);

        // Add parameters
        insertCommand.Parameters.AddWithValue("@Name", "John Doe");
        insertCommand.Parameters.AddWithValue("@Age", 30);
        insertCommand.Parameters.AddWithValue("@Department",
"Engineering");

        int rowsAffected = insertCommand.ExecuteNonQuery();
        Console.WriteLine($"{rowsAffected} row(s) inserted.");
    }
    catch (SqlException ex)
    {
        Console.WriteLine("Error inserting data:");
        Console.WriteLine(ex.Message);
    }
}
```

2. Read (Select)

- **Purpose:** To retrieve data from one or more tables in the database.
- **Method:** Use the `SqlCommand` object with a `SELECT` SQL statement. Execute the command using `ExecuteReader()` to get a `SqlDataReader`, or use a `SqlDataAdapter` and `DataSet` for disconnected access.
- **Example (using SqlDataReader - Connected Model):**

```
using System.Data.SqlClient;

string connectionString = "Data Source=.;Initial
Catalog=TestDB;Integrated Security=True;";
string selectCommandText = "SELECT EmployeeID, Name, Age, Department
FROM Employees";
```

```
using (SqlConnection connection = new SqlConnection(connectionString))
{
    try
    {
        connection.Open();
        SqlCommand selectCommand = new SqlCommand(selectCommandText, connection);
        SqlDataReader reader = selectCommand.ExecuteReader();

        Console.WriteLine("Employee Data:");
        while (reader.Read())
        {
            Console.WriteLine($"ID: {reader["EmployeeID"]}, Name: {reader["Name"]}, Age: {reader["Age"]}, Department: {reader["Department"]}");
        }
        reader.Close();
    }
    catch (SqlException ex)
    {
        Console.WriteLine("Error reading data:");
        Console.WriteLine(ex.Message);
    }
}
```

- **Example (using SqlDataAdapter and DataSet - Disconnected Model):**

```
using System.Data;
using System.Data.SqlClient;

string connectionString = "Data Source=.;Initial Catalog=TestDB;Integrated Security=True;";
string selectCommandText = "SELECT EmployeeID, Name, Age, Department FROM Employees";

using (SqlConnection connection = new SqlConnection(connectionString))
{
    try
    {
        SqlDataAdapter dataAdapter = new SqlDataAdapter(selectCommandText, connection);
        DataSet dataSet = new DataSet();
        dataAdapter.Fill(dataSet, "Employees");  // Fill the DataSet

        Console.WriteLine("Employee Data (from DataSet):");
        foreach (DataRow row in dataSet.Tables["Employees"].Rows)
        {
            Console.WriteLine($"ID: {row["EmployeeID"]}, Name: {row["Name"]}, Age: {row["Age"]}, Department: {row["Department"]}");
```

```
        }
    }
    catch (SqlException ex)
    {
        Console.WriteLine("Error reading data:");
        Console.WriteLine(ex.Message);
    }
}
```

3. Update

- **Purpose:** To modify existing data in a table.
- **Method:** Use the `SqlCommand` object with an `UPDATE` SQL statement. Use parameters to specify the new values and the condition for which rows to update. Execute the command using `ExecuteNonQuery()`.
- **Example:**

```
using System.Data.SqlClient;

string connectionString = "Data Source=.;Initial Catalog=TestDB;Integrated Security=True;";
string updateCommandText = "UPDATE Employees SET Age = @NewAge, Department = @NewDepartment WHERE EmployeeID = @EmployeeID";

using (SqlConnection connection = new SqlConnection(connectionString))
{
    try
    {
        connection.Open();
        SqlCommand updateCommand = new SqlCommand(updateCommandText, connection);

        // Add parameters
        updateCommand.Parameters.AddWithValue("@NewAge", 35);
        updateCommand.Parameters.AddWithValue("@NewDepartment", "Sales");
        updateCommand.Parameters.AddWithValue("@EmployeeID", 1); // Update the employee with ID 1

        int rowsAffected = updateCommand.ExecuteNonQuery();
        Console.WriteLine($"{rowsAffected} row(s) updated.");
    }
    catch (SqlException ex)
    {
        Console.WriteLine("Error updating data:");
        Console.WriteLine(ex.Message);
    }
}
```

4. Delete

- **Purpose:** To remove data from a table.
- **Method:** Use the `SqlCommand` object with a `DELETE` SQL statement. Use parameters to specify the condition for which rows to delete. Execute the command using `ExecuteNonQuery()`.
- **Example:**

```
using System.Data.SqlClient;

string connectionString = "Data Source=.;Initial Catalog=TestDB;Integrated Security=True;";
string deleteCommandText = "DELETE FROM Employees WHERE EmployeeID = @EmployeeID";

using (SqlConnection connection = new SqlConnection(connectionString))
{
    try
    {
        connection.Open();
        SqlCommand deleteCommand = new SqlCommand(deleteCommandText, connection);

        // Add parameter
        deleteCommand.Parameters.AddWithValue("@EmployeeID", 1); // Delete the employee with ID 1

        int rowsAffected = deleteCommand.ExecuteNonQuery();
        Console.WriteLine($"{rowsAffected} row(s) deleted.");
    }
    catch (SqlException ex)
    {
        Console.WriteLine("Error deleting data:");
        Console.WriteLine(ex.Message);
    }
}
```

Summary

- ADO.NET provides both connected and disconnected approaches to data access.
- SqlConnection, SqlCommand, SqlDataReader allow fast, real-time data operations.
- SqlDataAdapter and DataSet enable in-memory, offline data manipulations.
- CRUD operations can be easily executed using parameterized queries.

10 PRACTICAL EXAMPLES WITH SOLUTION

1. Retrieve a list of students from the database and display them in a console application.

* **Topic:** Connection, Command, DataReader
* **Solution:**

    ```csharp
    using System;
    using System.Data.SqlClient;

    class Program
    {
        static void Main(string[] args)
        {
            string connectionString = "Data Source=.;Initial Catalog=UniversityDB;Integrated Security=True;"; // Or provide User ID/Password

            try
            {
                using (SqlConnection connection = new SqlConnection(connectionString))
                {
                    connection.Open();

                    string selectQuery = "SELECT StudentID, FirstName, LastName, EnrollmentDate FROM Students";
                    SqlCommand command = new SqlCommand(selectQuery, connection);
                    SqlDataReader reader = command.ExecuteReader();

                    Console.WriteLine("List of Students:");
                    while (reader.Read())
                    {
                        Console.WriteLine($"ID: {reader["StudentID"]}, Name: {reader["FirstName"]} {reader["LastName"]}, Enrolled: {reader["EnrollmentDate"]}");
                    }
                    reader.Close();
                }
            }
            catch (SqlException ex)
            {
                Console.WriteLine("Error: " + ex.Message);
            }
            Console.ReadKey();
        }
    }
    // Create a database named UniversityDB
    // Create a table named Students
    // insert few records
    ```

2. Insert a new student record into the database.

* **Topic:** Connection, Command (INSERT), Parameters

* **Solution:**

```csharp
using System;
using System.Data.SqlClient;

class Program
{
    static void Main(string[] args)
    {
        string connectionString = "Data Source=.;Initial Catalog=UniversityDB;Integrated Security=True;";

        Console.Write("Enter First Name: ");
        string firstName = Console.ReadLine();
        Console.Write("Enter Last Name: ");
        string lastName = Console.ReadLine();
        Console.Write("Enter Enrollment Date (YYYY-MM-DD): ");
        DateTime enrollmentDate = DateTime.Parse(Console.ReadLine());

        try
        {
            using (SqlConnection connection = new SqlConnection(connectionString))
            {
                connection.Open();

                string insertQuery = "INSERT INTO Students (FirstName, LastName, EnrollmentDate) VALUES (@FirstName, @LastName, @EnrollmentDate)";
                SqlCommand command = new SqlCommand(insertQuery, connection);
                command.Parameters.AddWithValue("@FirstName", firstName);
                command.Parameters.AddWithValue("@LastName", lastName);
                command.Parameters.AddWithValue("@EnrollmentDate", enrollmentDate);

                int rowsAffected = command.ExecuteNonQuery();
                Console.WriteLine($"{rowsAffected} row(s) inserted successfully.");
            }
        }
        catch (SqlException ex)
        {
            Console.WriteLine("Error: " + ex.Message);
        }
        Console.ReadKey();
    }
}
```

3. Update a student's enrollment date.

* **Topic:** Connection, Command (UPDATE), Parameters
* **Solution:**

```csharp
using System;
using System.Data.SqlClient;

class Program
{
    static void Main(string[] args)
    {
        string connectionString = "Data Source=.;Initial
Catalog=UniversityDB;Integrated Security=True;";

        Console.Write("Enter Student ID to update: ");
        int studentId = int.Parse(Console.ReadLine());
        Console.Write("Enter new Enrollment Date (YYYY-MM-DD): ");
        DateTime newEnrollmentDate = DateTime.Parse(Console.ReadLine());

        try
        {
            using (SqlConnection connection = new
SqlConnection(connectionString))
            {
                connection.Open();

                string updateQuery = "UPDATE Students SET EnrollmentDate
= @NewEnrollmentDate WHERE StudentID = @StudentID";
                SqlCommand command = new SqlCommand(updateQuery,
connection);
                command.Parameters.AddWithValue("@NewEnrollmentDate",
newEnrollmentDate);
                command.Parameters.AddWithValue("@StudentID", studentId);

                int rowsAffected = command.ExecuteNonQuery();
                if (rowsAffected > 0)
                    Console.WriteLine("Enrollment date updated
successfully.");
                else
                    Console.WriteLine("Student not found.");
            }
        }
        catch (SqlException ex)
        {
            Console.WriteLine("Error: " + ex.Message);
        }
        Console.ReadKey();
    }
}
```

4. Delete a student from the database.

* **Topic:** Connection, Command (DELETE), Parameters
* **Solution:**

```csharp
using System;
```

```
using System.Data.SqlClient;

class Program
{
    static void Main(string[] args)
    {
        string connectionString = "Data Source=.;Initial
Catalog=UniversityDB;Integrated Security=True;";

        Console.Write("Enter Student ID to delete: ");
        int studentId = int.Parse(Console.ReadLine());

        try
        {
            using (SqlConnection connection = new
SqlConnection(connectionString))
            {
                connection.Open();

                string deleteQuery = "DELETE FROM Students WHERE
StudentID = @StudentID";
                SqlCommand command = new SqlCommand(deleteQuery,
connection);
                command.Parameters.AddWithValue("@StudentID", studentId);

                int rowsAffected = command.ExecuteNonQuery();
                if (rowsAffected > 0)
                    Console.WriteLine("Student deleted successfully.");
                else
                    Console.WriteLine("Student not found.");
            }
        }
        catch (SqlException ex)
        {
            Console.WriteLine("Error: " + ex.Message);
        }
        Console.ReadKey();
    }
}
```

5. Retrieve student data using a stored procedure.

* **Topic:** Connection, Command (Stored Procedure), Parameters, DataReader
* **Solution:**

```csharp
using System;
using System.Data.SqlClient;
using System.Data;

class Program
{
    static void Main(string[] args)
    {
```

```
            string connectionString = "Data Source=.;Initial
Catalog=UniversityDB;Integrated Security=True;";

            try
            {
                using (SqlConnection connection = new
SqlConnection(connectionString))
                {
                    connection.Open();

                    string storedProcedureName = "GetStudentDetails"; //
Create this stored procedure in SQL Server
                    SqlCommand command = new SqlCommand(storedProcedureName,
connection);
                    command.CommandType = CommandType.StoredProcedure;

                    command.Parameters.AddWithValue("@StudentID", 1); //
Example: Get details for StudentID = 1

                    SqlDataReader reader = command.ExecuteReader();

                    Console.WriteLine("Student Details:");
                    if (reader.Read())
                    {
                        Console.WriteLine($"ID: {reader["StudentID"]}, Name:
{reader["FirstName"]} {reader["LastName"]}, Enrolled:
{reader["EnrollmentDate"]}");
                    }
                    else
                    {
                        Console.WriteLine("Student not found.");
                    }
                    reader.Close();
                }
            }
            catch (SqlException ex)
            {
                Console.WriteLine("Error: " + ex.Message);
            }
            Console.ReadKey();
        }
    }

    // SQL Server Stored Procedure Example (Create this in your database):
    /*
    CREATE PROCEDURE GetStudentDetails
        @StudentID INT
    AS
    BEGIN
        SELECT StudentID, FirstName, LastName, EnrollmentDate
        FROM Students
        WHERE StudentID = @StudentID;
    END
    */
    ```
```
```

6. Get a list of courses and their instructors using DataAdapter and DataSet.

```
* **Topic:** DataAdapter, DataSet, DataRelation
* **Solution:**

    ```csharp
    using System;
    using System.Data;
    using System.Data.SqlClient;

    class Program
    {
        static void Main(string[] args)
        {
            string connectionString = "Data Source=.;Initial
Catalog=UniversityDB;Integrated Security=True;";

            try
            {
                using (SqlConnection connection = new
SqlConnection(connectionString))
                {
                    string coursesQuery = "SELECT CourseID, Title,
InstructorID FROM Courses";
                    string instructorsQuery = "SELECT InstructorID,
FirstName, LastName FROM Instructors";

                    SqlDataAdapter coursesAdapter = new
SqlDataAdapter(coursesQuery, connection);
                    SqlDataAdapter instructorsAdapter = new
SqlDataAdapter(instructorsQuery, connection);

                    DataSet universityDataSet = new DataSet();
                    coursesAdapter.Fill(universityDataSet, "Courses");
                    instructorsAdapter.Fill(universityDataSet,
"Instructors");

                    // Create a DataRelation
                    DataRelation courseInstructorRelation = new
DataRelation("CourseInstructorRelation",

universityDataSet.Tables["Instructors"].Columns["InstructorID"],

universityDataSet.Tables["Courses"].Columns["InstructorID"]);

universityDataSet.Relations.Add(courseInstructorRelation);

                    // Display courses and instructor names
                    Console.WriteLine("Courses and Instructors:");
                    foreach (DataRow courseRow in
universityDataSet.Tables["Courses"].Rows)
                    {
                        Console.Write($"Course: {courseRow["Title"]},
Instructor: ");
                        DataRow instructorRow =
courseRow.GetParentRow(courseInstructorRelation); // Get Parent
```
```

```
                        if (instructorRow != null)
                        {
                            Console.WriteLine($"{instructorRow["FirstName"]}
{instructorRow["LastName"]}");
                        }
                        else
                        {
                            Console.WriteLine("N/A");
                        }
                    }
                }
            }
            catch (SqlException ex)
            {
                Console.WriteLine("Error: " + ex.Message);
            }
            Console.ReadKey();
        }
    }

    //SQL
    /*
    CREATE TABLE Courses (
        CourseID INT PRIMARY KEY,
        Title VARCHAR(255),
        InstructorID INT,
    );

    CREATE TABLE Instructors (
        InstructorID INT PRIMARY KEY,
        FirstName VARCHAR(255),
        LastName VARCHAR(255),
    );

    ALTER TABLE Courses
    ADD CONSTRAINT FK_Courses_Instructors
    FOREIGN KEY (InstructorID) REFERENCES Instructors(InstructorID);
    */
```

7. Update course information in the database using a DataSet and DataAdapter.

* **Topic:** DataAdapter, DataSet, UpdateCommand
* **Solution:**

```csharp
    using System;
    using System.Data;
    using System.Data.SqlClient;

    class Program
    {
        static void Main(string[] args)
        {
```

```
            string connectionString = "Data Source=.;Initial
Catalog=UniversityDB;Integrated Security=True;";
            string coursesQuery = "SELECT CourseID, Title, Credits FROM
Courses";

            using (SqlConnection connection = new
SqlConnection(connectionString))
            {
                SqlDataAdapter coursesAdapter = new
SqlDataAdapter(coursesQuery, connection);

                // 1.  Define the UpdateCommand (Important!)
                string updateCommandText = "UPDATE Courses SET Title =
@Title, Credits = @Credits WHERE CourseID = @CourseID";
                SqlCommand updateCommand = new SqlCommand(updateCommandText,
connection);
                updateCommand.Parameters.Add("@Title", SqlDbType.VarChar,
255, "Title"); // SourceColumn
                updateCommand.Parameters.Add("@Credits", SqlDbType.Int, 0,
"Credits");     // SourceColumn
                updateCommand.Parameters.Add("@CourseID", SqlDbType.Int, 0,
"CourseID");    // SourceColumn
                coursesAdapter.UpdateCommand = updateCommand;

                DataSet universityDataSet = new DataSet();
                coursesAdapter.Fill(universityDataSet, "Courses");

                // 2.  Modify data in the DataSet
                DataTable coursesTable = universityDataSet.Tables["Courses"];
                DataRow courseRow = coursesTable.Rows.Find(1); // Find course
with CourseID = 1
                if (courseRow != null)
                {
                    courseRow["Title"] = "Updated Course Title";
                    courseRow["Credits"] = 4;
                }

                // 3.  Send changes back to the database
                try
                {
                    int rowsAffected =
coursesAdapter.Update(universityDataSet, "Courses");
                    Console.WriteLine($"{rowsAffected} row(s) updated.");
                }
                catch (SqlException ex)
                {
                    Console.WriteLine("Error updating database: " +
ex.Message);
                }
            }
            Console.ReadKey();
        }
    }
```

8. Delete a course using DataAdapter.

* **Topic:** DataAdapter, DataSet, DeleteCommand
* **Solution:**

```csharp
using System;
using System.Data;
using System.Data.SqlClient;

class Program
{
    static void Main(string[] args)
    {
        string connectionString = "Data Source=.;Initial
Catalog=UniversityDB;Integrated Security=True;";
        string coursesQuery = "SELECT CourseID, Title, Credits FROM
Courses";

        using (SqlConnection connection = new
SqlConnection(connectionString))
        {
            SqlDataAdapter coursesAdapter = new
SqlDataAdapter(coursesQuery, connection);

            // 1.  Define the DeleteCommand
            string deleteCommandText = "DELETE FROM Courses WHERE
CourseID = @CourseID";
            SqlCommand deleteCommand = new SqlCommand(deleteCommandText,
connection);
            deleteCommand.Parameters.Add("@CourseID", SqlDbType.Int, 0,
"CourseID"); // SourceColumn
            coursesAdapter.DeleteCommand = deleteCommand;

            DataSet universityDataSet = new DataSet();
            coursesAdapter.Fill(universityDataSet, "Courses");

            // 2. Delete from the DataSet
            DataTable coursesTable = universityDataSet.Tables["Courses"];
            DataRow rowToDelete = coursesTable.Rows.Find(2);
            if (rowToDelete != null)
            {
                rowToDelete.Delete();
                Console.WriteLine("Course Deleted from Dataset");
             }

            // 3.  Update the database
            try
            {
                int rowsAffected =
coursesAdapter.Update(universityDataSet, "Courses");
                Console.WriteLine($"{rowsAffected} row(s) deleted from
database.");
            }
            catch (SqlException ex)
            {
```

```
                    Console.WriteLine("Error deleting from database: " +
ex.Message);
                }
            }
            Console.ReadKey();
        }
    }
    ```
```

## 9. Insert a new course using DataAdapter.

```
* **Topic**: DataAdapter, DataSet, InsertCommand
* **Solution**:
    ```csharp
    using System;
    using System.Data;
    using System.Data.SqlClient;
    class Program
    {
        static void Main(string[] args)
        {
            string connectionString = "Data Source=.;Initial
Catalog=UniversityDB;Integrated Security=True;";
            string coursesQuery = "SELECT CourseID, Title, Credits FROM
Courses";
            using (SqlConnection connection = new
SqlConnection(connectionString))
            {
                SqlDataAdapter coursesAdapter = new
SqlDataAdapter(coursesQuery, connection);
                // 1. Define the InsertCommand
                string insertCommandText = "INSERT INTO Courses (CourseID,
Title, Credits) VALUES (@CourseID, @Title, @Credits)";
                SqlCommand insertCommand = new SqlCommand(insertCommandText,
connection);
                insertCommand.Parameters.Add("@CourseID", SqlDbType.Int, 0,
"CourseID");
                insertCommand.Parameters.Add("@Title", SqlDbType.VarChar,
255, "Title");
                insertCommand.Parameters.Add("@Credits", SqlDbType.Int, 0,
"Credits");
                coursesAdapter.InsertCommand = insertCommand;

                DataSet universityDataSet = new DataSet();
                coursesAdapter.Fill(universityDataSet, "Courses");
//Important to fill

                // 2. Add a new row to the DataSet
                DataTable coursesTable = universityDataSet.Tables["Courses"];
                DataRow newCourseRow = coursesTable.NewRow();
                newCourseRow["CourseID"] = 4;
                newCourseRow["Title"] = "New Course";
                newCourseRow["Credits"] = 3;
                coursesTable.Rows.Add(newCourseRow);
                Console.WriteLine("New Course Added To Dataset");
```

```
                // 3. Update the database
                try
                {
                    int rowsAffected =
coursesAdapter.Update(universityDataSet, "Courses");
                    Console.WriteLine($"{rowsAffected} row(s) inserted into
database.");
                }
                catch (SqlException ex)
                {
                    Console.WriteLine("Error inserting into database: " +
ex.Message);
                }
            }
            Console.ReadKey();
        }
    }
    ```
```

## 10. Perform a transaction to enroll a student in a course.

* **Topic:** Connection, Command, Transactions
* **Solution:**

```csharp
    using System;
    using System.Data.SqlClient;

    class Program
    {
        static void Main(string[] args)
        {
            string connectionString = "Data Source=.;Initial
Catalog=UniversityDB;Integrated Security=True;";

            using (SqlConnection connection = new
SqlConnection(connectionString))
            {
                connection.Open();
                SqlTransaction transaction = connection.BeginTransaction();
// Start a transaction

                try
                {
                    // 1. Insert into Enrollments table
                    string enrollQuery = "INSERT INTO Enrollments (StudentID,
CourseID, Grade) VALUES (@StudentID, @CourseID, @Grade)";
                    SqlCommand enrollCommand = new SqlCommand(enrollQuery,
connection, transaction); // Pass the transaction
                    enrollCommand.Parameters.AddWithValue("@StudentID", 1);
// Example StudentID
                    enrollCommand.Parameters.AddWithValue("@CourseID", 101);
// Example CourseID
                    enrollCommand.Parameters.AddWithValue("@Grade", "A");
```
```

```
                    enrollCommand.ExecuteNonQuery();

                    // 2. Update Course Capacity (assuming there's a Capacity
column in Courses table)
                    string updateCapacityQuery = "UPDATE Courses SET Capacity
= Capacity - 1 WHERE CourseID = @CourseID";
                    SqlCommand updateCapacityCommand = new
SqlCommand(updateCapacityQuery, connection, transaction); // Pass the
transaction

updateCapacityCommand.Parameters.AddWithValue("@CourseID", 101);
                    updateCapacityCommand.ExecuteNonQuery();

                    // If both operations were successful, commit the
transaction
                    transaction.Commit();
                    Console.WriteLine("Transaction committed: Student
enrolled and course capacity updated.");
                }
                catch (SqlException ex)
                {
                    // If any error occurs, roll back the transaction
                    transaction.Rollback();
                    Console.WriteLine("Transaction rolled back: " +
ex.Message);
                }
                finally
                {
                    connection.Close();
                }
            }
            Console.ReadKey();
        }
    }
    /*
    -- Create Enrollments Table
    CREATE TABLE Enrollments (
        EnrollmentID INT PRIMARY KEY IDENTITY,
        StudentID INT,
        CourseID INT,
        Grade VARCHAR(2),
        FOREIGN KEY (StudentID) REFERENCES Students(StudentID),
        FOREIGN KEY (CourseID) REFERENCES Courses(CourseID)
    );

    -- Add a Capacity Column to Courses Table
    ALTER TABLE Courses
    ADD Capacity INT;

    -- Initialize Capacity
    UPDATE Courses SET Capacity = 10;
    */
```

30 MCQ QUESTION WITH ANSWER

Connection, Command, DataReader

1. Which class is used to establish a connection to a SQL Server database in ADO.NET?
   a) SqlCommand
   b) SqlConnection
   c) SqlDataReader
   d) SqlDataAdapter
   Answer: b
2. Which method of the SqlConnection class is used to open a database connection?
   a) Connect()
   b) Open()
   c) Begin()
   d) Start()
   Answer: b
3. Which class represents a SQL statement or stored procedure to execute against a database?
   a) SqlConnection
   b) SqlCommand
   c) SqlDataReader
   d) SqlDataAdapter
   Answer: b
4. Which property of the SqlCommand class holds the SQL query to be executed?
   a) CommandText
   b) QueryString
   c) SQLStatement
   d) Text
   Answer: a
5. Which method of the SqlCommand class is used to execute a query and return a SqlDataReader?
   a) Execute()
   b) ExecuteQuery()
   c) ExecuteReader()
   d) ExecuteScalar()
   Answer: c
6. Which class provides a fast, forward-only, read-only stream of data from a SQL Server database?
   a) SqlConnection
   b) SqlCommand
   c) SqlDataReader
   d) SqlDataAdapter
   Answer: c
7. Does the SqlDataReader hold the data in memory?
   a) Yes
   b) No
   Answer: b
8. Which method is used to move to the next record in a SqlDataReader?
   a) Next()

b) Read()
c) Move()
d) NextRow()
Answer: b

9. Which of the following is true about SqlDataReader?
   a) It is read-only and forward-only.
   b) It is read-write and can move backward.
   c) It is read-only and can move backward.
   d) It is read-write and forward-only.
   Answer: a
10. What happens to the SqlConnection when the SqlDataReader is closed?
   a) The SqlConnection is also closed.
   b) The SqlConnection remains open.
   c) It depends on the connection string.
   d) An exception is thrown.
   Answer: b

DataAdapter and DataSet

11. Which class acts as a bridge between a DataSet and a data source?
   a) SqlConnection
   b) SqlCommand
   c) SqlDataReader
   d) SqlDataAdapter
   Answer: d
12. Which class represents an in-memory cache of data?
   a) SqlConnection
   b) SqlCommand
   c) SqlDataReader
   d) DataSet
   Answer: d
13. Which method of the SqlDataAdapter is used to fill a DataSet with data?
   a) FillData()
   b) Populate()
   c) Fill()
   d) Load()
   Answer: c
14. Which method of the SqlDataAdapter is used to update the database with changes from a DataSet?
   a) UpdateData()
   b) SaveChanges()
   c) Update()
   d) Modify()
   Answer: c
15. Can a DataSet contain multiple tables?
   a) Yes
   b) No
   Answer: a

16. Which of the following is NOT a valid property of a DataAdapter?
    a) SelectCommand
    b) InsertCommand
    c) UpdateCommand
    d) ExecuteCommand
    Answer: d
17. What is the primary purpose of a DataSet?
    a) To connect to a database.
    b) To execute SQL commands.
    c) To store data in memory for disconnected access.
    d) To read data in a forward-only manner.
    Answer: c
18. Does the DataSet maintain an active connection to the database?
    a) Yes
    b) No
    Answer: b
19. Which component of ADO.NET is used to define relationships between tables?
    a) DataRelation
    b) Data связи
    c) TableRelation
    d) Relation
    Answer: a
20. Which is the correct order of operations for retrieving data into a DataSet?
    a) Create DataAdapter, Create DataSet, Fill DataSet
    b) Create DataSet, Create DataAdapter, Fill DataSet
    c) Create DataSet, Fill DataSet, Create DataAdapter
    d) Create DataAdapter, Fill DataSet, Create DataSet
    Answer: a

Performing CRUD Operations with SQL Server

21. What does CRUD stand for?
    a) Create, Read, Update, Delete
    b) Connect, Retrieve, Update, Disconnect
    c) Control, Run, Upgrade, Destroy
    d) Compile, Run,Debug, Edit
    Answer: a
22. Which SQL statement is used to insert new data into a table?
    a) SELECT
    b) INSERT
    c) UPDATE
    d) DELETE
    Answer: b
23. Which SQL statement is used to retrieve data from a table?
    a) SELECT
    b) INSERT
    c) UPDATE
    d) DELETE

Answer: a

24. Which SQL statement is used to modify existing data in a table?
    a) SELECT
    b) INSERT
    c) UPDATE
    d) DELETE
    Answer: c
25. Which SQL statement is used to remove data from a table?
    a) SELECT
    b) INSERT
    c) UPDATE
    d) DELETE
    Answer: d
26. Which method of the SqlCommand object is typically used to execute an INSERT, UPDATE, or DELETE statement?
    a) ExecuteReader()
    b) ExecuteNonQuery()
    c) ExecuteScalar()
    d) Execute()
    Answer: b
27. Which of the following is the best practice to prevent SQL Injection?
    a) Using dynamic SQL.
    b) Using inline SQL.
    c) Using parameterized queries.
    d) Using string concatenation.
    Answer: c
28. In ADO.NET, which object is used to represent a parameter in a SQL query?
    a) SqlParameter
    b) Parameter
    c) QueryParameter
    d) SqlParam
    Answer: a
29. Which isolation level provides the most protection from concurrency issues in a transaction?
    a) Read Uncommitted
    b) Read Committed
    c) Repeatable Read
    d) Serializable
    Answer: d
30. What is the purpose of the using statement when working with SqlConnection?
    a) To improve performance
    b) To automatically close and dispose of the connection.
    c) To handle exceptions
    d) To open the connection asynchronously **Answer: b**

10 MID SIZE QUESTION WITH ANSWER

Connection, Command, DataReader

1. **Explain the purpose of the SqlConnection class in ADO.NET. Describe its key properties and methods with examples.**
   - **Answer:**
     - The SqlConnection class is used to establish a connection to a SQL Server database. It acts as a bridge between a .NET application and the database server.
     - Key Properties and Methods:
       - ConnectionString: Specifies the details required to connect to the database (e.g., server name, database name, authentication).
         - Example: "Data Source=.;Initial Catalog=MyDatabase;Integrated Security=True;"
       - Open(): Opens the database connection.
         - Example: connection.Open();
       - Close(): Closes the database connection, releasing resources.
         - Example: connection.Close();
       - State: Gets the current state of the connection (e.g., Open, Closed).
         - Example: Console.WriteLine(connection.State);
       - BeginTransaction(): Starts a database transaction.
         - Example: SqlTransaction transaction = connection.BeginTransaction();
2. **Describe the role of the SqlCommand class. Explain how to execute a SQL SELECT query and retrieve data using a SqlDataReader.**
   - **Answer:**
     - The SqlCommand class represents a SQL statement or stored procedure to be executed against the database.
     - Executing a SELECT query with SqlDataReader:
       - Create a SqlCommand object, providing the SQL SELECT statement and the SqlConnection.
       - Open the SqlConnection.
       - Call the SqlCommand.ExecuteReader() method to get a SqlDataReader object.
       - Use the SqlDataReader.Read() method to iterate through the result set, accessing column values using reader["ColumnName"] or reader[columnIndex].
       - Close the SqlDataReader and the SqlConnection.

```
using (SqlConnection connection = new
SqlConnection(connectionString))
{
    connection.Open();
    SqlCommand command = new SqlCommand("SELECT * FROM Products",
connection);
    SqlDataReader reader = command.ExecuteReader();
    while (reader.Read())
    {
        Console.WriteLine($"{reader["ProductID"]} -
{reader["ProductName"]}");
    }
```

```
o        reader.Close();
o    }
```

3. **What is a SqlDataReader? Explain its characteristics, advantages, and disadvantages.**
   - **Answer:**
     - A SqlDataReader provides a fast, forward-only, read-only stream of data from a SQL Server database.
     - Characteristics:
       - Forward-only: Data is read sequentially.
       - Read-only: Data cannot be modified.
       - Connected: Requires an open SqlConnection.
       - Lightweight: Minimal overhead, efficient for large datasets.
     - Advantages:
       - High performance: Optimized for fast data retrieval.
       - Low memory usage: Doesn't buffer the entire result set.
     - Disadvantages:
       - Limited functionality: Cannot move backward or modify data.
       - Connection dependency: Requires an open connection for the duration of data retrieval.
       - Not suitable for disconnected scenarios.

DataAdapter and DataSet

4. **Explain the purpose of the SqlDataAdapter and how it facilitates disconnected data access in ADO.NET.**
   - **Answer:**
     - The SqlDataAdapter acts as a bridge between a DataSet and a data source (SQL Server).
     - It enables disconnected data access by:
       - Using the SelectCommand to retrieve data from the database and populate a DataSet.
       - Using the InsertCommand, UpdateCommand, and DeleteCommand to propagate changes made in the DataSet back to the database.
     - The DataAdapter manages the connection, opening it to retrieve or update data and then closing it, allowing the DataSet to be used independently.
5. **Describe the DataSet and its key components. How is it different from a SqlDataReader?**
   - **Answer:**
     - The DataSet is an in-memory cache of data, representing a disconnected data store.
     - Key Components:
       - DataTable: Represents a table of data with rows and columns.
       - DataRow: Represents a single row in a DataTable.
       - DataColumn: Represents a single column in a DataTable.

- DataRelation: Represents a relationship between two tables.
- Difference from SqlDataReader:
  - SqlDataReader: Connected, forward-only, read-only, fast, low memory.
  - DataSet: Disconnected, can navigate and modify data, higher memory usage, supports multiple tables and relationships.

6. **Explain how to retrieve data from a database into a DataSet using a SqlDataAdapter. Provide a C# code example.**
   - **Answer:**
     - Steps:
       - Create a SqlConnection object.
       - Create a SqlDataAdapter object, providing a SelectCommand (SQL SELECT statement) and the SqlConnection.
       - Create a DataSet object.
       - Call the SqlDataAdapter.Fill() method, passing the DataSet and a table name (to create a DataTable within the DataSet).

```
using (SqlConnection connection = new SqlConnection(connectionString))
{
    SqlDataAdapter adapter = new SqlDataAdapter("SELECT * FROM Customers", connection);
    DataSet dataSet = new DataSet();
    adapter.Fill(dataSet, "Customers"); // Fills DataSet and creates a DataTable named "Customers"
} // Connection is automatically closed by the DataAdapter
```

Performing CRUD Operations with SQL Server

7. **Explain the importance of using parameterized queries when performing CRUD operations. Provide an example of how to use parameters with an INSERT statement.**
   - **Answer:**
     - Parameterized queries are crucial for preventing SQL injection attacks, which occur when malicious SQL code is inserted into a query through user input. They also improve performance by allowing the database to cache and reuse query execution plans.
     - Example (INSERT with parameters):

```
using (SqlConnection connection = new SqlConnection(connectionString))
{
    connection.Open();
    SqlCommand command = new SqlCommand("INSERT INTO Products (Name, Price) VALUES (@Name, @Price)", connection);
    command.Parameters.AddWithValue("@Name", productName); //simplest way
    command.Parameters.Add("@Price", SqlDbType.Decimal);
    command.Parameters["@Price"].Value = productPrice;

    command.ExecuteNonQuery();
}
```

8. **Describe the steps involved in updating data in a SQL Server database using ADO.NET. Provide a C# code example.**
   - **Answer:**
   - using System.Data.SqlClient;
   - string connectionString = "Data Source=.;Initial Catalog=testdb;Integrated security=true";
   - string updateQuery = "Update products set price = @Price where productId = @productId";
   -
   - using(SqlConnection connection = new SqlConnection(connectionString)){
   -     connection.Open();
   -     SqlCommand updateCommand = new SqlCommand(updateQuery,connection);
   -     updateCommand.Parameters.AddWithValue("@Price",123.45);
   -     updateCommand.Parameters.AddWithValue("@productId",1);
   -     int rowsAffected = updateCommand.ExecuteNonQuery();
   -     Console.WriteLine($"{rowsAffected} rows updated");
   - }

9. **Explain how to delete data from a SQL Server database using ADO.NET. Discuss the importance of specifying a WHERE clause in the DELETE statement.**
   - **Answer:**
     - Steps:
       - Create a SqlConnection and SqlCommand object.
       - Set the SqlCommand.CommandText to a DELETE statement.
       - Add parameters to the SqlCommand (especially for the WHERE clause).
       - Open the connection.
       - Call SqlCommand.ExecuteNonQuery().
       - Close the connection.
     - Importance of WHERE clause: The WHERE clause specifies which rows to delete. If it's omitted, *all* rows in the table will be deleted, which is rarely the intended behavior. It is critical to use a WHERE clause to avoid accidental data loss.
   - using (SqlConnection connection = new SqlConnection(connectionString))
   - {
   -     connection.Open();
   -     SqlCommand command = new SqlCommand("DELETE FROM Orders WHERE CustomerID = @CustomerID", connection);
   -     command.Parameters.AddWithValue("@CustomerID", customerId);
   -     int rowsAffected = command.ExecuteNonQuery();
   -     connection.Close();
   - }

10. **You have a scenario where you need to perform multiple database operations (an insert and an update) as a single unit of work. Explain how you would use a transaction to ensure data consistency. Provide a C# code snippet.**
    - **Answer:**
        - A transaction ensures that multiple database operations are treated as a single logical unit. If all operations succeed, the transaction is committed, and the changes are saved. If any operation fails, the transaction is rolled back, and all changes are discarded, maintaining data consistency.
        - C# Code with SqlTransaction:

```
using (SqlConnection connection = new SqlConnection(connectionString))
{
    connection.Open();
    SqlTransaction transaction = connection.BeginTransaction(); // Begin the transaction
    try
    {
        // 1. Insert an order
        SqlCommand insertCommand = new SqlCommand("INSERT INTO Orders (CustomerID, OrderDate) VALUES (@CustomerID, @OrderDate)", connection, transaction);
        insertCommand.Parameters.AddWithValue("@CustomerID", "CUST001");
        insertCommand.Parameters.AddWithValue("@OrderDate", DateTime.Now);
        insertCommand.ExecuteNonQuery();

        // 2. Update product quantity
        SqlCommand updateCommand = new SqlCommand("UPDATE Products SET Quantity = Quantity - @Quantity WHERE ProductID = @ProductID", connection, transaction);
        updateCommand.Parameters.AddWithValue("@Quantity", 2);
        updateCommand.Parameters.AddWithValue("@ProductID", 101);
        updateCommand.ExecuteNonQuery();

        transaction.Commit(); // Commit the transaction if all operations succeed
        Console.WriteLine("Transaction successful.");
    }
    catch (SqlException ex)
    {
        transaction.Rollback(); // Rollback on error
        Console.WriteLine("Transaction failed: " + ex.Message);
    }
    finally
    {
        connection.Close();
    }
}
```

CHAPTER 9: DATA BINDING IN ASP.NET

Data binding is a critical aspect of ASP.NET web development, enabling dynamic interactions between UI elements and backend data sources such as databases. In this chapter, we delve into the tools and techniques available in ASP.NET for efficiently binding data to web controls, especially for displaying and managing records in applications.

ASP.NET DataSource Controls

ASP.NET provides several data source controls that simplify the process of connecting to and retrieving data from various data stores. These controls act as intermediaries between your data-bound controls (like GridView, ListView, DetailsView) and the actual data source, abstracting away much of the data access code. Here's a breakdown of the two you mentioned, with more detail:

1. SqlDataSource

- **Purpose:** The `SqlDataSource` control allows you to work directly with SQL databases (like SQL Server, MySQL, Oracle, etc.) without writing manual ADO.NET code. It's designed for scenarios where you want to execute SQL queries or stored procedures.
- **Key Features:**
  - **Connection Management:** It manages the database connection for you.
  - **Command Execution:** It executes SQL `SELECT`, `INSERT`, `UPDATE`, and `DELETE` commands.
  - **Parameters:** Supports parameterized queries to prevent SQL injection and improve performance.
  - **Caching:** Can cache data to reduce database load.
  - **Data Binding:** Provides a simple way to bind data to data-bound controls.
- **Properties:**

    - ConnectionString: Specifies the connection string used to connect to the database. You can store connection strings in the Web.config file for better security and maintainability, and reference them using the <%$ ConnectionStrings:YourConnectionName %> syntax, as shown in your example.
    - SelectCommand: The SQL SELECT statement or the name of a stored procedure to retrieve data.
    - InsertCommand, UpdateCommand, DeleteCommand: The SQL statements or stored procedure names for modifying data.
    - DataSourceMode: Specifies whether the data is retrieved as a DataSet or a DataReader. The default is DataSet.
    - SelectParameters, InsertParameters, UpdateParameters, DeleteParameters: Collections of parameters used in the corresponding commands.
- **Example (Retrieving and Displaying Data with GridView):**

  ASPX:

```
<asp:SqlDataSource ID="SqlDataSource1" runat="server"
    ConnectionString="<%$ ConnectionStrings:MyDatabase %>"
    SelectCommand="SELECT ProductID, ProductName, Price FROM Products">
</asp:SqlDataSource>

<asp:GridView ID="GridView1" runat="server"
DataSourceID="SqlDataSource1" AutoGenerateColumns="true">
</asp:GridView>
```

  Explanation:

    - The SqlDataSource is configured with a connection string (assumed to be in Web.config) and a SELECT command.
    - The GridView's DataSourceID property is set to the ID of the SqlDataSource, establishing the data binding.
    - AutoGenerateColumns="true" tells the GridView to automatically create columns based on the data source.
- **Example (Inserting Data with FormView): FormView for Inserting Data**

```
<asp:SqlDataSource ID="SqlDataSource2" runat="server"
    ConnectionString="<%$ ConnectionStrings:MyDatabase %>"
    SelectCommand="SELECT CategoryID, CategoryName FROM Categories"
    InsertCommand="INSERT INTO Categories (CategoryName) VALUES
(@CategoryName)">
    <InsertParameters>
        <asp:Parameter Name="CategoryName" Type="String" />
    </InsertParameters>
</asp:SqlDataSource>

```

- <asp:FormView ID="FormView1" runat="server" DataSourceID="SqlDataSource2" DefaultMode="Insert">
- <InsertItemTemplate>
- Category Name:
- <asp:TextBox ID="CategoryNameTextBox" runat="server" Text='<%# Bind("CategoryName") %>' />
- <asp:Button ID="InsertButton" runat="server" CommandName="Insert" Text="Insert" />
- <asp:Label ID="MessageLabel" runat="server" Text=""></asp:Label>
- </InsertItemTemplate>
- </asp:FormView>

Code Behind (C#):

```
protected void FormView1_ItemInserted(object sender,
FormViewInsertedEventArgs e)
{
    if (e.Exception == null)
    {
        // Optionally, display a success message
    }
    else
    {
       //Error Message
    }
}
```

Explanation

- The `SqlDataSource` is configured with `InsertCommand` and `InsertParameters`.
- The `FormView` is in `Insert` mode, and its `InsertItemTemplate` defines the input controls.
- The `Bind("CategoryName")` creates a binding between the TextBox and the `CategoryName` parameter.
- When the Insert button is clicked, the FormView uses the `SqlDataSource` to execute the insert command.

2. ObjectDataSource

- **Purpose:** The `ObjectDataSource` control enables you to bind UI controls to *business objects* (classes you create) rather than directly to a database. This promotes a layered architecture, separating data access logic from the presentation layer.
- **Key Features:**
  - **Binding to Business Logic:** Binds to methods in your custom classes.
  - **CRUD Operations:** Supports `Select`, `Insert`, `Update`, and `Delete` operations through method calls.
  - **Parameters:** Passes parameters to the methods.

- **Flexibility:** Provides more control over data retrieval and manipulation logic.

- **Properties:**
  - `TypeName`: The fully qualified name of the class that provides the data.
  - `SelectMethod`: The name of the method in the class that retrieves the data.
  - `InsertMethod`, `UpdateMethod`, `DeleteMethod`: The names of the methods for data modification.
  - `SelectParameters`, `InsertParameters`, `UpdateParameters`, `DeleteParameters`: Collections of parameters for the methods.
- **Example (Binding to a Business Object with GridView):**

  C# (Business Object):

```
using System;
using System.Collections.Generic;
using System.Linq;

public class Student
{
    public int StudentID { get; set; }
    public string FirstName { get; set; }
    public string LastName { get; set; }
}

public class StudentManager
{
    // Simulate data retrieval (in a real application, this would come
from a database)
    private static List<Student> _students = new List<Student>
    {
        new Student { StudentID = 1, FirstName = "John", LastName =
"Doe" },
        new Student { StudentID = 2, FirstName = "Jane", LastName =
"Smith" },
        new Student { StudentID = 3, FirstName = "Bob", LastName =
"Johnson" }
    };

    public List<Student> GetAllStudents()
    {
        return _students;
    }
     public Student GetStudentById(int studentId)
    {
        return _students.FirstOrDefault(s => s.StudentID == studentId);
    }
}
```

  ASPX:

```
<asp:ObjectDataSource ID="ObjectDataSource1" runat="server"
    TypeName="StudentManager"
    SelectMethod="GetAllStudents">
```

```
</asp:ObjectDataSource>

<asp:GridView ID="GridView1" runat="server"
DataSourceID="ObjectDataSource1" AutoGenerateColumns="true">
</asp:GridView>
```

Explanation

- The `TypeName` is set to the fully qualified name of the `StudentManager` class.
- The `SelectMethod` is set to `GetAllStudents`.
- The `ObjectDataSource` calls the `GetAllStudents()` method of the `StudentManager` class and retrieves the list of students.

- **Example (Inserting a Student using ObjectDataSource and FormView):**

ASPX:

```
<asp:ObjectDataSource ID="ObjectDataSource2" runat="server"
    TypeName="StudentManager"
    InsertMethod="InsertStudent">
    <InsertParameters>
        <asp:Parameter Name="firstName" Type="String" />
        <asp:Parameter Name="lastName" Type="String" />
    </InsertParameters>
</asp:ObjectDataSource>

<asp:FormView ID="FormView2" runat="server"
DataSourceID="ObjectDataSource2" DefaultMode="Insert" >
    <InsertItemTemplate>
        First Name: <asp:TextBox ID="FirstNameTextBox" runat="server"
Text='<%# Bind("firstName") %>'></asp:TextBox><br />
        Last Name: <asp:TextBox ID="LastNameTextBox" runat="server"
Text='<%# Bind("lastName") %>'></asp:TextBox><br />
        <asp:Button ID="InsertButton" runat="server"
CommandName="Insert" Text="Insert" />
    </InsertItemTemplate>
</asp:FormView>
```

C# (Business Object - StudentManager):

```
public class StudentManager
{
    // ... (existing code for GetAllStudents and _students)

    public void InsertStudent(string firstName, string lastName)
    {
        int newId = _students.Max(s => s.StudentID) + 1;
        _students.Add(new Student { StudentID = newId, FirstName =
firstName, LastName = lastName });
        // In a real application, you would insert into the database
here
    }
```

```
}
```

Explanation

- The `InsertMethod` is set to the `InsertStudent` method in the `StudentManager` class.
- The `InsertParameters` define the parameters expected by the `InsertStudent` method.
- The `Bind("firstName")` and `Bind("lastName")` in the FormView's InsertItemTemplate bind the TextBox values to the `firstName` and `lastName` parameters of the `InsertStudent` method.

GridView, DetailsView, and FormView Controls in ASP.NET

These are data-bound controls in ASP.NET that are used to display data from a data source. They provide different ways to present and interact with data.

1. GridView

- **Purpose:** The `GridView` control is used to display data in a tabular format (rows and columns). It's ideal for presenting multiple records at once.
- **Key Features:**
  - **Tabular Display:** Presents data in a grid-like structure.
  - **Data Binding:** Binds to various data sources (e.g., `SqlDataSource`, `ObjectDataSource`, `DataSet`, `List`).
  - **Automatic Column Generation:** Can automatically generate columns based on the data source.
  - **Sorting, Paging, and Editing:** Supports built-in features for sorting, paging, and editing data.
  - **Customization:** Offers extensive customization options for appearance and behavior.
- **Example:**

  ASPX:

```
<asp:SqlDataSource ID="SqlDataSource1" runat="server"
    ConnectionString="<%$ ConnectionStrings:MyDatabase %>"
    SelectCommand="SELECT ProductID, ProductName, Price, CategoryName
FROM Products p JOIN Categories c ON p.CategoryID = c.CategoryID">
</asp:SqlDataSource>

<asp:GridView ID="GridView1" runat="server"
    DataSourceID="SqlDataSource1"
    AutoGenerateColumns="True"
    AllowPaging="True"
```

```
    PageSize="5"
    AllowSorting="True"
    CssClass="mydatagrid"
    PagerStyle-CssClass="pager"
    AlternatingRowStyle-CssClass="alt">
    <Columns>
         <asp:BoundField DataField="ProductID" HeaderText="Product ID"
/>
         <asp:BoundField DataField="ProductName" HeaderText="Product
Name" />
         <asp:BoundField DataField="Price" HeaderText="Price"
DataFormatString="{0:C}" />  <%--  Currency format --%>
         <asp:HyperLinkField DataTextField="CategoryName"
HeaderText="Category"
DataNavigateUrlFormatString="CategoryDetails.aspx?ID={0}"
DataNavigateUrlFields="CategoryID" />
    </Columns>
</asp:GridView>
```

Explanation:

- The `GridView` is bound to a `SqlDataSource` that retrieves product data along with the category name using a JOIN.
- `AutoGenerateColumns="True"` creates columns automatically.
- `AllowPaging="True"` and `PageSize="5"` enable paging, displaying 5 records per page.
- `AllowSorting="True"` enables sorting by clicking on column headers.
- `CssClass` and `PagerStyle-CssClass`, `AlternatingRowStyle-CssClass`: Applies CSS classes for styling.
- `Columns`: Explicitly defines the columns to display, formats the Price as currency, and creates a hyperlink to a "CategoryDetails.aspx" page, passing the CategoryID in the query string.

2. DetailsView

- **Purpose:** The `DetailsView` control displays the details of a *single* record from a data source. It presents the data in a table-like layout, with field names and values.
- **Key Features:**
    - **Single-Record Display:** Shows one record at a time.
    - **Table Layout:** Presents data in a row-column format.
    - **Data Binding:** Binds to various data sources.
    - **Editing, Inserting, and Deleting:** Supports built-in functionality for editing, inserting, and deleting records.
    - **Templates:** Allows customization of the layout using templates.
- **Example:**

  ASPX:

```
<asp:SqlDataSource ID="SqlDataSource2" runat="server"
```

```
    ConnectionString="<%$ ConnectionStrings:MyDatabase %>"
    SelectCommand="SELECT ProductID, ProductName, Price, Description,
CategoryID FROM Products WHERE ProductID = @ProductID">
    <SelectParameters>
        <asp:QueryStringParameter Name="ProductID"
QueryStringField="ID" Type="Int32" />
    </SelectParameters>
</asp:SqlDataSource>

<asp:DetailsView ID="DetailsView1" runat="server"
    DataSourceID="SqlDataSource2"
    AutoGenerateRows="False"
    DataKeyNames="ProductID"
    CssClass="mydetailsview">
    <Fields>
        <asp:BoundField DataField="ProductName" HeaderText="Product
Name" />
        <asp:BoundField DataField="Price" HeaderText="Price"
DataFormatString="{0:C}" />
        <asp:BoundField DataField="Description"
HeaderText="Description" />
         <asp:HyperLinkField DataTextField="CategoryID"
HeaderText="Category"
DataNavigateUrlFormatString="CategoryDetails.aspx?ID={0}"
DataNavigateUrlFields="CategoryID" />
        <asp:CommandField ShowEditButton="True" ShowDeleteButton="True"
/>
    </Fields>
</asp:DetailsView>
```

Explanation:

- The `DetailsView` is bound to a `SqlDataSource` that retrieves a single product based on the `ProductID` from the query string (`QueryStringField="ID"`). This is common when navigating from a `GridView`.
- `AutoGenerateRows="False"` prevents automatic row generation, giving you full control over the fields.
- `DataKeyNames="ProductID"` specifies the primary key, which is necessary for editing and deleting.
- `Fields`: Defines the fields to display.
- `CommandField`: Adds built-in "Edit" and "Delete" buttons.

3. FormView

- **Purpose:** The `FormView` is similar to `DetailsView` in that it displays a single record, but it offers greater flexibility in terms of layout and appearance through the use of templates. It's useful when you need a more customized presentation than the table-like structure of `DetailsView`.
- **Key Features:**
    - **Single-Record Display:** Shows one record.

- **Template-Driven:** Uses templates to define the layout of the control.
- **Data Binding:** Binds to various data sources.
- **Editing, Inserting, and Deleting:** Supports editing, inserting, and deleting using templates.
- **Highly Customizable:** Provides maximum control over the UI.

- **Templates:**
  - `ItemTemplate`: Defines the layout for displaying the data.
  - `EditItemTemplate`: Defines the layout for editing the data.
  - `InsertItemTemplate`: Defines the layout for inserting a new record.
  - `EmptyDataTemplate`: Displayed when the data source contains no records.
- **Example:**

  ASPX:

```
<asp:SqlDataSource ID="SqlDataSource3" runat="server"
    ConnectionString="<%$ ConnectionStrings:MyDatabase %>"
    SelectCommand="SELECT ProductID, ProductName, Price, Description
FROM Products WHERE ProductID = @ProductID"
    UpdateCommand="UPDATE Products SET ProductName = @ProductName,
Price = @Price, Description = @Description WHERE ProductID =
@ProductID">
    <SelectParameters>
        <asp:QueryStringParameter Name="ProductID"
QueryStringField="ID" Type="Int32" />
    </SelectParameters>
    <UpdateParameters>
        <asp:Parameter Name="ProductName" Type="String" />
        <asp:Parameter Name="Price" Type="Decimal" />
        <asp:Parameter Name="Description" Type="String" />
        <asp:Parameter Name="ProductID" Type="Int32" />
    </UpdateParameters>
</asp:SqlDataSource>

<asp:FormView ID="FormView1" runat="server"
    DataSourceID="SqlDataSource3"
    DataKeyNames="ProductID"
    DefaultMode="ReadOnly">
    <ItemTemplate>
        <h3><%# Eval("ProductName") %></h3>
        <p>Price: <%# Eval("Price", "{0:C}") %></p>
        <p>Description: <%# Eval("Description") %></p>
         <asp:HyperLink ID="EditLink" runat="server" CommandName="Edit"
Text="Edit" />
    </ItemTemplate>
    <EditItemTemplate>
        Product Name: <asp:TextBox ID="ProductNameTextBox"
runat="server" Text='<%# Bind("ProductName") %>' /><br />
        Price: <asp:TextBox ID="PriceTextBox" runat="server" Text='<%#
Bind("Price", "{0:F2}") %>' /><br />
        Description: <asp:TextBox ID="DescriptionTextBox"
runat="server" Text='<%# Bind("Description") %>' /><br />
        <asp:Button ID="UpdateButton" runat="server"
CommandName="Update" Text="Update" />
```

```
        <asp:Button ID="CancelButton" runat="server"
CommandName="Cancel" Text="Cancel" />
    </EditItemTemplate>
</asp:FormView>
```

Explanation:

- The `FormView` is bound to a `SqlDataSource` with `SelectCommand` and `UpdateCommand`.
- `DataKeyNames="ProductID"` is essential for updates.
- `DefaultMode="ReadOnly"` sets the initial mode to display data.
- `ItemTemplate`: Defines how the data is displayed in read-only mode.
- `EditItemTemplate`: Defines the layout for editing, using `TextBox` controls and the `Bind()` expression for two-way binding.
- The `EditLink` button's `CommandName="Edit"` switches the FormView to Edit mode. The `UpdateButton` and `CancelButton` handle the update operation.

Data Binding Expressions

ASP.NET uses data binding expressions to connect data-bound controls to data sources.

- `Eval()`:
  - Purpose: Performs one-way data binding. It's used to *display* data in a template.
  - Syntax: `<%# Eval("ColumnName", formatString) %>`
  - `ColumnName`: The name of the data field.
  - `formatString`: (Optional) A format string to apply to the data (e.g., "{0:C}" for currency).
  - Example: `<asp:Label ID="NameLabel" runat="server" Text='<%# Eval("FirstName") %>' />` Displays the value of the "FirstName" column.
- `Bind()`:
  - Purpose: Performs two-way data binding. It's used in *editing* or *inserting* scenarios to both display data and allow users to modify it.
  - Syntax: `<%# Bind("ColumnName", formatString) %>`
  - Example: `<asp:TextBox ID="NameTextBox" runat="server" Text='<%# Bind("FirstName") %>' />` Displays the "FirstName" value in a TextBox, and when the user edits the text, the changes are automatically bound back to the data source during an update operation.
- `XPath()`:
  - Purpose: Used for binding to XML data sources.
  - Not commonly used with SQL Server and the controls discussed above.

Key Differences:

- `Eval()`: Read-only data binding. Use for displaying data.
- `Bind()`: Read-write (two-way) data binding. Use for editing and inserting.

Paging, Sorting, and Editing in GridView

The `GridView` control in ASP.NET provides built-in support for common data interaction features like paging, sorting, and editing. These features enhance the user experience by allowing them to navigate through large datasets, order data, and modify records directly within the grid.

1. Paging

- **Purpose:** Paging divides a large dataset into smaller, more manageable pages. This improves performance and user experience by displaying only a subset of the data at a time.
- **Implementation:**
  - `AllowPaging="True"`: Enables paging for the `GridView`.
  - `PageSize="n"`: Specifies the number of records to display per page (e.g., `PageSize="5"` displays 5 records per page).
  - The `GridView` automatically adds a pager row (usually at the bottom) with navigation controls (page numbers, "Next," "Previous," "First," "Last" links).
- **Customization:**
  - `PagerStyle`: Provides properties to customize the appearance of the pager row (e.g., `CssClass`, `BackColor`, `ForeColor`).
  - `PagerSettings`: Offers more control over the pager's behavior (e.g., `Mode`, `Position`, `PageButtonCount`).
  - `PageIndexChanging` Event: Allows you to handle the page change event and perform custom logic (though this is rarely needed for basic paging).
- **Example:**

  ASPX:

```
<asp:SqlDataSource ID="SqlDataSource1" runat="server"
    ConnectionString="<%$ ConnectionStrings:MyDatabase %>"
    SelectCommand="SELECT ProductID, ProductName, Price, CategoryName
FROM Products p JOIN Categories c ON p.CategoryID = c.CategoryID">
</asp:SqlDataSource>

<asp:GridView ID="GridView1" runat="server"
    DataSourceID="SqlDataSource1"
    AutoGenerateColumns="True"
    AllowPaging="True"
    PageSize="5"
    CssClass="myGridview"
    PagerStyle-CssClass="pager"
    PagerSettings-Mode="NumericFirstLast"
    PagerSettings-PageButtonCount="3">
    <Columns>
        <asp:BoundField DataField="ProductID" HeaderText="Product ID"
/>
        <asp:BoundField DataField="ProductName" HeaderText="Product
Name" />
```

```
        <asp:BoundField DataField="Price" HeaderText="Price"
DataFormatString="{0:C}" />
        <asp:BoundField DataField="CategoryName" HeaderText="Category"
/>
    </Columns>
</asp:GridView>
```

Explanation:

- `AllowPaging="True"` enables paging.
- `PageSize="5"` displays 5 products per page.
- `CssClass` and `PagerStyle-CssClass`: Apply CSS styles to the GridView and pager row.
- `PagerSettings-Mode="NumericFirstLast"`: Displays page numbers along with "First" and "Last" links.
- `PagerSettings-PageButtonCount="3"`: Shows a maximum of 3 page number buttons at a time in the pager.

2. Sorting

- **Purpose:** Sorting allows users to arrange the data in ascending or descending order based on the values in one or more columns.
- **Implementation:**
  - `AllowSorting="True"`: Enables sorting for the `GridView`.
  - When sorting is enabled, the `GridView` automatically adds sort arrows to the column headers.
  - Clicking a column header triggers a postback and sorts the data.
- **Data Source Support:**
  - The `GridView` relies on the underlying data source to perform the actual sorting.
  - `SqlDataSource`: The `SqlDataSource` appends an `ORDER BY` clause to the `SelectCommand` based on the clicked column. For this to work, the `SelectCommand` should not already contain an `ORDER BY` clause.
  - `ObjectDataSource`, `DataSet`, `DataTable`, `List`: The `GridView` uses the data source's built-in sorting capabilities (if available). For example, `DataTable` has a `DefaultView.Sort` property.
- **Customization:**
  - `SortExpression`: Specifies the column to sort when a header is clicked. If not specified for a `BoundField`, it defaults to the `DataField`.
  - `Sorting` Event: Allows you to handle the sorting event and perform custom sorting logic (e.g., sorting by multiple columns).
- **Example:**

  ASPX:

```
<asp:SqlDataSource ID="SqlDataSource2" runat="server"
    ConnectionString="<%$ ConnectionStrings:MyDatabase %>"
```

```
    SelectCommand="SELECT ProductID, ProductName, Price, CategoryName
FROM Products p JOIN Categories c ON p.CategoryID = c.CategoryID">
</asp:SqlDataSource>

<asp:GridView ID="GridView2" runat="server"
    DataSourceID="SqlDataSource2"
    AutoGenerateColumns="True"
    AllowSorting="True"
    CssClass="myGridview">
    <Columns>
        <asp:BoundField DataField="ProductID" HeaderText="Product ID"
SortExpression="ProductID" />
        <asp:BoundField DataField="ProductName" HeaderText="Product
Name" SortExpression="ProductName"/>
        <asp:BoundField DataField="Price" HeaderText="Price"
DataFormatString="{0:C}" SortExpression="Price"/>
        <asp:BoundField DataField="CategoryName" HeaderText="Category"
SortExpression="CategoryName"/>
    </Columns>
</asp:GridView>
```

Explanation:

- `AllowSorting="True"` enables sorting.
- `SortExpression`: Explicitly sets the column to sort for each `BoundField`. In this case, it's the same as `DataField`, but you might use a different `SortExpression` if you need to sort by a different field or expression.
- When a user clicks a column header, the `GridView` adds an `ORDER BY` clause to the `SelectCommand` (e.g., `ORDER BY ProductID ASC` or `ORDER BY ProductID DESC`).

3. Editing

- **Purpose:** Editing allows users to modify the data in the `GridView` directly.
- **Implementation:**
  - `AutoGenerateEditButton="True"`: Adds an "Edit" button to each row in the `GridView`.
  - When the "Edit" button is clicked, the row switches to edit mode, and the columns are typically displayed as `TextBox` controls.
  - The `GridView` also adds "Update" and "Cancel" buttons.
- **Data Source Interaction:**
  - The `GridView` relies on the data source to perform the actual update operation.
  - `SqlDataSource`: The `SqlDataSource` must have an `UpdateCommand` defined to handle the update. The `UpdateCommand` should use parameters to prevent SQL injection.
  - `ObjectDataSource`: The `ObjectDataSource` must have an `UpdateMethod` defined in the associated business object.
- **Manual Editing with Events:**

- For more control over the editing process, you can handle the `RowEditing`, `RowUpdating`, and `RowCancelingEdit` events.
- `RowEditing`: Allows you to perform custom logic before the row enters edit mode.
- `RowUpdating`: Allows you to handle the update operation manually, retrieve the new values from the `GridView`, and call your own data access code.
- `RowCancelingEdit`: Allows you to handle the cancel operation.

- **Example (with SqlDataSource UpdateCommand):**

ASPX:

```
<asp:SqlDataSource ID="SqlDataSource3" runat="server"
    ConnectionString="<%$ ConnectionStrings:MyDatabase %>"
    SelectCommand="SELECT ProductID, ProductName, Price, CategoryID
FROM Products"
    UpdateCommand="UPDATE Products SET ProductName = @ProductName,
Price = @Price, CategoryID = @CategoryID WHERE ProductID = @ProductID">
    <UpdateParameters>
        <asp:Parameter Name="ProductName" Type="String" />
        <asp:Parameter Name="Price" Type="Decimal" />
         <asp:Parameter Name="CategoryID" Type="Int32" />
        <asp:Parameter Name="ProductID" Type="Int32" />  <%--  For the
WHERE clause --%>
    </UpdateParameters>
</asp:SqlDataSource>

<asp:GridView ID="GridView3" runat="server"
    DataSourceID="SqlDataSource3"
    AutoGenerateColumns="False"
    AutoGenerateEditButton="True"
    DataKeyNames="ProductID"
    CssClass="myGridview">
    <Columns>
        <asp:BoundField DataField="ProductName" HeaderText="Product
Name" />
        <asp:BoundField DataField="Price" HeaderText="Price"
DataFormatString="{0:C}" />
        <asp:DropDownListField DataField="CategoryID"
HeaderText="Category"
            DataSourceID="SqlDataSourceCategories"
            DataTextField="CategoryName"
            DataValueField="CategoryID"
            />
        <asp:BoundField DataField="ProductID" HeaderText="Product ID"
ReadOnly="True" />
    </Columns>
</asp:GridView>
<asp:SqlDataSource ID="SqlDataSourceCategories" runat="server"
    ConnectionString="<%$ ConnectionStrings:MyDatabase %>"
    SelectCommand="SELECT CategoryID, CategoryName FROM Categories" />
```

Explanation:

  - `AutoGenerateEditButton="True"` adds the "Edit," "Update," and "Cancel" buttons.
  - `DataKeyNames="ProductID"` specifies the primary key, which is used in the `WHERE` clause of the `UpdateCommand`.
  - The `SqlDataSource` has an `UpdateCommand` with parameters. The parameter names *must* match the column names in the `UPDATE` statement.
  - The `DropDownListField` displays a dropdown list for the `CategoryID` column, allowing the user to select a category. It uses a separate `SqlDataSource` (`SqlDataSourceCategories`) to populate the dropdown.
  - When the "Update" button is clicked, the `GridView` automatically populates the `UpdateParameters` with the values from the edited row and calls the `SqlDataSource` to execute the `UpdateCommand`.
- **Example (Manual Editing with Events): ASPX** ```html <asp:GridView ID="GridView4" runat="server" DataSourceID="SqlDataSource4" AutoGenerateColumns="False" AutoGenerateEditButton="True" DataKeyNames="ProductID" OnRowUpdating="GridView4_RowUpdating" OnRowCancelingEdit="GridView4_RowCancelingEdit" OnRowEditing="GridView4_RowEditing" CssClass="myGridview"> <asp:BoundField DataField="ProductName" HeaderText="Product Name" /> <asp:BoundField DataField="Price" HeaderText="Price" DataFormatString="{0:C}" /> <asp:BoundField DataField="ProductID" HeaderText="Product ID" ReadOnly="True" /> </asp:GridView>

~~~
  <asp:SqlDataSource ID="SqlDataSource4" runat="server"
      ConnectionString="<%$ ConnectionStrings:MyDatabase %>"
      SelectCommand="SELECT ProductID, ProductName, Price FROM
Products">
  </asp:SqlDataSource>
  ```

  **Code Behind (C#)**
  ```csharp
  protected void GridView4_RowEditing(object sender,
GridViewEditEventArgs e)
  {
      GridView4.EditIndex = e.NewEditIndex;
      GridView4.DataBind();
  }

  protected void GridView4_RowCancelingEdit(object sender,
GridViewCancelEditEventArgs e)
  {
      GridView4.EditIndex = -1;
      GridView4.DataBind();
  }

  protected void GridView4_RowUpdating(object sender,
GridViewUpdateEventArgs e)
  {
      // Get the ProductID from the DataKeyNames
~~~

```
        int productID = (int)GridView4.DataKeys[e.RowIndex].Value;

        // Get the new values from the TextBox controls in the GridView
        string productName =
((TextBox)GridView4.Rows[e.RowIndex].FindControl("ProductName")).Text;
        decimal price =
decimal.Parse(((TextBox)GridView4.Rows[e.RowIndex].FindControl("Price")
).Text);

        // Perform the update in the database (using ADO.NET)
        string connectionString =
ConfigurationManager.ConnectionStrings["MyDatabase"].ConnectionString;
        string updateQuery = "UPDATE Products SET ProductName =
@ProductName, Price = @Price WHERE ProductID = @ProductID";

        using (SqlConnection connection = new
SqlConnection(connectionString))
        {
            connection.Open();
            SqlCommand command = new SqlCommand(updateQuery, connection);
            command.Parameters.AddWithValue("@ProductName", productName);
            command.Parameters.AddWithValue("@Price", price);
            command.Parameters.AddWithValue("@ProductID", productID);

            command.ExecuteNonQuery();
        }

        // Exit edit mode and rebind the GridView
        GridView4.EditIndex = -1;
        GridView4.DataBind();
        e.Cancel = true;

    }
    ```
```

---

🔍 **Conclusion:** Data binding in ASP.NET greatly simplifies working with data-centric applications. Mastery of `SqlDataSource`, `ObjectDataSource`, and display controls like `GridView`, along with their built-in functionalities like paging and editing, equips developers with powerful tools to create robust and interactive web applications efficiently.

## 10 PRACTICAL EXAMPLES WITH SOLUTION

### 1. Display a list of products from a database using GridView and SqlDataSource.

- **Topic:** SqlDataSource, GridView
```

- **Solution:**

  ASPX:

```
<asp:SqlDataSource ID="SqlDataSource1" runat="server"
    ConnectionString="<%$ ConnectionStrings:MyDatabase %>"
    SelectCommand="SELECT ProductID, ProductName, Price, CategoryName
FROM Products p INNER JOIN Categories c ON p.CategoryID =
c.CategoryID">
</asp:SqlDataSource>

<asp:GridView ID="GridView1" runat="server"
DataSourceID="SqlDataSource1" AutoGenerateColumns="True"
CssClass="myGridview">
</asp:GridView>
```

  Explanation: This example retrieves product data (including the category name using an INNER JOIN) and displays it in a GridView. The AutoGenerateColumns="True" automatically creates the columns. The CssClass is for styling.

2. Display details of a selected product using DetailsView and SqlDataSource.

- **Topic:** SqlDataSource, DetailsView, Data Binding Expression (Eval)
- **Solution:**

  ASPX:

```
<asp:SqlDataSource ID="SqlDataSource2" runat="server"
    ConnectionString="<%$ ConnectionStrings:MyDatabase %>"
    SelectCommand="SELECT ProductID, ProductName, Price, Description
FROM Products WHERE ProductID = @ProductID">
    <SelectParameters>
        <asp:QueryStringParameter Name="ProductID"
QueryStringField="ID" Type="Int32" />
    </SelectParameters>
</asp:SqlDataSource>

<asp:DetailsView ID="DetailsView1" runat="server"
DataSourceID="SqlDataSource2" AutoGenerateRows="False"
DataKeyNames="ProductID" CssClass="mydetailsview">
    <Fields>
        <asp:BoundField DataField="ProductName" HeaderText="Product
Name" />
        <asp:BoundField DataField="Price" HeaderText="Price"
DataFormatString="{0:C}" />
        <asp:BoundField DataField="Description"
HeaderText="Description" />
    </Fields>
</asp:DetailsView>
```

Explanation: This example displays the details of a single product. It assumes that the ProductID is passed in the query string (e.g., ProductDetails.aspx?ID=1). The SelectParameters retrieves the product based on the ID. AutoGenerateRows="False" gives explicit control over displayed fields.

3. Display a list of students from a business object using ObjectDataSource and GridView.

- **Topic:** ObjectDataSource, GridView
- **Solution:**

  C# (Business Object):

```
using System;
using System.Collections.Generic;

public class Student
{
    public int StudentID { get; set; }
    public string FirstName { get; set; }
    public string LastName { get; set; }
    public string Major { get; set; }
}

public class StudentManager
{
    private static List<Student> _students = new List<Student>
    {
        new Student { StudentID = 1, FirstName = "John", LastName =
"Doe", Major = "Computer Science" },
        new Student { StudentID = 2, FirstName = "Jane", LastName =
"Smith", Major = "Engineering" },
        new Student { StudentID = 3, FirstName = "Bob", LastName =
"Johnson", Major = "Business" }
    };

    public List<Student> GetAllStudents()
    {
        return _students;
    }
}
```

  ASPX:

```
<asp:ObjectDataSource ID="ObjectDataSource1" runat="server"
TypeName="StudentManager" SelectMethod="GetAllStudents">
</asp:ObjectDataSource>

<asp:GridView ID="GridView1" runat="server"
DataSourceID="ObjectDataSource1" AutoGenerateColumns="True"
CssClass="myGridview">
</asp:GridView>
```

Explanation: This example retrieves student data from a StudentManager class and displays it in a GridView. The ObjectDataSource acts as the intermediary.

4. Display a single student's details using FormView and ObjectDataSource.

- **Topic:** ObjectDataSource, FormView, Data Binding (Eval)
- **Solution:**

C# (Business Object):

```
using System;
using System.Collections.Generic;
using System.Linq;

public class Student
{
    public int StudentID { get; set; }
    public string FirstName { get; set; }
    public string LastName { get; set; }
    public string Major { get; set; }
}

public class StudentManager
{
     private static List<Student> _students = new List<Student>
    {
        new Student { StudentID = 1, FirstName = "John", LastName =
"Doe", Major = "Computer Science" },
        new Student { StudentID = 2, FirstName = "Jane", LastName =
"Smith", Major = "Engineering" },
        new Student { StudentID = 3, FirstName = "Bob", LastName =
"Johnson", Major = "Business" }
    };
    public Student GetStudentDetails(int studentId)
    {
        return _students.FirstOrDefault(s => s.StudentID == studentId);
    }
}
```

ASPX:

```
<asp:ObjectDataSource ID="ObjectDataSource2" runat="server"
TypeName="StudentManager" SelectMethod="GetStudentDetails">
    <SelectParameters>
        <asp:QueryStringParameter Name="studentId"
QueryStringField="ID" Type="Int32" />
    </SelectParameters>
</asp:ObjectDataSource>

<asp:FormView ID="FormView1" runat="server"
DataSourceID="ObjectDataSource2"  CssClass="myformview">
    <ItemTemplate>
        <h3><%# Eval("FirstName") %> <%# Eval("LastName") %></h3>
```

```
            <p><strong>ID:</strong> <%# Eval("StudentID") %></p>
            <p><strong>Major:</strong> <%# Eval("Major") %></p>
        </ItemTemplate>
    </asp:FormView>
```

Explanation: This example displays a single student's details using a FormView. The ObjectDataSource calls the GetStudentDetails method in the StudentManager class, passing the studentId from the query string.

5. Display a list of courses with paging using GridView and SqlDataSource.

````
* **Topic:** SqlDataSource, GridView, Paging
* **Solution:**

    **ASPX:**

    ```html
    <asp:SqlDataSource ID="SqlDataSource3" runat="server"
        ConnectionString="<%$ ConnectionStrings:UniversityDB %>"
        SelectCommand="SELECT CourseID, Title, Credits, DepartmentName FROM
Courses c INNER JOIN Departments d ON c.DepartmentID = d.DepartmentID">
    </asp:SqlDataSource>

    <asp:GridView ID="GridView2" runat="server"
        DataSourceID="SqlDataSource3"
        AutoGenerateColumns="True"
        AllowPaging="True"
        PageSize="5"
        CssClass="myGridview">
    </asp:GridView>
    ```

    **Explanation:** This example displays a list of courses with paging
enabled.  `AllowPaging="True"` and `PageSize="5"` divide the courses into
pages of 5 records each.
````

6. Display a list of employees with sorting using GridView and SqlDataSource.

````
* **Topic:** SqlDataSource, GridView, Sorting
* **Solution:**

    **ASPX:**

    ```html
    <asp:SqlDataSource ID="SqlDataSource4" runat="server"
        ConnectionString="<%$ ConnectionStrings:HRDB %>"
        SelectCommand="SELECT EmployeeID, FirstName, LastName, JobTitle FROM
Employees">
    </asp:SqlDataSource>

    <asp:GridView ID="GridView3" runat="server"
        DataSourceID="SqlDataSource4"
````
````

```
        AutoGenerateColumns="True"
        AllowSorting="True"
        CssClass="myGridview">
    </asp:GridView>
```

Explanation: This example displays a list of employees with sorting enabled. `AllowSorting="True"` adds sort arrows to the column headers, allowing users to sort the data.

7. Allow editing of product information in a GridView using SqlDataSource.

* **Topic:** SqlDataSource, GridView, Editing
* **Solution:**

ASPX:

```html
<asp:SqlDataSource ID="SqlDataSource5" runat="server"
    ConnectionString="<%$ ConnectionStrings:StoreDB %>"
    SelectCommand="SELECT ProductID, ProductName, Price, StockQuantity FROM Products"
    UpdateCommand="UPDATE Products SET ProductName = @ProductName, Price = @Price, StockQuantity = @StockQuantity WHERE ProductID = @ProductID">
    <UpdateParameters>
        <asp:Parameter Name="ProductName" Type="String" />
        <asp:Parameter Name="Price" Type="Decimal" />
        <asp:Parameter Name="StockQuantity" Type="Int32" />
        <asp:Parameter Name="ProductID" Type="Int32" />
    </UpdateParameters>
</asp:SqlDataSource>

<asp:GridView ID="GridView4" runat="server"
    DataSourceID="SqlDataSource5"
    AutoGenerateColumns="False"
    AutoGenerateEditButton="True"
    DataKeyNames="ProductID"
    CssClass="myGridview">
    <Columns>
        <asp:BoundField DataField="ProductName" HeaderText="Product Name" />
        <asp:BoundField DataField="Price" HeaderText="Price" DataFormatString="{0:C}" />
        <asp:BoundField DataField="StockQuantity" HeaderText="Stock Quantity" />
        <asp:BoundField DataField="ProductID" HeaderText="Product ID" ReadOnly="True" />
    </Columns>
</asp:GridView>
```

Explanation: This example allows users to edit product information directly in the `GridView`. `AutoGenerateEditButton="True"` adds the edit functionality. The `SqlDataSource` has an `UpdateCommand` to handle the database update. `DataKeyNames` is crucial for identifying the record to update.

8. Display a list of books from a data source and use data binding expressions in FormView.

* **Topic:** SqlDataSource, FormView, Data Binding (Eval)
* **Solution:**

    ASPX:

```html
    <asp:SqlDataSource ID="SqlDataSource6" runat="server"
        ConnectionString="<%$ ConnectionStrings:LibraryDB %>"
        SelectCommand="SELECT BookID, Title, Author, PublicationDate FROM Books">
    </asp:SqlDataSource>

    <asp:FormView ID="FormView2" runat="server" DataSourceID="SqlDataSource6" CssClass="myformview">
        <ItemTemplate>
            <h3><%# Eval("Title") %></h3>
            <p><strong>Author:</strong> <%# Eval("Author") %></p>
            <p><strong>Published:</strong> <%# Eval("PublicationDate", "{0:d}") %></p>  <%-- Short date format --%>
        </ItemTemplate>
    </asp:FormView>
```

Explanation: This example displays book information in a `FormView` using `Eval()` expressions for one-way data binding. The `PublicationDate` is formatted as a short date.

9. Display a paginated and sortable list of customers using GridView and SqlDataSource * **Topic**: SqlDataSource, GridView, Paging, Sorting * **Solution**: **ASPX**: ```html <asp:SqlDataSource ID="SqlDataSource7" runat="server" ConnectionString="<%$ ConnectionStrings:SalesDB %>" SelectCommand="SELECT CustomerID, FirstName, LastName, City, Country FROM Customers"> </asp:SqlDataSource>

```html
    <asp:GridView ID="GridView5" runat="server"
        DataSourceID="SqlDataSource7"
        AutoGenerateColumns="True"
        AllowPaging="True"
        PageSize="10"
        AllowSorting="True"
        CssClass="mygridview"
        PagerStyle-CssClass="pager">
    </asp:GridView>
```

Explanation: This example shows a list of customers with both paging and sorting enabled. Users can navigate through pages of 10 customers and sort by clicking on the column headers.

10. Edit student information using ObjectDataSource and GridView. * **Topic**: ObjectDataSource, GridView, Editing, Data Binding (Bind) * **Solution**: **C# (Business Object)**: ```csharp using System; using System.Collections.Generic; using System.Linq;

```
    public class Student
    {
        public int StudentID { get; set; }
        public string FirstName { get; set; }
        public string LastName { get; set; }
        public string Major { get; set; }
    }

    public class StudentManager
    {
        private static List<Student> _students = new List<Student>
        {
            new Student { StudentID = 1, FirstName = "John", LastName =
"Doe", Major = "Computer Science" },
            new Student { StudentID = 2, FirstName = "Jane", LastName =
"Smith", Major = "Engineering" },
            new Student { StudentID = 3, FirstName = "Bob", LastName =
"Johnson", Major = "Business" }
        };

        public List<Student> GetAllStudents()
        {
            return _students;
        }

        public void UpdateStudent(int studentId, string firstName, string
lastName, string major)
        {
            Student studentToUpdate = _students.FirstOrDefault(s =>
s.StudentID == studentId);
            if (studentToUpdate != null)
            {
                studentToUpdate.FirstName = firstName;
                studentToUpdate.LastName = lastName;
                studentToUpdate.Major = major;
                // In a real application, you'd update the database here.
            }
        }
         public Student GetStudentById(int studentId)
        {
            return _students.FirstOrDefault(s => s.StudentID == studentId);
        }
    }
    ```
    ASPX:
    ```html
    <asp:ObjectDataSource ID="ObjectDataSource8" runat="server"
        TypeName="StudentManager"
        SelectMethod="GetStudentById"
        UpdateMethod="UpdateStudent">
```

```
        <SelectParameters>
            <asp:QueryStringParameter Name="studentId" QueryStringField="ID"
Type="Int32" />
        </SelectParameters>
        <UpdateParameters>
            <asp:Parameter Name="studentId" Type="Int32" />
            <asp:Parameter Name="firstName" Type="String" />
            <asp:Parameter Name="lastName" Type="String" />
            <asp:Parameter Name="major" Type="String" />
        </UpdateParameters>
    </asp:ObjectDataSource>

    <asp:GridView ID="GridView6" runat="server"
        DataSourceID="ObjectDataSource8"
        AutoGenerateColumns="False"
        AutoGenerateEditButton="True"
        DataKeyNames="StudentID"
        CssClass="mygridview">
        <Columns>
            <asp:BoundField DataField="FirstName" HeaderText="First Name" />
            <asp:BoundField DataField="LastName" HeaderText="Last Name" />
            <asp:BoundField DataField="Major" HeaderText="Major" />
            <asp:BoundField DataField="StudentID" HeaderText="Student ID"
ReadOnly="True" />
        </Columns>
    </asp:GridView>
```

Explanation: This example allows editing student information using an ObjectDataSource. The `GridView` is bound to the `StudentManager` class. `AutoGenerateEditButton="True"` enables editing, and `DataKeyNames` identifies the `StudentID` for updates. The `ObjectDataSource` calls the `UpdateStudent` method in the `StudentManager` class.

30 multiple-choice questions (MCQs) on DataSource Controls and data-bound controls in ASP.NET:

SqlDataSource, ObjectDataSource

1. Which data source control is used to directly interact with SQL databases?
   a) ObjectDataSource
   b) XmlDataSource
   c) SqlDataSource
   d) AccessDataSource
   Answer: c
2. Which data source control is used to bind to custom business objects?
   a) SqlDataSource
   b) XmlDataSource
   c) ObjectDataSource
   d) LinqDataSource
   Answer: c
3. Which property of the SqlDataSource control specifies the database connection string?

a) Database
b) Connection
c) ConnectionString
d) Source
Answer: c

4. Which property of the ObjectDataSource control specifies the class name of the business object?
a) ClassName
b) ObjectType
c) TypeName
d) ObjectName
Answer: c

5. Which property of the SqlDataSource control holds the SQL SELECT statement?
a) SelectQuery
b) SQLSelect
c) SelectCommand
d) Query
Answer: c

6. Which property of the ObjectDataSource control specifies the method to retrieve data?
a) GetDataMethod
b) SelectMethod
c) FetchMethod
d) RetrieveMethod
Answer: b

7. Which data source control uses `InsertCommand`, `UpdateCommand`, and `DeleteCommand`?
a) ObjectDataSource
b) SqlDataSource
c) Both a and b
d) None of the above
Answer: b

8. Which data source control offers more control over data retrieval logic?
a) SqlDataSource
b) ObjectDataSource
c) Both
d) Depends on the situation
Answer: b

9. Which is the correct way to specify a connection string in Web.config and use it in SqlDataSource?
a) `ConnectionString="MyConnectionString"`
b) `ConnectionString="<% ConnectionStrings:MyConnectionString %>"`
c) `ConnectionString="<%$ ConnectionStrings:MyConnectionString %>"`
d)
`ConnectionString=ConfigurationManager.ConnectionStrings["MyConnectionString"].ConnectionString`
Answer: c

10. Which data source control is suitable for a 3-tier architecture?
a) SqlDataSource

b) ObjectDataSource
c) Both
d) Neither
Answer: b

GridView, DetailsView, FormView

11. Which control displays data in a tabular format?
a) DetailsView
b) FormView
c) GridView
d) ListView
Answer: c
12. Which control displays a single record at a time in a table layout?
a) GridView
b) FormView
c) DetailsView
d) Repeater
Answer: c
13. Which control offers the most flexibility in terms of layout using templates?
a) GridView
b) DetailsView
c) FormView
d) DataList
Answer: c
14. Which property is used to bind a data source to a GridView?
a) DataSource
b) DataMember
c) DataSourceID
d) SourceID
Answer: c
15. Which control uses templates like `ItemTemplate`, `EditItemTemplate`, and `InsertItemTemplate`?
a) GridView
b) DetailsView
c) FormView
d) All of the above
Answer: c
16. Which control automatically generates columns based on the data source?
a) DetailsView
b) FormView
c) GridView (with AutoGenerateColumns=True)
d) All of the above
Answer: c
17. Which control is best suited for displaying a summary of a single record?
a) GridView
b) DetailsView
c) FormView

d) Any of the above
Answer: b

18. Which control provides built-in editing capabilities with automatically generated UI?
    a) GridView and DetailsView
    b) GridView and FormView
    c) GridView and DetailsView (with AutoGenerateRows=True)
    d) GridView and DetailsView (with CommandField)
    Answer: d
19. Which control uses `Eval()` and `Bind()` for data binding?
    a) GridView
    b) DetailsView
    c) FormView
    d) All of the above
    Answer: d
20. Which control is best for displaying a catalog of products?
    a) GridView
    b) DetailsView
    c) FormView
    d) It depends on the layout requirements
    Answer: d

Data Binding Expressions

21. Which data binding expression is used for one-way data binding?
    a) Bind()
    b) Eval()
    c) XPath()
    d) Format()
    Answer: b
22. Which data binding expression is used for two-way data binding?
    a) Eval()
    b) Bind()
    c) XPath()
    d) ToString()
    Answer: b
23. In which scenario is `Bind()` typically used?
    a) Displaying data in a label.
    b) Displaying data in a GridView.
    c) Editing data in a TextBox.
    d) Displaying data in a FormView's ItemTemplate.
    Answer: c
24. In which scenario is `Eval()` typically used?
    a) Updating data in a database.
    b) Displaying data in a GridView or FormView.
    c) Inserting new data.
    d) Binding to a session variable.
    Answer: b
25. What is the purpose of the format string in a data binding expression (e.g., `{0:C}`)?

a) To specify the data type.
b) To format the displayed data.
c) To filter the data.
d) To sort the data.
Answer: b

26. Which is the correct syntax for using `Eval()` to display a product name?
    a) `<%# Eval[ProductName] %>`
    b) `<%# Eval("ProductName") %>`
    c) `<%= Eval("ProductName") %>`
    d) `<asp:Label Text='Eval("ProductName")' runat='server'/>`
    Answer: b
27. Which is the correct syntax for using `Bind()` with a TextBox for editing a price?
    a) `<asp:TextBox Text='<%# Bind("Price") %>' runat="server" />`
    b) `<asp:TextBox Text='<%= Bind("Price") %>' runat="server" />`
    c) `<asp:TextBox Text='<%# Eval("Price") %>' runat="server" />`
    d) `<asp:TextBox Text='<% Bind("Price") %>' runat="server" />`
    Answer: a
28. Can you use `Bind()` in a FormView's ItemTemplate?
    a) Yes
    b) No
    c) Sometimes
    d) Only with specific data sources
    Answer: b
29. What is the default binding mode if you don't specify `Eval()` or `Bind()`?
    a) One-way binding
    b) Two-way binding
    c) No binding
    d) It depends on the control
    Answer: d
30. Which data binding expression is specifically designed for XML data?
    a) Eval()
    b) Bind()
    c) XPath()
    d) Format()
    Answer: c

10 MID SIZE QUESTION WITH ANSWER

10 mid-size questions with answers on DataSource Controls and data-bound controls in ASP.NET:

SqlDataSource, ObjectDataSource

1. **Explain the difference between SqlDataSource and ObjectDataSource. When would you choose one over the other?**
    - **Answer:**

- `SqlDataSource`: Connects directly to a SQL database. You provide SQL queries or stored procedure names. It's simpler for basic database interactions.
- `ObjectDataSource`: Connects to your own business objects (classes). You specify methods in your class for data retrieval and manipulation. It promotes a layered architecture and provides more control.
- Choice:
  - Use `SqlDataSource` for quick data binding to a single database table, especially in simpler applications.
  - Use `ObjectDataSource` when you have a business layer, need more control over data access logic, or are working with complex data retrieval/manipulation scenarios.

2. **How do you configure a SqlDataSource to retrieve data from a database? Provide an example, including how to use a connection string from Web.config.**
   - **Answer:**
     - Configuration involves setting the `ConnectionString` and `SelectCommand` properties.
     - Example:

```
<configuration>
    <connectionStrings>
        <add name="MyDatabase" connectionString="Data Source=.;Initial Catalog=MyDatabase;Integrated Security=True;" />
    </connectionStrings>
</configuration>

<asp:SqlDataSource ID="SqlDataSource1" runat="server"
    ConnectionString="<%$ ConnectionStrings:MyDatabase %>"
    SelectCommand="SELECT ProductID, ProductName, Price FROM Products">
</asp:SqlDataSource>
```

- The connection string is stored in `Web.config` for security and maintainability. The `<%$ ConnectionStrings:MyDatabase %>` syntax retrieves it in the `SqlDataSource`.

3. **Explain how to use ObjectDataSource to bind a GridView to data from a custom class. Provide a C# and ASPX example.**
   - **Answer:**
     - C# (Business Object):

```
public class Student
{
    public int StudentID { get; set; }
    public string FirstName { get; set; }
    public string LastName { get; set; }
}

public class StudentManager
{
    private static List<Student> _students = new List<Student>
    {
```

o   new Student { StudentID = 1, FirstName = "John", LastName = "Doe" },
o   new Student { StudentID = 2, FirstName = "Jane", LastName = "Smith" }
o   };
o
o   public List<Student> GetStudents()
o   {
o   return _students;
o   }
o }

- ASPX:

```
<asp:ObjectDataSource ID="ObjectDataSource1" runat="server"
    TypeName="StudentManager"
    SelectMethod="GetStudents">
</asp:ObjectDataSource>

<asp:GridView ID="GridView1" runat="server"
DataSourceID="ObjectDataSource1" AutoGenerateColumns="True">
</asp:GridView>
```

- The `TypeName` specifies the class (`StudentManager`), and `SelectMethod` specifies the method to call (`GetStudents()`).

GridView, DetailsView, FormView

4. **Compare and contrast GridView, DetailsView, and FormView. What are the key differences in their purpose and usage?**
   - **Answer:**
     - `GridView`: Displays data in a table (rows and columns). For displaying multiple records. Supports paging, sorting, editing.
     - `DetailsView`: Displays a single record in a table-like layout (field names and values). For detailed view of one record. Supports editing, inserting, deleting.
     - `FormView`: Displays a single record, but uses templates for highly customizable layout. For maximum control over presentation.
     - Key Differences:
       - `GridView`: Multiple records, tabular, feature-rich.
       - `DetailsView`: Single record, table-like, simple display/editing.
       - `FormView`: Single record, template-driven, highly customizable.
5. **Explain how to use a DetailsView to display the details of a selected item from a GridView. Assume you are passing the selected item's ID in the query string.**
   - **Answer:**
   - <asp:SqlDataSource ID="SqlDataSource2" runat="server"
   -     ConnectionString="<%$ ConnectionStrings:MyDatabase %>"

```
    SelectCommand="SELECT ProductID, ProductName, Price,
Description FROM Products WHERE ProductID = @ProductID">
    <SelectParameters>
        <asp:QueryStringParameter Name="ProductID"
QueryStringField="ID" Type="Int32" />
    </SelectParameters>
</asp:SqlDataSource>

<asp:DetailsView ID="DetailsView1" runat="server"
DataSourceID="SqlDataSource2" AutoGenerateRows="False"
DataKeyNames="ProductID">
    <Fields>
        <asp:BoundField DataField="ProductName"
HeaderText="Product Name" />
        <asp:BoundField DataField="Price" HeaderText="Price"
DataFormatString="{0:C}" />
        <asp:BoundField DataField="Description"
HeaderText="Description" />
    </Fields>
</asp:DetailsView>
```

- The `SqlDataSource` retrieves the product based on the `ProductID` from the query string (`QueryStringField="ID"`).
- `AutoGenerateRows="False"` is set so that only the fields specified are displayed.
- `DataKeyNames` is set to the primary key.

6. **Describe how to customize the layout of a FormView using templates. Provide an example of an ItemTemplate.**
   - **Answer:**
     - `FormView` uses templates to define its layout. The `ItemTemplate` specifies how the data is displayed in read-only mode.
     - Example:

```
<asp:FormView ID="FormView1" runat="server"
DataSourceID="SqlDataSource1">
    <ItemTemplate>
        <h3><%# Eval("ProductName") %></h3>
        <p>Price: <%# Eval("Price", "{0:C}") %></p>
        <p>Description: <%# Eval("Description") %></p>
    </ItemTemplate>
</asp:FormView>
```

- This template displays the product name as a heading, and the price and description as paragraphs. `Eval()` is used for one-way data binding.

Data Binding Expressions

7. **Explain the difference between Eval() and Bind() data binding expressions. In what scenarios would you use each?**
   - **Answer:**
     - `Eval()`: One-way data binding. Used to *display* data. Read-only.

- `Bind()`: Two-way data binding. Used for *editing* and *inserting* data. Read-write.
- Use `Eval()` in `ItemTemplate` of `FormView` and `DetailsView`, and in `GridView` columns to display data.
- Use `Bind()` in `EditItemTemplate` and `InsertItemTemplate` of `FormView`, and in editable `GridView` columns (with controls like `TextBox`) to allow users to modify data.

8. **Provide examples of using data binding expressions to format data (e.g., currency, dates) in a GridView or FormView.**
   - **Answer:**

```
<asp:GridView ID="GridView1" runat="server" DataSourceID="SqlDataSource1">
    <Columns>
        <asp:BoundField DataField="Price" HeaderText="Price" DataFormatString="{0:C}" />  <%-- Currency --%>
        <asp:BoundField DataField="OrderDate" HeaderText="Order Date" DataFormatString="{0:d}" />  <%-- Short date --%>
    </Columns>
</asp:GridView>

<asp:FormView ID="FormView1" runat="server" DataSourceID="SqlDataSource1">
    <ItemTemplate>
        <p>Price: <%# Eval("Price", "{0:F2}") %></p>  <%-- Two decimal places --%>
        <p>Date: <%# Eval("OrderDate", "{0:D}") %></p>    <%-- Long date --%>
    </ItemTemplate>
    <EditItemTemplate>
         <asp:TextBox ID="PriceTextBox" runat="server" Text='<%# Bind("Price", "{0:F2}") %>' />
    </EditItemTemplate>
</asp:FormView>
```

- The format string is applied within the `Eval()` or `Bind()` expression.

Paging, Sorting, and Editing in GridView

9. **Explain how to enable paging and sorting in a GridView control. What are the key properties involved, and how does the SqlDataSource support these features?**
   - **Answer:**
     - Paging:
       - `AllowPaging="True"`: Enables paging.
       - `PageSize="n"`: Sets the number of records per page.
       - `GridView` adds a pager row.
     - Sorting:
       - `AllowSorting="True"`: Enables sorting.
       - `GridView` adds sort arrows to column headers.
     - `SqlDataSource` Support:

        - Paging: `SqlDataSource` retrieves only the data for the current page.
        - Sorting: `SqlDataSource` automatically adds an `ORDER BY` clause to the `SelectCommand` based on the clicked column. The original `SelectCommand` should not have its own `ORDER BY` clause.

10. **Describe the process of enabling editing in a GridView using a SqlDataSource. What are the roles of AutoGenerateEditButton, DataKeyNames, and the SqlDataSource's UpdateCommand?**
    - **Answer:**
        - `AutoGenerateEditButton="True"`: Adds "Edit," "Update," and "Cancel" buttons to the `GridView`.
        - `DataKeyNames="PrimaryKeyColumnName"`: Specifies the primary key column(s). This is *essential* for the `GridView` to know which record to update.
        - `SqlDataSource UpdateCommand`:
            - The `SqlDataSource` must have an `UpdateCommand` defined. This is a SQL `UPDATE` statement with parameters.
            - The parameter names in the `UpdateCommand` *must* match the column names in the `UPDATE` statement. One parameter must be for the primary key (from `DataKeyNames`) to identify the row to update in the `WHERE` clause.
        - When the user clicks "Update," the `GridView` populates the `UpdateCommand`'s parameters with the new values and executes the command.

CHAPTER 10: STATE MANAGEMENT TECHNIQUES

State management is a critical concept in web development, especially with ASP.NET, because HTTP is a stateless protocol. This means that every request sent from a browser to a server is treated as an independent request without any knowledge of previous interactions. ASP.NET provides multiple techniques to maintain state across web requests.

Understanding Web Application State

Web application state refers to the ability of a web application to store and manage data across multiple requests and user sessions. Because HTTP is a stateless protocol, web applications need mechanisms to maintain information about the user and the application. This is crucial for providing a personalized and interactive user experience.

There are two main categories of state management:

1. Client-Side State Management

- **Definition:** Stores data on the client's browser. The server sends data to the client, and the client's browser is responsible for storing it.
- **Characteristics:**
  - Data is stored on the user's machine.
  - Reduces server load, as the server doesn't need to store the data.
  - Can improve performance for some operations, as data can be accessed directly on the client.

- Less secure, as data is accessible to the user.
- Limited storage capacity compared to server-side.
- Data is lost if the user clears their browser's cache or cookies.

- **Methods:**
  - **Cookies:**
    - Small text files that websites store on a user's computer.
    - Used to remember user preferences, track browsing behavior, and manage sessions.
    - Limited in size (around 4KB per cookie).
    - Can be accessed by JavaScript on the client-side and by server-side code.
    - Example (JavaScript):

```
// Set a cookie
document.cookie = "username=JohnDoe; expires=Thu, 18 Dec 2024 12:00:00 UTC; path=/;";

// Get a cookie
function getCookie(name) {
  let nameEQ = name + "=";
  let ca = document.cookie.split(';');
  for(let i=0; i < ca.length; i++) {
    let c = ca[i];
    while (c.charAt(0)==' ') {
      c = c.substring(1,c.length);
    }
    if (c.indexOf(nameEQ) == 0) {
      return c.substring(nameEQ.length,c.length);
    }
  }
  return null;
}
let username = getCookie("username");
if (username != null) {
  alert("Welcome again, " + username);
}

// Set cookie from C#
HttpCookie myCookie = new HttpCookie("LastVisit");
myCookie.Value = DateTime.Now.ToString();
myCookie.Expires = DateTime.Now.AddDays(30);  // Expires in 30 days.
Response.Cookies.Add(myCookie);

//Read Cookie
if (Request.Cookies["LastVisit"] != null)
{
    string lastVisit = Request.Cookies["LastVisit"].Value;
    Response.Write("Your last visit: " + lastVisit);
}
```

  - **Query Strings:**
    - Data appended to the end of a URL.

- Used to pass data between pages.
- Visible in the browser's address bar.
- Limited in length (due to URL length restrictions).
- Example:
    - URL: `mypage.aspx?id=123&name=John`
    - Retrieving values (C#):

```
string id = Request.QueryString["id"];    // "123"
string name = Request.QueryString["name"]; // "John"
```

- **Hidden Fields:**
    - HTML input elements that are not visible to the user.
    - Used to store small amounts of data within a form.
    - Data is sent to the server when the form is submitted.
    - Can be manipulated by the user if they view the page source.
    - Example:

```
<input type="hidden" id="ProductID" name="ProductID"
value="456">
```

    - Retrieving the value (C#):

```
string productId = Request.Form["ProductID"];   // "456"
```

- **View State (ASP.NET):**
    - ASP.NET mechanism to preserve the state of controls (e.g., TextBox text, GridView data) across postbacks (when the page is submitted to the server).
    - Stores data as a base64-encoded string within a hidden field (`__VIEWSTATE`).
    - Automatically managed by ASP.NET.
    - Can increase page size, especially if large amounts of data are stored.
    - Example:
        - A TextBox's Text property is automatically saved in View State across postbacks.

```
<asp:TextBox ID="MyTextBox" runat="server" Text="Initial
Value"></asp:TextBox>
```

- **Local Storage (HTML5):**
    - Stores data persistently in the browser. Data remains available even after the browser is closed and reopened.
    - Larger storage capacity than cookies (around 5MB per domain).
    - Data is only accessible by the website that created it.
    - Key-value storage.
    - Example (JavaScript):

```
// Store data
localStorage.setItem("username", "JohnDoe");
```

```
localStorage.setItem("theme", "dark");

// Retrieve data
let username = localStorage.getItem("username");  // "JohnDoe"
let theme = localStorage.getItem("theme");      // "dark"

// Remove data
localStorage.removeItem("username");

// Clear all data
localStorage.clear();
```

- **Session Storage (HTML5):**
  - Similar to Local Storage, but data is only stored for the duration of the user's session (until the browser tab or window is closed).
  - Key-value storage.
  - Example (JavaScript):

```
// Store data
sessionStorage.setItem("currentPage", "/products.aspx");
sessionStorage.setItem("itemsInCart", "3");

// Retrieve data
let currentPage = sessionStorage.getItem("currentPage"); // "/products.aspx"
let itemsInCart = sessionStorage.getItem("itemsInCart"); // "3"

// Remove data
sessionStorage.removeItem("currentPage");

// Clear all session data
sessionStorage.clear();
```

2. Server-Side State Management

- **Definition:** Stores data on the web server. The client sends a request, and the server stores the data and associates it with the user or application.
- **Characteristics:**
  - Data is stored on the server, making it more secure.
  - Greater storage capacity.
  - Can be accessed across multiple pages and user sessions (depending on the method).
  - Increases server load, as the server must manage the stored data.
  - Data is not lost when the user closes their browser.
- **Methods:**
  - **Application State:**
    - Stores data that is shared by *all* users of the application.

- Data persists as long as the application is running.
- Stored in the `HttpApplicationState` object.
- Accessed using the `Application` property of the `Page` or `HttpContext` class.
- Example (C#):
- `// Store data`
- `Application["TotalVisitors"] = 1000;   //int or object`
-
- `// Retrieve data`
- `int totalVisitors = (int)Application["TotalVisitors"];`
- `Response.Write("Total Visitors: " + totalVisitors);`
-
- `//Thread Safety`
- `Application.Lock();  //important`
- `Application["MyData"] = myObject;`
- `Application.UnLock();`

- **Session State:**
  - Stores data specific to a *single user's session.*
  - Data persists while the user is active on the website (until the session times out or is explicitly ended).
  - Stored in the `HttpSessionState` object.
  - Accessed using the `Session` property of the `Page` or `HttpContext` class.
  - Session data can be stored in various ways:
    - **InProc:** Stores session data in the web server's memory (fastest, but lost if the web application restarts).
    - **State Server:** Stores session data in a separate process (survives web application restarts, but slower than InProc).
    - **SQL Server:** Stores session data in a SQL Server database (persistent, supports web farms, but slowest).
    - **Custom Provider:** You can create your own storage mechanism.
  - Example (C#):
  - `// Store data`
  - `Session["Username"] = "JohnDoe";`
  - `Session["Cart"] = new List<string>();`
  -
  - `// Retrieve data`
  - `string username = Session["Username"].ToString();`
  - `List<string> cart = (List<string>)Session["Cart"];`
  -
  - `// Remove data`
  - `Session.Remove("Username");`
  -
  - `// Clear all session data`
  - `Session.Clear();`
  - `Session.Abandon(); // Ends the session`

- **Database:**

- Stores data in a relational database (e.g., SQL Server, MySQL).
- Provides persistent storage that can be accessed across multiple user sessions and application instances.
- Used for storing user profiles, product catalogs, order history, etc.
- Requires writing ADO.NET code (or using an ORM like Entity Framework) to interact with the database.
- Example (C# with ADO.NET):

```
string connectionString = "Data Source=.;Initial Catalog=MyDatabase;Integrated Security=True;";
using (SqlConnection connection = new SqlConnection(connectionString))
{
    connection.Open();
    string query = "SELECT * FROM Users WHERE UserID = @UserID";
    SqlCommand command = new SqlCommand(query, connection);
    command.Parameters.AddWithValue("@UserID", 123);
    SqlDataReader reader = command.ExecuteReader();
    if (reader.Read())
    {
        string username = reader["Username"].ToString();
        // ...
    }
    reader.Close();
}
```

- **Profile Properties (ASP.NET):**
  - ASP.NET feature that allows you to store user-specific data in a database, associated with the user's authentication information.
  - Provides a strongly-typed way to access user data.
  - Configured in the `Web.config` file.
  - Example (C#):
    - Web.config:

```
<profile>
  <properties>
    <add name="FirstName" type="System.String" />
    <add name="LastName" type="System.String" />
    <add name="City" type="System.String" />
  </properties>
</profile>
```

    - C#:

```
// Store profile data
Profile.FirstName = "John";
Profile.LastName = "Doe";
Profile.City = "New York";
Profile.Save();
```

```
// Retrieve profile data
string firstName = Profile.FirstName;
string lastName = Profile.LastName;
string city = Profile.City;
```

ViewState, Session State, and Cookies in ASP.NET

These are common techniques used in ASP.NET to manage state (data) in web applications. Because HTTP is stateless, these mechanisms are necessary to maintain information across multiple requests.

□ ViewState

- **Definition:** ViewState is a client-side mechanism used by ASP.NET to preserve the state of a web page (specifically, the values of controls) between postbacks. A postback occurs when a page is submitted to the server (e.g., when a button is clicked).
- **How it Works:**
  - When a page is rendered, ASP.NET serializes the current values of controls that have their `EnableViewState` property set to `true` (which is the default) into a base64-encoded string.
  - This string is stored in a hidden HTML input field named `__VIEWSTATE`.
  - When the page is posted back to the server, the `__VIEWSTATE` hidden field is sent along with the form data.
  - ASP.NET deserializes the ViewState data and restores the controls to their previous state.
- **Example:**

  ASPX:

```
<asp:TextBox ID="txtName" runat="server" Text="Initial
Value"></asp:TextBox>
<asp:Button ID="btnSubmit" runat="server" Text="Submit"
OnClick="btnSubmit_Click" />
<asp:Label ID="lblResult" runat="server"></asp:Label>
```

  Code-Behind (C#):

```
protected void btnSubmit_Click(object sender, EventArgs e)
{
    // Store the TextBox value in ViewState
    ViewState["UserName"] = txtName.Text;

    // Display the value from ViewState
    lblResult.Text = "Name Saved in ViewState: " +
ViewState["UserName"].ToString();
    txtName.Text = ""; //clear the textbox
}
```

Explanation:

- The `txtName` TextBox's `Text` property is automatically saved in ViewState by ASP.NET.
- In the `btnSubmit_Click` event handler:
  - `ViewState["UserName"] = txtName.Text;` stores the current text from the `txtName` TextBox into ViewState with the key "UserName".
  - `lblResult.Text = "Name Saved in ViewState: " + ViewState["UserName"].ToString();` retrieves the stored value from ViewState and displays it in the `lblResult` Label.

- **Pros:**
  - Simple to use: ASP.NET largely manages it automatically for controls.
  - No server resources required: Data is stored on the client's browser.
- **Cons:**
  - Increases page size: The `__VIEWSTATE` hidden field can become quite large, especially for pages with many controls or large amounts of data, leading to increased bandwidth usage and slower page loads.
  - Not suitable for sensitive information: ViewState data is base64-encoded, which is *not* encryption. It can be decoded, so it's not secure for storing sensitive data like passwords or credit card numbers.
  - Can lead to performance issues if used excessively.

□ Session State

- **Definition:** Session State is a server-side mechanism used to store data that is specific to a single user's session. A session represents the period during which a user interacts with a web application.
- **How it Works:**
  - When a user first accesses a web application, the server creates a unique session ID.
  - This session ID is sent to the client's browser, typically as a cookie.
  - For subsequent requests from that user, the browser sends the session ID back to the server.
  - The server uses the session ID to retrieve the data associated with that user's session.
  - Session data is stored on the server.
- **Example:**

  ASPX:

```
<asp:TextBox ID="txtName" runat="server"></asp:TextBox>
<asp:Button ID="btnSubmit" runat="server" Text="Submit"
OnClick="btnSubmit_Click" />
<asp:Label ID="lblResult" runat="server"></asp:Label>
```

Code-Behind (C#):

```
protected void btnSubmit_Click(object sender, EventArgs e)
{
    // Store the TextBox value in Session State
    Session["UserName"] = txtName.Text;

    // Display a welcome message using the Session value
    lblResult.Text = "Welcome " + Session["UserName"].ToString();
    txtName.Text = "";
}
```

Explanation:

- `Session["UserName"] = txtName.Text;` stores the value of the `txtName` TextBox in the user's session with the key "UserName".
- `lblResult.Text = "Welcome " + Session["UserName"].ToString();` retrieves the value from the session and displays it.

- **Pros:**
  - Stores data on the server: More secure than ViewState, as the data is not exposed to the client.
  - Can store various data types: You can store objects, collections, and other complex data.
- **Cons:**
  - Uses server memory: Session data consumes server resources. Storing large amounts of data for many users can impact performance.
  - Session timeout issues: Session data is lost when the user's session expires (due to inactivity or a server restart). Managing session timeouts can be complex.
  - Scalability challenges: In web farm scenarios (where a website is hosted on multiple servers), session data needs to be shared between servers, which can add complexity (e.g., using a state server or SQL Server for session storage).

🍪 Cookies

- **Definition:** Cookies are small text files that websites store on a user's computer through the user's web browser. They are used to store small amounts of data that can be retrieved by the website on subsequent visits.
- **How they Work:**
  - The server sends an HTTP response to the client that includes a `Set-Cookie` header.
  - The browser receives the response and stores the cookie on the user's machine.
  - For subsequent requests to the same website, the browser automatically includes the cookie in the HTTP request headers.
  - The server can then read the cookie's value.
- **Example:**

  ASPX:

```
<asp:TextBox ID="txtName" runat="server"></asp:TextBox>
<asp:Button ID="btnSubmit" runat="server" Text="Set Cookie"
OnClick="btnSubmit_Click" />
<asp:Label ID="lblResult" runat="server"></asp:Label>
```

Code-Behind (C#):

```
protected void btnSubmit_Click(object sender, EventArgs e)
{
    // Create a cookie
    HttpCookie userCookie = new HttpCookie("UserName");
    userCookie.Value = txtName.Text; // Set the cookie's value
    userCookie.Expires = DateTime.Now.AddDays(7); // Set the cookie's
expiration date (optional)

    // Add the cookie to the response
    Response.Cookies.Add(userCookie);

    lblResult.Text = "Cookie set!";
    txtName.Text = "";

}

protected void Page_Load(object sender, EventArgs e)
{
    // Retrieve the cookie
    if (Request.Cookies["UserName"] != null)
    {
        string cookieValue = Request.Cookies["UserName"].Value;
        lblResult.Text = "Cookie Value: " + cookieValue;
    }
    else
    {
        lblResult.Text = "Cookie not found!";
    }
}
```

Explanation:

- `HttpCookie userCookie = new HttpCookie("UserName");` creates a new cookie with the name "UserName".
- `userCookie.Value = txtName.Text;` sets the value of the cookie to the text entered in the `txtName` TextBox.
- `userCookie.Expires = DateTime.Now.AddDays(7);` sets the cookie to expire in 7 days. If you don't set an expiration, it's a session cookie and will be deleted when the browser closes.
- `Response.Cookies.Add(userCookie);` adds the cookie to the HTTP response, which tells the browser to store it.
- `Request.Cookies["UserName"]` retrieves the cookie from the HTTP request. The `Value` property gets the cookie's data.

- **Pros:**
  - Stores data across sessions: Cookies can persist even after the user closes and reopens their browser (if an expiration is set).
  - Useful for personalization: Can be used to remember user preferences, login status, and other information to customize the user experience.
- **Cons:**
  - Size limitation (~4KB per cookie): Cookies can only store small amounts of data.
  - Can be disabled in the browser: Users can disable cookies in their browser settings, which can prevent your website from functioning correctly if it relies on them.
  - Security concerns: Cookies can be intercepted or tampered with, so they are not suitable for storing highly sensitive information. You should avoid storing passwords or credit card details in cookies.
  - Privacy concerns: Cookies are often used for tracking user behavior, which raises privacy issues. Many websites are now required to obtain user consent before setting cookies.
-

Query Strings and Hidden Fields in ASP.NET

These are two methods used in ASP.NET to pass data between web pages or maintain data across postbacks.

🔗 Query Strings

- **Definition:** Query strings are a way to append data to the end of a URL. They consist of one or more name-value pairs, separated by ampersands (&), and are preceded by a question mark (?).
- **Purpose:**
  - Passing data between pages: Query strings are commonly used to send data from one page to another.
  - Filtering data: They can be used to pass parameters that filter the results on the destination page (e.g., displaying a specific product category).
  - Maintaining state in simple scenarios: They can help maintain some state information, especially when bookmarking is important.
- **Example:**

  Sending Data (C#):

```
protected void btnSubmit_Click(object sender, EventArgs e)
{
    // Construct the query string
```

```
    string url = "Welcome.aspx?user=" + txtName.Text + "&age=" +
txtAge.Text;

    // Redirect to the Welcome.aspx page with the query string
    Response.Redirect(url);
}
```

Receiving Data (Welcome.aspx.cs):

```
protected void Page_Load(object sender, EventArgs e)
{
    // Retrieve the values from the query string
    string userName = Request.QueryString["user"];
    string userAge = Request.QueryString["age"];

    // Display the values
    lblResult.Text = "Hello, " + userName + ". You are " + userAge + "
years old.";
}
```

Explanation:

- In `btnSubmit_Click`, the code constructs a URL with a query string:
  - `?user=" + txtName.Text`: Appends the user's name with the parameter name "user".
  - `&age=" + txtAge.Text`: Appends the user's age with the parameter name "age".
- `Response.Redirect(url);` sends the user to the new page with the constructed URL.
- In `Welcome.aspx.cs`, `Request.QueryString["user"]` retrieves the value of the "user" parameter, and `Request.QueryString["age"]` retrieves the value of the "age" parameter.

- **Pros:**
  - Simple and easy to implement: Query strings are straightforward to add to URLs and retrieve on the receiving page.
  - Bookmarked URLs retain state: Users can bookmark URLs with query strings, preserving the data and allowing them to return to the same state later. This is useful for search results, product listings, etc.
- **Cons:**
  - Visible in the URL: Data passed in the query string is visible in the browser's address bar, which can be a security concern for sensitive information.
  - Limited to text: Query strings can only transmit string data. You may need to convert other data types (e.g., integers, dates) to strings before adding them to the URL and parse them back on the receiving page.
  - Length limitations: URLs have a maximum length (which varies between browsers and servers), limiting the amount of data you can pass in a query string.

- Encoding issues: Special characters in the data (e.g., spaces, &, ?, #) need to be properly encoded (using `Server.UrlEncode()` in C# or `encodeURIComponent()` in JavaScript) to ensure they are transmitted correctly.
- Can make URLs less user-friendly: URLs with long or complex query strings can be difficult to read and understand.

□□♂□ Hidden Fields

- **Definition:** Hidden fields are HTML input elements that are not displayed to the user in the browser. They are used to store data within an HTML form that needs to be sent to the server when the form is submitted.
- **Purpose:**
  - Maintaining data across postbacks: Hidden fields are a simple way to preserve small amounts of data between postbacks (when a page is submitted to the server).
  - Storing values that are not directly editable by the user: They can be used to store values that the server needs but that the user should not be able to modify (e.g., a primary key, a record ID).
- **Example:**

  ASPX:

```
<form id="myForm" runat="server">
    <asp:Label ID="lblUserName" runat="server" Text="User
Name:"></asp:Label>
    <asp:TextBox ID="txtUserName" runat="server"></asp:TextBox>
    <asp:HiddenField ID="HiddenUserID" runat="server" Value="12345" />
    <asp:Button ID="btnSubmit" runat="server" Text="Submit"
OnClick="btnSubmit_Click" />
    <asp:Label ID="lblResult" runat="server"></asp:Label>
</form>
```

  Code-Behind (C#):

```
protected void btnSubmit_Click(object sender, EventArgs e)
{
    // Retrieve the values from the TextBox and Hidden Field
    string userName = txtUserName.Text;
    string userID = HiddenUserID.Value;

    // Display the values
    lblResult.Text = "User Name: " + userName + ", User ID: " + userID;
}
```

  Explanation:

- `<asp:HiddenField ID="HiddenUserID" runat="server" Value="12345" />` creates a hidden field with the ID "HiddenUserID" and sets its initial value to "12345".
  - In `btnSubmit_Click`, `HiddenUserID.Value` retrieves the value of the hidden field.

- **Pros:**
  - Maintains data across postbacks: Hidden fields preserve their values when the form is submitted to the server.
  - Simple to use: They are easy to add to a form and retrieve their values on the server.
- **Cons:**
  - Can be tampered with using browser developer tools: Users can view the HTML source of the page and modify the values of hidden fields. This makes them unsuitable for storing sensitive data.
  - Limited to string data: Like query strings, hidden fields store data as strings.
  - Adds to page size: Hidden fields increase the size of the HTML form, although usually by a small amount.
  - Not suitable for large amounts of data: Hidden fields are best for storing small pieces of data.
- **Security Note:** Never store sensitive information (passwords, credit card numbers, etc.) in hidden fields, as they are easily visible and modifiable by the user.

🖫 Application State

- **Definition:** Application State is a server-side mechanism in ASP.NET that allows you to store data that is shared by *all* users of a web application. The data stored in Application State is global to the application and persists as long as the application is running.
- **How it Works:**
  - Application State is stored in the `HttpApplicationState` object.
  - You access this object through the `Application` property of the `Page` class or the `HttpContext` class.
  - Data is stored as key-value pairs, similar to a dictionary or hash table.
  - When the web application starts (e.g., when the first user accesses the site), the Application State object is initialized.
  - The data remains in Application State until the application is stopped (e.g., due to a server restart, an application pool recycle, or a code change).
- **Example:**

  Global.asax (Application_Start):

```
void Application_Start(object sender, EventArgs e)
{
    // Code that runs on application startup
    Application["TotalVisitors"] = 0;  // Initialize the visitor
counter
```

```
    Application["ApplicationStartTime"] = DateTime.Now;
}
```

ASPX Page (e.g., Default.aspx.cs):

```
protected void Page_Load(object sender, EventArgs e)
{
    // Increment the visitor counter
    Application.Lock();  // Important:  Lock before modifying
Application State
    Application["TotalVisitors"] = (int)Application["TotalVisitors"] +
1;
    Application.UnLock(); // Important: Unlock after modifying

    // Display the visitor count and application start time
    lblVisitors.Text = "Visitors: " +
Application["TotalVisitors"].ToString();
    lblStartTime.Text = "Application started at: " +
((DateTime)Application["ApplicationStartTime"]).ToString();
}
```

Explanation:

- In `Global.asax`, the `Application_Start` event handler is used to initialize the `TotalVisitors` counter to 0 and store the application start time. This event handler runs only once when the application first starts.
- In `Default.aspx.cs`, the `Page_Load` event handler:
    - `Application.Lock();` and `Application.UnLock();` are crucial. Application State is a shared resource, and you *must* lock it before modifying it to prevent data corruption if multiple users try to update it simultaneously. Locking ensures that only one thread can write to the Application State at a time.
    - Increments the `TotalVisitors` counter.
    - Retrieves the current visitor count and application start time from Application State and displays them in labels.

- **Pros:**
    - Global scope: Data is accessible to all users and all pages within the web application.
    - Useful for storing application-wide data: Suitable for storing data that doesn't change frequently and is relevant to the entire application, such as:
        - Application settings or configuration values.
        - The number of online users.
        - Shared resources (e.g., database connection objects, although this is less common with modern practices like dependency injection).
        - Application start time or other application-level information.
- **Cons:**
    - Uses server memory: Application State consumes server resources. Storing large amounts of data can impact performance.

- Not user-specific: Data is shared by all users, so it's not appropriate for storing user-specific information (use Session State for that).
- Potential for data loss: Application State data is lost when the web application is stopped or restarted.
- Requires careful handling: You *must* use `Application.Lock()` and `Application.UnLock()` when modifying Application State to prevent race conditions and data corruption. Forgetting to lock can lead to unpredictable behavior and data loss.

□ Caching

- **Definition:** Caching is a technique that stores frequently accessed data in memory (or another fast storage location) to improve the performance of a web application. Instead of repeatedly retrieving the data from its original source (e.g., a database, a file), the application retrieves it from the cache, which is much faster.
- **Types of Caching in ASP.NET:**
  1. **Page Output Caching:**
     - Caches the entire output of a page (the HTML generated by the page) for a specified duration.
     - When a user requests the page, if the cached version is still valid, ASP.NET sends the cached HTML directly to the browser, bypassing the page's code execution.
     - Improves performance significantly for pages that don't change frequently.
     - Example (ASPX):
     - ```
       <%@ Page Language="C#" AutoEventWireup="true"
       CodeFile="MyPage.aspx.cs" Inherits="MyPage" OutputCache
       Duration="60" VaryByParam="none" %>
       ```
       - `Duration="60"`: Caches the page for 60 seconds.
       - `VaryByParam="none"`: Caches the same version of the page for all users. You can use `VaryByParam="ID"` to cache different versions based on the value of the "ID" query string parameter.
  2. **Fragment Caching (User Control Caching):**
     - Caches only a portion of a page, specifically the output of a user control (.ascx file).
     - Allows you to cache parts of a page that are static or change infrequently, while dynamically generating the rest of the page.
     - Provides more granular control than page output caching.
     - Example (ASPX):
     - ```
       <%@ Register TagPrefix="uc" TagName="MyControl"
       Src="MyControl.ascx" %>
       ```
     - ```
       <uc:MyControl ID="MyControl1" runat="server" />
       ```
       - In MyControl.ascx:
       ```

```
▪ <%@ Control Language="C#" AutoEventWireup="true"
  CodeFile="MyControl.ascx.cs" Inherits="MyControl"
  OutputCache Duration="300" %>
▪ <div>
▪     <% // Dynamic content here %>
▪     <p>This part is cached for 5 minutes.</p>
▪ </div>
```

3. **Data Caching:**
   - Caches specific data (e.g., a `DataTable`, a `DataSet`, a collection of objects) in the application's memory.
   - You explicitly add and retrieve data from the cache using the `Cache` object (which is an instance of `System.Web.Caching.Cache`).
   - Provides the most flexibility, allowing you to cache any type of data and control when it expires.
   - Example (C#):

```
▪ protected void Page_Load(object sender, EventArgs e)
▪ {
▪     if (Cache["Products"] == null)
▪     {
▪         // Retrieve product data from the database
▪         DataTable dt = GetProductsFromDB();
▪
▪         // Store the data in the cache
▪         Cache.Insert(
▪             "Products",  // Key to identify the cached data
▪             dt,          // The data to cache
▪             null,        // Dependencies (e.g., files,
other cache keys) - null for none
▪             DateTime.Now.AddMinutes(60), // Absolute
expiration time (60 minutes from now)
▪             Cache.NoSlidingExpiration,    // Sliding
expiration (data expires if not accessed) - None
▪             CacheItemPriority.Normal,     // Priority (used
when the cache is full)
▪             null                         // Callback method
when the item is removed
▪         );
▪         lblMessage.Text = "Data Loaded from Database.";
▪     }
▪     else
▪     {
▪         // Retrieve the data from the cache
▪         DataTable cachedProducts =
(DataTable)Cache["Products"];
▪         // Use the cached data (e.g., bind it to a
GridView)
▪         GridView1.DataSource = cachedProducts;
▪         GridView1.DataBind();
▪         lblMessage.Text = "Data Loaded from Cache.";
▪     }
▪ }
```

```
private DataTable GetProductsFromDB()
{
    // Code to retrieve product data from the database using ADO.NET
    // ...
    return new DataTable(); // Replace this with your actual data retrieval code
}
```

- **Pros of Caching:**
  - Improves performance: Retrieving data from the cache is much faster than retrieving it from the original source (especially a database).
  - Reduces database load: Caching reduces the number of queries sent to the database, which can significantly improve the scalability and responsiveness of the application.
  - Enhances user experience: Faster page loads and data retrieval lead to a better user experience.
- **Cons of Caching:**
  - Data staleness: Cached data can become outdated if the original data source changes. You need to implement a strategy to ensure that the cache is updated when the data changes (e.g., using expiration policies, cache dependencies, or manual updates).
  - Memory usage: Caching consumes server memory. Caching large amounts of data can impact performance if not managed carefully.
  - Complexity: Implementing caching effectively can add complexity to your application, especially when dealing with cache dependencies and expiration.
- Risk of stale data

Summary Table of State Management Techniques

Technique	Storage	Scope	Pros	Cons
ViewState	Client	Page-level	Easy to use	Increases page size
Session	Server	User-session	Secure, user-specific	Memory-intensive
Cookies	Client	Browser	Persistent storage	Can be disabled
Query String	Client	Page-level	Simple, bookmarkable	Visible, limited size
Hidden Fields	Client	Page-level	Hidden data transfer	Can be tampered

Application State	Server	Global	Shared across users	Not user-specific
Caching	Server	App-level	Fast data retrieval	Risk of stale data

---

10 PRACTICAL EXAMPLES WITH SOLUTION

ViewState, Session State, Cookies

1. **Example: Remember a user's preferred theme (light/dark) across postbacks on a single page.**
   - **Topic:** ViewState
   - **Solution:**

     ASPX:

```
<asp:DropDownList ID="ddlTheme" runat="server"
AutoPostBack="True"
OnSelectedIndexChanged="ddlTheme_SelectedIndexChanged">
    <asp:ListItem Value="light">Light</asp:ListItem>
    <asp:ListItem Value="dark">Dark</asp:ListItem>
</asp:DropDownList>
<div id="themeDiv" runat="server">
    <p>This is a themed section.</p>
</div>
```

     Code-Behind (C#):

```
protected void Page_Load(object sender, EventArgs e)
{
    if (ViewState["CurrentTheme"] != null)
    {
        // Retrieve theme from ViewState
        string theme = ViewState["CurrentTheme"].ToString();
        if (theme == "dark")
        {
            themeDiv.Attributes.Add("class", "dark-theme"); //
Apply CSS class
            ddlTheme.SelectedValue = "dark";
        }
        else
        {
            themeDiv.Attributes.Add("class", "light-theme");
            ddlTheme.SelectedValue = "light";
        }
    }
    else
    {
```

```
            //default
            ViewState["CurrentTheme"] = "light";
            themeDiv.Attributes.Add("class", "light-theme");
            ddlTheme.SelectedValue = "light";
        }
    }

    protected void ddlTheme_SelectedIndexChanged(object sender,
    EventArgs e)
    {
        // Store selected theme in ViewState
        string selectedTheme = ddlTheme.SelectedValue;
        ViewState["CurrentTheme"] = selectedTheme;

        if (selectedTheme == "dark")
        {
            themeDiv.Attributes.Add("class", "dark-theme");
        }
        else
        {
            themeDiv.Attributes.Add("class", "light-theme");
        }
    }
```

- **Explanation:** This example uses ViewState to store the user's selected theme. The ddlTheme_SelectedIndexChanged event stores the selected value in ViewState, and the Page_Load event retrieves it and applies the appropriate CSS class.

2. **Example: Implement a simple shopping cart to store product IDs across multiple pages within a user's session.**
   - **Topic:** Session State
   - **Solution:**

   Page 1 (e.g., ProductList.aspx.cs):

```
protected void btnAddToCart_Click(object sender, EventArgs e)
{
    // Get the product ID (e.g., from a hidden field or query
string)
    int productID =
Convert.ToInt32(((Button)sender).CommandArgument);

    // Get the current cart from Session, or create a new one if
it doesn't exist
    List<int> cart = Session["Cart"] as List<int>;
    if (cart == null)
    {
        cart = new List<int>();
    }

    // Add the product ID to the cart
    cart.Add(productID);
```

```
    Session["Cart"] = cart; // Store the updated cart back in
Session

    lblMessage.Text = "Product added to cart!";
}
```

Page 2 (e.g., ViewCart.aspx.cs):

```
protected void Page_Load(object sender, EventArgs e)
{
    // Retrieve the cart from Session
    List<int> cart = Session["Cart"] as List<int>;
    if (cart != null && cart.Count > 0)
    {
        // Display the products in the cart (e.g., in a GridView
or Label)
        string productList = string.Join(", ", cart.ToArray());
//convert the list to string
        lblCart.Text = "Products in your cart: " + productList;
    }
    else
    {
        lblCart.Text = "Your cart is empty.";
    }
}
```

- **Explanation:** This example uses Session State to store a list of product IDs. When a user adds a product to the cart, the ID is added to the list in Session. The ViewCart.aspx page retrieves the list from Session and displays the products.

3. **Example: Remember a user's last visited page using cookies.**
    - **Topic:** Cookies
    - **Solution:**

Base Page (or a common function):

```
protected void Page_Load(object sender, EventArgs e)
{
    // Store the current page URL in a cookie
    HttpCookie lastVisitedCookie = new HttpCookie("LastVisited");
    lastVisitedCookie.Value = Request.RawUrl; // Get the current
URL
    lastVisitedCookie.Expires = DateTime.Now.AddDays(30); //
Expire in 30 days
    Response.Cookies.Add(lastVisitedCookie);

    // Retrieve and display the last visited page
    if (Request.Cookies["LastVisited"] != null)
    {
        string lastVisited =
Request.Cookies["LastVisited"].Value;
```

```
        lblLastVisited.Text = "Your last visited page: " +
lastVisited;
    }
    else
    {
        lblLastVisited.Text = "This is your first visit!";
    }
}
```

- **Explanation:** This example stores the URL of the current page in a cookie named "LastVisited". The cookie is set to expire in 30 days. The Page_Load event retrieves the cookie (if it exists) and displays the last visited URL.

Query String and Hidden Fields

4. **Example: Pass a product ID from a product listing page to a product details page.**
   - **Topic:** Query String
   - **Solution:**

   Product Listing Page (e.g., ProductList.aspx):

```
<asp:Repeater ID="rptProducts" runat="server"
DataSourceID="SqlDataSource1">
    <ItemTemplate>
        <h3><%# Eval("ProductName") %></h3>
        <p>Price: <%# Eval("Price", "{0:C}") %></p>
        <a href="ProductDetails.aspx?ProductID=<%#
Eval("ProductID") %>">View Details</a>
    </ItemTemplate>
</asp:Repeater>

<asp:SqlDataSource ID="SqlDataSource1" runat="server"
    ConnectionString="<%$ ConnectionStrings:MyDatabase %>"
    SelectCommand="SELECT ProductID, ProductName, Price FROM
Products">
</asp:SqlDataSource>
```

   Product Details Page (e.g., ProductDetails.aspx.cs):

```
protected void Page_Load(object sender, EventArgs e)
{
    if (Request.QueryString["ProductID"] != null)
    {
        int productID =
Convert.ToInt32(Request.QueryString["ProductID"]);
        // Retrieve product details from the database based on
productID
        // and display them in Labels or other controls.
        // Example:
        // lblProductName.Text = GetProductName(productID);
```

```
        }
        else
        {
            lblError.Text = "Product ID is missing.";
        }
    }
```

- **Explanation:** The product listing page generates links to the details page, appending the ProductID to the URL as a query string parameter. The details page retrieves the ProductID from the query string and uses it to fetch and display the product details.

5. **Example: Store a non-editable record ID on a page across postbacks.**
   - **Topic:** Hidden Field
   - **Solution:**

   ASPX:

```
<form id="myForm" runat="server">
    <asp:HiddenField ID="hdnRecordID" runat="server" Value="123"
/>
    <asp:Label ID="lblMessage" runat="server"></asp:Label>
    <asp:Button ID="btnSubmit" runat="server" Text="Submit"
OnClick="btnSubmit_Click" />
</form>
```

   Code-Behind (C#):

```
protected void Page_Load(object sender, EventArgs e)
{
    // You can set the value of the hidden field in code-behind
if needed
    // hdnRecordID.Value = "456";
}

protected void btnSubmit_Click(object sender, EventArgs e)
{
    // Retrieve the value of the hidden field
    string recordID = hdnRecordID.Value;
    lblMessage.Text = "Record ID: " + recordID;
}
```

- **Explanation:** The hdnRecordID hidden field stores the record ID. The Page_Load event could be used to set the initial value (if it's dynamic), and the btnSubmit_Click event retrieves the value after the form is submitted.

Application State and Caching

6. **Example: Display the total number of visits to a website since it was deployed.**

- **Topic:** Application State
- **Solution:**

  Global.asax (Application_Start):

```
void Application_Start(object sender, EventArgs e)
{
    Application["TotalVisits"] = 0; // Initialize the counter
}
```

  Any Page (e.g., Default.aspx.cs):

```
protected void Page_Load(object sender, EventArgs e)
{
    Application.Lock();
    Application["TotalVisits"] = (int)Application["TotalVisits"]
+ 1;
    Application.UnLock();

    lblVisits.Text = "Total Visits: " +
Application["TotalVisits"].ToString();
}
```

  - **Explanation:** The Application_Start event initializes the counter. The Page_Load event increments the counter each time the page is loaded and displays the total. Application.Lock() and Application.UnLock() are essential for thread safety.

7. **Example: Cache a static list of categories retrieved from a database to improve performance.**
   - **Topic:** Caching (Data Caching)
   - **Solution:**

     ASPX (e.g., Default.aspx.cs):

```
protected void Page_Load(object sender, EventArgs e)
{
    if (Cache["Categories"] == null)
    {
        // Retrieve categories from the database
        DataTable categories = GetCategoriesFromDatabase();

        // Store categories in the cache for 60 minutes
        Cache.Insert("Categories", categories, null,
DateTime.Now.AddMinutes(60), Cache.NoSlidingExpiration);
        lblMessage.Text = "Categories loaded from database.";
    }
    else
    {
        // Retrieve categories from the cache
        DataTable categories = (DataTable)Cache["Categories"];
```

```
            // Bind the categories to a DropDownList or other control
            ddlCategories.DataSource = categories;
            ddlCategories.DataTextField = "CategoryName";
            ddlCategories.DataValueField = "CategoryID";
            ddlCategories.DataBind();
            lblMessage.Text = "Categories loaded from cache.";
        }
    }

    private DataTable GetCategoriesFromDatabase()
    {
        // Code to retrieve categories from the database using
    ADO.NET
        // ...
        return new DataTable(); // Replace with your actual database
    retrieval logic
    }
```

- **Explanation:** This example caches a list of categories. The Page_Load event checks if the "Categories" data is in the cache. If not, it retrieves the data from the database, stores it in the cache, and displays it. If the data is in the cache, it retrieves it from the cache instead of the database.

8. **Example: Cache the output of a user control that displays a frequently accessed but infrequently changing news feed.**
   - **Topic**: Caching (Fragment Caching)
   - **Solution**:

     User Control (NewsFeed.ascx):

```
<%@ Control Language="C#" AutoEventWireup="true"
CodeFile="NewsFeed.ascx.cs" Inherits="NewsFeed" OutputCache
Duration="300" VaryByParam="none" %>
<div>
    <h2>Latest News</h2>
    <ul>
        <li>News Item 1: <%# Eval("Title") %> - <%# Eval("Date")
%></li>
        <li>News Item 2: <%# Eval("Title") %> - <%# Eval("Date")
%></li>
        ...
    </ul>
</div>
```

     Page using the control (e.g., HomePage.aspx):

```
<%@ Register TagPrefix="uc" TagName="NewsFeed"
Src="NewsFeed.ascx" %>
<uc:NewsFeed ID="NewsFeedControl" runat="server" />
```

- **Explanation**: The OutputCache directive in the user control caches its output for 300 seconds (5 minutes). The HomePage.aspx page registers and uses the control. The news feed data is retrieved (presumably from a database or XML file) within the user control's code-behind.

9. **Example: Store a logged-in user's role and display personalized content based on that role.**
   - **Topic:** Session State
   - **Solution:**

     Login Page (e.g., Login.aspx.cs):

```
protected void btnLogin_Click(object sender, EventArgs e)
{
    // Authenticate the user (e.g., against a database)
    string username = txtUsername.Text;
    string password = txtPassword.Text;
    bool isAuthenticated = AuthenticateUser(username, password);
// Replace with your authentication logic

    if (isAuthenticated)
    {
        // Get the user's role from the database
        string userRole = GetUserRole(username); // Replace with
your role retrieval logic

        // Store the user's role in Session
        Session["UserRole"] = userRole;

        // Redirect to the home page
        Response.Redirect("Default.aspx");
    }
    else
    {
        lblLoginError.Text = "Invalid username or password.";
    }
}

private bool AuthenticateUser(string username, string password)
{
    // Replace this with your actual authentication logic (e.g.,
database query)
    // Return true if the user is authenticated, false otherwise
    return true; // Placeholder
}

private string GetUserRole(string username)
{
    // Replace this with your logic to retrieve the user's role
from the database
    // based on the username.
    return "Admin"; // Placeholder
}
```

Default.aspx (or any page):

```
protected void Page_Load(object sender, EventArgs e)
{
    if (Session["UserRole"] != null)
    {
        string userRole = Session["UserRole"].ToString();
        if (userRole == "Admin")
        {
            // Display admin-specific content
            pnlAdminContent.Visible = true;
            pnlUserContent.Visible = false;
        }
        else
        {
            // Display regular user content
            pnlUserContent.Visible = true;
            pnlAdminContent.Visible = false;
        }
    }
    else
    {
        // User is not logged in or role is not set
        pnlUserContent.Visible = false;
        pnlAdminContent.Visible = false;
    }
}
```

- **Explanation:** The login page stores the user's role in Session after successful authentication. Other pages can then retrieve the role from Session and display content accordingly.

10. **Example: Store a list of recently viewed products for a user using a combination of Session and Cookies.**
    - **Topic**: Session State, Cookies
    - **Solution**: **Product Details Page (e.g., ProductDetails.aspx.cs)**:

```
protected void Page_Load(object sender, EventArgs e)
{
    int productId =
Convert.ToInt32(Request.QueryString["ProductID"]);
    List<int> recentlyViewed = Session["RecentlyViewed"] as
List<int>;
    if (recentlyViewed == null)
    {
        recentlyViewed = new List<int>();
    }

    // Check if the product is already in the list
    if (!recentlyViewed.Contains(productId))
    {
        recentlyViewed.Insert(0, productId); // Add to the
beginning
        if (recentlyViewed.Count > 5) // Limit to 5 products
        {
```

```
                recentlyViewed.RemoveAt(5);
            }
            Session["RecentlyViewed"] = recentlyViewed;
        }
        //Store in Cookie
        string productString = string.Join(",", recentlyViewed);
        HttpCookie recentlyViewedCookie = new
    HttpCookie("RecentlyViewedProducts", productString);
        recentlyViewedCookie.Expires = DateTime.Now.AddDays(7);
        Response.Cookies.Add(recentlyViewedCookie);

        // Display Product Details
        // ...
    }
```

Any Page (e.g., Default.aspx.cs):

```
protected void Page_Load(object sender, EventArgs e)
{
     if (Request.Cookies["RecentlyViewedProducts"] != null)
    {
        string productString =
Request.Cookies["RecentlyViewedProducts"].Value;
        string[] productIds = productString.Split(',');
        List<int> recentlyViewed =
productIds.Select(int.Parse).ToList();
        // Display the recently viewed products (e.g., in a
repeater)
        // ...
    }
}
```

- **Explanation**: This example stores recently viewed product IDs. Session is used to maintain the list during the user's session. A cookie is also used to persist the list across sessions (for a limited time). When a user views a product, its ID is added to the list in Session and the cookie. The cookie stores a comma-separated string of product IDs.

30 multiple-choice questions (MCQs) on web application state management in ASP.NET:

ViewState, Session State, Cookies

1. Which state management technique is client-side?
   a) Session State
   b) Application State
   c) ViewState
   d) Server State
   Answer: c
2. Which state management technique stores data on the server?
   a) ViewState

b) Cookies
c) Session State
d) Hidden Fields
Answer: c

3. Which state management technique is most suitable for storing small amounts of non-sensitive data on the client?
   a) Session State
   b) Application State
   c) ViewState
   d) Cookies
   Answer: d
4. Which state management technique automatically maintains control values across postbacks in ASP.NET?
   a) Session State
   b) Application State
   c) ViewState
   d) Cookies
   Answer: c
5. Which state management technique stores data specific to a single user's interaction with the application?
   a) Application State
   b) ViewState
   c) Session State
   d) Cookies
   Answer: c
6. Which state management technique uses a hidden field (`__VIEWSTATE`) to store data?
   a) Session State
   b) Application State
   c) ViewState
   d) Cookies
   Answer: c
7. Which state management technique has a size limitation of approximately 4KB?
   a) ViewState
   b) Session State
   c) Cookies
   d) Application State
   Answer: c
8. Which state management technique can be disabled by the user in their browser?
   a) ViewState
   b) Session State
   c) Cookies
   d) Application State
   Answer: c
9. Which state management technique is generally considered the least secure for storing sensitive data?
   a) Session State

b) Application State
c) ViewState
d) Cookies
Answer: d

10. Which of the following is true about Session State?
    a) Data is stored on the client's browser.
    b) Data is available to all users of the application.
    c) Data is lost when the user closes the browser.
    d) Data is automatically encrypted.
    Answer: c

Query String and Hidden Fields

11. Which method appends data directly to the URL?
    a) ViewState
    b) Session State
    c) Query String
    d) Hidden Fields
    Answer: c
12. Which method stores data within an HTML form element?
    a) Query String
    b) Cookies
    c) Session State
    d) Hidden Fields
    Answer: d
13. Which method is suitable for passing data between pages?
    a) ViewState and Hidden Fields
    b) Session State and Cookies
    c) Query String and Hidden Fields
    d) Application State and Caching
    Answer: c
14. Which method makes data visible in the browser's address bar?
    a) Hidden Fields
    b) ViewState
    c) Query String
    d) Cookies
    Answer: c
15. Which method can be easily tampered with by the user?
    a) Session State
    b) Application State
    c) Cookies
    d) Hidden Fields
    Answer: d
16. Which method is limited to storing string data?
    a) Query String
    b) Hidden Fields
    c) Both Query String and Hidden Fields
    d) Neither Query String nor Hidden Fields

Answer: c

17. Which method can be used to maintain state across postbacks on the same page?
    a) Query String
    b) Cookies
    c) Session State
    d) Hidden Fields
    Answer: d
18. Which method has limitations on the amount of data that can be stored due to URL length restrictions?
    a) Hidden Fields
    b) ViewState
    c) Query String
    d) Cookies
    Answer: c
19. Which is the correct way to retrieve a value from a query string in C#?
    a) `Request.Form["myValue"]`
    b) `Request.Cookies["myValue"]`
    c) `Request.QueryString["myValue"]`
    d) `Session["myValue"]`
    Answer: c
20. Which is the correct way to set the value of a hidden field in ASPX?
    a) `<asp:HiddenField ID="myHidden" runat="server" Value="myValue" />`
    b) `<input type="hidden" id="myHidden" value="myValue" />`
    c) Both a and b
    d) Neither a nor b
    Answer: a

Application State and Caching

21. Which state management technique stores data that is shared by all users of an application?
    a) Session State
    b) ViewState
    c) Application State
    d) Cookies
    Answer: c
22. Which state management technique stores frequently accessed data in memory for faster retrieval?
    a) Application State
    b) Session State
    c) Caching
    d) ViewState
    Answer: c
23. Which of the following is a type of caching in ASP.NET?
    a) User Caching
    b) Page Output Caching
    c) Session Caching
    d) Client Caching

Answer: b

24. Which state management technique requires the use of `Application.Lock()` and `Application.UnLock()` when modifying data?
    a) Session State
    b) ViewState
    c) Application State
    d) Cookies
    Answer: c
25. Which type of caching caches only a portion of a web page?
    a) Page Output Caching
    b) Data Caching
    c) Fragment Caching
    d) Application Caching
    Answer: c
26. Which state management technique consumes server memory?
    a) Application State
    b) Session State
    c) Caching
    d) All of the above
    Answer: d
27. Which of the following is a benefit of caching?
    a) Increased database load
    b) Improved performance
    c) Data is always up-to-date
    d) Reduced server memory usage
    Answer: b
28. Which state management technique is most appropriate for storing a global counter for website visits?
    a) Session State
    b) ViewState
    c) Application State
    d) Cookies
    Answer: c
29. Which type of caching allows you to cache specific data objects like DataTables?
    a) Page Output Caching
    b) Fragment Caching
    c) Data Caching
    d) Application Caching
    Answer: c
30. Which is a potential drawback of caching?
    a) Increased server load
    b) Data staleness
    c) Reduced performance
    d) Increased database hits
    Answer: b

CHAPTER 11: INTRODUCTION TO ASP.NET MVC

Evolution from Web Forms to MVC in ASP.NET: A Detailed Explanation with Examples

The evolution from ASP.NET Web Forms to ASP.NET MVC represents a significant shift in web development paradigms within the Microsoft ecosystem. Web Forms, the initial offering, aimed to simplify web development by providing an event-driven model similar to Windows Forms. However, as web applications grew in complexity and the demands for better control, testability, and separation of concerns increased, the Model-View-Controller (MVC) architectural pattern emerged as a more suitable solution.

Let's delve into the details of each framework and illustrate the key differences with examples.

1. ASP.NET Web Forms (Before MVC)

As the initial description states, ASP.NET Web Forms was designed to abstract away the stateless nature of the web by providing a stateful, event-driven programming model familiar to developers with Windows Forms experience.

Key Features Explained with Examples:

- **Event-driven programming (like Windows apps):** Web Forms allowed developers to handle user interactions (like button clicks, text changes) through server-side event handlers. These events were tied to specific controls on the web page.

  Example (Conceptual):

  Imagine a simple form with a textbox (`txtName`) and a button (`btnSubmit`). In Web Forms, you would write an event handler for the `Click` event of `btnSubmit`.

  C#

```
// Code-behind (YourPage.aspx.cs)
protected void btnSubmit_Click(object sender, EventArgs e)
{
    string name = txtName.Text;
    lblMessage.Text = "Hello, " + name + "!"; // lblMessage is another
control
}
```

  When the user clicks the "Submit" button, the `btnSubmit_Click` method on the server is executed.

- **Uses ViewState to manage control states:** HTTP is stateless, meaning each request is treated independently. Web Forms introduced ViewState, a mechanism to persist the state of controls (like the text in a textbox, the selected item in a dropdown) across postbacks (form submissions to the same page). This state information was serialized and embedded within the HTML of the page as a hidden field.

  Example (Conceptual):

  If a user enters "John" in the `txtName` textbox and then clicks `btnSubmit`, the value "John" needs to be available on the server-side event handler. ViewState automatically handles this by storing "John" in the hidden field and restoring it when the page is posted back.

- **Drag-and-drop UI development:** Visual Studio provided a WYSIWYG (What You See Is What You Get) designer for Web Forms. Developers could drag and drop controls from a toolbox onto the design surface, visually arranging the UI elements. The IDE would then automatically generate the corresponding HTML markup in the `.aspx` file.

  Example (Conceptual):

  You could drag a `TextBox` control onto the designer, position it, and set its properties (like `ID`, `Width`) through the Properties window. The IDE would generate something like:

HTML

```
<asp:TextBox ID="txtName" runat="server"></asp:TextBox>
```

- **Tight coupling of UI and logic (code-behind):** Web Forms followed a "code-behind" model, where the UI (defined in the `.aspx` file) and the server-side logic (written in a separate `.aspx.cs` or `.aspx.vb` file) were tightly coupled. While this seemed convenient initially, it often led to large and complex code-behind files, making it difficult to separate presentation concerns from business logic.

  Example (Conceptual Structure):

  - `YourPage.aspx`: Contains the HTML markup and ASP.NET server controls.
  - `YourPage.aspx.cs`: Contains the C# code with event handlers and business logic that directly manipulates the controls in `YourPage.aspx`.

Limitations of Web Forms Explained:

- **Poor separation of concerns:** The tight coupling between the UI (ASPX) and the logic (code-behind) made it challenging to adhere to the principle of Separation of Concerns (SoC). Business logic, data access, and UI presentation often got mixed within the code-behind, leading to less maintainable and less readable code.
- **Difficult to unit test:** Due to the tight coupling and the heavy reliance on the ASP.NET runtime environment (including the `Page` lifecycle, `HttpContext`, and server controls), unit testing Web Forms applications was notoriously difficult. Mocking or isolating components for testing was cumbersome.
- **ViewState bloats the page:** ViewState, while convenient for maintaining state, could significantly increase the size of the HTML sent to the browser, especially for complex pages with many controls. This extra data overhead could impact page load times and bandwidth usage.
- **Harder control over HTML, CSS, and JavaScript:** Web Forms abstracted away much of the underlying HTML, CSS, and JavaScript. While this simplified development for basic scenarios, it became a limitation when developers needed fine-grained control over the rendered HTML structure, apply complex CSS styling, or integrate advanced JavaScript frameworks. The server controls often generated complex and sometimes unpredictable HTML.

2. ASP.NET MVC (The Evolution)

ASP.NET MVC was introduced as an alternative framework to address the limitations of Web Forms. It embraced the Model-View-Controller architectural pattern, promoting a clear separation of concerns and providing greater control over the web development process.

Key Concepts of MVC:

- **Model:** Represents the application's data and business logic. It is responsible for retrieving, storing, and manipulating data. [1] The Model is independent of the UI and how the data is presented.
- **View:** Represents the user interface. It is responsible for displaying the data provided by the Model. Views are typically written using HTML, CSS, and JavaScript, often with the help of a templating engine (like Razor in ASP.NET MVC). Views should contain minimal application logic.
- **Controller:** Acts as an intermediary between the Model and the View. It handles incoming requests from the user, interacts with the Model to retrieve or update data, and then selects the appropriate View to display the results to the user.

Benefits of MVC over Web Forms:

- **Improved Separation of Concerns:** MVC enforces a clear separation between the Model (data and logic), the View (presentation), and the Controller (request handling and coordination). This leads to more modular, maintainable, and testable code.
- **Enhanced Testability:** The decoupled nature of MVC components makes unit testing much easier. Controllers and Models can be tested independently without relying on the ASP.NET runtime or the complexities of the page lifecycle. Views can also be tested to ensure they render correctly based on the data provided.
- **Better Control over HTML, CSS, and JavaScript:** MVC gives developers direct control over the generated HTML markup. Views are essentially HTML files with embedded server-side code (using Razor syntax in ASP.NET MVC) for dynamic content. This allows for cleaner HTML, better adherence to web standards, and easier integration with CSS frameworks and JavaScript libraries.
- **Stateless Nature:** MVC embraces the stateless nature of HTTP. State management is handled explicitly by the developer using mechanisms like sessions, cookies, or query strings, rather than relying on automatic ViewState. This can lead to more predictable behavior and potentially better performance in some scenarios.
- **Better Support for Modern Web Development Practices:** MVC aligns well with modern web development practices, including RESTful API design, client-side frameworks (like Angular, React, Vue.js), and test-driven development (TDD).

Example Illustrating the MVC Pattern:

Let's consider the same scenario as before: a form to greet a user by name.

Model (`User.cs`):

C#

```
public class User
{
    public string Name { get; set; }
}
```

View (`GreetingView.cshtml`):

HTML

```
@model WebMvcExample.Models.User

@{
    ViewBag.Title = "Greeting";
}

<h2>Hello, @Model.Name!</h2>

@using (Html.BeginForm("SubmitName", "Home"))
{
    <div>
        @Html.LabelFor(m => m.Name, "Your Name:")
        @Html.TextBoxFor(m => m.Name)
    </div>
    <button type="submit">Submit</button>
}
```

Controller (`HomeController.cs`):

C#

```
using Microsoft.AspNetCore.Mvc;
using WebMvcExample.Models;

public class HomeController : Controller
{
    public IActionResult Index()
    {
        return View(); // Returns the default view (likely containing the
form)
    }

    [HttpPost]
    public IActionResult SubmitName(User model)
    {
        // Process the submitted name (e.g., save to database)
        // For this example, we'll just create a new User model for the
greeting view
        var greetingUser = new User { Name = model.Name };
        return View("GreetingView", greetingUser); // Returns the
GreetingView with the user data
    }
}
```

Explanation of the MVC Example:

1. **Model (`User.cs`):** Defines a simple `User` class with a `Name` property. This represents the data we are working with.
2. **View (`GreetingView.cshtml`):** This is an HTML file with Razor syntax (`@`).
    - `@model WebMvcExample.Models.User` declares that this view expects an instance of the `User` model.
    - `@Model.Name` displays the `Name` property of the passed-in `User` object.

   - `@using (Html.BeginForm("SubmitName", "Home"))` creates an HTML form that will submit data to the `SubmitName` action in the `HomeController`.
   - `@Html.LabelFor` and `@Html.TextBoxFor` are HTML helper methods that generate HTML elements based on the model properties, providing features like automatic ID and name generation.
3. **Controller (`HomeController.cs`):**
   - The `Index()` action likely renders an initial view containing the form (not shown explicitly for brevity).
   - The `[HttpPost]` attribute indicates that the `SubmitName` action handles HTTP POST requests.
   - The `SubmitName` action takes a `User` object as a parameter. ASP.NET MVC's model binding automatically populates this object with the values submitted from the form.
   - It then creates a new `User` object (`greetingUser`) and passes it to the `GreetingView`. The `View("GreetingView", greetingUser)` method tells MVC to render the `GreetingView.cshtml` and provide it with the `greetingUser` model.

---

2. MVC Design Pattern Overview: A Detailed Explanation with Examples

The Model-View-Controller (MVC) is a widely adopted architectural design pattern used in software engineering, particularly for building user interfaces. It promotes a clear separation of concerns within an application, dividing it into three interconnected components: the **Model**, the **View**, and the **Controller**. This separation leads to more organized, maintainable, testable, and flexible codebases.

Let's break down each component and illustrate their roles with a detailed example.

The Three Pillars of MVC:

1. Model:

- **Responsibility:** The Model is the heart of the application. It encapsulates the application's data, business logic, and rules. It is responsible for managing and manipulating the data, interacting with data sources (like databases, APIs, or files), and implementing the core functionality of the application.
- **Characteristics:**
   - It is independent of the user interface (View) and the user input handling (Controller).
   - It notifies the View whenever its data changes, allowing the View to update accordingly.
   - It contains the application's state and the logic to modify that state.
   - It can represent a single object, a collection of objects, or even more complex data structures.

- **Analogy:** Think of the Model as the data warehouse and the business analysts. The warehouse stores the raw data, and the analysts process and transform this data based on business rules.

Example (Conceptual C# Model):

Let's say we are building a simple blog application. A possible Model could be a `Post` class:

C#
```
public class Post
{
    public int Id { get; set; }
    public string Title { get; set; }
    public string Content { get; set; }
    public DateTime CreationDate { get; set; }
    public string Author { get; set; }

    // Business logic related to a Post could go here,
    // for example, methods to format the content or check for profanity.
}

public interface IPostRepository
{
    Post GetPostById(int id);
    List<Post> GetAllPosts();
    void AddPost(Post post);
    void UpdatePost(Post post);
    void DeletePost(int id);
}

public class BlogPostRepository : IPostRepository
{
    // In a real application, this would interact with a database.
    private static List<Post> _posts = new List<Post>
    {
        new Post { Id = 1, Title = "First Blog Post", Content = "This is the
content of the first post.", CreationDate = DateTime.Now.AddDays(-2), Author
= "John Doe" },
        new Post { Id = 2, Title = "Second Blog Entry", Content = "Another
interesting article.", CreationDate = DateTime.Now.AddDays(-1), Author =
"Jane Smith" }
    };

    public Post GetPostById(int id)
    {
        return _posts.FirstOrDefault(p => p.Id == id);
    }

    public List<Post> GetAllPosts()
    {
        return _posts;
    }

    public void AddPost(Post post)
    {
```

```
        post.Id = _posts.Count + 1;
        _posts.Add(post);
    }

    public void UpdatePost(Post post)
    {
        var existingPost = _posts.FirstOrDefault(p => p.Id == post.Id);
        if (existingPost != null)
        {
            existingPost.Title = post.Title;
            existingPost.Content = post.Content;
            existingPost.Author = post.Author;
        }
    }

    public void DeletePost(int id)
    {
        _posts.RemoveAll(p => p.Id == id);
    }
}
```

In this example, `Post` is the data model, and `IPostRepository` and `BlogPostRepository` handle the data access logic (simulated in memory here).

2. View:

- **Responsibility:** The View is responsible for presenting the data to the user. It takes the data provided by the Model and renders it in a user-friendly format. Ideally, the View should contain minimal application logic and focus primarily on display.
- **Characteristics:**
    - It is passive and does not directly handle user input.
    - It observes the Model and updates itself when the Model's data changes.
    - It is typically implemented using UI frameworks and templating engines (e.g., HTML, CSS, JavaScript, Razor in ASP.NET MVC, JSX in React).
    - Multiple Views can represent the same Model data in different ways.
- **Analogy:** The View is like the user interface designer and the presentation layer. They take the processed data and create visual representations that users can understand.

Example (Conceptual ASP.NET MVC Razor View - `Details.cshtml`):

Assuming the Controller passes a `Post` object to this View:

HTML
```
@model YourWebAppNamespace.Models.Post

@{
    ViewBag.Title = Model.Title;
}

<h2>@Model.Title</h2>
```

```
<p>
    <strong>Author:</strong> @Model.Author
</p>

<p>
    <strong>Published On:</strong> @Model.CreationDate.ToShortDateString()
</p>

<div>
    @Html.Raw(Model.Content)
</div>

<p>
    @Html.ActionLink("Back to List", "Index")
</p>
```

This View receives a `Post` object (`@model YourWebAppNamespace.Models.Post`) and displays its properties (Title, Author, CreationDate, Content) using HTML and Razor syntax. It also includes a link to go back to the list of posts.

3. Controller:

- **Responsibility:** The Controller acts as the intermediary between the Model and the View. It receives user input (e.g., button clicks, form submissions, URL requests), interacts with the Model to update data or retrieve data, and then selects the appropriate View to display the results back to the user.
- **Characteristics:**
    - It contains the application's control flow and decision-making logic.
    - It receives user actions and translates them into operations on the Model.
    - It selects which View to render based on the outcome of the Model interactions.
    - A single Controller can manage multiple Views, and a single Model can be used by multiple Controllers.
- **Analogy:** The Controller is like the event coordinator or the traffic cop. It listens for user actions, decides what needs to happen based on those actions (interacting with the data), and then directs the user to the appropriate display.

Example (Conceptual ASP.NET MVC Controller - `PostsController.cs`):

C#
```
using Microsoft.AspNetCore.Mvc;
using YourWebAppNamespace.Models;

public class PostsController : Controller
{
    private readonly IPostRepository _postRepository;

    public PostsController(IPostRepository postRepository)
    {
        _postRepository = postRepository;
    }
```

```
    // Action to display a list of all posts
    public IActionResult Index()
    {
        var allPosts = _postRepository.GetAllPosts();
        return View(allPosts); // Passes the list of posts to the Index View
    }

    // Action to display the details of a specific post
    public IActionResult Details(int id)
    {
        var post = _postRepository.GetPostById(id);
        if (post == null)
        {
            return NotFound(); // Return a 404 if the post is not found
        }
        return View(post); // Passes the specific post to the Details View
    }

    // Action to display a form for creating a new post (HTTP GET)
    public IActionResult Create()
    {
        return View(); // Returns the Create View
    }

    // Action to handle the submission of the new post form (HTTP POST)
    [HttpPost]
    public IActionResult Create(Post post)
    {
        if (ModelState.IsValid) // Check if the submitted data is valid
        {
            _postRepository.AddPost(post);
            return RedirectToAction("Index"); // Redirect to the list of
posts
        }
        return View(post); // If invalid, redisplay the form with validation
errors
    }

    // Similar actions for Edit and Delete would also exist.
}
```

In this Controller:

- The `Index` action retrieves all posts from the `BlogPostRepository` (Model) and passes them to the `Index` View.
- The `Details` action takes an `id` from the URL, retrieves the corresponding post, and passes it to the `Details` View.
- The `Create` actions handle both displaying the creation form (GET request) and processing the submitted form data (POST request), interacting with the Model to add a new post.

Why MVC? (Revisited with More Detail)

- **Promotes Separation of Concerns:** This is the core benefit. By dividing the application into Model, View, and Controller, each component has a specific responsibility. This makes the codebase more organized, easier to understand, and less prone to tightly coupled dependencies. Changes in one part of the application are less likely to affect other parts.
- **Easier to Maintain and Test:** The separation of concerns makes it easier to maintain the application over time. Bugs are easier to isolate and fix, and new features can be added without significantly impacting existing code. Furthermore, each component can be tested independently (unit testing). For example, you can test the Controller's logic without needing to render a UI, and you can test the Model's data manipulation logic without involving the Controller or View.
- **Cleaner Code Structure:** MVC enforces a structured way of organizing code. This consistency makes it easier for developers (especially new team members) to understand the application's architecture and navigate the codebase.
- **Full Control over HTML, CSS, and JavaScript:** In web development, the View in MVC typically consists of HTML, CSS, and JavaScript. Unlike some earlier UI frameworks that abstracted these away, MVC gives developers direct control over the generated front-end code. This allows for better optimization, adherence to web standards, and seamless integration with front-end frameworks and libraries.
- **Improved Team Collaboration:** The clear separation of responsibilities allows different team members to focus on specific parts of the application. For example, front-end developers can work on the Views while back-end developers focus on the Models and Controllers.
- **Flexibility and Adaptability:** The MVC pattern makes it easier to adapt the application to changing requirements or to support different presentation layers (e.g., a web interface and a mobile app can potentially share the same Model and Controller logic).

MVC Workflow Example (Detailed):

Let's expand on the provided example: **User requests URL `/products/details/1`**

1. **User Action:** The user clicks a link or enters the URL `/products/details/1` in their web browser. This initiates an HTTP GET request to the server.
2. **Routing:** The web server (e.g., IIS with ASP.NET Core) receives the request. The routing engine within the application examines the URL and maps it to a specific Controller and Action based on predefined routing rules. In this case, it likely maps `/products/details/1` to the `Details` action method within the `ProductsController`, with the parameter `id` having the value `1`.
3. **Controller Action Invoked:** The `Details` action method in the `ProductsController` is executed.
4. **Model Interaction:** Inside the `Details` action, the Controller interacts with the Model (e.g., a `ProductService` or a `ProductRepository`) to retrieve the product data with an ID of `1`. This might involve querying a database.

   C#

```
public class ProductsController : Controller
{
    private readonly IProductService _productService;

    public ProductsController(IProductService productService)
    {
        _productService = productService;
    }

    public IActionResult Details(int id)
    {
        var product = _productService.GetProductById(id);
        if (product == null)
        {
            return NotFound();
        }
        return View(product); // Pass the product data to the View
    }
}
```

5. **Data Passed to the View:** The Controller retrieves the `product` object from the Model. It then calls the `View(product)` method, which tells the framework to locate the appropriate View (typically `Details.cshtml` in a `Views/Products` folder) and pass the `product` object to it as the model for rendering.
6. **View Rendering:** The `Details.cshtml` View receives the `product` data. It uses HTML and potentially a templating engine (like Razor) to dynamically generate the HTML response that will be sent to the browser. The View accesses the properties of the `product` object (e.g., `Model.Name`, `Model.Description`, `Model.Price`) to display the product details.
7. **HTTP Response:** The web server sends the generated HTML response back to the user's browser.
8. **Browser Rendering:** The user's browser receives the HTML, CSS, and any JavaScript, and renders the product details page to the user.

This detailed workflow highlights how the different components of the MVC pattern collaborate to handle a user request and present information. The Controller orchestrates the process, the Model provides the data, and the View is responsible for the presentation. This separation makes the application more organized, testable, and maintainable.

---

3. Comparing ASP.NET MVC vs. Web Forms

The choice between ASP.NET MVC and ASP.NET Web Forms often depends on the specific requirements of a web development project, the team's expertise, and the desired level of control and testability. While both frameworks allow building dynamic web applications using the .NET platform, they differ significantly in their underlying architecture, features, and development paradigms.

Let's delve into each of the features listed in the comparison table and illustrate the differences with examples where applicable.

Feature-by-Feature Comparison:

1. Architecture:

- **ASP.NET Web Forms: Event-driven, Page Controller**
  - **Explanation:** Web Forms adopted an event-driven model similar to Windows Forms development. Each web page (`.aspx` file) behaves like a form with server-side controls. Interactions on these controls (like button clicks, text changes) trigger events that are handled in the associated "code-behind" file (`.aspx.cs` or `.aspx.vb`). The `Page` class itself acts as a central controller for the request lifecycle of that specific page.
  - **Analogy:** Imagine a traditional desktop application where you interact with buttons and text boxes, and event handlers directly respond to those actions on the same form.
  - **Example (Conceptual):** When a button (`btnSubmit`) is clicked on a Web Forms page, the `btnSubmit_Click` event handler in the code-behind is executed, potentially accessing data from other controls on the same page.
- **ASP.NET MVC: Request-driven, Front Controller**
  - **Explanation:** MVC follows a request-driven architecture. Each incoming HTTP request is routed to a specific Controller. The Controller then interacts with the Model to retrieve or update data and selects a View to render the response. A central `Front Controller` (within the ASP.NET MVC framework) handles all incoming requests and dispatches them to the appropriate Controller.
  - **Analogy:** Think of a dispatcher at a call center. All incoming calls (requests) go through the dispatcher (Front Controller), who then directs them to the appropriate agent (Controller) to handle the specific issue.
  - **Example (Conceptual):** A request to `/products/details/1` is routed to the `Details` action of the `ProductsController`. This action then fetches the product with ID 1 from the Model and passes it to the `Details` View for rendering.

2. ViewState:

- **ASP.NET Web Forms: Used to persist state**
  - **Explanation:** Due to the stateless nature of HTTP, Web Forms employed ViewState as a mechanism to automatically maintain the state of server-side controls across postbacks (form submissions to the same page). The state of controls (e.g., text in a textbox, selected item in a dropdown) was serialized and embedded as a hidden field (`__VIEWSTATE`) in the HTML. Upon postback, this data was sent back to the server, and Web Forms used it to restore the control states.
  - **Benefit:** Simplified development for maintaining control states without explicit server-side session management for every control.

- **Drawback:** Could lead to significant page bloat, especially for complex pages with many controls, impacting performance and bandwidth. Also made it harder to predict the exact HTML structure.
- **Example (Conceptual HTML):**

  HTML

  ```
  <input type="hidden" name="__VIEWSTATE" id="__VIEWSTATE" value="
  طويل جدا string of encoded state information ">
  ```

- **ASP.NET MVC: No ViewState**
  - **Explanation:** MVC embraces the stateless nature of HTTP. It does not have an automatic ViewState mechanism. If you need to persist state between requests, you have to do it explicitly using techniques like:
    - **Session:** Storing data on the server associated with a user's session.
    - **Cookies:** Storing small pieces of data on the client's browser.
    - **TempData:** Short-lived data passed between consecutive requests (typically used for redirects).
    - **Query Strings or Form Fields:** Passing data directly in the URL or within form submissions.
  - **Benefit:** Results in cleaner and smaller HTML, providing more control over the output and potentially better performance. Encourages a more explicit understanding of state management.
  - **Example (Conceptual - Using Session):**

    C#

    ```
    // Controller action to store data in session
    HttpContext.Session.SetString("UserName", "JohnDoe");

    // Controller action to retrieve data from session
    string userName = HttpContext.Session.GetString("UserName");
    ```

3. Testability:

- **ASP.NET Web Forms: Hard to test**
  - **Explanation:** The tight coupling between the UI (ASPX files) and the logic (code-behind), along with the heavy reliance on the ASP.NET page lifecycle and server controls, made unit testing Web Forms applications challenging. To test the code-behind logic, you often needed to instantiate the `Page` class and its dependencies, which could be cumbersome and require mocking the ASP.NET runtime environment.
  - **Challenge:** Difficult to isolate components for testing, leading to more integration-style tests which are slower and harder to pinpoint the source of failures.

- **ASP.NET MVC: Easy to test (supports unit testing)**
    - **Explanation:** The separation of concerns in MVC makes unit testing much more straightforward. Controllers are simple classes that can be instantiated and tested independently. You can easily mock or stub dependencies (like repositories or services) passed to the Controller. Views are primarily for presentation and can be tested to ensure they render correctly based on the data provided. Models are also easily testable as they contain the application's data and business logic.
    - **Benefit:** Enables Test-Driven Development (TDD) and facilitates writing comprehensive unit tests, leading to more robust and maintainable applications.

4. Control over HTML:

- **ASP.NET Web Forms: Limited**
    - **Explanation:** Web Forms server controls often abstract away the underlying HTML. While this simplified development for basic UI elements, it could lead to the generation of complex and sometimes unpredictable HTML structures. Developers had less direct control over the exact HTML rendered to the browser, which could be a limitation for achieving specific styling or integrating with certain JavaScript frameworks.
    - **Challenge:** Difficult to fine-tune the HTML for SEO optimization, accessibility, or specific front-end framework requirements.
- **ASP.NET MVC: Full control**
    - **Explanation:** In MVC, Views are essentially HTML files with embedded server-side code (using Razor syntax in ASP.NET MVC). Developers have direct control over the HTML markup, CSS, and JavaScript used in their Views. This allows for cleaner and more semantic HTML, better adherence to web standards, easier integration with front-end frameworks (like Angular, React, Vue.js), and greater flexibility in styling and client-side behavior.
    - **Benefit:** Enables developers to create highly optimized and standards-compliant front-ends.

5. Separation of Concerns:

- **ASP.NET Web Forms: Weak**
    - **Explanation:** The code-behind model in Web Forms often led to a mixing of UI logic, business logic, and data access code within the same class. While developers could strive for separation, the framework itself didn't strongly enforce it, making it easy to create "God Objects" and tightly coupled code.
- **ASP.NET MVC: Strong**
    - **Explanation:** MVC inherently promotes and enforces a clear separation of concerns between the Model (data and business logic), the View (presentation), and the Controller (request handling and application flow). This architectural pattern makes it easier to manage complexity, improve code organization, and enhance maintainability.

6. URL Routing:

- **ASP.NET Web Forms: File-based (e.g., Page.aspx)**
  - **Explanation:** In Web Forms, URLs were typically tied directly to the physical file structure of the application (e.g., `www.example.com/Products.aspx`). While URL rewriting could be used to create more user-friendly URLs, the default mapping was file-centric.
- **ASP.NET MVC: Pattern-based (e.g., /products/1)**
  - **Explanation:** MVC utilizes a powerful routing engine that maps incoming URLs to specific Controller actions based on defined patterns. This allows for the creation of clean, SEO-friendly, and RESTful URLs that are not tied to the physical file structure.
  - **Example (Conceptual Routing Rule):**

    C#

    ```
    app.MapControllerRoute(
        name: "productDetails",
        pattern: "products/{id}",
        defaults: new { controller = "Products", action = "Details" }
    );
    ```

    This route maps URLs like `/products/1`, `/products/123` to the `Details` action of the `ProductsController`, with the `{id}` segment being passed as a parameter to the action.

7. Performance:

- **ASP.NET Web Forms: Slower (ViewState overhead)**
  - **Explanation:** The automatic ViewState management in Web Forms could introduce performance overhead due to the serialization and deserialization of potentially large amounts of data on each request. The larger page sizes resulting from ViewState could also impact page load times. The more complex page lifecycle of Web Forms could also contribute to slightly slower processing compared to MVC.
- **ASP.NET MVC: Faster (lightweight)**
  - **Explanation:** MVC is generally considered more lightweight as it doesn't have the overhead of ViewState and the complex page lifecycle of Web Forms. Developers have more control over what is sent to the client. The request-driven nature and the focus on explicit state management can lead to better performance, especially for high-traffic applications.

Summary Table:

Feature	ASP.NET Web Forms	ASP.NET MVC
Architecture	Event-driven, Page Controller	Request-driven, Front Controller
ViewState	Used to persist state	No ViewState
Testability	Hard to test	Easy to test (supports unit testing)

Control over HTML	Limited	Full control
Separation of Concerns	Weak	Strong
URL Routing	File-based (e.g., Page.aspx)	Pattern-based (e.g., /products/1)
Performance	Slower (ViewState overhead)	Faster (lightweight)

Export to Sheets

Conclusion:

While ASP.NET Web Forms provided a rapid development environment for developers familiar with Windows Forms, its limitations in terms of testability, control over HTML, and separation of concerns became increasingly apparent as web applications grew in complexity.

ASP.NET MVC addressed these limitations by embracing the Model-View-Controller pattern, offering better testability, greater control over the front-end, cleaner code organization, and improved performance. As a result, MVC (and later ASP.NET Core MVC) has become the preferred framework for building modern, scalable, and maintainable ASP.NET web applications.

Although Web Forms is still supported for legacy applications, new development typically favors the MVC architecture due to its numerous advantages in line with modern web development best practices.

---

4. Creating a Basic MVC Project (Step-by-Step Example

This section provides a detailed, step-by-step guide to creating a fundamental ASP.NET MVC (.NET Framework) project using Visual Studio. We'll elaborate on each step mentioned in your outline, explaining the purpose and significance of the actions and the generated code.

Prerequisites:

- **Visual Studio:** You need to have Visual Studio installed on your system. The instructions are generally applicable to recent versions (e.g., 2019, 2022). Make sure you have the ASP.NET and web development workload installed.

Step 1: Create a New Project

1. **Open Visual Studio:** Launch your Visual Studio application.
2. **Select "Create a new project":** On the Visual Studio start screen, you'll see options to open existing projects or create a new one. Click on "Create a new project."
3. **Search for "ASP.NET Web Application (.NET Framework)":** In the "Create a new project" window, you'll see a list of project templates. Use the search bar at the top to find "ASP.NET Web Application (.NET Framework)" using C# or VB.NET as the language (we'll assume C# for this example). Select this template and click "Next."

4. **Configure your new project:**
    - **Project name:** Enter a name for your project (e.g., `MyBasicMvcApp`).
    - **Location:** Choose the directory where you want to save your project files.
    - **Solution name:** By default, this will be the same as your project name. A solution can contain one or more projects.
    - Click "Create."
5. **Choose the "MVC" template:** In the "New ASP.NET Web Application (.NET Framework)" dialog box, you'll be presented with different project templates. Select the **"MVC"** template.
    - **Authentication:** You might be asked about authentication. For a basic project, you can choose "No Authentication" for simplicity. You can always add authentication later if needed.
    - **Enable Docker Support:** You can optionally enable Docker support if you plan to containerize your application. For this basic example, we'll leave it unchecked.
    - **Configure HTTPS:** You can optionally configure HTTPS. For a basic local development setup, you can leave it unchecked, but it's recommended for production environments.
    - Click "Create."

Visual Studio will now scaffold a basic ASP.NET MVC project structure with essential files and folders.

Step 2: Project Structure Overview

The generated project structure is crucial to understanding how an MVC application is organized. Here's a breakdown of the key folders and files mentioned:

```
MyBasicMvcApp/
│
├── Controllers/
│   └── HomeController.cs
├── Models/
│   └── (Empty initially, will contain Product.cs)
├── Views/
│   ├── Home/
│   │   └── Index.cshtml
│   └── Shared/         // Contains layout files (_Layout.cshtml), error
views, etc.
├── App_Start/
│   └── RouteConfig.cs  // Defines URL routing rules
├── Content/          // Contains static content like CSS files
├── Fonts/            // Contains font files
├── Scripts/          // Contains JavaScript files and libraries
├── Global.asax         // Handles application-level events
├── Web.config          // Application configuration file
├── Properties/       // Contains project properties (e.g., AssemblyInfo.cs)
├── packages.config   // Lists NuGet packages used by the project
```

- **`Controllers/`:** This folder houses the Controller classes. Controllers are responsible for handling user input, interacting with the Model, and selecting the appropriate View to render. The default project includes `HomeController.cs`.
- **`Models/`:** This folder is intended to contain the Model classes. Models represent the data of your application and often contain business logic related to that data.
- **`Views/`:** This folder contains the View files (`.cshtml` files when using the Razor view engine). Views are responsible for displaying the data provided by the Model to the user. Views are typically organized into subfolders that correspond to the names of the Controllers (e.g., `Views/Home/` for views used by `HomeController`). The `Shared/` subfolder contains views that are shared across multiple controllers, such as the layout template (`_Layout.cshtml`).
- **`App_Start/`:** This folder contains configuration classes that are executed when the application starts. `RouteConfig.cs` is particularly important as it defines how URLs are mapped to Controller actions.
- **`Global.asax`:** This file contains code for handling application-level events, such as application start and session start.
- **`Web.config`:** This is the main configuration file for the ASP.NET application. It contains settings related to authentication, database connections, custom error pages, and more.
- **`Content/`, `Fonts/`, `Scripts/`:** These folders typically contain static assets like CSS stylesheets, font files, and JavaScript libraries used by the application's front-end.
- **`Properties/`:** Contains project-level settings, such as the assembly information.
- **`packages.config`:** Lists the NuGet packages (reusable components) that your project depends on.

Step 3: Add a Model

1. **Locate the `Models` folder:** In the Solution Explorer (usually on the right side of Visual Studio), find and expand the `Models` folder.
2. **Add a new class:** Right-click on the `Models` folder, navigate to "Add" -> "Class...".
3. **Name the class:** In the "Add New Item" dialog, name the class `Product.cs` and click "Add."
4. **Define the `Product` class:** Replace the default content of `Product.cs` with the following C# code:

   C#

   ```
   public class Product
   {
       public int Id { get; set; }
       public string Name { get; set; }
       public decimal Price { get; set; }
   }
   ```

   - **`public class Product`:** This declares a public class named `Product`.
   - **`public int Id { get; set; }`:** This defines a public integer property named `Id`. The `{ get; set; }` part creates automatic properties with getter and setter accessors, allowing you to read and write the value of this property.

- **`public string Name { get; set; }`:** This defines a public string property named `Name`.
- **`public decimal Price { get; set; }`:** This defines a public decimal property named `Price`, suitable for representing currency values.

This `Product` class serves as a simple representation of product data within our application.

Step 4: Add a Controller

1. **Locate the `Controllers` folder:** In the Solution Explorer, find and expand the `Controllers` folder.
2. **Add a new controller:** Right-click on the `Controllers` folder, navigate to "Add" -> "Controller...".
3. **Choose "MVC 5 Controller - Empty":** In the "Add Scaffold" dialog, select "MVC 5 Controller - Empty" (or a similar option depending on your Visual Studio version) and click "Add." This will create a basic controller without any pre-generated action methods.
4. **Name the controller:** In the "Add Controller" dialog, name the controller `ProductController` (it's convention to append "Controller" to the name of the controller class) and click "Add."
5. **Define the `ProductController`:** Replace the default content of `ProductController.cs` with the following C# code:

C#

```
using System.Web.Mvc;
using MyBasicMvcApp.Models; // Replace YourApp with your actual project
name

public class ProductController : Controller
{
    public ActionResult Details()
    {
        // Create an instance of the Product model
        var product = new Product()
        {
            Id = 1,
            Name = "Laptop",
            Price = 1200.00M
        };

        // Pass the Product model to the View
        return View(product);
    }
}
```

- **`using System.Web.Mvc;`:** This line imports the necessary namespace for working with MVC-related classes, including the `Controller` base class and `ActionResult`.

- **`using MyBasicMvcApp.Models;`: Important:** Replace `YourApp` with the actual name of your project's namespace. This line imports the namespace where our `Product` model is defined, allowing us to use the `Product` class.
- **`public class ProductController : Controller`:** This declares a public class named `ProductController` that inherits from the `Controller` base class. This inheritance provides the controller with various helper methods for handling requests and responses.
- **`public ActionResult Details()`:** This defines a public action method named `Details`. Action methods are the entry points for handling specific user requests. `ActionResult` is a base class for various types of results that a controller action can return (e.g., a View, a Redirect, JSON data).
- **`var product = new Product() { ... };`:** Inside the `Details` action, we create a new instance of our `Product` model and initialize its properties with some sample data. In a real application, this data would likely come from a database or another data source.
- **`return View(product);`:** This line is crucial. It tells MVC to render a View. The `View()` helper method, when passed an object (in this case, our `product` object), will look for a View named `Details.cshtml` within the `Views/Product/` folder and make the `product` object available to that View as its model.

Step 5: Add a View

1. **Locate the `Views` folder:** In the Solution Explorer, find and expand the `Views` folder.
2. **Create a `Product` subfolder:** Right-click on the `Views` folder, navigate to "Add" -> "New Folder," and name the folder `Product`. It's important to name this folder the same as your controller name (without the "Controller" suffix) so that MVC can automatically discover the associated views.
3. **Add a new View:** Right-click on the newly created `Views/Product` folder, navigate to "Add" -> "MVC 5 View (Razor)..." (or a similar option).
4. **Configure the View:**
   - **View name:** Enter `Details`. This name should match the name of the action method in the controller that returns this view (`Details()` in `ProductController`).
   - **Select a template:** Choose "Empty (without model)" from the dropdown initially. We'll modify it to use the model.
   - **Create as a partial view:** Leave this unchecked.
   - **Use a layout page:** You can leave this checked to use the default layout (`_Layout.cshtml` in `Views/Shared/`), which provides a consistent look and feel for your application.
   - **Click "Add."**
5. **Modify `Views/Product/Details.cshtml`:** Replace the default content of `Details.cshtml` with the following HTML and Razor code:

   HTML

```
@model MyBasicMvcApp.Models.Product // Replace YourApp with your actual
project name

@{
    ViewBag.Title = "Product Details"; // Sets the title of the page
}

<h2>Product Details</h2>

<p><strong>ID:</strong> @Model.Id</p>
<p><strong>Name:</strong> @Model.Name</p>
<p><strong>Price:</strong> $@Model.Price</p>
```

- **`@model MyBasicMvcApp.Models.Product`: Important:** Replace `YourApp` with the actual name of your project's namespace. This directive tells the View that it will be receiving an object of type `MyBasicMvcApp.Models.Product` (our `Product` model) from the Controller. This allows us to access the properties of the `Product` object within the View.
- **`@{ ViewBag.Title = "Product Details"; }`:** This sets the value of the `Title` property in the `ViewBag`, which is typically used to set the `<title>` tag of the HTML page (often within the `_Layout.cshtml` file).
- **`<h2>Product Details</h2>`:** This is a standard HTML heading.
- **`<p><strong>ID:</strong> @Model.Id</p>`:** This displays the `Id` property of the `Product` model. The `@Model` syntax provides access to the model object passed from the Controller, and `@Model.Id` accesses its `Id` property.
- **`<p><strong>Name:</strong> @Model.Name</p>`:** Similarly, this displays the `Name` property.
- **`<p><strong>Price:</strong> $@Model.Price</p>`:** This displays the `Price` property, formatted as currency using the `@$` syntax.

Step 6: Run the App

1. **Build the project:** In Visual Studio, go to "Build" -> "Build Solution" (or press Ctrl+Shift+B). This compiles your code and checks for any errors.
2. **Run the application:** Press F5 or click the "Start" button (the green play icon) in the Visual Studio toolbar. This will build and run your application in a development web server (IIS Express by default). Your default web browser should open automatically.
3. **Navigate to `/Product/Details`:** In your browser's address bar, manually navigate to the URL `/Product/Details`.
    - **Explanation:**
        - `/Product`: This part of the URL maps to the `ProductController` (based on the default routing configuration in `App_Start/RouteConfig.cs`, which typically maps `[Controller]/[Action]/[Id]` to controller and action names).
        - `/Details`: This part of the URL maps to the `Details()` action method within the `ProductController`.

4. **Observe the output:** You should see a web page rendered in your browser displaying the product information that was created in the `ProductController` and passed to the `Details.cshtml` View:
5. `Product Details`
6.
7. `ID: 1`
8. `Name: Laptop`
   `Price: $1200.00`

Conclusion

ASP.NET MVC brought a cleaner, more testable and maintainable approach compared to Web Forms. It uses the powerful MVC pattern to separate application logic and UI, giving developers full control over the web stack.

30 multiple-choice questions with answers covering the evolution from Web Forms to MVC, MVC design pattern overview, comparing ASP.NET MVC vs. Web Forms, and creating a basic MVC project:

Evolution from Web Forms to MVC

1. Which of the following is the original web development framework from Microsoft?
   - a) ASP.NET MVC
   - b) ASP.NET Core
   - c) ASP.NET Web Forms
   - d) Razor Pages
   - **Answer: c) ASP.NET Web Forms**
2. ASP.NET Web Forms uses which of the following to manage control states?
   - a) Session
   - b) Cookies
   - c) ViewState
   - d) TempData
   - **Answer: c) ViewState**
3. In ASP.NET Web Forms, UI and logic are typically...
   - a) Loosely coupled
   - b) Tightly coupled
   - c) Separated by interfaces
   - d) Managed by routing
   - **Answer: b) Tightly coupled**
4. Which of the following is a limitation of ASP.NET Web Forms?
   - a) Strong separation of concerns
   - b) Easy unit testing
   - c) ViewState bloat
   - d) Full control over HTML
   - **Answer: c) ViewState bloat**
5. ASP.NET Web Forms follows which programming model?

- a) Request-driven
- b) Event-driven
- c) Component-based
- d) Service-oriented
- **Answer: b) Event-driven**

6. Which framework was introduced to address the limitations of Web Forms?
   - a) ASP.NET Web API
   - b) ASP.NET MVC
   - c) ASP.NET Core
   - d) Silverlight
   - **Answer: b) ASP.NET MVC**
7. Which of the following is NOT a characteristic of ASP.NET Web Forms?
   - a) Drag-and-drop UI development
   - b) Server-side controls
   - c) Pattern-based URLs
   - d) Code-behind model
   - **Answer: c) Pattern-based URLs**
8. What does the term "code-behind" refer to in ASP.NET Web Forms?
   - a) Client-side JavaScript code
   - b) Server-side code that handles events for a web page
   - c) CSS stylesheets
   - d) Database access logic
   - **Answer: b) Server-side code that handles events for a web page**
9. Which of the following is a challenge in testing ASP.NET Web Forms applications?
   - a) Simplicity of mocking dependencies
   - b) Tight coupling with the ASP.NET runtime
   - c) Clear separation of concerns
   - d) Stateless nature of the framework
   - **Answer: b) Tight coupling with the ASP.NET runtime**
10. In ASP.NET Web Forms, which of the following is true about HTML?
    - a) Developers have full control over generated HTML.
    - b) HTML is generated by server controls.
    - c) HTML is written in Razor syntax.
    - d) HTML is primarily client-side.
    - **Answer: b) HTML is generated by server controls.**

MVC Design Pattern Overview

11. What does MVC stand for?
    - a) Model-View-Communication
    - b) Model-View-Controller
    - c) Module-View-Component
    - d) Main-View-Control
    - **Answer: b) Model-View-Controller**
12. Which component of MVC is responsible for managing application data and business logic?

- a) View
- b) Controller
- c) Model
- d) Router
- **Answer: c) Model**

13. Which component of MVC is responsible for displaying data to the user?
    - a) Model
    - b) Controller
    - c) View
    - d) Router
    - **Answer: c) View**
14. Which component of MVC handles user input and updates the Model?
    - a) View
    - b) Model
    - c) Controller
    - d) Router
    - **Answer: c) Controller**
15. What is a primary benefit of the MVC pattern?
    - a) Reduced code complexity
    - b) Improved performance
    - c) Separation of concerns
    - d) Automatic state management
    - **Answer: c) Separation of concerns**
16. In MVC, the View typically interacts directly with the...
    - a) Controller
    - b) Model
    - c) Database
    - d) Router
    - **Answer: b) Model**
17. Which of the following is NOT a typical responsibility of a Controller?
    - a) Handling user input
    - b) Updating the Model
    - c) Rendering the UI
    - d) Selecting a View
    - **Answer: c) Rendering the UI**
18. In MVC, the flow of data when a user makes a request is typically:
    - a) Model -> View -> Controller
    - b) View -> Controller -> Model
    - c) Controller -> Model -> View
    - d) Controller -> View -> Model
    - **Answer: c) Controller -> Model -> View**
19. Which MVC component is responsible for application's control flow?
    - a) Model
    - b) View
    - c) Controller
    - d) Router

- **Answer: c) Controller**

20. Which design pattern does ASP.NET MVC implement?
    - a) Singleton
    - b) Factory
    - c) Model-View-Controller
    - d) Observer
    - **Answer: c) Model-View-Controller**

Comparing ASP.NET MVC vs. Web Forms

21. Which architecture does ASP.NET MVC follow?
    - a) Event-driven
    - b) Component-based
    - c) Request-driven
    - d) Page-based
    - **Answer: c) Request-driven**
22. Which of the following is used to persist state in ASP.NET Web Forms?
    - a) Session
    - b) Cookies
    - c) ViewState
    - d) TempData
    - **Answer: c) ViewState**
23. Which framework offers better control over HTML?
    - a) ASP.NET Web Forms
    - b) ASP.NET MVC
    - c) Both offer the same control
    - d) Neither offers control
    - **Answer: b) ASP.NET MVC**
24. Which framework is generally easier to unit test?
    - a) ASP.NET Web Forms
    - b) ASP.NET MVC
    - c) Both are equally easy to test
    - d) Neither is easy to test
    - **Answer: b) ASP.NET MVC**
25. Which framework uses pattern-based URL routing?
    - a) ASP.NET Web Forms
    - b) ASP.NET MVC
    - c) Both use file-based routing
    - d) Both use pattern-based routing
    - **Answer: b) ASP.NET MVC**
26. Which framework generally results in faster performance?
    - a) ASP.NET Web Forms
    - b) ASP.NET MVC
    - c) Both have similar performance
    - d) Performance depends on the server
    - **Answer: b) ASP.NET MVC**

27. In ASP.NET MVC, URLs are mapped to controller actions using...
    - a) File paths
    - b) Configuration files
    - c) Routing rules
    - d) Server controls
    - **Answer: c) Routing rules**
28. Which of the following is a characteristic of ASP.NET MVC?
    - a) Server-side controls
    - b) Code-behind files
    - c) Razor view engine
    - d) Event-driven programming
    - **Answer: c) Razor view engine**
29. Which of the following is a primary difference between ASP.NET MVC and Web Forms?
    - a) Language used for development
    - b) Server-side vs. client-side scripting
    - c) Architectural pattern
    - d) Database connectivity
    - **Answer: c) Architectural pattern**
30. Which framework provides a more explicit control over state management?
    - a) ASP.NET Web Forms
    - b) ASP.NET MVC
    - c) Both abstract state management
    - d) Neither manages state
    - **Answer: b) ASP.NET MVC**

10 mid-size questions with detailed answers, covering the evolution from Web Forms to MVC:

Evolution from Web Forms to MVC

1. **Explain the primary architectural difference between ASP.NET Web Forms and ASP.NET MVC. How does this difference impact state management?**
    - **Answer:** The primary architectural difference lies in how each framework handles requests and manages application structure.
        - **ASP.NET Web Forms** is event-driven and uses a Page Controller pattern. The page itself handles both UI and logic, with events triggering server-side code. State is managed automatically using ViewState, which embeds control states in the page's HTML.
        - **ASP.NET MVC** is request-driven and employs a Front Controller pattern. A central routing system directs requests to Controllers, which then interact with Models and select Views. MVC does not use ViewState, promoting explicit state management via Session, Cookies, or other methods.
    - This difference significantly impacts state management. Web Forms' ViewState simplifies state maintenance but adds overhead and reduces control over the generated HTML. MVC's stateless nature requires developers to handle state

explicitly, leading to cleaner HTML and potentially better performance but demanding more coding.

2. **Compare and contrast the approach to UI development in ASP.NET Web Forms and ASP.NET MVC. What are the advantages and disadvantages of each?**
    - **Answer:**
        - **ASP.NET Web Forms** offers a visual, drag-and-drop approach with server controls. This simplifies UI development for those familiar with desktop application development. However, it often results in less control over the generated HTML and can lead to bloated pages due to ViewState.
        - **ASP.NET MVC** provides full control over HTML, CSS, and JavaScript. Views are created using HTML and a templating engine (like Razor), allowing for cleaner, more semantic markup and easier integration with client-side frameworks. This approach requires more manual work but offers greater flexibility and adherence to web standards.
    - **Advantages:** Web Forms: Rapid development for simple UIs. MVC: Clean HTML, separation of concerns, and front-end framework integration.
    - **Disadvantages:** Web Forms: Limited control over HTML, ViewState overhead. MVC: Steeper learning curve, more manual coding for UI.
3. **Discuss the concept of "separation of concerns" and how it is addressed in ASP.NET Web Forms and ASP.NET MVC.**
    - **Answer:** Separation of concerns (SoC) is a design principle that advocates dividing an application into distinct parts, each responsible for a specific aspect.
        - **ASP.NET Web Forms** often struggles with SoC. The code-behind model can lead to a mixing of UI logic, business logic, and data access code within the same page, making the application harder to maintain and test.
        - **ASP.NET MVC** strongly enforces SoC. The Model handles data and business logic, the View handles presentation, and the Controller manages application flow. This separation improves code organization, maintainability, and testability.
4. **Explain the role of routing in ASP.NET MVC and how it differs from URL handling in ASP.NET Web Forms.**
    - **Answer:**
        - **ASP.NET Web Forms** traditionally relies on file-based URLs (e.g., `page.aspx`). While URL rewriting is possible, the default behavior maps URLs directly to physical files.
        - **ASP.NET MVC** uses a routing system to map URLs to Controller actions based on defined patterns (e.g., `/products/details/1`). This allows for creating user-friendly, SEO-friendly URLs that are decoupled from the file structure.
    - MVC routing provides greater flexibility, enabling RESTful URLs and easier management of application flow.
5. **Compare the testability of applications built with ASP.NET Web Forms and ASP.NET MVC. Why is MVC generally considered more testable?**
    - **Answer:**

        - **ASP.NET Web Forms** applications are often difficult to test due to the tight coupling between UI and code-behind, the reliance on server controls, and the complex page lifecycle.
        - **ASP.NET MVC** applications are more testable because of the separation of concerns. Controllers are simple classes that can be easily unit-tested in isolation. Views are primarily focused on presentation and can also be tested.
    - MVC's architecture allows for mocking dependencies and testing components independently, leading to more robust and maintainable code.

MVC Design Pattern Overview

6. **Describe the responsibilities of each component in the MVC design pattern (Model, View, Controller) and explain how they interact with each other.**
    - **Answer:**
        - **Model:** Represents the application's data and business logic. It retrieves and manipulates data, enforcing business rules.
        - **View:** Displays data to the user. It receives data from the Controller and renders it in a user-friendly format (HTML, etc.).
        - **Controller:** Handles user input, interacts with the Model to process data, and selects the appropriate View to display the result.
    - **Interaction:** The Controller receives a user request, uses the Model to get or modify data, and passes that data to the View. The View then renders the data for the user.
7. **Explain the benefits of using the MVC pattern in web application development.**
    - **Answer:**
        - **Separation of Concerns:** Divides the application into manageable parts.
        - **Improved Testability:** Enables unit testing of individual components.
        - **Increased Maintainability:** Makes the code easier to understand, modify, and debug.
        - **Enhanced Reusability:** Allows for reuse of Models and Views across different parts of the application.
        - **Parallel Development:** Facilitates concurrent work by different developers on different components.
        - **Better Organization:** Provides a structured approach to application development.

Creating a Basic MVC Project

8. **Outline the essential steps involved in creating a basic ASP.NET MVC project in Visual Studio, explaining the purpose of each step.**
    - **Answer:**
        1. **Create a New Project:** Select the ASP.NET Web Application (.NET Framework) template and choose the MVC template to set up the basic project structure.

2. **Add a Model:** Define classes that represent the data and business logic of the application (e.g., a `Product` class).
3. **Add a Controller:** Create classes that handle user requests, interact with the Model, and choose a View to render (e.g., a `ProductController`).
4. **Add a View:** Design the user interface using HTML and a templating engine (like Razor) to display data from the Model.
5. **Configure Routing (if necessary):** Define URL patterns that map to Controller actions (though the default route often suffices for simple projects).
6. **Run the Application:** Build and run the project to see the application in action.

9. **`Explain the significance of the App\_Start folder and the RouteConfig.cs file in an ASP.NET MVC project.`**
   - **Answer:**
     - **`App_Start`** Folder: Contains classes that configure the application when it starts.
     - **`RouteConfig.cs`** File: Defines the routing rules for the application. These rules determine how URLs are mapped to Controller actions. The default route is typically defined here, and custom routes can be added to handle specific URL patterns.
10. **Describe the role of a "View Model" in ASP.NET MVC. How does it differ from a "Model," and when would you use it?**
    - **Answer:**
      - **Model:** Represents data and business logic, often mapping directly to database tables or entities.
      - **View Model:** A class specifically created to hold the data required by a particular View. It might combine data from multiple Models or contain additional properties needed for presentation.
      - **When to use:** When a View needs data from multiple Models, or when the data needs to be formatted or transformed specifically for the View. View Models help to keep Views clean and avoid over-exposing the domain Model.

CHAPTER 12: ROUTING AND CONTROLLERS

1. URL Routing in ASP.NET MVC: A Deep Dive

✅ What is Routing?

In traditional web development, like in ASP.NET Web Forms, URLs often correspond directly to physical files on the server. For example, a request for `http://example.com/Products.aspx` would typically load the `Products.aspx` file.

ASP.NET MVC introduces a different approach. **Routing** is a pattern-matching system that maps incoming URLs to specific controller actions. Instead of a one-to-one mapping between URLs and files, MVC uses rules to interpret the URL and determine which code should handle the request.

Key Concepts:

- **URL Pattern:** A template that defines the structure of a URL.
- **Route:** A specific rule that associates a URL pattern with a controller and action.
- **Controller:** A class that handles requests and prepares data for the view.
- **Action:** A method within a controller that performs a specific task.

✅ Example:

Let's consider your example:

```
http://localhost:1234/Product/Details/5
```

In an ASP.NET MVC application, this URL is interpreted as follows:

- **`http://localhost:1234`**: This is the server address (domain name and port).
- **`/Product`**: This part of the URL maps to the `ProductController` class. MVC uses convention to find the controller class by adding "Controller" to this URL segment.
- **`/Details`**: This maps to the `Details` action method within the `ProductController`.
- **`/5`**: This is a parameter. In this case, it represents the product ID, and it's passed to the `Details` action as the `id` parameter.

Code Example:

Here's how this would be handled in ASP.NET MVC:

1. Controller:

```
public class ProductController : Controller
{
    public ActionResult Details(int id)
    {
        // Retrieve product details from a database or other source
        var product = GetProductById(id);

        // Pass the product data to the view
        return View(product);
    }

    private Product GetProductById(int id)
    {
        // Implementation to fetch product from database
        // For example:
        // using (var db = new MyDbContext())
        // {
        //     return db.Products.Find(id);
        // }
        return new Product { Id = id, Name = "Sample Product", Price = 19.99M
}; // Placeholder
```

```
    }
}
```

2. Model (Product.cs):

```
public class Product
{
    public int Id { get; set; }
    public string Name { get; set; }
    public decimal Price { get; set; }
    // Other properties
}
```

3. View (Views/Product/Details.cshtml):

```
@model Product

<h2>Product Details</h2>

<p>ID: @Model.Id</p>
<p>Name: @Model.Name</p>
<p>Price: @Model.Price</p>
```

4. Routing Configuration (App_Start\RouteConfig.cs):

```
public class RouteConfig
{
    public static void RegisterRoutes(RouteCollection routes)
    {
        routes.IgnoreRoute("{resource}.axd/{*pathInfo}");

        routes.MapRoute(
            name: "Default",
            url: "{controller}/{action}/{id}",
            defaults: new { controller = "Home", action = "Index", id =
UrlParameter.Optional }
        );
    }
}
```

Explanation:

1. **`ProductController`**: This controller has a `Details` action method that takes an integer `id` as a parameter. It retrieves the product data (in a real application, this would come from a database) and passes it to the `View`.
2. **`Product`** Model: This simple class defines the structure of a product.

3. **`Details.cshtml`** View: This view displays the product details, using the `@Model` directive to access the data passed from the controller.
4. **`RouteConfig.cs`**:
    - `routes.IgnoreRoute()`: This tells MVC to ignore requests for certain files, such as `.axd` files (used by Web Forms).
    - `routes.MapRoute()`: This is where the default route is defined.
        - `name`: A name for the route ("Default" in this case).
        - `url`: The URL pattern:
            - `{controller}`: The name of the controller.
            - `{action}`: The name of the action method.
            - `{id}`: An optional parameter named "id".
        - `defaults`: Specifies default values if the URL doesn't provide them. Here, if no controller is specified, it defaults to "Home"; if no action is specified, it defaults to "Index"; and the "id" parameter is optional.

How it Works:

When a user enters the URL `http://localhost:1234/Product/Details/5`, the MVC routing engine parses the URL and matches it against the route defined in `RouteConfig.cs`. The default route pattern `{controller}/{action}/{id}` matches the URL. MVC then creates an instance of the `ProductController` and calls the `Details` action method, passing the value `5` as the `id` parameter.

Benefits of Routing:

- **Clean URLs:** Routing enables you to create user-friendly URLs that are easy to read and remember (e.g., `/Product/Details/5` instead of `ProductDetails.aspx?ID=5`).
- **SEO Friendliness:** Clean URLs are better for search engine optimization, improving your site's ranking.
- **Decoupling:** Routing decouples URLs from the physical file structure, making your application more flexible and easier to reorganize.
- **RESTful URLs:** Routing makes it easier to design RESTful APIs, which use URLs to represent resources (e.g., `/api/products/5` to get product with ID 5).
- **Maintainability:** Routing centralizes URL mapping, making it easier to manage and modify URLs.

`2. Defining Routes in RouteConfig.cs`

The `RouteConfig.cs` file, located within the `App_Start` folder, is the heart of URL routing in ASP.NET MVC. It's where you tell your application how to interpret incoming URLs and map them to the appropriate controller actions.

`Understanding the RegisterRoutes Method`

The key part of `RouteConfig.cs` is the `RegisterRoutes` method:

```
public static void RegisterRoutes(RouteCollection routes)
{
    // Your routes are defined here
}
```

This method is automatically called by the ASP.NET MVC framework when the application starts. The `routes` parameter is an instance of `RouteCollection`, which is where you add your routing rules.

Anatomy of a Route

Each route is defined using the `MapRoute` method:

```
routes.MapRoute(
    name: "RouteName",
    url: "URLPattern",
    defaults: new { /* Default values */ },
    constraints: new { /* Optional constraints */ } // Introduced later
);
```

- **`name`**: A unique name for the route. This is essential for generating URLs later in your application (e.g., using `Html.ActionLink`). It should be descriptive.
- **`url`**: The URL pattern. This is a string that defines the structure of the URL. It can contain:
    - **Static segments**: Fixed parts of the URL (e.g., "Products", "Details").
    - **Parameter placeholders**: Parts of the URL enclosed in curly braces (`{}`). These placeholders extract values from the URL and make them available as action method parameters (e.g., `{controller}`, `{id}`).
- **`defaults`**: An anonymous object that specifies default values for the URL parameters. If a parameter is not present in the URL, its default value is used.
- **`constraints`**: An optional anonymous object that defines restrictions on the values of the URL parameters (e.g., requiring an `id` to be an integer). We'll cover this later.

Default Route Pattern in Detail

Let's examine the default route:

```
routes.MapRoute(
    name: "Default",
    url: "{controller}/{action}/{id}",
    defaults: new { controller = "Home", action = "Index", id =
UrlParameter.Optional }
);
```

- `name: "Default"`: The route is named "Default".
- `url: "{controller}/{action}/{id}"`: This pattern matches URLs with the following structure:
    - `{controller}`: The name of the controller (e.g., "Product", "Blog"). ASP.NET MVC will look for a class named `ProductController`, `BlogController`, etc.
    - `{action}`: The name of the action method within the controller (e.g., "Details", "Edit", "Index").
    - `{id}`: An optional parameter named "id" (e.g., a product ID, a blog post ID).
- **`defaults`**:
    - `controller = "Home"`: If the URL doesn't specify a controller (e.g., `/`), the `HomeController` will be used.
    - `action = "Index"`: If the URL doesn't specify an action (e.g., `/Home`), the `Index` action method will be called.
    - `id = UrlParameter.Optional`: The `id` parameter is optional. The URL may or may not include it.

Example Scenarios with the Default Route

Here's how the default route handles various URLs:

- **`http://localhost:1234/`**:
    - `controller` = "Home" (from `defaults`)
    - `action` = "Index" (from `defaults`)
    - This calls: `HomeController.Index()`
- **`http://localhost:1234/Home`**:
    - `controller` = "Home"
    - `action` = "Index" (from `defaults`)
    - This calls: `HomeController.Index()`
- **`http://localhost:1234/Products/Details/5`**:
    - `controller` = "Products"
    - `action` = "Details"
    - `id` = 5
    - This calls: `ProductsController.Details(5)`
- **`http://localhost:1234/Blog/Posts/Latest`**:
    - `controller` = "Blog"
    - `action` = "Posts"
    - `id` = "Latest" (The action method parameter will be a string)
    - This calls: `BlogController.Posts("Latest")`
- **`http://localhost:1234/Account/Login`**:
    - `controller` = "Account"
    - `action` = "Login"
    - `id` = null
    - This calls: `AccountController.Login()`

Creating Custom Routes

While the default route is very useful, you'll often need to create custom routes to handle specific URL patterns. Here's how:

```
routes.MapRoute(
    name: "ProductCategory",
    url: "Products/Category/{categoryName}",
    defaults: new { controller = "Products", action = "Category" }
);
```

In this example:

- We've created a route named "ProductCategory".
- The URL pattern is `"Products/Category/{categoryName}"`.
- If a user goes to a URL like `http://localhost:1234/Products/Category/Electronics`, the `Category` action of the `ProductsController` will be called, and the value "Electronics" will be passed as the `categoryName` parameter.

Example with a Custom Route

1. Route Configuration (RouteConfig.cs):

```
public static void RegisterRoutes(RouteCollection routes)
{
    routes.IgnoreRoute("{resource}.axd/{*pathInfo}");

    // Custom Route for Product Categories
    routes.MapRoute(
        name: "ProductCategory",
        url: "Products/Category/{categoryName}",
        defaults: new { controller = "Products", action = "Category" }
    );

    // Default Route
    routes.MapRoute(
        name: "Default",
        url: "{controller}/{action}/{id}",
        defaults: new { controller = "Home", action = "Index", id =
UrlParameter.Optional }
    );
}
```

2. Controller (ProductsController.cs):

```
public class ProductsController : Controller
{
    public ActionResult Category(string categoryName)
    {
        // Retrieve products for the specified category from the database
        var products = GetProductsByCategory(categoryName);
```

```
        // Pass the products to the view
        return View(products);
    }

    private List<Product> GetProductsByCategory(string categoryName)
    {
        // Implementation to fetch products by category
        // ...
        return new List<Product>
        {
            new Product { Id = 1, Name = $"Product 1 ({categoryName})", Price
= 10.00M },
            new Product { Id = 2, Name = $"Product 2 ({categoryName})", Price
= 20.00M }
        }; // Placeholder
    }
}
```

Key Points

- **Route Order:** The order in which you define routes in `RouteConfig.cs` is crucial. MVC matches routes in the order they are defined. More specific routes should come before more general routes (like the default route).
- **Flexibility:** Routing provides immense flexibility in designing your application's URL structure, allowing you to create clean, SEO-friendly, and RESTful URLs.

---

3. Creating Controllers and Action Methods

Controllers are a fundamental part of the ASP.NET MVC framework. They act as intermediaries between the user's request and the application's data and logic. They are responsible for handling incoming requests, processing them, and determining what response to send back to the user.

✅ What is a Controller?

As you mentioned, a controller is a C# class that typically inherits from the `System.Web.Mvc.Controller` base class. This base class provides a set of helper methods and properties that are useful for handling web requests, such as:

- `View()`: Renders a view.
- `RedirectToAction()`: Redirects to another action.
- `Json()`: Returns JSON data.
- `File()`: Returns a file.
- `HttpContext`: Provides access to the current HTTP request and response.
- `Request`: Provides access to HTTP request data.
- `Response`: Provides access to HTTP response data.

Controllers are named by convention with the suffix "Controller" (e.g., `ProductController`, `HomeController`, `OrderController`).

Action Methods

Within a controller, **action methods** are public methods that handle specific requests. Each action method typically corresponds to a specific URL. For example, a `Details` action in a `ProductController` might handle requests for `/Product/Details/{id}`.

Action methods can:

- Receive input from the user (e.g., from URL parameters, form data, or query strings).
- Interact with models to retrieve or modify data.
- Prepare data to be displayed in a view.
- Return a result, such as a view, a redirection, JSON data, or a file.

✅ **Example: Creating a ProductController**

Let's expand on your `ProductController` example:

Controllers/ProductController.cs

```
using System;
using System.Web.Mvc;
using YourApp.Models; // Assuming your models are in this namespace
using System.Collections.Generic; // Add this for lists

public class ProductController : Controller
{
    // Action method to display a single product's details
    public ActionResult Details(int id)
    {
        // Simulate getting a product (usually from a database)
        var product = GetProductById(id);

        if (product == null)
        {
            return HttpNotFound(); // Return a 404 if the product is not
found
        }

        // Pass the product data to the view
        return View(product);
    }

    // Action method to display a list of products
    public ActionResult List()
    {
        // Get a list of products (from database or other source)
        List<Product> products = GetAllProducts();

        // Pass the list of products to the view
```

```
        return View(products);
    }

     // Action to create a new product (GET version for the form)
    public ActionResult Create()
    {
        return View(); // Render the Create.cshtml form
    }

    // Action to create a new product (POST version to handle form
submission)
    [HttpPost]
    public ActionResult Create(Product newProduct)
    {
        if (ModelState.IsValid) // Check if the posted data is valid
        {
            // Save the new product to the database
            SaveNewProduct(newProduct);

            // Redirect to the List action to show the updated list
            return RedirectToAction("List");
        }
        else
        {
            // If the data is not valid, redisplay the form with validation
errors
            return View(newProduct);
        }
    }

    // Simulate getting a product by ID
    private Product GetProductById(int id)
    {
        // In a real application, you'd fetch from a database:
        // using (var db = new YourDbContext())
        // {
        //     return db.Products.Find(id);
        // }

        // Placeholder for demonstration:
        if (id == 1)
        {
             return new Product
            {
                Id = id,
                Name = "Gaming Laptop",
                Price = 1500.00M,
                Description = "High-performance laptop for gaming", //added
description
                Category = "Electronics"
            };
        }
        else if (id == 2)
        {
            return new Product
            {
                Id = id,
```

```
                Name = "Ergonomic Mouse",
                Price = 75.00M,
                Description = "Comfortable mouse for long hours",
                Category = "Electronics"
            };
        }
        return null; // Or throw an exception if you prefer
    }

    private List<Product> GetAllProducts()
    {
           return new List<Product>
        {
            new Product { Id = 1, Name = "Gaming Laptop", Price = 1500.00M,
Description = "High-performance laptop for gaming", Category = "Electronics"
},
            new Product { Id = 2, Name = "Ergonomic Mouse", Price = 75.00M,
Description = "Comfortable mouse for long hours", Category = "Electronics" },
            new Product { Id = 3, Name = "Office Chair", Price = 250.00M,
Description = "Adjustable chair for office use", Category = "Furniture" }
        };
    }

    private void SaveNewProduct(Product product)
    {
        // In a real application, you'd save to a database:
        // using (var db = new YourDbContext())
        // {
        //     db.Products.Add(product);
        //     db.SaveChanges();
        // }

        // Placeholder for demonstration:
        Console.WriteLine($"Saving new product: {product.Name}, Price:
{product.Price}");
    }
}
```

Models/Product.cs

```
using System.ComponentModel.DataAnnotations; // Needed for validation
attributes

namespace YourApp.Models
{
    public class Product
    {
        public int Id { get; set; }

        [Required(ErrorMessage = "Product name is required")]
        [StringLength(100, ErrorMessage = "Name cannot exceed 100
characters")]
        public string Name { get; set; }

        [Required(ErrorMessage = "Price is required")]
```

```
        [Range(0.01, double.MaxValue, ErrorMessage = "Price must be greater
than 0")]
        public decimal Price { get; set; }

        public string Description { get; set; }

        public string Category{get; set;}
    }
}
```

Explanation:

- **`ProductController`**:
    - Inherits from `Controller`.
    - Contains action methods to handle product-related requests.
- **`Details(int id)`**:
    - Handles requests for a single product's details (e.g., `/Product/Details/1`).
    - Takes an `id` parameter from the URL.
    - Retrieves the product data (simulated here).
    - Returns a `ViewResult`, passing the product data to the `Details.cshtml` view. If the product is not found, it returns `HttpNotFound()`.
- **`List()`**:
    - Displays a list of all products (e.g., `/Product/List`).
    - Retrieves a list of products.
    - Returns a `ViewResult`, passing the list to the `List.cshtml` view.
- **`Create()`** (GET):
    - Displays the form for creating a new product (`/Product/Create`).
    - Returns a `ViewResult`, rendering the `Create.cshtml` view (which contains the form).
- **`Create()`** (POST):
    - Handles the submission of the new product form.
    - The `[HttpPost]` attribute specifies that this action only handles POST requests.
    - ASP.NET MVC's model binding automatically maps the form data to the `newProduct` parameter.
    - `ModelState.IsValid` checks if the submitted data is valid based on the validation attributes in the `Product` model (e.g., `[Required]`, `[Range]`).
    - If the data is valid, the new product is saved (simulated here), and the user is redirected to the `List` action using `RedirectToAction()`.
    - If the data is invalid, the `Create.cshtml` view is re-rendered, and the validation errors are displayed to the user.
- **`GetProductById(int id)`** and **`GetAllProducts()`** and **`SaveNewProduct(Product product)`**: These are private methods that simulate data access (in a real application, these would interact with a database).
- **`Product`** Model:
    - Defines the properties of a product.
    - Uses data annotation attributes (`[Required]`, `[Range]`, `[StringLength]`) to specify validation rules.

Key Takeaways

- Controllers are classes that handle requests.
- Action methods are public methods within controllers that respond to specific URLs.
- Controllers interact with models to work with data.
- Controllers use `ViewResult` to render views and display data.
- Controllers can use other action results like `RedirectToAction`, `Json`, and `File`.
- `[HttpPost]` attribute is used to specify that an action method handles POST requests (form submissions).
- `ModelState.IsValid` is used to validate user input based on data annotations in the model.

---

4. Passing Data Between Controller and View

In ASP.NET MVC, controllers are responsible for retrieving and preparing data, while views are responsible for displaying that data to the user. Therefore, it's essential to have mechanisms to pass data from the controller to the view. Here are the three primary methods:

✅ 1. Strongly-Typed Model (Best Practice)

- **Concept:** This is the preferred and most robust way to pass data. You create a class (the model) that represents the data you want to display in the view. The controller creates an instance of this model and passes it to the view. The view then uses the model's properties to access the data.
- **Advantages:**
  - **Strong Typing:** Provides compile-time type checking, reducing the risk of errors. You get IntelliSense in the view, making development easier.
  - **Testability:** Models are simple classes that are easy to create and test.
  - **Maintainability:** Clear separation of data and presentation logic.
  - **Readability:** Code is more self-documenting and easier to understand.
- **Example:**
  - **Model (Models/Product.cs):**

```
namespace YourApp.Models
{
    public class Product
    {
        public int Id { get; set; }
        public string Name { get; set; }
        public decimal Price { get; set; }
        public string Description { get; set; } // Added Description
        public string Category { get; set; }
    }
}
```

  - **Controller (Controllers/ProductController.cs):**

```
using System.Web.Mvc;
using YourApp.Models;

namespace YourApp.Controllers
{
    public class ProductController : Controller
    {
        public ActionResult Details(int id)
        {
            // Simulate getting a product (usually from the database)
            var product = new Product
            {
                Id = id,
                Name = "Gaming Laptop",
                Price = 1500.00M,
                Description = "High-performance laptop for gaming",
                Category = "Electronics"
            };

            // In a real application, you would check if the product exists
            // and return HttpNotFound() if it doesn't.

            // Pass the strongly-typed model to the view
            return View(product);
        }

        public ActionResult List()
        {
             var products = new List<Product>
            {
                new Product { Id = 1, Name = "Gaming Laptop", Price = 1500.00M, Description = "High-performance laptop for gaming", Category = "Electronics" },
                new Product { Id = 2, Name = "Ergonomic Mouse", Price = 75.00M, Description = "Comfortable mouse for long hours", Category = "Electronics" },
                new Product { Id = 3, Name = "Office Chair", Price = 250.00M, Description = "Adjustable chair for office use", Category = "Furniture" }
            };
            return View(products);
        }
    }
}
```

- **View (Views/Product/Details.cshtml):**

```
@model YourApp.Models.Product

<h2>@Model.Name</h2>
<p>Price: $@Model.Price</p>
<p>Description: @Model.Description</p>
<p>Category: @Model.Category</p>
```

- **`View (Views/Product/List.cshtml)`:**

```
@model List<YourApp.Models.Product>

<h2>Product List</h2>
<ul>
    @foreach (var product in Model)
    {
        <li>
            <strong>@product.Name</strong> - $@product.Price
            <p>@product.Description</p>
            <p>Category: @product.Category</p>
        </li>
    }
</ul>
```

- **Explanation:**
  - The `@model` directive at the top of the view specifies the type of data the view expects. In `Details.cshtml`, it's `@model YourApp.Models.Product`, and in `List.cshtml` it is `@model List<YourApp.Models.Product>`.
  - The `Controller` creates an instance of the `Product` model (or a list of products) and passes it to the `View` using the `View(model)` method.
  - Inside the view, you use `@Model` to access the model's properties. This gives you strongly-typed access to the data, with IntelliSense support.

✅ 2. ViewBag (Dynamic Object)

- **Concept:** `ViewBag` is a dynamic object that allows you to pass data from the controller to the view without defining a specific model class. It's a wrapper around `ViewData`, providing a more convenient syntax.
- **Use Case:** Best suited for passing small, simple pieces of data, such as messages, titles, or flags. Avoid using it for complex data structures.
- **Advantages:**
  - Simpler syntax than `ViewData`.
  - Dynamic, so you don't need to define properties in advance.
- **Disadvantages:**
  - **Weak Typing:** No compile-time type checking, which can lead to runtime errors if you misspell a property name or assign the wrong type of data.
  - **Limited IntelliSense:** Less IDE support in the view.
  - **Maintainability:** Can make code harder to maintain and understand, especially for larger projects.
- **Example:**
  - **`Controller (Controllers/HomeController.cs)`:**

```
using System.Web.Mvc;

namespace YourApp.Controllers
{
    public class HomeController : Controller
```

```
    {
        public ActionResult About()
        {
            ViewBag.Message = "Your application description page.";
            ViewBag.CurrentTime = System.DateTime.Now; // Example of passing dynamic data
            return View();
        }
    }
}
```

- **View (Views/Home/About.cshtml):**

```
<h2>About</h2>
<h3>@ViewBag.Message</h3>
<p>Current Time: @ViewBag.CurrentTime</p>
```

- **Explanation:**
  - In the controller, you assign values to properties of the `ViewBag` object (e.g., `ViewBag.Message`, `ViewBag.CurrentTime`). `ViewBag` is dynamic, so you can create properties on the fly.
  - In the view, you access these values using `@ViewBag.PropertyName`.

✅ 3. ViewData (Dictionary Object)

- **Concept:** `ViewData` is a dictionary-like object that allows you to pass data from the controller to the view using key-value pairs.
- **Use Case:** Similar to `ViewBag`, it's suitable for passing small amounts of data.
- **Advantages:**
  - Can be useful for passing data when you need more control over the keys.
- **Disadvantages:**
  - **Weak Typing:** Like `ViewBag`, it lacks compile-time type checking.
  - **Verbose Syntax:** More cumbersome to use than `ViewBag`.
  - **Maintainability:** Less readable than strongly-typed models.
- **Example:**
  - **Controller (Controllers/HomeController.cs):**

```
using System.Web.Mvc;

namespace YourApp.Controllers
{
    public class HomeController : Controller
    {
        public ActionResult Contact()
        {
            ViewData["Title"] = "Contact Us";
            ViewData["Email"] = "support@example.com";
            return View();
        }
    }
}
```

- **View (Views/Home/Contact.cshtml):**
- <h2>@ViewData["Title"]</h2>
- <p>Contact Email: @ViewData["Email"]</p>

- **Explanation:**
  - In the controller, you store data in the `ViewData` dictionary using string keys (e.g., `ViewData["Title"]`, `ViewData["Email"]`).
  - In the view, you retrieve the data using the same keys (e.g., `@ViewData["Title"]`).

Summary and Best Practices

- **Strongly-Typed Models:** Always use strongly-typed models whenever you're passing more than a couple of simple values to a view. This provides the best combination of performance, maintainability, and code clarity.
- **ViewBag/ViewData:** Use `ViewBag` or `ViewData` for small, one-off pieces of data, such as titles, messages, or flags. `ViewBag` is generally preferred over `ViewData` due to its simpler syntax.

By following these guidelines, you can ensure that your ASP.NET MVC applications are well-structured, maintainable, and less prone to errors.

📌 Summary Table

Feature	Description
Routing	Maps URLs to controller actions
RouteConfig.cs	Defines URL patterns for the app
Controller	Class that handles web requests
Action Method	A method inside the controller
Passing Data	Use Model (preferred), ViewBag, or ViewData

30 multiple-choice questions with answers covering URL Routing, Defining Routes, Controllers, Action Methods, and Passing Data in ASP.NET MVC:

URL Routing in ASP.NET MVC

1. What is the primary purpose of routing in ASP.NET MVC?

- a) To define the visual layout of a page
- b) To map URLs to controller actions
- c) To manage database connections
- d) To handle user authentication
- Answer: b

2. In ASP.NET MVC, URLs are typically mapped to:
   - a) Physical files on the server
   - b) Controller classes and action methods
   - c) Database tables
   - d) HTML elements
   - Answer: b
3. Which of the following is NOT a benefit of using routing in ASP.NET MVC?
   - a) Clean URLs
   - b) SEO friendliness
   - c) Tighter coupling between URLs and server files
   - d) Improved maintainability
   - Answer: c
4. What does the term "URL pattern" refer to in ASP.NET MVC routing?
   - a) A regular expression for validating URLs
   - b) A template that defines the structure of a URL
   - c) A list of all URLs in the application
   - d) A class that handles URL requests
   - Answer: b
5. Which file typically contains the routing configuration in an ASP.NET MVC application?
   - a) Web.config
   - b) Global.asax
   - c) RouteConfig.cs
   - d) App_Start.cs
   - Answer: c

Defining Routes in RouteConfig.cs

6. Which method is used to define a route in `RouteConfig.cs`?
   - a) `AddRoute()`
   - b) `MapRoute()`
   - c) `RegisterRoute()`
   - d) `CreateRoute()`
   - Answer: b
7. In a route definition, what does the `{controller}` placeholder represent?
   - a) The name of a view file
   - b) The name of a controller class
   - c) The name of an action method
   - d) A parameter in the URL
   - Answer: b
8. What does the `defaults` parameter in `MapRoute()` specify?
   - a) The URL pattern for the route

- b) The HTTP methods allowed for the route (e.g., GET, POST)
- c) Default values for URL parameters
- d) Constraints on URL parameters
- Answer: c

9. Which of the following is true about the default route in ASP.NET MVC?
   - a) It is defined in Global.asax
   - b) It cannot be modified
   - c) It uses the pattern `{controller}/{action}/{id}`
   - d) It is only used for the home page
   - Answer: c
10. What is the purpose of `routes.IgnoreRoute("{resource}.axd/{*pathInfo}");`?
    - a) To define a default route
    - b) To ignore requests for certain file types
    - c) To redirect users to a specific page
    - d) To handle errors in routing
    - Answer: b
11. In RouteConfig.cs, which order should routes be registered?
    - a) From least specific to most specific
    - b) The order does not matter
    - c) From most specific to least specific
    - d) Alphabetical order
    - Answer: c
12. What will the URL "http://example.com/Products/Details/10" map to, assuming the default route?
    - a) ProductsController.Details()
    - b) ProductsController.Details(10)
    - c) DetailsController.Index(10)
    - d) ProductsController.Index(10)
    - Answer: b
13. Which of the following is NOT a valid parameter for the MapRoute method?
    - a) name
    - b) url
    - c) defaults
    - d) method
    - Answer: d
14. If a URL does not match any defined routes, what happens?
    - a) The user is redirected to the home page.
    - b) The application throws an error (404 Not Found).
    - c) The default route is used.
    - d) The first route defined is used.
    - Answer: b
15. How do you make a parameter optional in a route definition?
    - a) By using the `Optional` keyword
    - b) By enclosing it in square brackets: `[{id}]`
    - c) By setting its default value to `UrlParameter.Optional`
    - d) By omitting it from the `url` parameter

- Answer: c

Creating Controllers and Action Methods

16. In ASP.NET MVC, what is a controller?
    - a) A class that defines the data model
    - b) A class that handles user interface elements
    - c) A class that handles requests and returns responses
    - d) A class that manages routing configuration
    - Answer: c
17. From which class do controllers typically inherit?
    - a) `System.Web.UI.Page`
    - b) `System.Web.Mvc.Controller`
    - c) `System.Web.Http.ApiController`
    - d) `System.Web.Routing.Route`
    - Answer: b
18. What is an action method?
    - a) A method that defines a URL route
    - b) A method that renders a view
    - c) A public method within a controller that handles a specific request
    - d) A method that interacts with the database
    - Answer: c
19. Which suffix is conventionally used for controller class names?
    - a) ControllerClass
    - b) Controller
    - c) MVCController
    - d) ActionController
    - Answer: b
20. What is the purpose of the `ActionResult` return type?
    - a) To define a view
    - b) To specify the data model
    - c) To represent the result of an action method
    - d) To handle exceptions
    - Answer: c
21. Which attribute is used to specify that an action method should only handle HTTP POST requests?
    - a) `[HttpGet]`
    - b) `[HttpPost]`
    - c) `[HttpPut]`
    - d) `[HttpDelete]`
    - Answer: b
22. What does the `View()` method in a controller do?
    - a) Redirects to another action
    - b) Returns JSON data
    - c) Renders a view
    - d) Returns a file

- Answer: c

Passing Data Between Controller and View

23. Which is the preferred way to pass data from a controller to a view in ASP.NET MVC?
    - a) ViewBag
    - b) ViewData
    - c) Strongly-typed model
    - d) Session variables
    - Answer: c
24. What is a "strongly-typed model"?
    - a) A dynamic object for passing data
    - b) A dictionary for storing data
    - c) A class that represents the data to be displayed in the view
    - d) A built-in data type in ASP.NET MVC
    - Answer: c
25. In a view, how do you access data passed from the controller using a strongly-typed model?
    - a) `@ViewBag.PropertyName`
    - b) `@ViewData["Key"]`
    - c) `@Model.PropertyName`
    - d) `@Session["Key"]`
    - Answer: c
26. What is `ViewBag`?
    - a) A strongly-typed model
    - b) A dynamic object for passing data from the controller to the view
    - c) A dictionary for storing view-specific data
    - d) A class for handling HTTP requests
    - Answer: b
27. What is the primary disadvantage of using `ViewBag` and `ViewData` for passing data?
    - a) They can only pass primitive data types
    - b) They require more code to use than strongly-typed models
    - c) They lack compile-time type checking
    - d) They cannot be used in partial views
    - Answer: c
28. Which of the following is true about `ViewData`?
    - a) It is a dynamic object.
    - b) It uses key-value pairs to store data.
    - c) It provides strongly-typed access to data.
    - d) It is the preferred way to pass data to a view.
    - Answer: b
29. When should you prefer using `ViewBag` or `ViewData` over strongly typed models?
    - a) When passing complex data structures
    - b) When needing compile-time type safety
    - c) For small, simple pieces of data
    - d) In scenarios requiring high performance

- Answer: c

30. In a .cshtml view, how do you declare the type of model being passed from the controller?
    - a) `@modeltype ModelName`
    - b) `@using ModelName`
    - c) `@model ModelName`
    - d) `@declare ModelName`
    - Answer: c

10 mid-size questions and answers on URL Routing in ASP.NET MVC, covering the areas you specified:

1. Defining Routes in RouteConfig.cs

1. **Question:** Explain the role of `RouteConfig.cs` in an ASP.NET MVC application. Describe the purpose of the `RegisterRoutes` method and the `RouteCollection` object.
    - **Answer:**
        - `RouteConfig.cs` is where URL routing for the ASP.NET MVC application is configured.
        - The `RegisterRoutes` method is called by the application at startup to define the application's routing rules.
        - The `RouteCollection` object, passed as a parameter to `RegisterRoutes`, is a collection that stores all the defined routes. Routes are added to this collection using the `MapRoute` method, which maps URL patterns to specific controller actions.
2. **Question:** Describe the structure of a typical route definition using the `MapRoute` method. Explain the purpose of the `name`, `url`, and `defaults` parameters. Provide an example.
    - **Answer:**
        - A route definition using `MapRoute` consists of:
            - `name`: A unique name for the route, used for route identification and URL generation.
            - `url`: A URL pattern with static segments and parameter placeholders (e.g., `{controller}/{action}/{id}`).
            - `defaults`: An object that provides default values for URL parameters, in case they are not present in the requested URL.
        - Example:

```
routes.MapRoute(
    name: "ProductDetails",
    url: "Products/{category}/{id}",
    defaults: new { controller = "Product", action =
"Details", category = "All" }
);
```

2. Defining Routes in RouteConfig.cs

3. **Question:** Explain the importance of route order in `RouteConfig.cs`. What can happen if routes are not defined in the correct order? Provide an example to illustrate your point.
   - **Answer:**
     - Route order is crucial because ASP.NET MVC matches incoming URLs to routes in the order they are defined in `RouteConfig.cs`. The first route that matches the URL is used.
     - If routes are not in the correct order, more general routes might match before more specific ones, leading to incorrect routing.
     - Example:
     - `routes.MapRoute(name: "Blog", url: "{controller}/{action}/{id}", defaults: new { controller = "Blog", action = "Index", id = UrlParameter.Optional });`
     - `routes.MapRoute(name: "BlogPosts", url: "Blog/Posts/{year}/{month}/{day}", defaults: new { controller = "Blog", action = "Posts" });`

     If the "Blog" route is defined *before* "BlogPosts", a URL like `/Blog/Posts/2024/10/27` would match the "Blog" route instead of "BlogPosts", causing an error or unexpected behavior. The more specific route ("BlogPosts") should be defined first.

4. **Question:** What are route constraints? Explain how they can be used to restrict the values of URL parameters. Provide an example of using a route constraint to ensure that an `id` parameter is an integer.
   - **Answer:**
     - Route constraints are optional restrictions on URL parameters that specify what values are allowed.
     - They are used to make routes more specific and prevent them from matching unintended URLs.
     - Example:

```
routes.MapRoute(
    name: "ProductDetails",
    url: "Products/{id}",
    defaults: new { controller = "Product", action =
"Details" },
    constraints: new { id = @"\d+" } // id must be a number
);
```

     In this example, the `constraints` parameter ensures that the `id` parameter must consist of one or more digits (`\d+`).

3. Creating Controllers and Action Methods

5. **Question:** Explain the role of a controller in the ASP.NET MVC framework. What are its main responsibilities?
   - **Answer:**
     - A controller is responsible for handling incoming HTTP requests.
     - Its main responsibilities include:
       - Receiving and processing user input.
       - Interacting with the model to retrieve or modify data.
       - Selecting which view to display to the user.
       - Preparing any data needed by the view (using a model, ViewBag, or ViewData).
       - Returning an appropriate `ActionResult` (e.g., `ViewResult`, `RedirectResult`, `JsonResult`).
6. **Question:** What is an action method? Explain the characteristics of an action method and its role in the MVC request lifecycle.
   - **Answer:**
     - An action method is a public method within a controller that handles a specific URL request.
     - Characteristics:
       - It must be a public method of a controller class.
       - It typically returns an `ActionResult` or a derived type.
       - It can receive parameters from the URL, query string, or form data.
     - Role in MVC request lifecycle:
       - The routing engine maps a URL to a specific action method.
       - The action method is executed to process the request.
       - The action method determines the response to be sent back to the client.

4. Passing Data Between Controller and View

7. **Question:** Describe the "strongly-typed model" approach for passing data from a controller to a view. What are the advantages of using this approach?
   - **Answer:**
     - In the strongly-typed model approach, a class is created to represent the data that the view needs. An instance of this class is created in the controller and passed to the view.
     - Advantages:
       - Strong compile-time type checking.
       - IntelliSense support in the view.
       - Improved code organization and maintainability.
       - Better testability.
8. **Question:** Explain the differences between `ViewBag` and `ViewData` for passing data from a controller to a view. In what scenarios might you choose to use them?
   - **Answer:**
     - `ViewBag` is a dynamic object, while `ViewData` is a dictionary. Both are used to pass data from a controller to a view.

- `ViewBag` provides a simpler syntax (e.g., `ViewBag.Message = "Hello"`) compared to `ViewData` (`ViewData["Message"] = "Hello"`).
- `ViewBag` and `ViewData` are suitable for passing small amounts of data, such as simple messages or flags, where strong typing is not critical. Strongly-typed models are preferred for more complex data scenarios.

5. Passing Data Between Controller and View

9. **Question:** You need to pass a list of products from a controller to a view. Demonstrate how you would do this using both a strongly-typed model and `ViewBag`. Compare the code in both the controller and the view.
   - **Answer:**
     - Controller (Strongly-Typed Model):

```
public ActionResult ProductList()
{
    List<Product> products = GetProducts(); // Assume this method retrieves the product list
    return View(products);
}
```

View (Strongly-Typed Model):

```
@model List<YourNamespace.Models.Product>
@foreach (var product in Model)
{
    <p>@product.Name - @product.Price</p>
}
```

- Controller (ViewBag):

```
public ActionResult ProductList()
{
    ViewBag.Products = GetProducts(); // Assume this method retrieves the product list
    return View();
}
```

View (ViewBag):

```
@foreach (var product in ViewBag.Products)
{
    <p>@product.Name - @product.Price</p>
}
```

- The strongly-typed model approach is generally preferred because it provides better type safety and IntelliSense support in the view.

10. **Question:** Describe a scenario where you would use TempData and explain why it is appropriate for that situation.
    - **Answer:**
        - TempData is useful for passing data between two consecutive requests, such as after a redirect.
        - Scenario: After successfully creating an order, you want to display a confirmation message to the user. You redirect them to a "Confirmation" action to display this message.
        - Why TempData?
            - You store the confirmation message in TempData in the "CreateOrder" action.
            - After the redirect, the "Confirmation" action retrieves the message from TempData and displays it.
            - TempData ensures that the message is only available for the next request and is then automatically removed, preventing it from being displayed indefinitely if the user refreshes the page.

CHAPTER 13: VIEWS AND RAZOR SYNTAX

1. Introduction to Razor View Engine

✅ What is Razor?

- Razor is a view engine developed by Microsoft for ASP.NET MVC (and later adopted in ASP.NET Core). A view engine is responsible for taking server-side code and data and combining it with HTML markup to generate dynamic web pages.
- Before Razor, ASP.NET MVC used the ASPX view engine, which had a more verbose and complex syntax. Razor was designed to provide a cleaner, more concise, and more developer-friendly way to write views.
- Razor allows developers to embed C# (or VB.NET, though C# is far more common) code directly into HTML markup. This enables you to display dynamic data, use control structures (like loops and conditional statements), and access server-side functionality within your views.

✅ Key Features of Razor:

- **Clean and Minimal Syntax:** Razor's syntax is designed to be unobtrusive and easy to read. It uses the `@` symbol to transition between HTML and C# code, reducing the amount of code clutter.
- **Fast and Easy to Write:** Razor's concise syntax makes it quicker to write views compared to older view engines. It also benefits from Visual Studio's IntelliSense, which provides code completion and error checking.
- **Supports Full C# Code:** Within a Razor code block, you can write any valid C# code. This gives you access to the full power of the .NET framework within your views.
- **File Extension:** Razor view files typically use the `.cshtml` extension for C# (and `.vbhtml` for VB.NET).

✅ How Razor Works

- When a controller action returns a view, the ASP.NET MVC framework uses the Razor view engine to process the `.cshtml` file.
- The Razor engine parses the file, identifying the HTML markup and the embedded C# code.
- The C# code is executed on the server, and the results are dynamically inserted into the HTML.
- The final HTML output is then sent to the client's browser.

✅ Example: Displaying a Product

Let's expand on your example and create a more complete scenario:

- **Model (Models/Product.cs):**

```
namespace MyWebApp.Models
{
    public class Product
    {
        public int Id { get; set; }
        public string Name { get; set; }
        public decimal Price { get; set; }
        public string Description { get; set; }
    }
}
```

- **Controller (Controllers/ProductController.cs):**

```
using System.Web.Mvc;
using MyWebApp.Models;

namespace MyWebApp.Controllers
{
    public class ProductController : Controller
    {
        public ActionResult Details(int id)
```

```
        {
            // Simulate retrieving product data from a database
            var product = new Product
            {
                Id = id,
                Name = "Wireless Mouse",
                Price = 25.99M,
                Description = "Ergonomic wireless mouse for comfortable
use."
            };

            // Pass the product model to the view
            return View(product);
        }
    }
}
```

- **View (Views/Product/Details.cshtml):**

```
@model MyWebApp.Models.Product  // Declare the model type

<h2>Product Details</h2>

<div class="product-info">
    <h3>@Model.Name</h3>  <p>Price: $@Model.Price</p> <p>Description:
@Model.Description</p>
    <p>Product ID: @Model.Id</p>
</div>

<p>
    @if (Model.Price > 50)
    {
        <span class="high-price">This is a high-priced item.</span>
    }
    else
    {
        <span>This is a reasonably priced item.</span>
    }
</p>

@* A comment in Razor.  This will not be rendered in the HTML. *@
```

Explanation:

- **`@model MyWebApp.Models.Product`**: This line at the top of the `.cshtml` file specifies the type of data that the view expects to receive from the controller. This is crucial for strong typing and IntelliSense.

- **`@Model.Name`, `@Model.Price`, and `@Model.Description`**: These are examples of how to embed C# code to display data from the model. The `@` symbol indicates the start of a C# expression. The value of the `Name`, `Price`, and `Description` properties of the `Model` object (which is an instance of the `Product` class) will be rendered as HTML.
- **`@if`** block: Razor allows you to use C# control structures like `if`, `else`, `for`, and `while` within your views. In this case, an `if` statement checks the product's price and displays a different message depending on whether it's above or below $50.
- **Razor Comments**: Comments within `@* *@` will not be rendered in the final HTML output.

Benefits of Razor

- **Improved Readability**: The blending of HTML and C# is more natural.
- **Cleaner Code**: Less code clutter compared to older view engines.
- **Better IDE Support**: Visual Studio provides excellent IntelliSense for Razor, including code completion, syntax highlighting, and error detection.
- **Testability**: Facilitates writing unit tests for view logic.

`2. Razor Syntax: @model, HTML Helpers, Loops, and Conditions`

Razor provides a concise way to embed C# code within your HTML markup in ASP.NET MVC views. Here's a breakdown of the elements you've mentioned, with more details:

✅ **`@model Directive`**

- **Purpose:**
  - The `@model` directive is used at the very top of a Razor view (`.cshtml` file) to specify the type of the data that the view expects to receive from the controller. This is also referred to as the view's model.
- **Syntax:**
  - `@model Namespace.ClassName`
- **Explanation:**
  - `Namespace.ClassName` should be the fully qualified name of the C# class that represents the data you want to use in the view.
  - For example, if you have a `Product` class in the `MyWebApp.Models` namespace, you would use `@model MyWebApp.Models.Product`.
- **Benefits:**
  - **Strong Typing:** The most important benefit. By specifying the model type, you enable strong typing within your view. This means that the Razor engine and Visual Studio know the properties and methods available on your model object.
  - **IntelliSense:** Strong typing enables IntelliSense in Visual Studio. When you use `@Model` in your view, Visual Studio will provide code completion, syntax highlighting, and error checking, making your development process much faster and less error-prone.

- **Compile-Time Checking:** In some cases, the Razor engine can perform some compile-time checks to ensure that you are using the model's properties correctly. This helps catch errors early in the development cycle.

- **Example:**
  - **`Model (Models/Product.cs):`**

```
namespace MyWebApp.Models
{
    public class Product
    {
        public int Id { get; set; }
        public string Name { get; set; }
        public decimal Price { get; set; }
        public string Description { get; set; }
    }
}
```

  - **`View (Views/Product/Details.cshtml):`**

```
@model MyWebApp.Models.Product

<h2>Product Details</h2>
<p>Name: @Model.Name</p>  <p>Price: $@Model.Price</p>
<p>Description: @Model.Description</p>

@if (Model.Price > 100)
{
   <p>This is an expensive product</p>
}
```

  - In this example, the `@model` directive tells the view that it will be working with a `Product` object. Then, within the view, you can use `@Model.Name`, `@Model.Price`, and `@Model.Description` to access the properties of that object.

✓ HTML Helpers

- **Purpose:**
  - HTML helpers are methods that generate HTML elements in your Razor views. They provide a more convenient and less error-prone way to create HTML, especially for form elements and elements that need to be bound to model properties.
- **Namespace:**
  - HTML helpers are accessed using the `Html` property of the view (which is of type `HtmlHelper`).
- **Benefits:**
  - **Code Reusability:** Helpers encapsulate the logic for generating common HTML structures, reducing code duplication.
  - **Strong Typing (for some helpers):** Helpers like `LabelFor` and `TextBoxFor` use lambda expressions to bind to model properties, providing some level of type safety and enabling features like automatic generation of element IDs and names.

- **Automatic Handling of Values:** Helpers like `TextBoxFor` automatically populate the input field with the value from the model, making it easier to display and edit data.
- **Simplified Syntax:** They often provide a more concise way to generate HTML than writing it manually.

- **Examples:**
  - **`@Html.LabelFor(m => m.Name)`**:
    - Generates an HTML `<label>` element for the `Name` property of the model.
    - The `m => m.Name` is a lambda expression that specifies the model property.
    - Output: `<label for="Name">Name</label>` (The `for` attribute is automatically set to the correct ID).
  - **`@Html.TextBoxFor(m => m.Name)`**:
    - Generates an HTML `<input type="text">` element for the `Name` property.
    - The input field's `id` and `name` attributes are automatically set to "Name", and its `value` attribute is set to the value of `Model.Name`.
    - Output: `<input type="text" id="Name" name="Name" value="[Value of Model.Name]" />`
  - **`@Html.DisplayFor(m => m.Price)`**:
    - Generates HTML to display the value of the `Price` property. The generated HTML might vary depending on the data type and any display attributes applied to the property.
    - Output: `<span>[Value of Model.Price]</span>`
  - **`@Html.DropDownListFor(m => m.CategoryId, ViewBag.Categories)`**
    - Generates a dropdown list.
    - `m => m.CategoryId`: Binds the dropdown to the `CategoryId` property of the model.
    - `ViewBag.Categories`: Provides the list of options for the dropdown.
  - **`@Html.ActionLink("View Details", "Details", "Products", new { id = Model.Id })`**:
    - Generates an HTML `<a>` (link) element.
    - "View Details": The text of the link.
    - "Details": The action method name.
    - "Products": The controller name.
    - `new { id = Model.Id }`: Route values (in this case, the `id` parameter).
    - Output: `<a href="/Products/Details?id=[Model.Id]">View Details</a>`

✅ Loops and Conditions

- **Purpose:**
  - Razor allows you to use standard C# control flow statements (loops and conditional statements) directly within your views to control the rendering of HTML.
- **Syntax:**

- You use the `@` symbol to enter a C# code block, and then you can write any valid C# code.

- **Examples:**
  - **`@if` / `@else`:**

```
@if (Model.Price > 100)
{
    <p>This product is expensive.</p>
}
else if (Model.Price > 50)
{
    <p>This product is moderately priced.</p>
}
else
{
    <p>This product is affordable.</p>
}
```

  - **`@for`** loop:

```
@for (int i = 0; i < Model.Quantity; i++)
{
    <p>Item @(i + 1)</p>  //  Parenthesis is used to render inline expression
}
```

  - **`@foreach`** loop:

```
 @model List<MyWebApp.Models.Product>

<ul>
    @foreach (var product in Model)
    {
        <li>@product.Name - $@product.Price</li>
    }
</ul>
```

  - **`@while`** loop

```
@{ int counter = 0; }
 @while (counter < 5) {
   <p>Current Counter: @counter</p>
   counter++;
 }
```

- **Explanation**
  - The `@` symbol is used to switch from HTML to C# context.
  - Inside the code block, you can use any C# syntax.
  - The code is executed on the server before the HTML is sent to the browser.
  - You can mix HTML and C# code within the loop or conditional statement.
  - In the `@foreach` example, `Model` is assumed to be a `List<Product>`. The loop iterates through each product in the list and displays its name and price.

```
}
```

---

3. Creating Layout Pages and Partial Views

✅ **`Layout Pages (_Layout.cshtml)`**

- **Purpose:**
    - Layout pages provide a way to define a consistent structure for the pages within your ASP.NET MVC web application. They allow you to avoid duplicating common HTML elements across multiple views.
    - Think of a layout page as a master template that defines the overall visual structure of your site, including elements like:
        - Header
        - Footer
        - Navigation menus
        - Sidebars
        - CSS and JavaScript references
    - Content from individual views is then inserted into specific sections of the layout page.
- **`_Layout.cshtml`**:
    - By convention, layout pages are named `_Layout.cshtml` and are typically located in the `Views/Shared` folder. This location makes them accessible to all views in your application. However, you can create layout pages in other folders as well.
- **`Example (Views/Shared/_Layout.cshtml)`**:

```
<!DOCTYPE html>
<html lang="en">
<head>
    <meta charset="utf-8" />
    <meta name="viewport" content="width=device-width, initial-
scale=1.0" />
    <title>@ViewBag.Title - My Web Application</title>
    <link rel="stylesheet" href="~/Content/site.css" />
    <script src="~/Scripts/jquery-3.7.1.js"></script>
    <script src="~/Scripts/bootstrap.js"></script>
</head>
<body>
    <header>
        <div class="container">
            <nav>
                <ul class="nav navbar-nav">
                    <li>@Html.ActionLink("Home", "Index", "Home")</li>
                    <li>@Html.ActionLink("Products", "Index",
"Products")</li>
                    <li>@Html.ActionLink("About", "About", "Home")</li>
                </ul>
            </nav>
```

```
            <h1 class="logo">My Application</h1>
        </div>
    </header>

    <div class="container body-content">
        @RenderBody()
        <hr />
        <footer>
            <p>&copy; @DateTime.Now.Year - My Web Application</p>
        </footer>
    </div>

    @RenderSection("scripts", required: false)
</body>
</html>
```

- **Explanation:**
    - **<!DOCTYPE html>** and **<html lang="en">**: Standard HTML5 declaration and language attribute.
    - **<head>**: Contains metadata, title, CSS links, and JavaScript references that are common to all pages.
    - **@ViewBag.Title**: This allows individual views to set the title of the page. The value assigned to ViewBag.Title in a view will be rendered here.
    - **<header>**, **<nav>**, **<footer>**: These define the common header, navigation, and footer sections of the website.
    - **@RenderBody()**: This is a placeholder where the content of the specific view being rendered will be inserted. Every view that uses this layout *must* have content that will be rendered here.
    - **@RenderSection("scripts", required: false)**: This allows individual views to include specific JavaScript files. The required: false argument means that views are not required to define this section.
- **Using the Layout in a View:**

```
@{
    Layout = "~/Views/Shared/_Layout.cshtml";  // Specify the layout
page
}

<h2>Welcome to the Home Page</h2>
<p>This is the content of the home page.</p>
```

- **Explanation:**
    - **Layout = "~/Views/Shared/_Layout.cshtml";**: This line at the top of the view specifies which layout page to use. The path is relative to the Views folder.
    - The content within the <h2> and <p> tags will be rendered inside the @RenderBody() section of the _Layout.cshtml page.

    - The view doesn't need to repeat the <!DOCTYPE html>, <head>, <body>, etc. tags, as they are already defined in the layout.
    - If you don't want to use a layout page for a specific view, you can set `Layout = null;`
- **Benefits of Layout Pages:**
    - **Consistency:** Ensures a consistent look and feel across all pages of your application.
    - **Reduced Code Duplication:** Avoids repeating common HTML markup in every view.
    - **Maintainability:** Changes to the layout (e.g., adding a new navigation item) only need to be made in one place (the layout page).
    - **Separation of Concerns:** Separates the overall page structure from the content of individual views.

✅ Partial Views

- **Purpose:**
    - Partial views are used to encapsulate reusable UI components or sections of a view. They allow you to break down complex views into smaller, more manageable pieces.
    - Common uses for partial views include:
        - Rendering a product summary card
        - Displaying a login form
        - Creating a navigation menu
        - Rendering a section of a page that is updated via AJAX
        - Displaying validation errors
- **`Partial View (Views/Shared/_ProductSummary.cshtml):`**

```
@model MyWebApp.Models.Product

<div class="product-summary">
    <h3>@Model.Name</h3>
    <p>Price: $@Model.Price</p>
    <p>
        @if (Model.Price > 50)
        {
            <span class="high-price">Expensive</span>
        }
        else
        {
           <span>Affordable</span>
        }
    </p>
    <p><a href="@Url.Action("Details", "Products", new { id = Model.Id
})">View Details</a></p>
</div>
```

- **Explanation:**

- Like regular views, partial views use the .cshtml extension and can contain HTML markup and Razor code.
  - The @model directive specifies the data that the partial view expects.
  - This partial view displays a summary of a product, including its name, price, and a link to the details page. It's designed to be reusable wherever a product summary needs to be displayed.
  - Partial views do *not* typically include the <!DOCTYPE html>, <head>, <body>, etc. tags. They are meant to be embedded within a larger view or layout.
- **Rendering a Partial View in a Main View:**

```
@model List<MyWebApp.Models.Product>  // The main view's model is a list of products

<h2>Featured Products</h2>
<div class="product-list">
    @foreach (var product in Model)
    {
        @Html.Partial("_ProductSummary", product)  // Render the partial view for each product
    }
</div>
```

- **Explanation:**
  - **@Html.Partial("_ProductSummary", product)**: This line renders the _ProductSummary.cshtml partial view.
    - The first argument is the name of the partial view. By convention, partial view names often start with an underscore (_).
    - The second argument (product) is the model data that is passed to the partial view. In this case, we're passing a Product object from the loop. Each product in the main view's model is passed to the partial view.
  - The @Html.Partial() method generates the HTML output of the partial view and inserts it into the main view's HTML.
- **Alternatives for Rendering Partial Views** * @Html.RenderPartial(): This method writes the output of the partial view directly to the response stream, which can be slightly more efficient in some cases. It doesn't return a string. * @Html.Action(): This is used to render the result of a child action within a view. It's more powerful than Partial or RenderPartial but also more complex, as it involves invoking a controller action.
- **Benefits of Partial Views:**
  - **Reusability:** Encapsulate reusable UI components.
  - **Modularity:** Break down complex views into smaller, more manageable pieces.
  - **Maintainability:** Changes to a reusable component only need to be made in one place (the partial view).
  - **Improved Organization:** Keep your views cleaner and more organized.

---

4. Strongly-Typed Views

In ASP.NET MVC, a strongly-typed view is a view that is explicitly associated with a specific model class. This association is established using the `@model` directive at the top of the view file.

Key Concepts

- **`@model`** Directive: As you mentioned, the `@model` directive is crucial. It declares the type of the object that the view expects to receive from the controller.
- **Model Class:** This is a C# class that defines the structure and data that the view needs to display. It's often a class within your application's `Models` namespace.
- **Strongly-Typed HTML Helpers:** These are versions of HTML helpers (like `@Html.TextBoxFor()`, `@Html.LabelFor()`, and `@Html.DisplayFor()`) that work in conjunction with the `@model` directive to provide type safety and IntelliSense.

Example

Let's expand on your example to illustrate the benefits of strongly-typed views:

- **Model (Models/Product.cs):**

```
namespace MyWebApp.Models
{
    public class Product
    {
        public int Id { get; set; }
        [Display(Name = "Product Name")] // Added Display attribute
        [Required(ErrorMessage = "The Product Name is required.")]
        public string Name { get; set; }
        [Display(Name = "Price")]
        [Range(0.01, 10000, ErrorMessage = "Price must be between 0.01
and 10,000")]
        public decimal Price { get; set; }
        public string Description { get; set; }
    }
}
```

- **Controller (Controllers/ProductController.cs):**

```
using System.Web.Mvc;
using MyWebApp.Models;

namespace MyWebApp.Controllers
{
    public class ProductController : Controller
    {
        public ActionResult Details(int id)
        {
            // In a real application, you'd fetch the product from a
database
            var product = new Product
```

```
            {
                Id = id,
                Name = "Wireless Mouse",
                Price = 25.99M,
                Description = "Ergonomic wireless mouse for comfortable use."
            };
            return View(product);
        }

        public ActionResult Edit(int id)
        {
             var product = new Product
            {
                Id = id,
                Name = "Wireless Mouse",
                Price = 25.99M,
                Description = "Ergonomic wireless mouse for comfortable use."
            };
            return View(product);
        }

        [HttpPost]
        public ActionResult Edit(Product product)
        {
            if (ModelState.IsValid)
            {
                // Update the product in the database (not implemented here)
                return RedirectToAction("Details", new { id = product.Id });
            }
            // If the model is not valid, return to the Edit view to display errors
            return View(product);
        }
    }
}
```

- **View (Views/Product/Details.cshtml):**

```
@model MyWebApp.Models.Product

<h2>Product Details</h2>

<p>@Html.LabelFor(m => m.Name): @Html.DisplayFor(m => m.Name)</p>
<p>@Html.LabelFor(m => m.Price): @Html.DisplayFor(m => m.Price)</p>
<p>Description: @Html.DisplayFor(m => m.Description)</p>

```

```
<p>
    @Html.ActionLink("Edit", "Edit", new { id = Model.Id })
</p>
```

- **View (Views/Product/Edit.cshtml):**

```
@model MyWebApp.Models.Product

<h2>Edit Product</h2>

@using (Html.BeginForm())
{
    @Html.AntiForgeryToken()
    @Html.ValidationSummary(true, "", new { @class = "text-danger" })

    <div class="form-group">
        @Html.LabelFor(m => m.Name, new { @class = "control-label col-md-2" })
        <div class="col-md-10">
            @Html.TextBoxFor(m => m.Name, new { @class = "form-control" })
            @Html.ValidationMessageFor(m => m.Name, "", new { @class = "text-danger" })
        </div>
    </div>

    <div class="form-group">
        @Html.LabelFor(m => m.Price, new { @class = "control-label col-md-2" })
        <div class="col-md-10">
            @Html.TextBoxFor(m => m.Price, new { @class = "form-control" })
            @Html.ValidationMessageFor(m => m.Price, "", new { @class = "text-danger" })
        </div>
    </div>

    <div class="form-group">
        @Html.LabelFor(m => m.Description, new { @class = "control-label col-md-2" })
        <div class="col-md-10">
            @Html.TextAreaFor(m => m.Description, new { @class = "form-control" })
        </div>
    </div>

    <div class="form-group">
        <div class="col-md-offset-2 col-md-10">
            <input type="submit" value="Save" class="btn btn-default" />
```

```
•         </div>
•     </div>
• }
•
• <div>
•     @Html.ActionLink("Back to Details", "Details", new { id = Model.Id })
• </div>
```

Explanation

- `@model MyWebApp.Models.Product`: In both views, this line specifies that the view is designed to work with a `Product` object.
- **Strongly-Typed HTML Helpers**:
    - `@Html.LabelFor(m => m.Name)`: Generates a label for the "Name" property. The `for` attribute of the label is set to the correct ID (which is "Name"). The display name is taken from the `[Display(Name = "Product Name")]` attribute on the model.
    - `@Html.DisplayFor(m => m.Name)`: Displays the value of the "Name" property. It uses the display format defined by the property's data type (or any display attributes).
    - `@Html.TextBoxFor(m => m.Name)`: Generates an input field for editing the "Name" property. It automatically sets the `id`, `name`, and `value` attributes.
    - `@Html.TextAreaFor()`: Generates a
    - `@Html.ValidationMessageFor()`: Displays validation messages for a specific property.
    - `@Html.ValidationSummary()`: Displays all validation errors.
- **Model Binding and Validation**:
    - In the `Edit` action, when the form is submitted, the ASP.NET MVC framework uses model binding to automatically create a `Product` object from the form data.
    - The `[Required]` and `[Range]` attributes in the `Product` model class define validation rules. ASP.NET MVC uses these rules to validate the data before the `Edit` action is executed. If the data is invalid, `ModelState.IsValid` will be false, and the view will be redisplayed with validation error messages.

Benefits of Strongly-Typed Views

- **Compile-Time Checking:** The compiler can detect some errors related to model properties at compile time. For example, if you try to access a property that doesn't exist on the `Product` class (e.g., `@Model.NonExistentProperty`), you'll get a compile-time error. This prevents runtime errors.
- **IntelliSense in Visual Studio:** Visual Studio provides excellent IntelliSense support for strongly-typed views. When you type `@Model.`, you'll see a list of the available properties on the `Product` class. This makes it much faster and easier to write your views, and it reduces the risk of typos and other errors.

- **Avoiding Runtime Errors:** Strong typing helps prevent runtime errors caused by accessing incorrect properties or using data in an unexpected format. This leads to more robust and reliable code.
- **Improved Code Readability and Maintainability:** Strongly-typed views make your code easier to read and understand because the structure of the data is clearly defined. This also makes it easier to maintain your code over time.
- **Automatic HTML Generation:** Strongly-typed HTML helpers can automatically generate the correct HTML for form elements, including IDs, names, and values, reducing the amount of manual HTML coding you have to do.
- **Metadata Integration**: Strongly-typed helpers can leverage metadata from model properties (e.g., display names from `[Display]`, validation rules from `[Required]`, etc.) to generate more accurate and user-friendly HTML.

📌 Summary Table

Feature	Description
Razor Engine	Embeds C# code in HTML with minimal syntax
@model	Declares the data type passed from the controller
Html Helpers	Generate HTML controls like textbox, labels, dropdowns
Conditions/Loops	Embed C# logic directly in views
Layout Pages	Common design templates for all views
Partial Views	Reusable small views for repeated UI components
Strongly-Typed Views	Provides type safety and better development experience

30 multiple-choice questions on the Razor View Engine, with answers:

1. Introduction to Razor View Engine

1. What is Razor?
   - a) A database management system
   - b) A client-side scripting language
   - c) A server-side view engine
   - d) A web server software
   - Answer: c) A server-side view engine
2. Razor is primarily used with which ASP.NET framework?
   - a) ASP.NET Web Forms
   - b) ASP.NET MVC/Core

- c) ASP.NET Web API
    - d) ASP.NET SignalR
    - Answer: b) ASP.NET MVC/Core
3. Which symbol is used to embed C# code within a Razor view?
    - a) $
    - b) #
    - c) @
    - d) %
    - Answer: c) @
4. What is the typical file extension for a Razor view?
    - a) .aspx
    - b) .html
    - c) .cshtml
    - d) .razor
    - Answer: c) .cshtml
5. Which of the following is a characteristic of Razor syntax?
    - a) Verbose and complex
    - b) Clean and minimal
    - c) Similar to XML
    - d) Requires extensive scripting
    - Answer: b) Clean and minimal
6. What is the primary purpose of a view engine?
    - a) To manage server-side logic
    - b) To define database schemas
    - c) To generate dynamic HTML
    - d) To handle HTTP requests
    - Answer: c) To generate dynamic HTML
7. In Razor, can you use the full range of C# code?
    - a) No, only a limited subset
    - b) Yes, any valid C# code
    - c) Only for simple expressions
    - d) Only within specific tags
    - Answer: b) Yes, any valid C# code
8. Razor views are processed on the:
    - a) Client-side (browser)
    - b) Server-side
    - c) Both client and server
    - d) Database server
    - Answer: b) Server-side
9. Which is NOT a feature of Razor?
    - a) Clean syntax
    - b) Strong typing
    - c) Client-side scripting
    - d) Full C# support
    - Answer: c) Client-side scripting
10. Razor helps in creating:

- a) Static web pages
- b) Dynamic web pages
- c) Client-side applications
- d) Database servers
- Answer: b) Dynamic web pages

2. Syntax: @model, HTML Helpers, Loops, and Conditions

11. What is the purpose of the `@model` directive in a Razor view?
    - a) To define a controller
    - b) To specify the view engine
    - c) To declare the data type of the model
    - d) To create a database connection
    - Answer: c) To declare the data type of the model
12. If your model is `MyWebApp.Models.Product`, how would you declare it in your Razor view?
    - a) `@using MyWebApp.Models.Product`
    - b) `@model = MyWebApp.Models.Product`
    - c) `@model MyWebApp.Models.Product`
    - d) `@import MyWebApp.Models.Product`
    - Answer: c) `@model MyWebApp.Models.Product`
13. What do HTML Helpers do?
    - a) Manage server-side logic
    - b) Generate HTML elements
    - c) Define CSS styles
    - d) Handle database queries
    - Answer: b) Generate HTML elements
14. Which HTML Helper generates an HTML input element for a model property?
    - a) `@Html.LabelFor()`
    - b) `@Html.DisplayFor()`
    - c) `@Html.TextBoxFor()`
    - d) `@Html.ActionLink()`
    - Answer: c) `@Html.TextBoxFor()`
15. What HTML output does `@Html.LabelFor(m => m.Name)` typically produce?
    - a) `<input type="text" id="Name" name="Name" />`
    - b) `<span>Name</span>`
    - c) `<label for="Name">Name</label>`
    - d) `<label>Name</label>`
    - Answer: c) `<label for="Name">Name</label>`
16. Which of the following is used to iterate over a collection in a Razor view?
    - a) `@if`
    - b) `@for` or `@foreach`
    - c) `@while`
    - d) All of the above
    - Answer: b) `@for` or `@foreach`
17. How do you write an `if` statement in Razor?

   - a) if (Model.Property) { ... }
   - b) <% if (Model.Property) { ... } %>
   - c) @if (Model.Property) { ... }
   - d) #if Model.Property { ... }
   - Answer: c) @if (Model.Property) { ... }
18. What is the correct Razor syntax to display the value of a model property called "Title"?
   - a) <% Title %>
   - b) {{ Title }}
   - c) @Model.Title
   - d) @Title
   - Answer: c) @Model.Title
19. Which helper is used to create a hyperlink?
   - a) @Html.LabelFor()
   - b) @Html.TextBoxFor()
   - c) @Html.ActionLink()
   - d) @Html.DisplayFor()
   - Answer: c) @Html.ActionLink()
20. What does the @Html.DisplayFor() helper method do?
   - a) Creates an editable input field.
   - b) Renders the value of a specified model property.
   - c) Creates a label for a form field.
   - d) Creates a dropdown list.
   - Answer: b) Renders the value of a specified model property.

3. Creating Layout Pages and Partial Views

21. What is the purpose of a layout page?
   - a) To define the content of a single page
   - b) To define the common structure of multiple pages
   - c) To define a database schema
   - d) To define a CSS stylesheet
   - Answer: b) To define the common structure of multiple pages
22. What is the name of the method used to render the content of a view within a layout page?
   - a) @RenderPage()
   - b) @RenderContent()
   - c) @RenderBody()
   - d) @RenderView()
   - Answer: c) @RenderBody()
23. Where are layout pages typically located in an ASP.NET MVC project?
   - a) In the root folder
   - b) In the Controllers folder
   - c) In the Views/Shared folder
   - d) In the Models folder
   - Answer: c) In the Views/Shared folder
24. What is a partial view?

- a) A complete web page
- b) A reusable portion of a view
- c) A database table
- d) A JavaScript file
- Answer: b) A reusable portion of a view

25. Which method is used to render a partial view?
    - a) `@Html.RenderView()`
    - b) `@Html.Partial()`
    - c) `@RenderPartial()`
    - d) Both `@Html.Partial()` and `@Html.RenderPartial()`
    - Answer: d) Both `@Html.Partial()` and `@Html.RenderPartial()`
26. Which is true about Layout pages?
    - a) They are used to render small, reusable components.
    - b) They define the overall structure of a web page.
    - c) They are placed inside the controller.
    - d) They have a .html extension.
    - Answer: b) They define the overall structure of a web page.
27. Which is NOT a benefit of using Layout pages?
    - a) Code reusability
    - b) Consistent look and feel
    - c) Improved maintainability
    - d) Increased code duplication
    - Answer: d) Increased code duplication
28. Partial views are useful for:
    - a) Defining the main layout of a page
    - b) Displaying reusable UI components
    - c) Handling form submissions
    - d) Defining routing rules
    - Answer: b) Displaying reusable UI components
29. What is the common naming convention for layout pages?
    - a) layout.cshtml
    - b) _layout.cshtml
    - c) layoutpage.cshtml
    - d) master.cshtml
    - Answer: b) _layout.cshtml
30. Which of the following is NOT typically included in a partial view?
    - a) HTML markup
    - b) Razor code
    - c) `@model` directive
    - d) `<!DOCTYPE html>` tag
    - Answer: d) `<!DOCTYPE html>` tag

10 mid-size questions and answers about the Razor View Engine:

1. Introduction to Razor View Engine

1. **Question:** Explain the role of the Razor View Engine in the ASP.NET MVC framework. How does it contribute to the development of dynamic web pages?
   - **Answer:** The Razor View Engine is a server-side technology in ASP.NET MVC that's responsible for generating dynamic HTML. It allows developers to embed C# code into HTML markup within a view. When a controller action renders a view, the Razor Engine processes the `.cshtml` file, executes the C# code, merges the output with the HTML, and sends the resulting HTML to the client's browser. This process enables the creation of web pages that display dynamic data from the server. It simplifies the process of building dynamic web pages by providing a cleaner syntax than previous view engines.

2. Syntax: @model, HTML Helpers, Loops, and Conditions

2. **Question:** Describe the purpose and benefits of the `@model` directive in a Razor view. Provide an example of its usage and explain how it improves the development process.
   - **Answer:** The `@model` directive is used at the top of a Razor view to declare the type of the data (the model) that the view expects to receive from the controller. For example: `@model MyWebApp.Models.Product`. The benefits are:
     - **Strong Typing**: It enables strong typing, allowing the Razor engine and Visual Studio to know the properties and methods of the model.
     - **IntelliSense**: Strong typing enables IntelliSense, providing code completion, syntax highlighting, and compile-time checking (in some cases).
     - **Compile-time checking**: Catches errors early. It improves the development process by reducing errors and improving developer productivity.
3. **Question:** Explain the concept of HTML Helpers in Razor. Provide three examples of commonly used HTML Helpers and describe the HTML they generate.
   - **Answer:** HTML Helpers are methods that generate HTML elements programmatically in Razor views. They simplify HTML generation, especially for form elements, and promote code reuse.
     - `@Html.LabelFor(m => m.Name)`: Generates a `<label>` element. Example output: `<label for="Name">Name</label>`
     - `@Html.TextBoxFor(m => m.Price)`: Generates an `<input type="text">` element. Example output: `<input type="text" id="Price" name="Price" value="19.99" />`
     - `@Html.ActionLink("Details", "Details", "Product", new { id = 1 })`: Generates an `<a>` element for a hyperlink. Example output: `<a href="/Product/Details/1">Details</a>`
4. **Question:** Discuss how loops and conditional statements are used within Razor views. Provide examples of using `@if`, `@foreach`, and `@while` to control the rendering of HTML.
   - **Answer:** Razor allows embedding C# control structures directly into views to dynamically control HTML output.
     - `@if`: Conditionally renders HTML.

```
@if (Model.IsActive) { <p>Active</p> } else {
<p>Inactive</p> }
```

- `@foreach`: Iterates over a collection.

```
<ul> @foreach (var item in Model.Items) {
<li>@item.Name</li> } </ul>
```

- `@while`: Executes a block of code as long as a condition is true

```
@{ int counter = 0; }
 @while (counter < 5) {
   <p>Current Counter: @counter</p>
   counter++;
 }
```

- These statements allow for dynamic content generation based on server-side data.

5. Creating Layout Pages and Partial Views

5. **Question:** Describe the purpose and structure of a layout page in ASP.NET MVC. Explain how layout pages promote consistency and reduce code duplication in web applications.
   - **Answer:** A layout page (`_Layout.cshtml`) defines the shared structure of a web application, including elements like headers, footers, and navigation. It contains placeholders like `@RenderBody()` where the content of individual views is inserted. By using a layout page, developers avoid repeating common HTML across multiple views. This promotes consistency in the user interface and reduces code duplication, making the application easier to maintain. Changes to the layout only need to be made in one place.
6. **Question:** Explain the concept of partial views and their role in creating reusable UI components. Provide an example of how to create and use a partial view to display a product summary.
   - **Answer:** Partial views are reusable Razor views that render a portion of a UI. They encapsulate reusable components, promoting modularity.
     - Example (Partial View `_ProductSummary.cshtml`):

```
@model MyWebApp.Models.Product
<div><h3>@Model.Name</h3><p>Price: @Model.Price</p></div>
```

- Example (Using in a View):

```
@foreach (var product in Model.Products) {
@Html.Partial("_ProductSummary", product) }
```

- This renders the product summary for each product in the collection.

7. **Question:** Compare and contrast `@Html.Partial()` and `@Html.RenderPartial()`. What are the key differences between these two methods, and when might you choose one over the other?
   - **Answer**:
      - `@Html.Partial()`: Returns an `MvcHtmlString`, which is then rendered.
      - `@Html.RenderPartial()`: Writes the output directly to the response stream.
      - The key difference is how the output is handled. `RenderPartial()` can be slightly more efficient as it avoids creating an intermediate string. In most common scenarios, `@Html.Partial()` is sufficient and often preferred for its more straightforward usage. Use `@Html.RenderPartial()` for performance-critical sections where minute optimizations matter.

6. Strongly-Typed Views

8. **Question:** What is a strongly-typed view in ASP.NET MVC? Explain how the `@model` directive is used to create strongly-typed views, and discuss the advantages of using them.
   - **Answer:** A strongly-typed view is a view that is associated with a specific model class using the `@model` directive. This enables strong typing within the view. For example, `@model MyWebApp.Models.Product` declares that the view will use a `Product` object.
      - **Advantages**:
         - Compile-time checking: Some errors can be caught during compilation.
         - IntelliSense: Provides better code completion in Visual Studio.
         - Reduced runtime errors: Less chance of accessing non-existent properties.
         - Improved code readability.
9. **Question:** Explain how strongly-typed HTML helpers enhance the development of strongly-typed views. Provide examples of using `@Html.TextBoxFor()` and `@Html.LabelFor()` in a strongly-typed view, and describe how they differ from their non-strongly-typed counterparts.
   - **Answer**: Strongly-typed HTML helpers work with the `@model` directive. Instead of using strings, they use lambda expressions to bind to model properties.
      - `@Html.TextBoxFor(m => m.Name)`: Generates an input field for the `Name` property. It automatically sets the `id`, `name`, and `value` attributes based on the model.
      - `@Html.LabelFor(m => m.Name)`: Generates a label for the `Name` property, with the 'for' attribute correctly set.
      - Non-strongly typed helpers, like `@Html.TextBox("Name")`, require you to manually specify the ID, name, and value as strings, which is more error-prone and doesn't benefit from IntelliSense or compile-time checking.
10. **Question:** Discuss the role of model validation in strongly-typed views. How do data annotation attributes in the model class interact with strongly-typed HTML helpers and the `ModelState` property to provide validation feedback to the user?

- **Answer**: Data annotation attributes (e.g., `[Required]`, `[StringLength]`) in the model class define validation rules. Strongly-typed HTML helpers like `@Html.TextBoxFor()` respect these rules. When a form is posted, ASP.NET MVC uses these attributes to validate the input. The `ModelState.IsValid` property in the controller indicates whether the data is valid. If not valid, `@Html.ValidationMessageFor()` displays the error messages in the view, providing feedback to the user. This integration of model validation with strongly-typed views ensures data integrity and a better user experience.

CHAPTER 14: WORKING WITH MODELS AND DATA ANNOTATIONS

1. Creating Models using Classes

In ASP.NET MVC, the Model component is responsible for handling the application's data and business logic. It acts as an interface between the data source (database, API, etc.) and the Controller, which processes user requests and interacts with the Model. The Model then passes data to the View, which displays it to the user.

Key Concepts

- **Model:** Represents the data and business rules of the application.
- **Class:** Models are typically implemented as C# classes.
- **Properties:** The attributes of the data are defined as properties of the class.
- **Data Annotations:** Attributes from the `System.ComponentModel.DataAnnotations` namespace can be used to define validation rules and metadata for model properties.

✅ Example: Product Model

You provided a good basic example. Let's add more detail:

```
using System.ComponentModel.DataAnnotations; // Import the namespace for data
annotations

namespace MyWebApp.Models
{
```

```
    public class Product
    {
        [Key] // Specifies that Id is the primary key (if mapping to a
database)
        public int Id { get; set; }

        [Required(ErrorMessage = "The Name is required")] // Validation: Name
is required
        [StringLength(100, ErrorMessage = "Name cannot exceed 100
characters")] // Validation: Max length
        [Display(Name = "Product Name")] // Metadata: Display name for labels
in views
        public string Name { get; set; }

        [Required(ErrorMessage = "The Price is required")]
        [Range(0.01, double.MaxValue, ErrorMessage = "Price must be greater
than 0")] // Validation: Range
        [Display(Name = "Price")]
        public decimal Price { get; set; }

        [DataType(DataType.MultilineText)]  // Metadata:  For text areas
        [Display(Name = "Description")]
        public string Description { get; set; }

        public int CategoryId { get; set; } // Foreign key to the Category
table (if mapping to DB)
        public Category Category { get; set; } // Navigation property:
Represents the related Category
    }

    public class Category
    {
        [Key]
        public int CategoryId { get; set; }
        public string CategoryName { get; set; }

        public ICollection<Product> Products { get; set; } // Navigation
property:  Products in this category
    }
}
```

Explanation

- **`namespace MyWebApp.Models`**: Models are typically placed in the `Models` namespace to organize your code.
- **`public class Product`**: Defines a class named `Product` to represent a product in the application.
- **Properties**:
  - `Id`: An integer property representing the unique identifier for the product.
  - `Name`: A string property for the product's name.
  - `Price`: A decimal property for the product's price.
  - `Description`: A string property for the product's description.
  - `CategoryId`: An integer representing the foreign key.

    - `Category Category`: A navigation property that represents the related `Category` object.
- **Data Annotation Attributes**:
    - `[Key]`: Specifies that the `Id` property is the primary key, especially important when working with a database and Entity Framework.
    - `[Required]`**: Specifies that the property is required and cannot be empty. The `ErrorMessage` provides a user-friendly message.
    - `[StringLength(100)]`: Specifies the maximum length of the string property.
    - `[Display(Name = "Product Name")]`: Provides a user-friendly name for the property, used in labels and display fields in views.
    - `[Range(0.01, double.MaxValue)]`: Specifies a range constraint for the `Price` property.
    - `[DataType(DataType.MultilineText)]`: Provides metadata about the property's data type, which can influence how it's rendered in a view (e.g., as a `<textarea>`).
- **Navigation Properties**:
    - `Category Category`: In the `Product` class, this is a navigation property. It allows you to access the `Category` object associated with a `Product`. This is essential for relating data, especially when working with databases and Entity Framework.
    - `ICollection<Product> Products`: In the `Category` class, this navigation property represents the collection of products within a specific category.
- **Relationship**: The `CategoryId` property in the `Product` model establishes a foreign key relationship with the `CategoryId` property in the `Category` model.

How Models Are Used

1. **Database Representation**: As you mentioned, a model class can represent a table in a database. Object-Relational Mapping (ORM) frameworks like Entity Framework use these classes to map database tables to objects, allowing you to interact with the database using C# code. For example, the `Product` class could correspond to a "Products" table in a database, with columns like "Id," "Name," "Price," and "Description."
2. **Data Transfer**: Models are also used to transfer data between controllers and views. A controller might retrieve data from a database (using Entity Framework), populate a model object (or a collection of model objects), and then pass that object to the view. The view then uses the data in the model to render the HTML that is displayed to the user.

Example of Controller and View Interaction

```
// Controller
using System.Web.Mvc;
using MyWebApp.Models;
using System.Linq; // For LINQ queries

public class ProductController : Controller
{
    public ActionResult Index()
    {
        //  Get a list of products from the database (using Entity Framework)
```

```
        var db = new MyDbContext(); //  Replace MyDbContext
        var products = db.Products.ToList();

        // Pass the list of products to the view
        return View(products);
    }

     public ActionResult Details(int id)
    {
        //  Get a single product from the database, based on its ID
        var db = new MyDbContext(); //  Replace MyDbContext
        var product = db.Products.Include(p => p.Category).FirstOrDefault(p
=> p.Id == id); //Eager loading

        if (product == null)
        {
             return HttpNotFound();
        }
        // Pass the product to the view
        return View(product);
    }
}

// View (Index.cshtml)
@model List<MyWebApp.Models.Product> // The view expects a list of Product
objects

<h2>Products</h2>
<ul>
    @foreach (var product in Model)
    {
        <li>@product.Name - $@product.Price</li>
    }
</ul>

// View (Details.cshtml)
@model MyWebApp.Models.Product

<h2>Product Details</h2>
<p>Name: @Model.Name</p>
<p>Price: $@Model.Price</p>
<p>Description: @Model.Description</p>
<p>Category: @Model.Category.CategoryName</p> //Access the category name
```

In this example, the controller retrieves product data from a database (using Entity Framework, though the database interaction is simplified here for brevity) and passes it to the view. The view then uses the model to display the product information.

---

2. Data Annotations for Validation

Data Annotations are a powerful feature in ASP.NET MVC that allows you to define validation rules for your model properties directly within the model class. These attributes, found in the System.ComponentModel.DataAnnotations namespace, provide a declarative way to specify constraints on the data that your model properties can hold. ASP.NET MVC leverages these annotations to automatically validate user input before it's processed by your application, ensuring data integrity and improving the user experience.

✅ Example with Annotations

You've provided a good example, let's add more context and elaborate:

```
using System.ComponentModel.DataAnnotations; // Import the namespace

namespace MyWebApp.Models
{
    public class Product
    {
        public int Id { get; set; }

        [Required(ErrorMessage = "Product Name is required")]
        [StringLength(100, MinimumLength = 3, ErrorMessage = "Product Name
must be between 3 and 100 characters")]
        [Display(Name = "Product Name")] // Added for better UI labels
        public string Name { get; set; }

        [Required(ErrorMessage = "Price is required")]
        [Range(0.01, 100000, ErrorMessage = "Price must be between 0.01 and
100000")]
        [Display(Name = "Price")]
        public decimal Price { get; set; }

        [StringLength(500, ErrorMessage = "Description cannot exceed 500
characters")]
        [DataType(DataType.MultilineText)] // Added to suggest a textarea in
the UI
        [Display(Name = "Description")]
        public string Description { get; set; }

        [EmailAddress(ErrorMessage = "Invalid Email Address")]
        [Display(Name = "Email")]
        public string Email { get; set; }

        [Compare("ConfirmPassword", ErrorMessage = "Password and confirmation
do not match.")]
        [DataType(DataType.Password)]
        [Display(Name = "Password")]
        public string Password { get; set; }

        [DataType(DataType.Password)]
        [Display(Name = "Confirm Password")]
        public string ConfirmPassword { get; set; }
    }
}
```

Explanation

- **using System.ComponentModel.DataAnnotations;**: This line imports the namespace that contains the Data Annotation attributes.
- **[Key]**: Although not strictly a validation attribute, [Key] is often used in conjunction with them. It specifies that a property is the primary key for a database table. While it doesn't directly cause validation errors, it can influence how the model is handled by Entity Framework.
- **[Required(ErrorMessage = "Product Name is required")]**: This attribute ensures that the Name property is not null or empty. If the user doesn't provide a value, the specified error message is displayed.
- **[StringLength(100, MinimumLength = 3, ErrorMessage = "Product Name must be between 3 and 100 characters")]**: This attribute specifies the maximum and minimum length of the Name string.
- **[Display(Name = "Product Name")]**: This attribute provides a user-friendly name for the Name property. This name is used in labels and display fields generated by HTML helpers in views (e.g., @Html.LabelFor()).
- **[Range(0.01, 100000, ErrorMessage = "Price must be between 0.01 and 100000")]**: This attribute ensures that the Price property falls within the specified range.
- **[DataType(DataType.MultilineText)]**: This attribute provides metadata about the data type of the property. In this case, it suggests that the Description property should be rendered as a multi-line text box (<textarea>) in the view. It doesn't perform validation in the same way as Required or Range, but it influences how the data is displayed and handled.
- **[EmailAddress(ErrorMessage = "Invalid Email Address")]**: Validates that the value of the Email property is a valid email address.
- **[Compare("ConfirmPassword", ErrorMessage = "Password and confirmation do not match.")]**: This attribute compares the value of the Password property with the value of the ConfirmPassword property. It's commonly used to ensure that password and password confirmation fields match during user registration or password changes.

✅ Common Data Annotations

Here's a more detailed table with explanations:

Annotation	Description
[Required]	Specifies that the field is required and cannot be empty.
[StringLength(int maximumLength, int minimumLength)]	Limits the length of a string. You can specify both a maximum and a minimum length.
[Range(object minimum, object maximum)]	Limits a numeric value to a specified range.
[EmailAddress]	Validates that the value is a valid email address format.
[Compare(string otherProperty)]	Compares the value of one property to the value of another property (e.g., for password confirmation).

[RegularExpression(string pattern)]	Validates that the value matches a specified regular expression. This allows for highly customized validation rules.
[DataType(DataType enum)]	Provides metadata about the type of data the property represents (e.g., EmailAddress, Password, Date, MultilineText). This influences how the data is displayed and handled in the UI but doesn't always provide validation.
[Display(Name = "Display Name")]	Specifies the display name for the property, which is used in labels and other UI elements.
[Key]	Specifies that a property is the primary key for an entity. While not a validation attribute, it's often used in conjunction with them and is important for database mapping.
[ConcurrencyCheck]	Specifies that a property should be checked for concurrency during updates.
[CreditCard]	Validates that a property is a credit card number.
[Phone]	Validates that a property is a phone number.
[Url]	Validates that a property is a URL.

How Data Annotations Work with Validation

1. **Attribute Application**: You apply Data Annotation attributes to the properties of your model classes.
2. **Automatic Validation**: When you use HTML helpers like @Html.EditorFor() or @Html.TextBoxFor() in your views, ASP.NET MVC automatically incorporates these validation rules into the generated HTML. For example, if you have a [Required] attribute, the generated HTML might include client-side validation (if enabled).
3. **Model Binding and Validation**: When a form is submitted, the ASP.NET MVC framework uses model binding to create an instance of your model class from the form data. During this process, the framework automatically validates the data against the rules specified by the Data Annotation attributes.
4. **ModelState.IsValid**: The results of the validation are stored in the ModelState property of the Controller. You check ModelState.IsValid in your controller action to determine if the data is valid.
5. **Displaying Errors**: If ModelState.IsValid is false, you redisplay the view, and you can use HTML helpers like @Html.ValidationMessageFor() and @Html.ValidationSummary() to display the validation error messages to the user.

Example of Controller and View

```
// Controller
using System.Web.Mvc;
using MyWebApp.Models;

public class ProductController : Controller
{
    public ActionResult Create()
```

```
    {
        return View(); // Display the empty form
    }

    [HttpPost]
    public ActionResult Create(Product product)
    {
        if (ModelState.IsValid)
        {
            //  Save the product to the database (not implemented here)
            return RedirectToAction("Index");
        }
        // If ModelState.IsValid is false, validation errors occurred.
        // Redisplay the form with the validation messages.
        return View(product);
    }
}

// View (Create.cshtml)
@model MyWebApp.Models.Product

<h2>Create Product</h2>

@using (Html.BeginForm())
{
    @Html.AntiForgeryToken()
    @Html.ValidationSummary(true, "", new { @class = "text-danger" }) //
Display a summary of all validation errors

    <div class="form-group">
        @Html.LabelFor(model => model.Name, htmlAttributes: new { @class =
"control-label col-md-2" })
        <div class="col-md-10">
            @Html.TextBoxFor(model => model.Name, new { @class = "form-
control" })
            @Html.ValidationMessageFor(model => model.Name, "", new { @class
= "text-danger" }) // Display error for Name
        </div>
    </div>

    <div class="form-group">
        @Html.LabelFor(model => model.Price, htmlAttributes: new { @class =
"control-label col-md-2" })
        <div class="col-md-10">
            @Html.TextBoxFor(model => model.Price, new { @class = "form-
control" })
            @Html.ValidationMessageFor(model => model.Price, "", new { @class
= "text-danger" })  // Display error for Price
        </div>
    </div>

    <div class="form-group">
        @Html.LabelFor(model => model.Description, htmlAttributes: new {
@class = "control-label col-md-2" })
        <div class="col-md-10">
            @Html.TextAreaFor(model => model.Description, new { @class =
"form-control" })
```

```
            @Html.ValidationMessageFor(model => model.Description, "", new {
@class = "text-danger" })
        </div>
    </div>

    <div class="form-group">
        <div class="col-md-offset-2 col-md-10">
            <input type="submit" value="Create" class="btn btn-default" />
        </div>
    </div>
}
```

In this example, the Create action handles both displaying the form and processing the form submission. The HttpPost version checks ModelState.IsValid. If it's false, the view is redisplayed with validation errors, which are rendered by the @Html.ValidationMessageFor() helpers.

✅ What is Model Binding?

Model Binding is a fundamental process in ASP.NET MVC that automatically maps data from an HTTP request (such as form data, query string parameters, or route data) to the properties of a model object. This simplifies the process of retrieving user input and converting it into a usable format for your application. Instead of manually extracting and converting each piece of data, the framework handles this for you.

How Model Binding Works

1. **Incoming Request**: When a user submits a form or makes a request to a URL, the browser sends an HTTP request to the server. This request contains data.
2. **Routing**: The ASP.NET MVC routing system determines which controller and action method should handle the request.
3. **Model Binder**: The ASP.NET MVC framework uses a component called a Model Binder to process the incoming data. There are default Model Binders for common data types, and you can also create custom Model Binders for more complex scenarios.
4. **Data Mapping**: The Model Binder examines the incoming data (e.g., form fields) and attempts to match the data keys (e.g., form field names) to the properties of the model class specified as a parameter to the action method.
5. **Object Creation and Population**: The Model Binder creates an instance of the model class and populates its properties with the corresponding values from the incoming data. It performs automatic type conversion (e.g., converting a string from a form field to an integer or decimal).

6. **Action Method Invocation**: The populated model object is then passed as a parameter to the controller action method.

✅ Example: Product Model and Binding

You've provided a good example. Let's add more detail and context.

- **Model (Models/Product.cs):**

```
using System.ComponentModel.DataAnnotations;

namespace MyWebApp.Models
{
    public class Product
    {
        public int Id { get; set; }

        [Required(ErrorMessage = "Product Name is required")]
        [StringLength(100, MinimumLength = 3)]
        [Display(Name = "Product Name")]
        public string Name { get; set; }

        [Required(ErrorMessage = "Price is required")]
        [Range(0.01, 100000, ErrorMessage = "Price must be between 0.01 and 100000")]
        [Display(Name = "Price")]
        public decimal Price { get; set; }

        [StringLength(500)]
        [Display(Name = "Description")]
        public string Description { get; set; }
    }
}
```

- **Form in View (Views/Product/Create.cshtml):**

```
@model MyWebApp.Models.Product

<h2>Create Product</h2>

@using (Html.BeginForm())
{
    @Html.AntiForgeryToken()
    @Html.ValidationSummary(true, "", new { @class = "text-danger" })

    <div class="form-group">
        @Html.LabelFor(m => m.Name, new { @class = "control-label col-md-2" })
        <div class="col-md-10">
```

```
            @Html.TextBoxFor(m => m.Name, new { @class = "form-control" })
            @Html.ValidationMessageFor(m => m.Name, "", new { @class = "text-danger" })
        </div>
    </div>

    <div class="form-group">
        @Html.LabelFor(m => m.Price, new { @class = "control-label col-md-2" })
        <div class="col-md-10">
            @Html.TextBoxFor(m => m.Price, new { @class = "form-control" })
            @Html.ValidationMessageFor(m => m.Price, "", new { @class = "text-danger" })
        </div>
    </div>

    <div class="form-group">
        @Html.LabelFor(m => m.Description, new { @class = "control-label col-md-2" })
        <div class="col-md-10">
            @Html.TextAreaFor(m => m.Description, new { @class = "form-control" })
            @Html.ValidationMessageFor(m => m.Description, "", new { @class = "text-danger" })
        </div>
    </div>

    <div class="form-group">
        <div class="col-md-offset-2 col-md-10">
            <input type="submit" value="Create" class="btn btn-default" />
        </div>
    </div>
}
```

- **Controller (Controllers/ProductController.cs):**

```
using System.Web.Mvc;
using MyWebApp.Models;

public class ProductController : Controller
{
    public ActionResult Create()
    {
        return View(); // Display the empty form
    }

    [HttpPost]
```

```
•       public ActionResult Create(Product product)
•       {
•           if (ModelState.IsValid)
•           {
•               //  Save to database (using Entity Framework, for example)
•               //  db.Products.Add(product);
•               //  db.SaveChanges();
•
•               return RedirectToAction("Index"); // Redirect to a success
    page
•           }
•
•           // If validation fails, return to the form with validation
    errors
•           return View(product);
•       }
•   }
```

Explanation of Model Binding in the Example

1. **Form Submission**: When the user fills out the "Create Product" form and clicks the "Create" button, the browser sends an HTTP POST request to the `/Product/Create` URL. The form data is included in the request body. The form field names (e.g., "Name", "Price", "Description") correspond to the property names in the `Product` model.
2. **Model Binder's Role**: The ASP.NET MVC framework's default Model Binder takes over. It sees that the `Create` action method has a parameter of type `Product`.
3. **Data Mapping**: The Model Binder looks at the incoming form data and finds the following values:
   - `Name` = (value entered by the user)
   - `Price` = (value entered by the user)
   - `Description` = (value entered by the user)
4. **Object Creation**: The Model Binder creates a new `Product` object.
5. **Property Population**: The Model Binder populates the properties of the `Product` object:
   - `product.Name` = (value from the "Name" form field)
   - `product.Price` = (value from the "Price" form field)
   - `product.Description` = (value from the "Description" form field)
6. **Action Method Execution**: The populated `Product` object is then passed to the `Create` action method as the `product` parameter.
7. **Validation**: Inside the `Create` action, `ModelState.IsValid` is checked. If the user entered "Name" as "ABC", then the `ModelState.IsValid` will be false, because we have specified the `StringLength` attribute with a minimum value of 3 in our Model class.

✓ ModelState

`ModelState` is a property of the `Controller` that represents the state of the model during the model binding and validation process. It contains information about:

- **Validity**: Whether the incoming data was successfully bound to the model and whether it conforms to any validation rules.
- **Errors**: A collection of validation errors, if any, that occurred during model binding or validation.
- **Values**: The raw values that were submitted in the request.

Key Points about ModelState

- **`ModelState.IsValid`**: This property returns a boolean value indicating whether the model is valid. It's crucial to check this property in your controller action *before* you attempt to use the model data (e.g., saving it to a database).
- **Validation Errors**: If `ModelState.IsValid` is false, the `ModelState` property contains a collection of `ModelStateEntry` objects, each of which represents a validation error. You can access these errors to display them to the user.
- **Automatic Validation**: Data Annotation attributes in your model class (e.g., `[Required]`, `[StringLength]`, `[Range]`) are a primary source of validation rules. ASP.NET MVC automatically uses these attributes to validate the model during model binding.
- **Manual Errors**: You can also manually add errors to `ModelState` in your controller action if you need to perform custom validation logic. For example: `ModelState.AddModelError("Name", "The Name must be unique.");`
- **Preserving State**: `ModelState` is preserved across postbacks. This means that if validation fails and you redisplay the form, the validation error messages will still be available.

How ModelState Works in the Example

1. **Validation in Action**: In the `[HttpPost] Create` action, the `product` parameter is populated by Model Binding. ASP.NET MVC automatically validates the `product` object based on the Data Annotation attributes in the `Product` class.
2. **Checking Validity**: The code checks `if (ModelState.IsValid)`.
3. **Success**: If the user provides valid data (e.g., a name between 3 and 100 characters, a positive price), `ModelState.IsValid` will be true. The code then saves the product (in a real application) and redirects to the "Index" action.
4. **Failure**: If the user provides invalid data (e.g., an empty name, a negative price), `ModelState.IsValid` will be false. The code does *not* save the product. Instead, it calls `return View(product);` again.
5. **Redisplaying with Errors**: The `View(product)` call redisplays the `Create.cshtml` view. The `@Html.ValidationMessageFor()` helpers in the view use the information in `ModelState` to display the appropriate error messages next to the input fields. The `@Html.ValidationSummary()` helper displays a summary of all validation errors.

---

4. Custom Validation Attributes

While ASP.NET MVC provides a rich set of built-in Data Annotation attributes, there are situations where you need to implement custom validation logic. This is where custom validation attributes come in. By creating your own attributes, you can encapsulate complex validation rules and apply them to your model properties in a declarative and reusable manner.

Creating Custom Validation Attributes

To create a custom validation attribute, you need to:

1. **Create a Class**: Define a new class that inherits from the `ValidationAttribute` class.
2. **`Override IsValid()`**: Override the `IsValid()` method. This method is where you implement your custom validation logic. It takes the value to be validated as an `object` parameter and returns a `bool` indicating whether the value is valid.
3. **Implement Validation Logic**: Inside the `IsValid()` method, cast the `object` parameter to the appropriate data type and perform your validation checks.
4. **Set Error Message (Optional)**: You can set the `ErrorMessage` property of the `ValidationAttribute` class in the constructor of your custom attribute class or within the `IsValid()` method to provide a user-friendly error message when validation fails.
5. **Apply the Attribute**: Apply your custom attribute to the model properties you want to validate.

✅ Example: Custom Attribute to Prevent "Test" as Product Name

Let's elaborate on your example and add more context:

- **`Custom Validator (NoTestNameAttribute.cs):`**

```
using System.ComponentModel.DataAnnotations;

namespace MyWebApp.Models //  Ensure this is in your project's Models namespace or a relevant namespace
{
    public class NoTestNameAttribute : ValidationAttribute
    {
        public NoTestNameAttribute() : base("Product name cannot be 'test'") // Best Practice: set default message in constructor
        {
        }
        public override bool IsValid(object value)
        {
            if (value == null)
            {
                return true; // null values might be handled by Required attribute
            }
            string name = value as string;
            if (name != null && name.ToLower() == "test")
            {
                return false;
```

```
•             }
•             return true;
•         }
•
•        //Optional: Override FormatErrorMessage
•         public override string FormatErrorMessage(string name)
•         {
•              return string.Format("The {0} field cannot be 'test'",
name);
•         }
•     }
• }
```

- **Apply to Model (Models/Product.cs):**

```
• using System.ComponentModel.DataAnnotations;
•
• namespace MyWebApp.Models
• {
•     public class Product
•     {
•         public int Id { get; set; }
•
•         [Required(ErrorMessage = "Product Name is required")]
•         [StringLength(100, MinimumLength = 3, ErrorMessage = "Product
Name must be between 3 and 100 characters")]
•         [NoTestName] // Apply the custom attribute
•         [Display(Name = "Product Name")]  //Added Display Attribute
•         public string Name { get; set; }
•
•         [Required(ErrorMessage = "Price is required")]
•         [Range(0.01, 10000, ErrorMessage = "Price must be between 0.01
and 10000")]
•          [Display(Name = "Price")]
•         public decimal Price { get; set; }
•
•         [StringLength(500, ErrorMessage = "Description cannot exceed
500 characters")]
•         [Display(Name = "Description")]
•         public string Description { get; set; }
•     }
• }
```

Explanation

- **`using System.ComponentModel.DataAnnotations;`**: This line imports the namespace that contains the `ValidationAttribute` class.

- **public class NoTestNameAttribute : ValidationAttribute**: This line defines a new class named `NoTestNameAttribute` that inherits from `ValidationAttribute`.
- **public NoTestNameAttribute() : base("Product name cannot be 'test'")**: This is the constructor for the attribute. It calls the base class constructor (`ValidationAttribute`) and sets the default error message. It's a best practice to set the default error message here.
- **public override bool IsValid(object value)**: This is the overridden `IsValid()` method. It contains the custom validation logic.
    - `if (value == null) { return true; }`: This check is important. Custom validation attributes should typically handle null values gracefully. In many cases, a `[Required]` attribute is used in conjunction with other attributes to handle null checks, and the other attributes don't need to repeat this check.
    - `string name = value as string;`: This line casts the `value` parameter to a string. It's crucial to check the type of the value before casting it to prevent errors.
    - `if (name != null && name.ToLower() == "test")`: This is the custom validation logic. It checks if the name is not null and, if not, checks if it's equal to "test" (case-insensitively).
    - `return false;`: If the name is "test", the method returns `false`, indicating that the validation failed.
    - `return true;`: If the name is not "test", the method returns `true`, indicating that the validation succeeded.
- **public override string FormatErrorMessage(string name)**: This is an override of the `FormatErrorMessage` method. This allows you to create a dynamic error message.
- **[NoTestName]**: This is how you apply the custom attribute to the `Name` property in the `Product` class. Now, whenever the `Name` property is validated, the `NoTestNameAttribute`'s `IsValid()` method will be executed.
- **[Display(Name = "Product Name")]**: This is added to the Name property so that the LabelFor Html helper will display "Product Name" instead of "Name".

How Custom Validation Attributes Work

1. **Attribute Definition**: You define your custom validation attribute class, inheriting from `ValidationAttribute` and overriding the `IsValid()` method.
2. **Attribute Application**: You apply your custom attribute to one or more properties in your model class.
3. **Validation Execution**: When ASP.NET MVC performs model validation (during model binding), it checks for all validation attributes applied to the model properties, including your custom ones.
4. **IsValid()** Invocation: For each applied attribute, the `IsValid()` method is called. The value of the model property being validated is passed as the `value` parameter.
5. **Validation Result**: The `IsValid()` method returns `true` if the value is valid according to your custom rule, and `false` if it's invalid.
6. **Error Message**: If `IsValid()` returns `false`, ASP.NET MVC uses the `ErrorMessage` property of the attribute to generate a validation error message. This message is then added to the `ModelState`, which can be displayed in the view using HTML helpers like `@Html.ValidationMessageFor()`.

Example of Controller and View

Here's how this custom validation attribute would be used in a controller and view:

```
// Controller
using System.Web.Mvc;
using MyWebApp.Models;

public class ProductController : Controller
{
    public ActionResult Create()
    {
        return View();
    }

    [HttpPost]
    public ActionResult Create(Product product)
    {
        if (ModelState.IsValid)
        {
            //  Save the product (not implemented here)
            return RedirectToAction("Index");
        }

        return View(product); // Redisplay the form with errors
    }
}

// View (Create.cshtml)
@model MyWebApp.Models.Product

<h2>Create Product</h2>

@using (Html.BeginForm())
{
    @Html.ValidationSummary(true, "", new { @class = "text-danger" })

    <div class="form-group">
        @Html.LabelFor(m => m.Name, new { @class = "control-label col-md-2"
})
        <div class="col-md-10">
            @Html.TextBoxFor(m => m.Name, new { @class = "form-control" })
            @Html.ValidationMessageFor(m => m.Name, "", new { @class = "text-
danger" })
        </div>
    </div>

    // Other form fields for Price, Description, etc.

    <div class="form-group">
        <div class="col-md-offset-2 col-md-10">
            <input type="submit" value="Create" class="btn btn-default" />
        </div>
    </div>
}
```

In this example, if the user enters "test" (or "TEST", etc.) in the "Product Name" field, the `NoTestNameAttribute` will cause validation to fail, and the error message "Product name cannot be 'test'" will be displayed in the view by `@Html.ValidationMessageFor(m => m.Name)`.

📌 Summary Table

Concept	Description
Model	Represents the data structure
Data Annotations	Add validation rules directly to the model class
Model Binding	Automatically maps form inputs to model properties
ModelState	Tracks whether the model passed validation checks
Custom Validation	Create reusable validation rules by extending `ValidationAttribute`

30 multiple-choice questions with answers.

1. Creating Models using Classes

1. In ASP.NET MVC, models are typically implemented as:
   - a) Interfaces
   - b) Abstract classes
   - c) C# classes
   - d) Structs
   - Answer: c) C# classes
2. Which namespace is commonly used for defining model classes in ASP.NET MVC?
   - a) System.Web.Mvc
   - b) System.ComponentModel
   - c) System.Data
   - d) YourApp.Models
   - Answer: d) YourApp.Models (or a similar namespace you define)
3. What is the primary purpose of a model in ASP.NET MVC?
   - a) To define the user interface
   - b) To handle HTTP requests
   - c) To represent the data and business logic of the application
   - d) To manage routing
   - Answer: c) To represent the data and business logic of the application
4. Which of the following is true about models in ASP.NET MVC?
   - a) They are only used to represent database tables.
   - b) They are used to transfer data between controllers and views.
   - c) They define the visual layout of a web page.

- d) They handle client-side scripting.
- Answer: b) They are used to transfer data between controllers and views.

5. Which of the following can a model class represent?
   - a) A database table
   - b) A form to be displayed in a view
   - c) A collection of data
   - d) All of the above
   - Answer: d) All of the above
6. Properties in a model class define:
   - a) Methods
   - b) Attributes of the data
   - c) Events
   - d) Interfaces
   - Answer: b) Attributes of the data
7. Which of the following is NOT a characteristic of a Model?
   - a) Represents application data
   - b) Contains business logic
   - c) Defines the user interface
   - d) Can map to a database table
   - Answer: c) Defines the user interface
8. What is an ORM?
   - a) Object-Relational Mapping
   - b) Object-Relational Model
   - c) Object Rendering Model
   - d) Object Request Mapping
   - Answer: a) Object-Relational Mapping
9. Which of the following is a benefit of using models?
   - a) Improved performance of client-side scripts
   - b) Separation of concerns
   - c) Automatic creation of controllers
   - d) Direct manipulation of HTML elements
   - Answer: b) Separation of concerns
10. In ASP.NET MVC, which folder conventionally holds the model classes?
   - a) Views
   - b) Controllers
   - c) Models
   - d) App_Data
   - Answer: c) Models

2. Data Annotations for Validation

11. Which namespace contains the Data Annotation attributes?
   - a) System.Web.Mvc
   - b) System.ComponentModel
   - c) System.ComponentModel.DataAnnotations
   - d) System.Data.SqlClient

- Answer: c) System.ComponentModel.DataAnnotations

12. What is the purpose of Data Annotations?
    - a) To define the layout of a view
    - b) To specify validation rules for model properties
    - c) To create database queries
    - d) To handle routing
    - Answer: b) To specify validation rules for model properties
13. Which Data Annotation attribute is used to specify that a field is required?
    - a) [RequiredField]
    - b) [Mandatory]
    - c) [Required]
    - d) [NotNull]
    - Answer: c) [Required]
14. Which Data Annotation attribute is used to limit the length of a string?
    - a) [MaxLength]
    - b) [StringLength]
    - c) [Length]
    - d) [LimitLength]
    - Answer: b) [StringLength]
15. Which Data Annotation attribute is used to specify a range for a numeric value?
    - a) [Range]
    - b) [NumericRange]
    - c) [ValueRange]
    - d) [LimitRange]
    - Answer: a) [Range]
16. What does the `[EmailAddress]` attribute validate?
    - a) That the field contains a valid URL
    - b) That the field contains a valid phone number
    - c) That the field contains a valid email address
    - d) That the field is not empty
    - Answer: c) That the field contains a valid email address
17. Which attribute is used to compare the values of two properties?
    - a) [Compare]
    - b) [Match]
    - c) [EqualTo]
    - d) [CompareTo]
    - Answer: a) [Compare]
18. Which attribute is used to validate a property against a regular expression?
    - a) [Regex]
    - b) [RegularExpression]
    - c) [Pattern]
    - d) [Expression]
    - Answer: b) [RegularExpression]
19. What is the purpose of the `ErrorMessage` property in a Data Annotation attribute?
    - a) To specify the name of the field
    - b) To provide a user-friendly error message

- c) To define the data type of the field
- d) To format the output of the field
- Answer: b) To provide a user-friendly error message

20. Which attribute is used to provide a user-friendly name for a model property?
    - a) [DisplayName]
    - b) [DisplayField]
    - c) [Display]
    - d) [FriendlyName]
    - Answer: c) [Display]

3. Model Binding and ModelState

21. What is Model Binding in ASP.NET MVC?
    - a) The process of creating a database schema
    - b) The process of mapping HTTP request data to model properties
    - c) The process of defining the layout of a view
    - d) The process of handling routing
    - Answer: b) The process of mapping HTTP request data to model properties
22. Which of the following is NOT a source of data for Model Binding?
    - a) Form data
    - b) Query string parameters
    - c) Route data
    - d) CSS files
    - Answer: d) CSS files
23. What is `ModelState` in ASP.NET MVC?
    - a) A class for defining database models
    - b) A property of the controller that represents the state of the model during binding and validation
    - c) A view engine for rendering HTML
    - d) A component for handling HTTP requests
    - Answer: b) A property of the controller that represents the state of the model during binding and validation
24. What does `ModelState.IsValid` indicate?
    - a) That the model has been successfully bound
    - b) That the model data is valid according to the validation rules
    - c) That the view has been successfully rendered
    - d) That the controller action has been executed
    - Answer: b) That the model data is valid according to the validation rules
25. If `ModelState.IsValid` is false, what should the controller typically do?
    - a) Redirect to a success page
    - b) Save the data to the database
    - c) Redisplay the view with validation errors
    - d) Throw an exception
    - Answer: c) Redisplay the view with validation errors
26. Which HTML helper is commonly used to display validation error messages in a view?
    - a) `@Html.DisplayFor()`

- b) `@Html.LabelFor()`
- c) `@Html.ValidationMessageFor()`
- d) `@Html.TextBoxFor()`
- Answer: c) `@Html.ValidationMessageFor()`

27. Can you manually add errors to `ModelState` in a controller?
    - a) No
    - b) Yes
    - c) Only for specific data types
    - d) Only in custom Model Binders
    - Answer: b) Yes
28. What is the purpose of `@Html.ValidationSummary()`?
    - a) To display a summary of all validation errors
    - b) To display a single validation error
    - c) To display the model's display name
    - d) To generate a form
    - Answer: a) To display a summary of all validation errors
29. Model Binding occurs:
    - a) Before the action method is executed
    - b) After the action method is executed
    - c) During view rendering
    - d) In the browser
    - Answer: a) Before the action method is executed
30. Which of the following is a responsibility of the Model Binder?
    - a) Generating HTML
    - b) Mapping HTTP request data to model properties
    - c) Defining routing rules
    - d) Interacting with the database
    - Answer: b) Mapping HTTP request data to model properties

10 mid-size questions and answers on the topics you requested:

1. Creating Models using Classes

1. **Question:** Explain the concept of a "model" in ASP.NET MVC. Discuss how models are created using C# classes, and describe the role they play in the MVC architecture.
    - **Answer:** In ASP.NET MVC, a model represents the data and business logic of the application. Models are created as C# classes, with properties defining the data attributes. They are a core part of the MVC architecture, responsible for:
        - Representing data structures.
        - Enforcing business rules.
        - Interacting with data sources (databases, APIs, etc.).
        - Transferring data between the controller and the view.
        - They promote separation of concerns, making applications more maintainable.

2. **Question:** Describe how model classes are used to represent database tables when working with an ORM like Entity Framework. Provide an example of a simple model class and explain how it might correspond to a table in a relational database.
   - **Answer:** ORMs like Entity Framework use model classes to define the structure of database tables. Each model class typically represents a table, and the properties of the class correspond to the columns in the table.
     - Example:

```
public class Customer
{
    public int CustomerId { get; set; } // Maps to a primary key column
    public string FirstName { get; set; }
    public string LastName { get; set; }
    public string Email { get; set; }
}
```

     - In a database, this would create a "Customers" table with columns like "CustomerId", "FirstName", "LastName", and "Email". Entity Framework uses this model to generate the database schema and perform CRUD operations.

2. Data Annotations for Validation

3. **Question:** Explain the purpose of Data Annotations in ASP.NET MVC. Describe how they are used to define validation rules for model properties, and discuss the benefits of using them.
   - **Answer:** Data Annotations are attributes from the `System.ComponentModel.DataAnnotations` namespace that are applied to model properties to specify validation rules and metadata.
     - Purpose:
       - Declarative validation: Define rules directly in the model.
       - Enforce data integrity: Ensure data meets specific criteria.
       - Provide metadata: For UI display (e.g., display names).
     - Benefits:
       - Simplified validation logic.
       - Improved code readability.
       - Automatic integration with Model Binding and ModelState.
       - Reduced code duplication.
4. **Question:** Describe how Data Annotations work. Explain how ASP.NET MVC uses these annotations to validate user input and how validation errors are handled.
   - **Answer:**

0. Annotations are applied to model properties.
1. During Model Binding, ASP.NET MVC reads these annotations.
2. It validates the incoming data against the rules.
3. Validation results are stored in `ModelState`.
4. `ModelState.IsValid` indicates success or failure.

5. If invalid, error messages from the attributes are added to `ModelState`.
6. These errors are then displayed in the View using HTML helpers.

3. Model Binding and ModelState

5. **Question:** Explain the process of Model Binding in ASP.NET MVC. Describe how data from an HTTP request is mapped to the properties of a model object, and discuss the role of the Model Binder in this process.
    - **Answer:** Model Binding is the automatic mapping of HTTP request data (form data, query string, route data) to model properties.
        - Process:
            1. Request is received.
            2. Routing determines the action method.
            3. The Model Binder component takes over.
            4. It matches request data keys to model properties.
            5. It converts the data to the property types.
            6. It creates an instance of the model and populates it.
            7. The populated model is passed to the action method.
        - The Model Binder is the component that performs the mapping and type conversion.
6. **Question:** What is `ModelState` in ASP.NET MVC? Explain its purpose and how it is used to track the validity of model data during the Model Binding and validation process.
    - **Answer:** `ModelState` is a property of the controller that holds the state of the model during binding and validation.
        - Purpose:
            - Tracks if the model is valid.
            - Stores validation errors.
            - Contains the raw data from the request.
        - It is used to:
            - Check `ModelState.IsValid` in the controller.
            - Retrieve validation errors to display in the view.
            - Ensure only valid data is processed.

4. Custom Validation Attributes

7. **Question:** Why might you need to create custom validation attributes in ASP.NET MVC? Explain the limitations of built-in Data Annotations and provide a scenario where a custom attribute would be necessary.
    - **Answer:**
        - Need for Custom Attributes: When validation logic is too complex or specific to be handled by the built-in Data Annotations.
        - Limitations of Built-in Attributes: Limited to common validation rules (required, range, string length, etc.). They lack the flexibility for complex business rules.

- Scenario: Validating that a username is unique in a database. This requires a database lookup, which cannot be done with standard Data Annotations. A custom attribute can perform this check.

8. **Question:** Describe the process of creating a custom validation attribute in ASP.NET MVC. Explain the key steps involved and provide a simple example.
   - **Answer:**

0. Create a class that inherits from `ValidationAttribute`.
1. Override the `IsValid(object value)` method.
2. Implement the validation logic within `IsValid()`.
3. Optionally, set the `ErrorMessage` property.
4. Apply the custom attribute to a model property.

- Example:

```
public class PositiveAttribute : ValidationAttribute
{
    public override bool IsValid(object value)
    {
        if (value is decimal number)
        {
            return number > 0;
        }
        return false;
    }
}
```

9. **Question:** How does a custom validation attribute interact with the ASP.NET MVC validation process? Explain how the `IsValid()` method is used and how error messages are handled.
   - **Answer:**

   0. When MVC validates a model, it calls the `IsValid()` method of each applied validation attribute.
   1. The value of the property being validated is passed to `IsValid()`.
   2. `IsValid()` returns `true` (valid) or `false` (invalid).
   3. If `IsValid()` returns `false`:
      - The `ErrorMessage` property of the attribute is used.
      - An error is added to `ModelState` for that property.
      - The error message is displayed in the view using `@Html.ValidationMessageFor()`.

10. **Question:** Explain how you can format the error message in a custom validation attribute, including using the property name in the message.
    - **Answer**:

      - Use the `ErrorMessage` property in the constructor.
      - Override the `FormatErrorMessage(string name)` method in your custom attribute class to create a dynamic error message.

- The name parameter in FormatErrorMessage is the name of the property being validated.
- Example:

```
public override string FormatErrorMessage(string name)
{
    return $"The {name} must be a valid date";
}
```

CHAPTER 15: HANDLING FORMS AND USER INPUT IN MVC

✅ 1. HTML Forms in Razor Views

In ASP.NET MVC, Razor views are used to generate the HTML that is sent to the browser. HTML forms are essential for allowing users to input data, which is then sent back to the server for processing. Razor provides the @Html.BeginForm() helper method to simplify the creation of HTML <form> elements.

Understanding HTML Forms

Before diving into Razor's helper methods, let's quickly review the basics of HTML forms:

- **<form>** Element: The <form> element defines an HTML form, which is used to collect user input.
- **action** Attribute: The action attribute specifies the URL where the form data should be submitted.

- `method` Attribute: The `method` attribute specifies the HTTP method to use when submitting the form data (e.g., "GET" or "POST").
- **Input Elements**: Form elements like `<input>`, `<textarea>`, `<select>`, and `<button>` allow users to enter and submit data.

`Using @Html.BeginForm()`

The `@Html.BeginForm()` helper method in Razor simplifies the process of generating the opening `<form>` tag in your HTML. It provides a more convenient and less error-prone way to create forms compared to manually writing the HTML.

`Syntax of @Html.BeginForm()`

The `@Html.BeginForm()` method has several overloads, but the most common one looks like this:

```
@using (Html.BeginForm(string actionName, string controllerName, FormMethod
method))
{
    // Form elements here
}
```

- **`actionName`**: The name of the controller action method that will handle the form submission.
- **`controllerName`**: The name of the controller that contains the action method.
- **`method`**: The HTTP method to use for the form submission (e.g., `FormMethod.Post` or `FormMethod.Get`).

Explanation

- **`@using`** Statement: `@Html.BeginForm()` is typically used within a `@using` statement. This ensures that the `<form>` tag is properly closed with a corresponding `</form>` tag, even if errors occur. The `@using` statement creates a code block, and when the block finishes (either normally or due to an exception), the `Dispose()` method of the object created by `BeginForm()` is called, which writes the closing `</form>` tag.
- **Generated HTML**: The `@Html.BeginForm()` helper generates the opening `<form>` tag with the specified `action` and `method` attributes.
- **Form Elements**: Inside the `@using` block, you place the HTML form elements (e.g., `<input>`, `<label>`, etc.) that make up the form.

◆ Example: Create Product Form

You've provided a good example. Let's break it down and add more detail.

```
@model MyWebApp.Models.Product // Declare the model for the view
```

```
@using (Html.BeginForm("Create", "Product", FormMethod.Post)) // Start the
form
{
    @Html.AntiForgeryToken() // Add anti-forgery token for security

    @Html.LabelFor(m => m.Name, new { @class = "control-label col-md-2" }) //
Label for Name
    <div class="col-md-10">
        @Html.TextBoxFor(m => m.Name, new { @class = "form-control" })
// Textbox for Name
        @Html.ValidationMessageFor(m => m.Name, "", new { @class = "text-
danger" })  // Validation message
    </div>

    @Html.LabelFor(m => m.Price, new { @class = "control-label col-md-2" })
// Label for Price
     <div class="col-md-10">
        @Html.TextBoxFor(m => m.Price, new { @class = "form-control" })
// Textbox for Price
        @Html.ValidationMessageFor(m => m.Price, "", new { @class = "text-
danger" }) // Validation message
     </div>
    <div class="form-group">
        @Html.LabelFor(model => model.Description, htmlAttributes: new {
@class = "control-label col-md-2" })
        <div class="col-md-10">
            @Html.TextAreaFor(model => model.Description, new { @class =
"form-control" })
            @Html.ValidationMessageFor(model => model.Description, "", new {
@class = "text-danger" })
        </div>
    </div>

    <input type="submit" value="Create" class="btn btn-default" /> // Submit
button
}
```

Explanation

- **`@model MyWebApp.Models.Product`**: This line declares that the view expects a model of type `Product`. This allows you to use strongly-typed HTML helpers.
- **`@using (Html.BeginForm("Create", "Product", FormMethod.Post))`**: This line starts the HTML form.
  - `"Create"`: The form will submit data to the `Create` action method.
  - `"Product"`: The `Create` action method is in the `ProductController`.
  - `FormMethod.Post`: The form will use the HTTP POST method to submit data.
- **`@Html.AntiForgeryToken()`**: This helper generates a hidden input field that contains an anti-forgery token. This token helps prevent Cross-Site Request Forgery (CSRF) attacks. It's crucial for security, especially with POST requests.
- **`@Html.LabelFor(m => m.Name, new { @class = "control-label col-md-2" })`**: This helper generates a `<label>` element for the "Name" field.

- `m => m.Name`: This lambda expression specifies that the label is for the `Name` property of the model.
- `new { @class = "control-label col-md-2" }`: This adds HTML attributes to the label. In this case, it adds CSS classes for styling (Bootstrap classes, in this example).

- **`@Html.TextBoxFor(m => m.Name, new { @class = "form-control" })`**: This helper generates an `<input type="text">` element for the "Name" field.
  - `m => m.Name`: This lambda expression binds the textbox to the `Name` property of the model. This means that the textbox's `name` attribute will be set to "Name", and if the model has a value for `Name`, that value will be displayed in the textbox.
  - `new { @class = "form-control" }`: Adds CSS classes for styling (Bootstrap).
- **`@Html.ValidationMessageFor(m => m.Name, "", new { @class = "text-danger" })`**: This helper displays any validation error message associated with the "Name" field.
  - `m => m.Name`: Specifies that the validation message is for the `Name` property.
  - `""`: An empty string. This is for the error message itself.
  - `new { @class = "text-danger" }`: Adds CSS classes for styling (Bootstrap error styling).
- **`@Html.TextAreaFor()`**: Generates a `<textarea>` element.
- **`<input type="submit" value="Create" class="btn btn-default" />`**: This is a standard HTML `<input>` element that creates the submit button. When the user clicks this button, the form data will be submitted to the server.

`Key Benefits of Using @Html.BeginForm() and HTML Helpers`

- **Simplified HTML Generation**: Reduces the amount of manual HTML coding.
- **Strong Typing**: HTML helpers like `@Html.TextBoxFor()` and `@Html.LabelFor()` are strongly typed, which means they work with the model and provide better IntelliSense support in Visual Studio, reducing errors.
- **Automatic Handling of Attributes**: HTML helpers automatically generate the correct `name` and `id` attributes for form elements, which is essential for model binding.
- **Integration with Routing**: `@Html.BeginForm()` automatically generates the correct URL for the form's `action` attribute based on the specified controller and action names.
- **Security**: `@Html.AntiForgeryToken()` helps prevent Cross-Site Request Forgery (CSRF) attacks.
- **Validation Integration**: HTML helpers like `@Html.ValidationMessageFor()` seamlessly integrate with ASP.NET MVC's validation framework to display validation errors.

✅ 2. Form Submission using HTTP POST in MVC

In ASP.NET MVC, HTTP POST is the standard method for submitting form data to the server when you want to create or update data. It's considered more secure than HTTP GET for submitting sensitive information because the data is sent in the request body, not in the URL.

Understanding HTTP POST

- **HTTP Methods**: HTTP defines several methods for interacting with web servers, including GET, POST, PUT, DELETE, etc.
- **POST**: The POST method is used to send data to the server to create or update a resource.
- **Request Body**: With POST, the data being submitted is included in the body of the HTTP request, which is not visible in the URL.
- **Security**: POST is generally preferred for submitting sensitive data (like passwords or credit card information) because it's less likely to be exposed in browser history or server logs.

Form Submission in MVC

When a user submits a form in an MVC application, the following steps typically occur:

1. **Form in View**: The view contains an HTML `<form>` element. The `method` attribute of the form is set to "post". The `@Html.BeginForm()` helper in Razor is used to generate this form.
2. **User Input**: The user enters data into the form fields.
3. **Form Submission**: The user clicks the submit button.
4. **HTTP Request**: The browser sends an HTTP POST request to the server. The form data is included in the request body.
5. **Routing**: The ASP.NET MVC routing system determines which controller and action method should handle the request.
6. **Model Binding**: The MVC framework's Model Binder automatically maps the form data from the request body to the properties of a model object.
7. **Action Method Execution**: The controller's action method is executed. The model object, populated with the form data, is passed as a parameter to the action method.
8. **Processing**: The action method processes the data (e.g., saves it to a database).
9. **Response**: The action method returns a response, which might be a view, a redirect, or some other type of data.

◆ Controller Example

You've provided a good example. Let's break it down and add more detail.

```
using System.Web.Mvc;
using MyWebApp.Models; // Assuming Product model is in this namespace

public class ProductController : Controller
{
    // GET: Product/Create
    public ActionResult Create()
    {
        // This action handles the initial request to display the empty form.
        return View(); // Returns the Create.cshtml view
    }
```

```
    // POST: Product/Create
    [HttpPost] // This attribute specifies that this action handles POST
requests.
    public ActionResult Create(Product product) // Model Binding happens here
    {
        if (ModelState.IsValid) // Check if the model is valid (based on Data
Annotations)
        {
            // Save to database (simulated)
            //  db.Products.Add(product); // Example using Entity Framework
            //  db.SaveChanges();

            TempData["Message"] = "Product saved successfully!"; // Store a
message for the next request
            return RedirectToAction("Success"); // Redirect to the Success
action
        }

        // If ModelState.IsValid is false, validation errors occurred.
        // Redisplay the Create view with the model (which contains the
user's input and validation errors).
        return View(product);
    }

    public ActionResult Success()
    {
        // This action displays a success message after the product is saved.
        ViewBag.Message = TempData["Message"]; // Retrieve the message from
TempData
        return View(); // Returns the Success.cshtml view
    }
}
```

Explanation

- **`using System.Web.Mvc;`**: Imports the necessary ASP.NET MVC classes.
- **`using MyWebApp.Models;`**: Imports the namespace where the `Product` model is defined.
- **`public class ProductController : Controller`**: Defines the controller that handles product-related actions.
- **`// GET: Product/Create`**: This is a comment indicating the purpose of the following action.
- **`public ActionResult Create()`**: This action method handles the initial GET request to display the "Create Product" form. It simply returns the `Create.cshtml` view.
- **`// POST: Product/Create`**: This comment indicates the purpose of the following action.
- **`[HttpPost]`**: This attribute is crucial. It tells ASP.NET MVC that this `Create` action method should only be invoked when the request is an HTTP POST request. This prevents this method from being called when the user initially requests the `Create` page (which is a GET request).

- **`public ActionResult Create(Product product)`**: This action method handles the POST request when the user submits the form.
    - **`Product product`**: This is where Model Binding occurs. ASP.NET MVC automatically creates a `Product` object and populates its properties with the values from the form data in the POST request.
- **`if (ModelState.IsValid)`**: This line checks if the model is valid. `ModelState` contains the results of the validation process. Validation rules are typically defined using Data Annotation attributes in the `Product` model class (e.g., `[Required]`, `[StringLength]`, `[Range]`).
- **`// Save to database (simulated)`**: This is a comment indicating where you would typically save the data to a database using an ORM like Entity Framework.
- **`TempData["Message"] = "Product saved successfully!";`**: `TempData` is a dictionary-like object that allows you to store data between consecutive requests. It's often used to pass messages (like success or error messages) after a redirect. The data is available in the next request and is then automatically discarded.
- **`return RedirectToAction("Success");`**: This line redirects the user to the `Success` action method. This is a common pattern after successfully processing a POST request. Redirecting prevents the user from accidentally resubmitting the form if they refresh the page (the "Post-Redirect-Get" pattern).
- **`return View(product);`**: If `ModelState.IsValid` is false (meaning there were validation errors), this line redisplays the `Create.cshtml` view. The `product` object is passed back to the view, which allows the view to display the user's input and the validation error messages (using `@Html.ValidationMessageFor()`).
- **`public ActionResult Success()`**: This action method handles the GET request for the "Success" page.
- **`ViewBag.Message = TempData["Message"];`**: This line retrieves the message from `TempData` and stores it in `ViewBag`. `ViewBag` is a dynamic object that allows you to pass data from the controller to the view.
- **`return View();`**: This line returns the `Success.cshtml` view, which can then display the message from `ViewBag`.

Key Points

- **Security**: Using HTTP POST for form submissions is more secure than using GET, as the data is not visible in the URL.
- **`[HttpPost]`** Attribute: This attribute is essential to specify which action methods should handle POST requests.
- **`ModelState.IsValid`**: Always check `ModelState.IsValid` before processing the submitted data.
- **`TempData`**: Use `TempData` to pass messages between redirects.
- **Post-Redirect-Get**: Use the Post-Redirect-Get pattern to prevent form resubmission issues.

✅ 3. Validating Form Data

In ASP.NET MVC, validating form data is crucial for ensuring the integrity of your application's data. It involves verifying that the data submitted by the user meets the rules and constraints defined by your application. ASP.NET MVC provides a robust validation framework that integrates seamlessly with model binding and view rendering.

Key Concepts

- **Data Annotations**: Attributes applied to model properties to specify validation rules.
- **Model Binding**: The process of mapping form data to model properties.
- **ModelState**: A property of the controller that tracks the validity of the model.
- **Validation in the Model**: Validation rules are defined within the model class, promoting a clean separation of concerns.
- **Automatic Validation**: ASP.NET MVC automatically validates the data during model binding.
- **User Feedback**: Validation errors are displayed in the view to provide feedback to the user.

How Validation Works in ASP.NET MVC

1. **Data Annotation Attributes**: You apply Data Annotation attributes to the properties of your model class to define validation rules.
2. **Form Submission**: The user submits a form, and the browser sends an HTTP request (usually POST) to the server.
3. **Model Binding**: The ASP.NET MVC framework's Model Binder attempts to map the form data to the properties of the model object that is passed as a parameter to the controller action method.
4. **Automatic Validation**: During the model binding process, ASP.NET MVC automatically validates the data against the rules specified by the Data Annotation attributes.
5. **ModelState**: The results of the validation are stored in the `ModelState` property of the controller. `ModelState` is a dictionary-like object that contains information about the validity of the model and any validation errors.
6. **Checking Validity**: In your controller action method, you check the `ModelState.IsValid` property. If it's `true`, the data is valid, and you can proceed with processing it (e.g., saving it to a database). If it's `false`, there are validation errors.
7. **Displaying Errors**: If `ModelState.IsValid` is `false`, you redisplay the view, and the view uses HTML helpers like `@Html.ValidationMessageFor()` and `@Html.ValidationSummary()` to display the validation error messages to the user.

◆ Example

You've provided a good example. Let's expand on it and provide a more complete scenario.

- **`Model (Models/Product.cs):`**
- `using System.ComponentModel.DataAnnotations;`
-

```
namespace MyWebApp.Models
{
    public class Product
    {
        public int Id { get; set; }

        [Required(ErrorMessage = "Product Name is required")]
        [StringLength(100, MinimumLength = 3, ErrorMessage = "Product Name must be between 3 and 100 characters")]
        [Display(Name = "Product Name")]
        public string Name { get; set; }

        [Required(ErrorMessage = "Price is required")]
        [Range(0.01, 10000, ErrorMessage = "Price must be between 0.01 and 10000")]
        [Display(Name = "Price")]
        public decimal Price { get; set; }

        [StringLength(500, ErrorMessage = "Description cannot exceed 500 characters")]
        [Display(Name = "Description")]
        public string Description { get; set; }
    }
}
```

- **Controller (Controllers/ProductController.cs):**

```
using System.Web.Mvc;
using MyWebApp.Models;

public class ProductController : Controller
{
    public ActionResult Create()
    {
        return View(); // Display the empty form
    }

    [HttpPost]
    public ActionResult Create(Product product)
    {
        if (ModelState.IsValid)
        {
            // Save to database (not implemented here)
            //  db.Products.Add(product);
            //  db.SaveChanges();

            TempData["Message"] = "Product saved successfully!";
            return RedirectToAction("Index");
        }

```

- // If ModelState.IsValid is false, redisplay the form with errors
- return View(product);
- }
- }

- **View (Views/Product/Create.cshtml):**

```
@model MyWebApp.Models.Product

<h2>Create Product</h2>

@using (Html.BeginForm())
{
    @Html.AntiForgeryToken()
    @Html.ValidationSummary(true, "", new { @class = "text-danger" })

    <div class="form-group">
        @Html.LabelFor(model => model.Name, htmlAttributes: new {
@class = "control-label col-md-2" })
        <div class="col-md-10">
            @Html.TextBoxFor(model => model.Name, new { @class = "form-
control" })
            @Html.ValidationMessageFor(model => model.Name, "", new {
@class = "text-danger" })
        </div>
    </div>

    <div class="form-group">
        @Html.LabelFor(model => model.Price, htmlAttributes: new {
@class = "control-label col-md-2" })
        <div class="col-md-10">
            @Html.TextBoxFor(model => model.Price, new { @class =
"form-control" })
            @Html.ValidationMessageFor(model => model.Price, "", new {
@class = "text-danger" })
        </div>
    </div>

    <div class="form-group">
        @Html.LabelFor(model => model.Description, htmlAttributes: new
{ @class = "control-label col-md-2" })
        <div class="col-md-10">
            @Html.TextAreaFor(model => model.Description, new { @class
= "form-control" })
            @Html.ValidationMessageFor(model => model.Description, "",
new { @class = "text-danger" })
        </div>
    </div>

    <div class="form-group">
```

```
•         <div class="col-md-offset-2 col-md-10">
•             <input type="submit" value="Create" class="btn btn-default"
  />
•         </div>
•     </div>
• }
```

Explanation

1. **Model with Data Annotations**: The `Product` model class is decorated with Data Annotation attributes:
    - `[Required]`: Ensures that the `Name` and `Price` properties are not empty.
    - `[StringLength]`: Specifies the maximum and minimum length for the `Name` property.
    - `[Range]`: Specifies the valid range for the `Price` property.
    - `[Display]`: Provides user-friendly names for the labels.
2. **Controller Actions**:
    - `Create()` (GET): Displays the empty form.
    - `Create(Product product)` (POST): Handles the form submission.
        - It checks `ModelState.IsValid`.
        - If valid, it saves the data and redirects.
        - If invalid, it redisplays the form with the `product` model (which now contains the user's input and validation errors).
3. **View**:
    - `@model MyWebApp.Models.Product`: Declares the model type.
    - `@Html.ValidationSummary()`: Displays a summary of all validation errors.
    - `@Html.LabelFor()`: Generates labels for the form fields.
    - `@Html.TextBoxFor()` and `@Html.TextAreaFor()`: Generate input elements for the form fields, bound to the model properties.
    - `@Html.ValidationMessageFor()`: Displays the validation error message for each specific field.

How Validation Errors are Displayed

If a user submits invalid data (e.g., an empty name, a price outside the valid range), the following happens:

1. `ModelState.IsValid` is `false` in the `HttpPost Create` action.
2. The action calls `return View(product);`, which redisplays the `Create.cshtml` view.
3. The `@Html.ValidationMessageFor()` helpers in the view use the information in `ModelState` to display the appropriate error messages next to the input fields. For example, if the user leaves the "Name" field empty, the `[Required]` attribute will cause a validation error, and `@Html.ValidationMessageFor(model => model.Name)` will render the error message "Product Name is required".

4. `@Html.ValidationSummary()` displays a summary of all the errors at the top of the form.

Key Benefits of this Approach

- **Declarative Validation**: Validation rules are defined directly in the model, making the code more readable and maintainable.
- **Automatic Validation**: ASP.NET MVC automatically performs validation during model binding, reducing the amount of manual validation code you need to write.
- **User Feedback**: Validation errors are seamlessly integrated with the view, providing a user-friendly way to inform users about data entry problems.
- **Separation of Concerns**: Validation logic is kept in the model, separating it from the controller and view logic.

✅ 4. Using TempData, ViewBag, and ViewData

In ASP.NET MVC, `TempData`, `ViewBag`, and `ViewData` are mechanisms for passing data from the controller to the view. They serve different purposes and have different lifecycles, making them suitable for various scenarios.

1. ViewBag

- **Type**: Dynamic object (late-bound).
- **Lifetime**: Available only during the current request.
- **Usage**: Primarily used for passing small amounts of data from the controller to the view.

Explanation

`ViewBag` is a dynamic property of the `Controller` base class. This means you can add properties to it at runtime, and you don't need to define them beforehand. It uses the `dynamic` keyword, so property resolution occurs at runtime.

- **Late-Bound**: Because it's dynamic, there's no compile-time type checking. If you misspell a property name, you'll only discover the error at runtime.
- **Single Request**: Data stored in `ViewBag` is only available to the view that's rendered by the current controller action. It's not persisted across redirects.

◆ Example

- **Controller:**

```
public ActionResult Welcome()
{
    ViewBag.Message = "Welcome to the form page!";
    ViewBag.CurrentTime = DateTime.Now;
```

```
    ViewBag.UserCount = 125; // Example of passing an integer
    return View();
}
```

- **View (Welcome.cshtml):**

```
<h2>@ViewBag.Message</h2>
<p>Current Time: @ViewBag.CurrentTime</p>
<p>User Count: @ViewBag.UserCount</p>
```

2. ViewData

- **Type**: `ViewDataDictionary` (dictionary-based, key-value pairs).
- **Lifetime**: Available only during the current request.
- **Usage**: Similar to `ViewBag`, used for passing data to the view, but it's an older approach.

Explanation

`ViewData` is a property of the `Controller` base class that is a dictionary. You store data in it using string keys and retrieve it using those keys in the view.

- **Dictionary**: It's a dictionary, so you use string keys to access the values. This can be slightly less convenient than `ViewBag`'s dynamic properties.
- **Single Request**: Like `ViewBag`, data in `ViewData` is only available to the view rendered by the current action.

◆ Example

- **Controller:**

```
public ActionResult Greet()
{
    ViewData["Greeting"] = "Hello from ViewData!";
    ViewData["UserName"] = "John Doe";
    ViewData["IsAdmin"] = true; // Example of passing a boolean
    return View();
}
```

- **View (Greet.cshtml):**

```
<h2>@ViewData["Greeting"]</h2>
<p>User Name: @ViewData["UserName"]</p>
@if ((bool)ViewData["IsAdmin"])
{
    <p>You are an administrator.</p>
}
```

3. TempData

- **Type**: `TempDataDictionary` (dictionary-based).
- **Lifetime**: Available for the *next* request (typically after a redirect).
- **Usage**: Best for passing short-lived messages, such as success or error messages, after a form submission and redirect.

Explanation

`TempData` is a dictionary that stores data temporarily. The data is available during the *next* HTTP request, and then it's automatically removed. This is particularly useful when you redirect from one action to another (e.g., after successfully saving data).

- **Redirect Scenario**: `TempData` solves the problem of needing to display a message after a redirect. If you used `ViewBag` or `ViewData`, the data wouldn't be available after the redirect because they only last for the current request.
- **Short-Lived**: The data is automatically removed after it's accessed in the next request, so it's not intended for long-term storage.

◆ Example

- **Controller:**

```
public ActionResult SaveData(string input)
{
    if (string.IsNullOrEmpty(input))
    {
        TempData["ErrorMessage"] = "Please enter some data.";
        return RedirectToAction("Index"); // Redirect back to the form
    }

    // Save the data
    TempData["SuccessMessage"] = "Data saved successfully!";
    return RedirectToAction("Success"); // Redirect to a success page
}

public ActionResult Success()
{
    string message = TempData["SuccessMessage"] as string; // Read the
value.
    ViewBag.Result = message;
    return View();
}

 public ActionResult Index()
{
    string errorMessage = TempData["ErrorMessage"] as string; // Read
the value.
    ViewBag.ErrorMessage = errorMessage;
```

```
        return View();
    }
```

- **View (Success.cshtml):**

```
<h2>Success!</h2>
@if (ViewBag.Result != null)
{
    <p>@ViewBag.Result</p>
}
```

- **View (Index.cshtml):**

```
<h2>Index Page</h2>
@if (ViewBag.ErrorMessage != null)
{
    <p style="color:red">@ViewBag.ErrorMessage</p>
}
```

□ Full Example Workflow

You've provided a good workflow example. Let's add some more detail.

1. **Create Form (View):**
    - Views/Product/Create.cshtml:

```
@model MyWebApp.Models.Product

<h2>Create Product</h2>

@using (Html.BeginForm())
{
    @Html.AntiForgeryToken()
    @Html.ValidationSummary(true, "", new { @class = "text-danger" })

    <div class="form-group">
        @Html.LabelFor(m => m.Name, new { @class = "control-label col-md-2" })
        <div class="col-md-10">
            @Html.TextBoxFor(m => m.Name, new { @class = "form-control" })
            @Html.ValidationMessageFor(m => m.Name, "", new { @class = "text-danger" })
        </div>
    </div>

    <div class="form-group">
        @Html.LabelFor(m => m.Price, new { @class = "control-label col-md-2" })
        <div class="col-md-10">
```

```
o             @Html.TextBoxFor(m => m.Price, new { @class = "form-
   control" })
o             @Html.ValidationMessageFor(m => m.Price, "", new {
   @class = "text-danger" })
o         </div>
o     </div>
o
o     <div class="form-group">
o         @Html.LabelFor(m => m.Description, htmlAttributes: new {
   @class = "control-label col-md-2" })
o         <div class="col-md-10">
o             @Html.TextAreaFor(model => model.Description, new {
   @class = "form-control" })
o             @Html.ValidationMessageFor(model =>
   model.Description, "", new { @class = "text-danger" })
o         </div>
o     </div>
o
o     <div class="form-group">
o         <div class="col-md-offset-2 col-md-10">
o             <input type="submit" value="Save" class="btn btn-
   default" />
o         </div>
o     </div>
o }
```

2. **Controller (Handles POST):**

```
o Controllers/ProductController.cs:
o using System.Web.Mvc;
o using MyWebApp.Models;
o
o public class ProductController : Controller
o {
o     [HttpPost]
o     public ActionResult Create(Product product)
o     {
o         if (ModelState.IsValid)
o         {
o             // Save to database
o             //  db.Products.Add(product);
o             //  db.SaveChanges();
o
o             TempData["Message"] = "Product added successfully!";
o             return RedirectToAction("Success"); // Redirect to
   Success action
o         }
o
o         // If ModelState is invalid, return to the form
o         return View(product);
o     }
o
o     public ActionResult Success()
o     {
o         string message = TempData["Message"] as string;
o         if(message != null)
```

- ```
              ViewBag.Message = message; // Get message from TempData
  ```
- ```
          return View(); // Render Success.cshtml
  ```
- ```
      }
  ```
- ```
  }
  ```

3. **Success View:**
   - `Views/Product/Success.cshtml:`
   - `<h2>Success!</h2>`
   - `@if (ViewBag.Message != null)`
   - `{`
   - `    <p>@ViewBag.Message</p>`
   - `}`

✅ Summary Table

Concept	Description
Html.BeginForm	Creates a form in Razor view
HttpPost	Used to handle form submission securely
ModelState	Checks if model input is valid
ViewBag	Passes data between controller and view (dynamic)
ViewData	Dictionary for passing data (request-limited)
TempData	Dictionary for persisting data across requests (like after a redirect)

30 MCQ QUESTION WITH ANSWER

1. HTML Forms in Razor Views

1. Which helper method is used to begin an HTML form in a Razor view?
   - a) `@Html.Form()`
   - b) `@Html.BeginForm()`
   - c) `@Html.FormStart()`
   - d) `@Html.CreateForm()`
   - Answer: b) `@Html.BeginForm()`
2. What is the purpose of the `action` attribute in an HTML `<form>` element?
   - a) Specifies the HTTP method

- b) Specifies the URL to submit the form data to
- c) Specifies the form's ID
- d) Specifies the form's title
- Answer: b) Specifies the URL to submit the form data to

3. Which attribute of the `<form>` element specifies the HTTP method used to submit the form data?
    - a) `method`
    - b) `type`
    - c) `action`
    - d) `submit`
    - Answer: a) `method`
4. Which HTTP method is typically used for submitting forms that create or update data?
    - a) GET
    - b) POST
    - c) PUT
    - d) DELETE
    - Answer: b) POST
5. What does the `@using` block do when used with `@Html.BeginForm()`?
    - a) Defines a code block
    - b) Ensures the form is correctly closed
    - c) Specifies the form's model
    - d) Includes a partial view
    - Answer: b) Ensures the form is correctly closed
6. Which helper generates an HTML `<label>` element in a Razor view?
    - a) `@Html.Label()`
    - b) `@Html.LabelFor()`
    - c) `@Html.FormLabel()`
    - d) `@Html.DisplayLabel()`
    - Answer: b) `@Html.LabelFor()`
7. Which helper generates an HTML `<input type="text">` element?
    - a) `@Html.TextBox()`
    - b) `@Html.TextInput()`
    - c) `@Html.TextBoxFor()`
    - d) `@Html.InputField()`
    - Answer: c) `@Html.TextBoxFor()`
8. What is the primary benefit of using `@Html.TextBoxFor()` over manually creating an input element?
    - a) Automatic styling
    - b) Strong typing and automatic attribute generation
    - c) Client-side validation
    - d) Improved performance
    - Answer: b) Strong typing and automatic attribute generation
9. Which helper is used to display validation messages for a specific form field?
    - a) `@Html.ValidationMessage()`
    - b) `@Html.ErrorMessageFor()`
    - c) `@Html.ValidationFor()`

- d) `@Html.ValidationMessageFor()`
- Answer: d) `@Html.ValidationMessageFor()`

10. What security feature does `@Html.AntiForgeryToken()` provide?
    - a) Prevents SQL injection
    - b) Prevents Cross-Site Scripting (XSS)
    - c) Prevents Cross-Site Request Forgery (CSRF)
    - d) Encrypts form data
    - Answer: c) Prevents Cross-Site Request Forgery (CSRF)

2. Form Submission using HTTP POST

11. Which HTTP method is used to submit form data in the request body?
    - a) GET
    - b) POST
    - c) PUT
    - d) DELETE
    - Answer: b) POST
12. Where is the form data located when using the POST method?
    - a) In the URL
    - b) In the request headers
    - c) In the request body
    - d) In a cookie
    - Answer: c) In the request body
13. Why is POST generally preferred over GET for submitting sensitive data?
    - a) It is faster
    - b) It is simpler
    - c) It is less likely to expose data in browser history or server logs
    - d) It is the default method
    - Answer: c) It is less likely to expose data in browser history or server logs
14. In an ASP.NET MVC controller, how do you specify that an action method should only handle POST requests?
    - a) `[HttpPostRequest]`
    - b) `[PostOnly]`
    - c) `[HttpPost]`
    - d) `[RequestType(Method = "POST")]`
    - Answer: c) `[HttpPost]`
15. What happens to the form data after it is submitted using the POST method?
    - a) It is displayed in the view
    - b) It is automatically saved to a file
    - c) It is processed by the controller action method
    - d) It is sent back to the client
    - Answer: c) It is processed by the controller action method
16. What is the role of routing in form submission?
    - a) To define the form's layout
    - b) To determine which controller and action method handles the request
    - c) To validate the form data

- d) To display the form
- Answer: b) To determine which controller and action method handles the request

17. What is Model Binding?
    - a) Creating database tables
    - b) Mapping HTTP request data to model properties
    - c) Generating HTML for a form
    - d) Defining URL patterns
    - Answer: b) Mapping HTTP request data to model properties
18. What does the `method="post"` attribute in an HTML form indicate?
    - a) The form data will be sent as part of the URL.
    - b) The form data will be sent in the request body.
    - c) The form will only accept file uploads.
    - d) The form will be submitted using JavaScript.
    - Answer: b) The form data will be sent in the request body.
19. Which of the following is true about HTTP POST requests?
    - a) They are idempotent.
    - b) They are typically used to retrieve data.
    - c) They are typically used to create or update data.
    - d) They are limited to small amounts of data.
    - Answer: c) They are typically used to create or update data.
20. What is the purpose of the submit button in an HTML form?
    - a) To reset the form data.
    - b) To display a preview of the form data.
    - c) To send the form data to the server.
    - d) To validate the form data.
    - Answer: c) To send the form data to the server.

3. Validating Form Data

21. Where are validation rules typically defined in ASP.NET MVC?
    - a) In the view
    - b) In the controller
    - c) In the model
    - d) In the web.config file
    - Answer: c) In the model
22. Which feature is commonly used to define validation rules for model properties?
    - a) HTML attributes
    - b) JavaScript
    - c) Data Annotations
    - d) CSS
    - Answer: c) Data Annotations
23. What is `ModelState` in ASP.NET MVC?
    - a) A class for defining views
    - b) A property of the controller that represents the state of the model during validation
    - c) A database table

- d) A JavaScript object
- Answer: b) A property of the controller that represents the state of the model during validation

24. What does `ModelState.IsValid` return?
    - a) The model object
    - b) A boolean indicating whether the model data is valid
    - c) The validation error messages
    - d) The view name
    - Answer: b) A boolean indicating whether the model data is valid
25. What should a controller do if `ModelState.IsValid` is false?
    - a) Save the data anyway
    - b) Redirect to a success page
    - c) Redisplay the view with validation errors
    - d) Throw an exception
    - Answer: c) Redisplay the view with validation errors
26. Which HTML helper is used to display validation errors for a specific property in a view?
    - a) `@Html.DisplayErrorFor()`
    - b) `@Html.ErrorMessage()`
    - c) `@Html.ValidationMessageFor()`
    - d) `@Html.ErrorFor()`
    - Answer: c) `@Html.ValidationMessageFor()`
27. Which of the following is NOT a Data Annotation attribute?
    - a) `[Required]`
    - b) `[StringLength]`
    - c) `[Range]`
    - d) `[Validate]`
    - Answer: d) `[Validate]`
28. Data Annotations are found in which namespace?
    - a) `System.Web`
    - b) `System.ComponentModel`
    - c) `System.ComponentModel.DataAnnotations`
    - d) `System.Web.Mvc`
    - Answer: c) `System.ComponentModel.DataAnnotations`
29. What happens if a user submits a form with invalid data, and the view uses `@Html.ValidationMessageFor()`?
    - a) The form submission is prevented.
    - b) The invalid data is automatically corrected.
    - c) An error message is displayed in the view.
    - d) The application crashes.
    - Answer: c) An error message is displayed in the view.
30. Which helper displays a summary of all validation errors in a view?
    - a) `@Html.ValidationSummary()`
    - b) `@Html.AllValidationMessages()`
    - c) `@Html.ErrorSummary()`
    - d) `@Html.DisplayAllErrors()`
    - Answer: a) `@Html.ValidationSummary()`

10 MID SIZE QUESTION WITH ANSWER

1. HTML Forms in Razor Views

1. **Question:** Explain the purpose of HTML forms in web development. Describe how HTML forms are created in ASP.NET MVC Razor views, including the role of the @Html.BeginForm() helper.
    - **Answer:** HTML forms are used to collect user input, which is then sent to the server for processing. In ASP.NET MVC Razor views, forms are created using the @Html.BeginForm() helper. This helper generates the opening <form> tag, specifying the action and method for form submission. It simplifies form creation and integrates with MVC's routing and security features.
2. **Question:** Describe the difference between using standard HTML input elements (e.g., <input type="text">) and using HTML helpers like @Html.TextBoxFor() in Razor views. What are the advantages of using HTML helpers?
    - **Answer:** Standard HTML input elements require manual coding of attributes (e.g., name, id, value). HTML helpers like @Html.TextBoxFor() are strongly typed, meaning they work with model properties. Advantages include:
        - Automatic generation of name and id attributes.
        - Binding to model properties.
        - Better IntelliSense support.
        - Integration with validation.
        - Reduced code and fewer errors.

2. Form Submission using HTTP POST

3. **Question:** Explain the difference between the HTTP GET and POST methods. Describe why HTTP POST is generally preferred for submitting form data that creates or updates data on the server.
    - **Answer:**
        - **GET:** Data is appended to the URL. Used for retrieving data. Limited data size. Data is visible in the URL.
        - **POST:** Data is sent in the request body. Used for creating/updating data. Larger data size. Data is not visible in the URL.
        - POST is preferred for creating/updating because it's more secure (data not in URL) and can handle larger amounts of data.
4. **Question:** Describe the process of form submission using HTTP POST in an ASP.NET MVC application. Explain how the data from the form is processed by the controller and what happens after the data is processed.
    - **Answer:**

0. User fills out the form in the view.
1. User clicks submit.
2. Browser sends an HTTP POST request.
3. MVC routing directs the request to the correct controller action.
4. Model binding maps form data to the action method's model parameter.

5. The action method processes the data (e.g., saves to the database).
6. The controller returns a response (e.g., a view, a redirect).

3. Validating Form Data

5. **Question:** Explain how form data validation is typically implemented in ASP.NET MVC. Describe the role of Data Annotations, ModelState, and HTML helpers in this process.
   - **Answer:**
     - Data Annotations: Attributes in the model that define validation rules (e.g., [Required], [StringLength]).
     - ModelState: A property of the controller that stores validation results. ModelState.IsValid indicates if the data is valid.
     - HTML Helpers: Like @Html.ValidationMessageFor(), display validation errors in the view.
     - MVC automatically validates during model binding. The controller checks ModelState.IsValid and redisplays the view with errors if needed.
6. **Question:** What is ModelState.IsValid, and why is it important to check its value in a controller action method that handles form submissions? Provide an example of how it is used.
   - **Answer:** ModelState.IsValid is a boolean property that indicates whether the model data is valid, according to the validation rules defined by Data Annotations.
   - It's crucial to check it to:
     - Prevent processing invalid data.
     - Ensure data integrity.
     - Provide feedback to the user.
   - Example:

```
[HttpPost]
public ActionResult Create(Product product)
{
    if (ModelState.IsValid)
    {
        // Save the product
    }
    return View(product); // Redisplay with errors
}
```

4. Using TempData, ViewBag, and ViewData

7. **Question:** Compare and contrast ViewBag and ViewData in ASP.NET MVC. Explain their purpose, lifetime, and how data is accessed in the view.
   - **Answer:**
     - Purpose: Both pass data from the controller to the view.
     - Lifetime: Both are available only during the current request.
     - ViewBag: Dynamic object. Access data using properties (e.g., @ViewBag.Message). Late-bound.

        - ViewData: Dictionary. Access data using string keys (e.g., @ViewData["Message"]). Requires casting.
8. **Question:** Explain the purpose of TempData in ASP.NET MVC. Describe its lifetime and provide a scenario where it is the most appropriate choice for passing data between the controller and view.
    - **Answer:**
        - Purpose: To pass data between controller actions, specifically across a redirect.
        - Lifetime: Data is available during the *next* request, then it's removed.
        - Scenario: Displaying a success/error message after a form submission and redirect. TempData ensures the message is shown on the success/error page.
9. **Question:** Explain when you would choose to use each of the following to pass data from a controller to a view:
    - ViewBag
    - ViewData
    - TempData
    - **Answer**:
        - ViewBag: For simple, short-lived data transfer to the view in the current request. For convenience and readability.
        - ViewData: Similar to ViewBag, but less preferred due to the need for string keys and casting. Use if you prefer a dictionary-based approach.
        - TempData: For data that needs to survive a redirect, such as success/error messages after a form submission.
10. **Question:** Describe a complete workflow example where a user submits a form, the data is processed, and a success message is displayed on a different page. Explain how TempData would be used in this scenario.
    - **Answer**:

0. User submits a form on Create.cshtml (POST).
1. Controller's Create action processes the data.
2. If successful, the controller sets TempData["Success"] = "Data saved!".
3. The controller redirects to Success.cshtml.
4. The Success action reads TempData["Success"] and passes it to the view.
5. Success.cshtml displays the message. TempData ensures the message survives the redirect.

www.ingramcontent.com/pod-product-compliance
Lightning Source LLC
LaVergne TN
LVHW060120070326
832902LV00019B/3042

* 9 7 9 8 2 8 0 3 1 8 5 1 9 *